Honda VT600 & VT750 Shadow V-Twins

Service and Repair Manual

by Mike Stubblefield

Models covered

(2312-6N5-2)

Honda VT600C Shadow VLX, 1988 and 1989
Honda VT600C Shadow VLX, 1991 through 2007
Honda VT600CD Shadow VLX Deluxe, 1993 through 2007
Honda VT750C/CD Shadow American Classic Edition, 1998 through 2003
Honda VT750C Shadow Aero, 2004 through 2009
Honda VT750C2 Shadow Spirit, 2007 through 2009

ABCDE
FGH

ISBN-13: 978-1-56392-852-9
ISBN-10: 1-56392-852-3

Library of Congress Control Number: 2010931221
Printed in the USA

Haynes Publishing
Sparkford, Nr Yeovil, Somerset BA22 7JJ, England

Haynes North America, Inc
861 Lawrence Drive, Newbury Park, California 91320, USA

© Haynes North America, Inc. 1999, 2000, 2003, 2008, 2010

With permission from J.H. Haynes & Co. Ltd.

A book in the Haynes Service and Repair Manual Series

10-288

Contents

LIVING WITH YOUR HONDA

Introduction

Pre-ride checks

MAINTENANCE

Routine maintenance and servicing

Contents

The Birth of a Dream

by Julian Ryder

There is no better example of the Japanese post-war industrial miracle than Honda. Like other companies which have become household names, it started with one man's vision. In this case the man was the 40-year old Soichiro Honda, who had sold his piston-ring manufacturing business to Toyota in 1945 and was happily spending the proceeds on prolonged parties for his friends. However, the difficulties of getting around in the chaos of post-war Japan irked Honda, so when he came across a job lot of generator engines, he realized that here was a way of getting people mobile again at low cost.

A 12 by 18-foot shack in Hamamatsu became his first bike factory, fitting the generator motors into pushbikes. Before long he'd used up all 500 generator motors and started manufacturing his own engine, known as the "chimney," either because of the elongated cylinder head or the smoky exhaust, or perhaps both. The chimney made all of half a horsepower from its 50 cc engine but it was a major success and became the Honda A-type.

Less than two years after he'd set up in Hamamatsu, Soichiro Honda founded the Honda Motor Company in September 1948. By then, the A-type had been developed into the 90 cc B-type engine, which Mr. Honda decided deserved its own chassis, not a bicycle frame. Honda was about to become Japan's first post-war manufacturer of complete motorcycles. In August 1949 the first prototype was ready. With an output of three horsepower, the 98 cc D-type was still a simple two-stroke, but it had a two-speed transmission and, most importantly, a pressed steel frame with telescopic forks and hard tail rear end. The frame was almost triangular in profile with the top rail going in a straight line from the massively braced steering head to the rear axle. Legend has it that after the D-type's first tests, the entire workforce went for a drink to celebrate and try and think of a name for the bike. One man broke one of those silences you get when people are thinking, exclaiming "This is like a dream!" "That's it!" shouted Honda, and so the Honda Dream was christened.

Mr. Honda was a brilliant, intuitive engineer and designer, but he did not bother himself with the marketing side of his business. With hindsight, it is possible to see that employing Takeo Fujisawa - who would both sort out the home market and plan the eventual expansion into overseas markets - was a masterstroke. He arrived in October 1949 and in 1950 was made Sales Director. Another vital new name was Kiyoshi Kawashima, who along with Honda himself, designed the company's first four-stroke after Kawashima had told them that the four-stroke opposition to Honda's two-strokes sounded nicer and therefore sold better. The result of that statement was the overhead-valve 148 cc E-type, which first ran in July 1951 just two months after the first drawings were made. Kawashima was made a director of the Honda Company at 34 years old.

The E-type was a massive success, over 32,000 were made in 1953 alone, a feat of

> ## 'This is like a dream!' 'That's it' shouted Honda

mass-production that was astounding by the standards of the day given the relative complexity of the machine. But Honda's lifelong pursuit of technical innovation sometimes distracted him from commercial reality. Fujisawa pointed out that they were in danger of ignoring their core business, the motorized bicycles that still formed Japan's main means of transport. In May 1952, the F-type Cub appeared, another two-stroke despite the top men's reservations. You could buy a complete machine or just the motor to attach to your own bicycle. The result was certainly distinctive, a white fuel tank with a circular profile went just below and behind the saddle on the left of the bike, and the motor with its horizontal cylinder and bright red cover just below the rear axle on the same side of the bike. This was the machine that turned Honda into the biggest bike maker in Japan, with 70% of the market for bolt-on bicycle motors. The F-type was also the first Honda to be exported. Next came the machine that would turn Honda into the biggest motorcycle manufacturer in the world.

The C100 Super Cub was a typically audacious piece of Honda engineering and marketing. For the first time, but not the last, Honda invented a completely new type of motorcycle, although the term "scooterette'" was coined to describe the new bike which had many of the characteristics of a scooter but the large wheels, and therefore stability, of a motorcycle. The first one was sold in August 1958; fifteen years later, over nine-million of them were on the roads of the world. If ever a machine can be said to have brought mobility

Honda C70 and C90 OHV-engined models

The CB250N Super Dream became a favorite with UK learner riders of the late seventies and early eighties

The GL1000 introduced in 1975, was the first in Honda's line of GoldWings

to the masses, it is the Super Cub. If you add in the electric starter that was added for the C102 model of 1961, the design of the Super Cub has remained substantially unchanged ever since, testament to how right Honda got it first time. The Super Cub made Honda the world's biggest manufacturer after just two years of production.

Honda's export drive started in earnest in 1957 when Britain and Holland got their first bikes; America got just two bikes the next year. By 1962, Honda had half the American market with 65,000 sales. But Soichiro Honda had already travelled abroad to Europe and the USA, making a special point of going to the Isle of Man TT, then the most important race in the GP calendar. He realized that no matter how advanced his products were, only racing success would convince overseas markets for whom "Made in Japan" still meant cheap and nasty. It took five years from Soichiro Honda's first visit to

the Island before his bikes were ready for the TT. In 1959 the factory entered five riders in the 125 class. They did not have a massive impact on the event, being benevolently regarded as a curiosity, but sixth, seventh and eighth were good enough for the team prize. The bikes were off the pace but they were well engineered and very reliable.

The TT was the only time the West saw the Hondas in '59, but they came back for more the following year with the first of a generation of bikes which shaped the future of motorcycling – the double-overhead-cam four-cylinder 250. It was fast and reliable – it revved to 14,000 rpm – but didn't handle anywhere near as well as the opposition. However, Honda had now signed up non-Japanese riders to lead their challenge. The first win didn't come until 1962 (Aussie Tom Phillis in the Spanish 125 GP) and was followed up with a world-shaking performance at the TT. Twenty-one year old Mike Hailwood

won both 125 and 250 cc TTs and Hondas filled the top five positions in both races. Soichiro Honda's master plan was starting to come to fruition; Hailwood and Honda won the 1961 250 cc World Championship. Next year Honda won three titles. The other Japanese factories fought back and inspired Honda to produce some of the most fascinating racers ever seen: the awesome six-cylinder 250, the five-cylinder 125, and the 500 four, with which the immortal Hailwood battled Agostini and the MV Agusta.

When Honda pulled out of racing in '67, they had won sixteen rider's titles, eighteen manufacturer's titles, and 137 GPs, including 18 TTs, and introduced the concept of the modern works team to motorcycle racing. Sales success followed racing victory as Soichiro Honda had predicted, but only because the products advanced as rapidly as the racing machinery. The Hondas that came to Britain in the early '60s were incredibly sophisticated. They had overhead cams where the British bikes had pushrods, they had electric starters when the Brits relied on the kickstart, they had 12V electrics when even the biggest British bike used a 6V system. There seemed no end to the technical wizardry. It wasn't that the technology itself was so amazing, but just like that first E-type, it was the fact that Honda could mass-produce it more reliably than the lower-tech competition that was so astonishing.

When, in 1968, the first four-cylinder CB750 road bike arrived, the world of motorcycling changed forever, they even had to invent a new word for it, "Superbike." Honda raced again with the CB750 at Daytona and won the World Endurance title with a prototype DOHC version that became the CB900 roadster. There was the six-cylinder CBX, the CX500T – the world's first turbocharged production bike. They invented the full-dress tourer with the GoldWing, and came back to GPs with the

Carl Fogarty in action at the Suzuka 8 Hour on the RC45

An early CB750 Four

revolutionary oval-pistoned NR500 four-stroke, a much-misunderstood bike that was more a rolling experimental laboratory than a racer. Just to show their versatility, Honda also came up with the weird CX500 shaft-drive V-twin, a rugged workhorse that powered a

new industry: the courier companies that oiled the wheels of commerce in London and other big cities.

It was true, though, that Mr. Honda was not keen on two-strokes – early motocross engines had to be explained away to him as lawnmower

motors! However, in 1982 Honda raced the NS500, an agile three-cylinder lightweight against the big four-cylinder opposition in 500 GPs. The bike won in its first year, and in '83 took the world title for Freddie Spencer. In four-stroke racing the V4 layout took over from the straight four, dominating TT, F1 and Endurance championships with the RVF750, the nearest thing ever built to a Formula 1 car on two wheels. And when Superbike arrived, Honda were ready with the RC30. On the roads the VFR V4 became an instant classic, while the CBR600 invented another new class of bike on its way to becoming a best-seller. The V4 road bikes had problems to start with, but the VFR750 sold world-wide over its lifetime while the VFR400 became a massive commercial success and cult bike in Japan. The original RC30 won the first two World Superbike Championships is 1988 and '89, but Honda had to wait until 1997 to win it again with the RC45, the last of the V4 roadsters. In Grands Prix, the NSR500 V4 two-stroke superseded the NS triple and became the benchmark racing machine of the '90s. Mick Doohan secured his place in history by winning five World Championships in consecutive years on it.

In yet another example of Honda inventing a new class of motorcycle, they came up with the astounding CBR900RR FireBlade, a bike with the punch of a 1000 cc motor in a package the size and weight of a 750. It became a cult bike as well as a best seller, and with judicious redesigns, it continues to give much more recent designs a run for their money.

When it became apparent that the high-tech V4 motor of the RC45 was too expensive to produce, Honda looked to a V-twin engine to power its flagship for the first time. Typically, the VTR1000 FireStorm was a much more rideable machine than its opposition, and once accepted by the market formed the basis of the next generation of Superbike racer, the VTR-SP-1.

One of Mr. Honda's mottos was that technology would solve the customers' problems, and no company has embraced cutting-edge technology more firmly than Honda. In fact, Honda often developed new technology, especially in the fields of materials science and metallurgy. The embodiment of that was the NR750, a bike that was misunderstood nearly as much as the original NR500 racer. This limited-edition technological tour-de-force embodied many of Soichiro Honda's ideals. It used the latest techniques and materials in every component, from the oval-piston, 32-valve V4 motor to the titanium coating on the windscreen, it was – as Mr Honda would have wanted – the best it could possibly be. A fitting memorial to the man who has shaped the motorcycle industry and motorcycles as we know them today.

The CX500 – Honda's first V-Twin and a favorite choice of dispatch riders

The VT600 and 750

Honda's current entries in the middleweight cruiser market appeared in 1988 with the introduction of the VT600. Its larger stablemate, the VT750, was introduced 10 years later. The VT600 continued in production through the 2007 model year, while the VT750 is still being produced. Both bikes feature a straightforward and economical design, with a V-twin engine having a 52-degree angle between the cylinders. The engine, which is basically the same in both bikes, has a single overhead cam and three valves (two intake, one exhaust) per cylinder.

Dual carburetors were used on the 1988 and 1989 VT600, as well as on the 1998 through 2003 VT750. Later models use a single carburetor with an accelerator pump.

Front suspension on all models is by damper rod forks. The VT600 rear suspension uses a swingarm that resembles a rigid-frame, with a concealed coil spring-shock absorber unit. The VT750 is equipped with a conventional swingarm and dual coil spring-shock absorber units.

All VT600 models, and 2003 and earlier VT750 models, use chain final drive. 2004 and later VT750 models use the same shaft drive design as the VT1100.

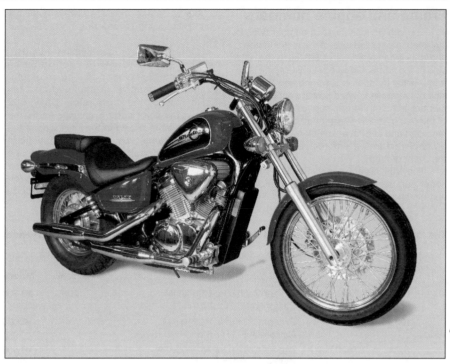

1999 Honda Shadow 600

Acknowledgements

Our thanks to Honda of Milpitas, Milpitas, CA for providing the motorcycles used in the teardown photographs; to Pete Sirett, service manager, for arranging the facilities and fitting the project into his shop's busy schedule; and to Bruce Farley, service technician, for doing the mechanical work and providing valuable technical information. Thanks also to The Motor Cafe, Sunnyvale, California, for providing the motorcycles used in the cover photographs.

About this Manual

The aim of this manual is to help you get the best value from your motorcycle. It can do so in several ways. It can help you decide what work must be done, even if you choose to have it done by a dealer; it provides information and procedures for routine maintenance and servicing; and it offers diagnostic and repair procedures to follow when trouble occurs.

We hope you use the manual to tackle the work yourself. For many simpler jobs, doing it yourself may be quicker than arranging an appointment to get the motorcycle into a dealer and making the trips to leave it and pick it up. More importantly, a lot of money can be saved by avoiding the expense the shop must pass on to you to cover its labour and overhead costs. An added benefit is the sense of satisfaction and accomplishment that you feel after doing the job yourself.

References to the left or right side of the motorcycle assume you are sitting on the seat, facing forward.

We take great pride in the accuracy of information given in this manual, but motorcycle manufacturers make alterations and design changes during the production run of a particular motorcycle of which they do not inform us. No liability can be accepted by the authors or publishers for loss, damage or injury caused by any errors in, or omissions from, the information given.

Frame and engine numbers

The vehicle identification number (VIN) is stamped into the left side of the steering head, and/or is located on a label affixed to the right side of the frame, below the exhaust pipe. The frame serial number is stamped into the right side of the steering head and the engine serial number is stamped into the lower right side of the rear cylinder. These numbers should be recorded and kept in a safe place so they can be furnished to law enforcement officials in the event of theft.

The VIN, frame serial number, engine serial number and carburetor identification number should be kept in a handy place (such as your wallet) so they are always available when purchasing or ordering parts for your machine.

Other important identification numbers include the carburetor identification number and the color code. The carburetor identification number is stamped into the intake side of the carburetor. On VT600 models, the color code is located under the seat, on a label affixed to the inner side of the left upper frame tube, next to the fuel filter; on VT750 models, it's on a label affixed to the front side of the left frame tube, right below the ignition switch and just ahead of the left passenger peg. Always refer to the color code when buying painted parts such as the fuel tank, fenders or side covers.

The models covered by this manual are as follows:

Honda VT600C Shadow VLX, 1988 and 1989
Honda VT600C Shadow VLX, 1991 through 2007
Honda VT600CD Shadow VLX Deluxe, 1993 through 2007
Honda VT750C/CD Shadow American Classic Edition, 1998 through 2003
Honda VT750C Shadow Aero, 2004 through 2009
Honda VT750C2 Shadow Spirit, 2007 through 2009

The following table is a breakdown of the initial frame numbers for each model and year of production:

Year	Model	Initial frame number	Year	Model	Initial frame number
1988	VT600	Except California: PC210 JM California PC211 JM	2000	VT600	Except California: PC210 YK or YM California: PC211 YK or YM
1989	VT600	Except California: PC210 KM California: PC211 KM		VT600CD	Except California: PC213 YK or YM California: PC214 YK or YM
1991	VT600	Except California: PC210 MM California: PC211 MM		VT600CD2	Except California: PC216 YK or YM California: PC217 YK or YM
1992	VT600	Except California: PC210 NM California: PC211 MM		VT750C	Except California: RC440 YK or YK California: RC441 YM or YK
1993	VT600	Except California: PC210 PM California: PC211 PM		VT750CD	Except California: RC443 YM or YK California: RC444 YM or YK
1994	VT600	Except California: PC210 RM California: PC211 RM		VT750CD2	Except California: RC446 YM or YK California: RC447 YM or YK
1995	VT600	Except California: PC210 SM California: PC211 SM	2001	VT600C	Except California: PC210 1K or 1M California: PC211 1K or 1M
	VT600D	Except California: PC213 SM California: PC214 SM		VT600CD	Except California: PC213 1K or 1M California: PC214 1K or 1M
1996	VT600	Except California: PC210 TM California: PC211 TM		VT750CD	Except California: RC443 1K California: RC444 1K
1996	VT600D	Except California: PC213 TM California: PC214 TM		VT750CD2	Except California: RC446 1K California: RC447 1K
1997		Not available at time of printing.		VT750DC	Except California: RC440 1K California: RC441 1K
1998	VT600	Not available at time of printing.	2002	VT600C	Except California: PC210 2K or 2M California: PC211 2K or 2M
	VT750C	Except California: RC440 WM California: RC441 WM		VT600CD	Except California: PC213 2K or 2M California: PC214 2K or 2M
	VT750CD	Except California: RC443 WM California: RC444 WM		VT750CD, VT750CD2	Not available at time of printing
	VT750CD2	Except California: RC446 WM California: RC447WM		VT750DC	Except California: RC440 2M California: RC441 2M
1999	VT600	Except California: PC210 XM9 California: PC211 XM9	2003	VT600C	Except California: PC210 3K or 3M California: PC211 3K or 3M
	VT600D	Except California: PC213 XM9 California: PC214 XM9		VT600CD	Except California: PC213 3K or 3M California: PC214 3K or 3M
	VT600D2	Except California: PC216 XM9 California: PC217 XM9		VT750CD, VT750CD2	Not available at time of printing
	VT750C	Except California: RC440 XM1 California: RC441 XM1		VT750DCA	Except California: RC440 3M California: RC441 3M
	VT750CD	Except California: RC443 XM1 California: RC444 XM1		VT750DCB	Except California: RC445 3M California: RC448 3M
	VT750CD2	Except California: RC446 XM1 California: RC447 XM1	2004 and later		Not available at time of printing

The engine number location

The frame number location

Buying spare parts

Once you have found all the identification numbers, record them for reference when buying parts. Since the manufacturers change specifications, parts and vendors (companies that manufacture various components on the machine), providing the ID numbers is the only way to be reasonably sure that you are buying the correct parts.

Whenever possible, take the worn part to the dealer so direct comparison with the new component can be made. Along the trail from the manufacturer to the parts shelf, there are numerous places that the part can end up with the wrong number or be listed incorrectly.

The two places to purchase new parts for your motorcycle – the accessory store and the franchised dealer – differ in the type of parts they carry. While dealers can obtain virtually every part for your motorcycle, the accessory dealer is usually limited to normal high wear items such as shock absorbers, tune-up parts, various engine gaskets, cables, chains, brake parts, etc. Rarely will an accessory outlet have major suspension components, cylinders, transmission gears, or cases.

Used parts can be obtained for roughly half the price of new ones, but you can't always be sure of what you're getting. Once again, take your worn part to the breaker's yard for direct comparison.

Whether buying new, used or rebuilt parts, the best course is to deal directly with someone who specializes in parts for your particular make.

Professional mechanics are trained in safe working procedures. However enthusiastic you may be about getting on with the job at hand, take the time to ensure that your safety is not put at risk. A moment's lack of attention can result in an accident, as can failure to observe simple precautions.

There will always be new ways of having accidents, and the following is not a comprehensive list of all dangers; it is intended rather to make you aware of the risks and to encourage a safe approach to all work you carry out on your bike.

Asbestos

● Certain friction, insulating, sealing and other products - such as brake pads, clutch linings, gaskets, etc. - contain asbestos. Extreme care must be taken to avoid inhalation of dust from such products since it is hazardous to health. If in doubt, assume that they do contain asbestos.

Fire

● Remember at all times that gasoline is highly flammable. Never smoke or have any kind of naked flame around, when working on the vehicle. But the risk does not end there - a spark caused by an electrical short-circuit, by two metal surfaces contacting each other, by careless use of tools, or even by static electricity built up in your body under certain conditions, can ignite gasoline vapor, which in a confined space is highly explosive. Never use gasoline as a cleaning solvent. Use an approved safety solvent.

● Always disconnect the battery ground terminal before working on any part of the fuel or electrical system, and never risk spilling fuel on to a hot engine or exhaust.

● It is recommended that a fire extinguisher of a type suitable for fuel and electrical fires is kept handy in the garage or workplace at all times. Never try to extinguish a fuel or electrical fire with water.

Fumes

● Certain fumes are highly toxic and can quickly cause unconsciousness and even death if inhaled to any extent. Gasoline vapor comes into this category, as do the vapors from certain solvents such as trichloro-ethylene. Any draining or pouring of such volatile fluids should be done in a well ventilated area.

● When using cleaning fluids and solvents, read the instructions carefully. Never use materials from unmarked containers - they may give off poisonous vapors.

● Never run the engine of a motor vehicle in an enclosed space such as a garage. Exhaust fumes contain carbon monoxide which is extremely poisonous; if you need to run the engine, always do so in the open air or at least have the rear of the vehicle outside the workplace.

The battery

● Never cause a spark, or allow a naked light near the vehicle's battery. It will normally be giving off a certain amount of hydrogen gas, which is highly explosive.

● Always disconnect the battery ground terminal before working on the fuel or electrical systems (except where noted).

● If possible, loosen the filler plugs or cover when charging the battery from an external source. Do not charge at an excessive rate or the battery may burst.

● Take care when topping up, cleaning or carrying the battery. The acid electrolyte, even when diluted, is very corrosive and should not be allowed to contact the eyes or skin. Always wear rubber gloves and goggles or a face shield. If you ever need to prepare electrolyte yourself, always add the acid slowly to the water; never add the water to the acid.

Electricity

● When using an electric power tool, inspection light etc., always ensure that the appliance is correctly connected to its plug and that, where necessary, it is properly grounded. Do not use such appliances in damp conditions and, again, beware of creating a spark or applying excessive heat in the vicinity of fuel or fuel vapor. Also ensure that the appliances meet national safety standards.

● A severe electric shock can result from touching certain parts of the electrical system, such as the spark plug wires (HT leads), when the engine is running or being cranked, particularly if components are damp or the insulation is defective. Where an electronic ignition system is used, the secondary (HT) voltage is much higher and could prove fatal.

Remember...

✗ **Don't** start the engine without first ascertaining that the transmission is in neutral.

✗ **Don't** suddenly remove the pressure cap from a hot cooling system - cover it with a cloth and release the pressure gradually first, or you may get scalded by escaping coolant.

✗ **Don't** attempt to drain oil until you are sure it has cooled sufficiently to avoid scalding you.

✗ **Don't** grasp any part of the engine or exhaust system without first ascertaining that it is cool enough not to burn you.

✗ **Don't** allow brake fluid or antifreeze to contact the machine's paintwork or plastic components.

✗ **Don't** siphon toxic liquids such as fuel, hydraulic fluid or antifreeze by mouth, or allow them to remain on your skin.

✗ **Don't** inhale dust - it may be injurious to health (see Asbestos heading).

✗ **Don't** allow any spilled oil or grease to remain on the floor - wipe it up right away, before someone slips on it.

✗ **Don't** use ill-fitting wrenches or other tools which may slip and cause injury.

✗ **Don't** lift a heavy component which may be beyond your capability - get assistance.

✗ **Don't** rush to finish a job or take unverified short cuts.

✗ **Don't** allow children or animals in or around an unattended vehicle.

✗ **Don't** inflate a tire above the recommended pressure. Apart from overstressing the carcass, in extreme cases the tire may blow off forcibly.

✔ **Do** ensure that the machine is supported securely at all times. This is especially important when the machine is blocked up to aid wheel or fork removal.

✔ **Do** take care when attempting to loosen a stubborn nut or bolt. It is generally better to pull on a wrench, rather than push, so that if you slip, you fall away from the machine rather than onto it.

✔ **Do** wear eye protection when using power tools such as drill, sander, bench grinder etc.

✔ **Do** use a barrier cream on your hands prior to undertaking dirty jobs - it will protect your skin from infection as well as making the dirt easier to remove afterwards; but make sure your hands aren't left slippery. Note that long-term contact with used engine oil can be a health hazard.

✔ **Do** keep loose clothing (cuffs, ties etc. and long hair) well out of the way of moving mechanical parts.

✔ **Do** remove rings, wristwatch etc., before working on the vehicle - especially the electrical system.

✔ **Do** keep your work area tidy - it is only too easy to fall over articles left lying around.

✔ **Do** exercise caution when compressing springs for removal or installation. Ensure that the tension is applied and released in a controlled manner, using suitable tools which preclude the possibility of the spring escaping violently.

✔ **Do** ensure that any lifting tackle used has a safe working load rating adequate for the job.

✔ **Do** get someone to check periodically that all is well, when working alone on the vehicle.

✔ **Do** carry out work in a logical sequence and check that everything is correctly assembled and tightened afterwards.

✔ **Do** remember that your vehicle's safety affects that of yourself and others. If in doubt on any point, get professional advice.

● If in spite of following these precautions, you are unfortunate enough to injure yourself, seek medical attention as soon as possible.

Note: *The Pre-ride checks outlined in the owner's manual covers those items which should be inspected before riding the motorcycle.*

Engine oil level

Before you start:

Caution: Do not run the engine in an enclosed space such as a garage or workshop.

✔ Start the engine and let it idle for several minutes to allow it to reach normal operating temperature.

✔ Stop the engine and support the motorcycle in an upright position, using an auxiliary stand if required. Make sure it is on level ground.

✔ Leave the motorcycle undisturbed for a few minutes to allow the oil level to stabilize.

Bike care:

● If you have to add oil frequently, you should check whether you have any oil leaks. If there is no sign of oil leakage from the joints and gaskets the engine could be burning oil (see *Troubleshooting*).

The correct oil:

● Modern, high-revving engines place great demands on their oil. It is very important that the correct oil for your bike is used.

● Always top up with a good quality oil of the specified type and viscosity and do not overfill the engine.

Oil type	API grade SF, SG or VASO standard MA
Oil viscosity	SAE 10W40 or 10W30

1 Remove the oil filler cap (arrow) from the right-hand side of the engine. The dipstick is integral with the cap and is used to check the engine oil level. Using a clean rag or paper towel, wipe all the oil off the dipstick. Insert the clean dipstick in the filler cap hole, but do not screw it in.

2 Remove the dipstick and observe the level of the oil, which should be somewhere in between the upper and lower lines (arrows). If the level is below the lower line, add the recommended grade and type of oil to bring the level up to the upper line on the dipstick. Do not overfill. Install the filler cap.

Coolant level

> ⚠ **Warning: DO NOT remove the radiator pressure cap to add coolant. Topping up is done via the coolant reservoir tank filler. DO NOT leave open containers of coolant about, as it is poisonous.**

Before you start:

✔ Make sure you have a supply of coolant available – a mixture of 50% distilled water and 50% corrosion inhibited ethylene glycol antifreeze is needed.

✔ Check the coolant level when the engine is at operating temperature and idling.

✔ Support the motorcycle in an upright position, using an auxiliary stand if required. Make sure it is on level ground.

Bike care:

● Use only the specified coolant mixture. It is important that antifreeze is used in the system all year round, and not just in the winter. Do not top the system up using only water, as the system will become too diluted.

● Do not overfill the reservoir. If the coolant is significantly above the FULL level line at any time, the surplus should be siphoned or drained off to prevent the possibility of it being expelled out of the overflow hose.

● If the coolant level falls steadily, check the system for leaks (see Chapter 1). If no leaks are found and the level continues to fall, it is recommended that the machine be taken to a Honda dealer for a pressure test.

1 The coolant reservoir is mounted behind the right passenger footpeg on VT600 models and below the front of the engine on early VT750 models (shown).

2 On later VT750 models, it's on the left side of the bike below the swingarm pivot. If the coolant level on the reservoir is below the lower line, remove the cap and top the coolant level up with the recommended coolant mixture.

Suspension, steering and drive chain

Suspension and Steering:

● Check that the front and rear suspension operates smoothly without binding.
● Check that the suspension is adjusted as required.
● Check that the steering moves smoothly from lock-to-lock.

Drive chain:

● Check that the drive chain slack isn't excessive, and adjust it if necessary (see Chapter 1).
● If the chain looks dry, lubricate it (see Chapter 1).

Legal and safety

Lighting and signalling:

● Take a minute to check that the headlight, tail light, brake light, instrument lights and turn signals all work correctly.
● Check that the horn sounds when the switch is operated.
● A working speedometer graduated in mph is a statutory requirement in the UK.

Safety:

● Check that the throttle grip rotates smoothly and snaps shut when released, in all steering positions. Also check for the correct amount of freeplay (see Chapter 1).
● Check that the engine shuts off when the kill switch is operated.
● Check that sidestand (and centerstand on CBF600 models) return spring holds the stand up securely when it is retracted.

Fuel:

● This may seem obvious, but check that you have enough fuel to complete your journey. If you notice signs of fuel leakage – rectify the cause immediately.
● Ensure you use the correct grade unleaded fuel – see Chapter 4 Specifications.

Brake fluid levels

> ⚠️ *Warning: Brake hydraulic fluid can harm your eyes and damage painted surfaces, so use extreme caution when handling and pouring it and cover surrounding surfaces with rag. Do not use fluid that has been standing open for some time, as it absorbs moisture from the air which can cause a dangerous loss of braking effectiveness.*

Before you start:

✔ Support the motorcycle in an upright position, using an auxiliary stand if required.

Turn the handlebars until the top of the front master cylinder is as level as possible. The rear master cylinder reservoir is located behind the right-hand side cover on CB600F and FS models.

✔ Make sure you have the correct hydraulic fluid. DOT 4 is recommended.

✔ Wrap a rag around the reservoir being worked on to ensure that any spillage does not come into contact with painted surfaces.

Bike care:

● The fluid in the front and rear brake master cylinder reservoirs will drop slightly as the brake pads wear down.

● If any fluid reservoir requires repeated topping-up this is an indication of an hydraulic leak somewhere in the system, which should be investigated immediately.

● Check for signs of fluid leakage from the hydraulic hoses and brake system components – if found, rectify immediately (see Chapter 7).

● Check the operation of both brakes before taking the machine on the road; if there is evidence of air in the system (spongy feel to lever or pedal), it must be bled as described in Chapter 7.

1 The front brake fluid level is visible through the sight glass in the reservoir body - it must be above the LOWER reservoir line. If the fluid is below the line, remove the cap screws and lift off the reservoir cap, diaphragm plate and diaphragm. Top up with new, clean DOT 4 brake fluid, until the level is just below the upper level line cast on the inside of the reservoir. Take care to avoid spills (see WARNING above) and do not overfill. Be sure the diaphragm is correctly seated before installing the plate and cap, then tighten the screws securely.

2 Press the brake pedal and look at the indicator. If the moving pointer (right arrow) aligns with the mark cast on the brake panel (left arrow), the brake shoes are worn and need to be replaced

Tires

The correct pressures:

● The tires must be checked when **cold**, not immediately after riding. Note that low tire pressures may cause the tire to slip on the rim or come off. High tire pressures will cause abnormal tread wear and unsafe handling.

● Use an accurate pressure gauge. Many garage forecourt gauges are wildly inaccurate. If you buy your own, spend as much as you can justify on a quality gauge.

● Correct air pressure will increase tire life and provide maximum stability, handling capability and ride comfort.

Front	2 Bar (29 psi)
Rear	
Up to 90 kg (198 lbs)	2 Bar (29 psi)
Above 90 kg (198 lbs)	2.5 Bar (36 psi)

Tire care:

● Check the tires carefully for cuts, tears, embedded nails or other sharp objects and excessive wear. Operation of the motorcycle with excessively worn tires is extremely hazardous, as traction and handling are directly affected.

● Check the condition of the tire valve and ensure the dust cap is in place.

● Pick out any stones or nails which may have become embedded in the tire tread. If left, they will eventually penetrate through the casing and cause a puncture.

● If tire damage is apparent, or unexplained loss of pressure is experienced, seek the advice of a tire fitting specialist without delay.

Tire tread depth:

● At the time of writing UK law requires that tread depth must be at least 1 mm over the entire tread breadth all the way around the tire, with no bald patches. Many riders, however, consider 2 mm tread depth minimum to be a safer limit. Honda recommends a minimum of 1.5 mm for the front tire and 2 mm for the rear tire.

● Many tires now incorporate wear indicators in the tread. Identify the triangular pointer or

1 Check the tire pressures when the tires are cold and keep them properly inflated.

TWI mark on the tire sidewall to locate the indicator bar and renew the tire if the tread has worn down to the bar.

2 Measure tread depth at the center of the tire using a tread depth gauge

3 Tire tread wear indicator bar (A) and its location marking (B) – usually either an arrow, a triangle or the letters TWI – on the sidewall. Look for the tire information label on the chainguard or swingarm

Chapter 1
Tune-up and routine maintenance

Contents

Degrees of difficulty

Easy, suitable for novice with little experience	**Fairly easy,** suitable for beginner with some experience	**Fairly difficult,** suitable for competent DIY mechanic	**Difficult,** suitable for experienced DIY mechanic	**Very difficult,** suitable for expert DIY or professional

Specifications

Engine
Spark plugs (all VT600, 2003 and earlier VT750)

Type

Standard	NGK DPR8EA-9 or ND X24EPR-U9
Cold climate	NGK DPR7EA-9 or ND X22EPR-U9
Extended high-speed riding	NGK DPR9EA-9 or ND X27EPR-U9
Gap	0.8 to 0.9 mm (0.031 to 0.035 inch)

Engine (continued)

Spark plugs (VT750, 2004 and later)	
Standard	NGK DPR6EA-9 or ND X20EPR-U9
Extended high-speed riding...	NGK DPR7EA-9 or ND X22EPR-U9
Valve clearances (COLD engine)	
Intake	0.13 to 0.17 mm (0.005 to 0.007 inch)
Exhaust	0.18 to 0.22 mm (0.007 to 0.009 inch)
Engine idle speed	
VT600	1100 to 1300 rpm
VT750	
2003 and earlier	900 to 1100 rpm
2004 and later	1100 to 1300 rpm
Cylinder compression pressure	
VT600	12.26 to 14.22 Bars (178 to 206 psi)
VT750	
2003 and earlier	11.77 to 13.73 Bars (171 to 199 psi)
2004 and later	13.73 to 14.69 Bars (199 to 213 psi)
Carburetor synchronization (dual carburetor models)	
Maximum vacuum difference between cylinders	
VT600	
1988 and 1989, 1991 through 1996......................................	40 mm Hg (1.6 inches Hg)
1997 on	20 mm Hg (0.7 inch Hg)
VT750	20 mm Hg (0.7 inch Hg)
Cylinder numbering	
Rear cylinder	1
Front cylinder	2

Miscellaneous

Battery electrolyte specific gravity	1.280 at 20 degrees C (68 degrees F)
Brake pedal position	
Pedal height (above top of footpeg)	
VT600	43 mm (1.7 inches)
VT750	
VT750C/CD ACE	50 mm (2.0 inches)
VT750DC Spirit...	Not specified
VT750C Aero, VT750 C2 Spirit (2004 and later)	75 mm (3.0 inches)
Pedal freeplay	20 to 30 mm (3/4 to 1-1/4 inches)
Clutch lever freeplay..	10 to 20 mm (3/8 to 3/4 inch)
Drive chain slack	
VT600...	20 to 30 mm (3/4 to 1-3/16 inches)
VT750...	15 to 25 mm (5/8 to 1 inch)
Throttle grip freeplay	2 to 6 mm (1/8 to 1/4 inch)
Minimum tire tread depth	
Front...	1.5 mm (0.06 inch)
Rear..	2.0 mm (0.08 inch)
Tire pressures (cold)	
Front...	2 Bars (29 psi)
Rear	
Up to 90 kg (198 lbs)	2 Bars (29 psi)
Above 90 kg (198 lbs)	2.5 Bars (36 psi)

Torque specifications

Cooling system drain plugs	
Water pump drain plug	13 Nm (116 in-lbs)
Rear cylinder drain plug	13 Nm (116 in-lbs)
Oil drain plug	
VT600	
1988 through 1998	34 Nm (25 ft-lbs)
1999 on	30 Nm (22 ft-lbs)
VT750	
2003 and earlier..	30 Nm (22 ft-lbs)
2004 and later	29 Nm (21 ft-lbs)
Spark plugs	
2003 and earlier	
Used	14 Nm (124 in-lbs)
New	Hand tighten until sealing washer touches seat, then tighten plug 1/2-turn

2004 and later
    VT750C Aero .... 16 Nm (12 ft-lbs)
    VT750C2 Spirit.. 18 Nm (13 ft-lbs)
Steering head bearing adjustment nut
    VT600... 25 Nm (18 ft-lbs)
    VT750... 21 Nm (16 ft-lbs)
Valve adjustment screw locknuts .... 23 Nm (17 ft-lbs)
Valve adjustment cover bolts (VT600) .... 12 Nm (106 in-lbs)
Final drive oil check plug .... 12 Nm (106 inch-lbs)
Final drive oil drain plug .... 29 Nm (22 ft-lbs)

Recommended lubricants and fluids

Fuel type... Unleaded
Fuel capacity
    VT600
        1988 and 1989, 1991 through 1993
            Total.. 9 liters (2.4 gallons)
            Reserve .... 1.9 liters (0.5 gallons)
        1994 on
            Total.. 11 liters (2.9 gallons)
            Reserve .... 3.4 liters (0.9 gallons)
    VT750C/CD ACE
        Total.. 14.0 liters (3.7 gallons)
        Reserve... 3.6 liters (0.95 gallons)
    VT750DC Spirit, VT750C Aero, VT750 C2 Spirit
        Total.. 13.0 liters (3.43 gallons)
        Reserve... 4.0 liters (1.06 gallons)
Engine/transmission oil
    Type... API grade SG or higher, meeting JASO standard MA
                                      (the MA standard is required to prevent clutch slippage)
    Viscosity.. 10W30 or 10W40
    Capacity
        VT600
            Oil change only.. 2.1 liters (2.21 quarts)
            With filter change .... 2.25 liters (2.38 quarts)
        VT750
            2003 and earlier
                Oil change only .... 2.2 liters (2.32 quarts)
                With filter change .... 2.4 liters (2.54 quarts)
            2004 and later
                Oil change only .... 2.5 liters (2.6 quarts)
                With filter change .... 2.6 liters (2.75 quarts)
Coolant
    Type... 50/50 mixture of ethylene glycol-based antifreeze and distilled water
    Capacity
        Radiator and engine
            VT600... 1.6 liters (1.51 quarts)
            VT750
                 2003 and earlier.. 1.75 liters (1.85 quarts)
                2004 and later .... 1.58 liters (1.67 quarts)
            Reservoir... 0.4 liter (0.42 quart)
Final drive oil (shaft drive)
    Type... SAE 80 hypoid gear oil
    Capacity (drain and fill) .... 160 cc (5.4 fl oz)
Brake fluid .... DOT 4
Wheel bearings.. Medium weight, lithium-based multi-purpose grease
Swingarm pivot bearings... Medium weight, lithium-based multi-purpose grease
Cables and lever pivots... Chain and cable lubricant or 10W30 motor oil
Sidestand pivot .... Chain and cable lubricant or 10W30 motor oil
Brake pedal/shift lever pivots.. Chain and cable lubricant or 10W30 motor oil
Throttle grip .... Multi-purpose grease or dry film lubricant

Maintenance points

1 Front brake master cylinder
2 Steering head bearing adjuster
3 Front brake pads
4 Rear brake light switch
5 Air filter (behind cover)
6 Cooling system lower drain plug (on left side)

7 Engine oil drain plug (on left side, behind water pump)
8 Oil filter (on lower rear of engine)
9 Drive chain adjuster location (chain drive models; one on each side of bike)
10 Rear brake adjuster

11 Rear brake wear indicator (behind muffler)
12 Battery (behind side cover)
13 Engine oil filler cap/dipstick
14 Cooling system upper drain plug (on rear of front cylinder)

1 Maintenance schedule

Note: *The pre-ride inspection outlined in the owner's manual covers checks and maintenance that should be carried out on a daily basis. It's condensed and included here to remind you of its importance. Always perform the pre-ride inspection at every maintenance interval (in addition to the procedures listed). The intervals listed below are the shortest intervals recommended by the manufacturer for each particular operation during the model years covered in this manual. Your owner's manual may have different intervals for your model.*

Daily or before riding
- [ ] Check the engine oil level
- [ ] Check the fuel level and inspect for leaks
- [ ] Check the engine coolant level and look for leaks
- [ ] Check the operation of both brakes - also check the front brake fluid level and look for leakage
- [ ] Check the tires for damage, the presence of foreign objects and correct air pressure
- [ ] Check the throttle for smooth operation and correct freeplay
- [ ] Check the operation of the clutch - make sure the freeplay is correct
- [ ] Make sure the steering operates smoothly, without looseness and without binding
- [ ] Check for proper operation of the headlight, taillight, brake light, turn signals, indicator lights and horn
- [ ] Make sure the sidestand fully returns to its "up" position and stays there under spring pressure
- [ ] Make sure the engine STOP switch works properly

After the initial 600 miles/1000 km
- [ ] Perform all of the daily checks plus:
- [ ] Check/adjust the carburetor synchronization
- [ ] Adjust the valve clearances
- [ ] Check/adjust the drive chain slack
- [ ] Change the engine oil and oil filter
- [ ] Check the tightness of all fasteners
- [ ] Check the steering
- [ ] Check/adjust clutch freeplay
- [ ] Check the front brake fluid level
- [ ] Check the cooling system hoses
- [ ] Inspect brake pads and shoes
- [ ] Check/adjust the brake pedal position
- [ ] Check the operation of the brake light
- [ ] Check the operation of the sidestand switch
- [ ] Lubricate the clutch cable, throttle cable(s) and speedometer cable

Every 300 miles/500 km
- [ ] Check/adjust the drive chain slack (if equipped)

Every 4000 miles/6000 km or 6 months
- [ ] Change the engine oil
- [ ] Clean the air filter element and replace it if necessary
- [ ] Adjust the valve clearances

- [ ] Clean and gap the spark plugs
- [ ] Lubricate the clutch cable, throttle cable(s) and speedometer cable
- [ ] Check/adjust throttle cable freeplay
- [ ] Check/adjust the idle speed
- [ ] Check/adjust the carburetor synchronization
- [ ] Check the front brake fluid level
- [ ] Adjust front brake freeplay
- [ ] Check the brake disc and pads
- [ ] Check the rear brake shoes for wear
- [ ] Check/adjust the brake pedal position
- [ ] Check the operation of the brake light
- [ ] Lubricate the clutch and brake lever pivots
- [ ] Lubricate the shift/brake pedal pivots and the sidestand pivot
- [ ] Check the steering
- [ ] Check the front forks for proper operation and fluid leaks
- [ ] Check the tires, wheels and wheel bearings
- [ ] Check the battery electrolyte level and specific gravity; inspect the breather tube
- [ ] Check the exhaust system for leaks and check the tightness of the fasteners
- [ ] Check the cleanliness of the fuel system and the condition of the fuel lines and vacuum hoses
- [ ] Inspect the crankcase ventilation system
- [ ] Check the operation of the sidestand switch
- [ ] Check and adjust clutch cable freeplay

Every 8,000 miles/12,000 km or 12 months
All of the items above plus:
- [ ] Change the engine oil and oil filter
- [ ] Replace the spark plugs
- [ ] Check the final drive oil

Every 12,000 miles/18,000 km
- [ ] Repack the swingarm bearings
- [ ] Inspect the cooling system and replace the coolant

Every 15,000 miles/24,000 km or two years
- [ ] Clean and lubricate the steering head bearings

Every 24,000 miles/38,600 km
- [ ] Change the final drive oil

Every 30,000 miles/50,000 km
- [ ] Replace the drive chain

Every two years
- [ ] Replace the brake master cylinder and caliper seals and change the brake fluid

Every four years
- [ ] Replace the brake hose

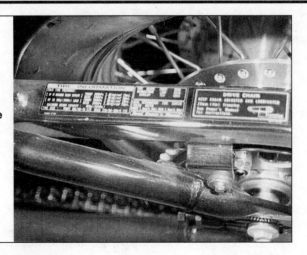

2.3 Decals at various locations on the motorcycle include such information as tire pressures and drive chain service procedures

References to additional information in applicable Chapters is also included and should not be overlooked.

Before beginning any maintenance or repair, the machine should be cleaned thoroughly, especially around the oil filter, spark plugs, cylinder head covers, side covers, carburetors, etc. Cleaning will help ensure that dirt does not contaminate the engine and will allow you to detect wear and damage that could otherwise easily go unnoticed.

3 Fluid levels - check

2 Introduction to tune-up and routine maintenance

This Chapter covers in detail the checks and procedures necessary for the tune-up and routine maintenance of your motorcycle. Section 1 includes the routine maintenance schedule, which is designed to keep the machine in proper running condition and prevent possible problems. The remaining Sections contain detailed procedures for carrying out the items listed on the maintenance schedule, as well as additional maintenance information designed to increase reliability.

Since routine maintenance plays such an important role in the safe and efficient operation of your motorcycle, it is presented here as a comprehensive check list. For the rider who does all his own maintenance, these lists outline the procedures and checks that should be done on a routine basis.

Maintenance information is printed on labels attached to the motorcycle **(see illustration)**. If the information on the labels differs from that included here, use the information on the label.

Deciding where to start, or "plug into," the routine maintenance schedule depends on several factors. If the warranty has recently expired, and if the motorcycle has been maintained according to the warranty standards, you may want to pick up routine maintenance as it coincides with the next mileage or calendar interval. If you have owned the machine for some time but have never performed any maintenance on it, then you may want to start at the nearest interval and include some additional procedures to ensure that nothing important is overlooked. If you have just had a major engine overhaul, then you may want to start the maintenance routine from the beginning. If you have a used machine and have no knowledge of its history or maintenance record, you may desire to combine all the checks into one large service initially and then settle into the maintenance schedule prescribed.

The Sections which outline the inspection and maintenance procedures are written as step-by-step comprehensive guides to the performance of the work. They explain in detail each of the routine inspections and maintenance procedures on the check list.

Engine oil

1   Run the engine and allow it to reach normal operating temperature.
Caution: Do not run the engine in an enclosed space such as a garage or shop.
2   Stop the engine and allow the machine to sit undisturbed for about five minutes.
3   Hold the motorcycle level. With the engine off, remove the filler cap from the right side of the crankcase and check the oil level on the dipstick. It should be between the Maximum and Minimum level marks on the dipstick **(see illustrations)**.
4   If the level is below the Minimum mark, add enough oil of the recommended grade and type to bring the level up to the Maximum mark. Do not overfill.

Brake fluid

5   In order to ensure proper operation of the hydraulic disc brake, the fluid level in the master cylinder reservoir must be properly maintained.
6   With the motorcycle held level, turn the handlebars until the top of the master cylinder is as level as possible.
7   Look closely at the inspection window in the master cylinder reservoir. Make sure that the fluid level is above the Lower mark

3.3a Remove the filler plug (arrow) . . .

3.3b . . . and add oil, if necessary, to bring the level up to the maximum mark

3.7 The level of the brake fluid in the master cylinder reservoir should be above the Lower line in the window; to remove the cover, remove these two screws (arrows)

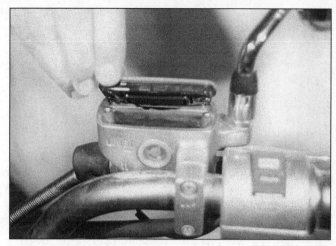

3.9 To add fluid, carefully remove the cover and diaphragm

on the reservoir **(see illustration)**.

8   If the level is low, the fluid must be replenished. Before removing the master cylinder cover, cover the fuel tank to protect it from brake fluid spills (which will damage the paint) and remove all dust and dirt from the area around the cover.

9   To add brake fluid, remove the reservoir cover screws **(see illustration 3.7)** and lift off the cover and rubber diaphragm **(see illustration)**.

Caution: Do not operate the front brake with the cover removed.

10   Add new, clean brake fluid of the recommended type until the level is above the inspection window. Do not mix different brands of brake fluid in the reservoir, as they may not be compatible.

11   Reinstall the rubber diaphragm and the cover. Tighten the screws evenly, but do not overtighten them.

12   Wipe any spilled fluid off the reservoir body.

13   If the brake fluid level was low, inspect the brake system for leaks.

Coolant

14   Warm up the engine and check the coolant level with the engine running at its normal temperature.

15   On VT600 models, the Upper and Lower level marks for the coolant are on the front right corner of the coolant reservoir, directly behind the oil filler cap/dipstick **(see illustration 3.3a)**. On VT750 models, the Upper and Lower level marks for the coolant are on the left side of the coolant reservoir, which is located below the radiator, in front of the engine.

16   The reservoir is translucent plastic, so the coolant level is easily visible in relation to the marks. The coolant level should be at the Upper mark on the reservoir.

17   To add coolant, shut off the engine and remove the coolant reservoir filler cap **(see illustrations)**. Using a 50/50 mixture of ethyl-

ene glycol and distilled water, bring the coolant level up to the Upper mark on the reservoir. Install the filler cap.

18   If the coolant level in the reservoir was low, or empty, inspect the cooling system (see Section 20). It might be leaking.

Final drive oil (shaft drive)

19   Check the final drive oil level as described in Section 30.

4   Battery electrolyte level/ specific gravity - check

> ⚠ *Warning: Be extremely careful when handling or working around the battery. The electrolyte is very caustic and an explosive gas (hydrogen) is given off when the battery is charging.*

3.17a On VT600 models, the coolant reservoir filler cap (arrow) is located on the right side of the bike, near the passenger footpeg

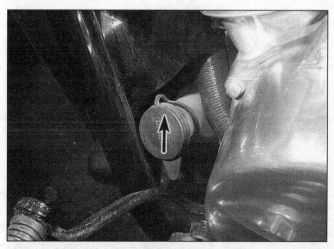

3.17b On VT750 models, the coolant reservoir filler cap (arrow) is located on the left side of the bike, near the shift lever, below the radiator

4.4 The electrolyte level should be between the marks on the battery case

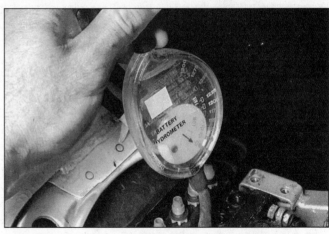

4.7 Check the specific gravity with a hydrometer

1   This procedure applies to conventional batteries with filler caps which can be removed to add water to the battery cells. The original-equipment battery is a sealed, maintenance-free battery; if the motorcycle is still equipped with the original battery, or an OEM replacement, it's unnecessary to check the electrolyte. However, if a conventional battery has been installed, it should be checked as follows.

2   Remove the battery (see Chapter 9).

3   Clean off the battery and place it on a workbench.

4   The electrolyte level, which is visible through the translucent battery case, should be between the Upper and Lower level marks **(see illustration)**.

5   If the electrolyte is low, remove the cell caps and fill each cell to the upper level mark with distilled water. Do not use tap water (except in an emergency), and do not overfill. The cell holes are quite small, so it may help to use a plastic squeeze bottle with a small spout to add the water. If the level is within the marks on the case, additional water is not necessary.

6   Next, check the specific gravity of the electrolyte in each cell with a small hydrometer made especially for motorcycle batteries. These are available from most dealer parts departments or motorcycle accessory stores.

7   Remove the caps, draw some electrolyte from the first cell into the hydrometer **(see illustration)** and note the specific gravity. Compare the reading to the Specifications listed in this Chapter. Add 0.004 points to the reading for every 10-degrees F above 20-degrees C (68-degrees F); subtract 0.004 points from the reading for every 10-degrees below 20-degrees C (68-degrees F). Return the electrolyte to the appropriate cell and repeat the check for the remaining cells. When the check is complete, rinse the hydrometer thoroughly with clean water.

8   If the specific gravity of the electrolyte in each cell is as specified, the battery is in good condition and is apparently being charged by the machine's charging system.

9   If the specific gravity is low, the battery is not fully charged. This may be due to corroded battery terminals, a dirty battery case, a malfunctioning charging system, or loose or corroded wiring connections. On the other hand, it may be that the battery is worn out, especially if the machine is old, or that infrequent use of the motorcycle prevents normal charging from taking place.

10   Be sure to correct any problems and charge the battery if necessary. Refer to Chapter 9 for additional battery maintenance and charging procedures.

11   Install the battery cell caps, tightening them securely.

12   Install the battery (see Chapter 9). When reconnecting the cables to the battery, attach the positive cable first, then the negative cable. Make sure to install the insulating boot over the positive terminal. Install all components removed for access. Be very careful not to pinch or otherwise restrict the battery vent tube, as the battery may build up enough internal pressure during normal charging system operation to explode.

5   Brake pads and shoes - wear check

1   The front brake pads and the rear brake shoes should be checked at the recommended intervals and replaced when worn beyond the limit listed in this Chapter's Specifications. Always replace pads and shoes as complete sets.

2   To check the thickness of the front brake pads, squeeze the front brake lever and look at the pads through the lower "window" of the caliper **(see illustration)**. Note whether

5.2b If there are no wear indicator marks on the lower end of the brake pads, inspect the pad rain grooves from the open front side of the caliper; when the grooves in the pads are no longer visible, replace the pads (caliper and pads removed from bike for clarity)

5.2a Using a small flashlight, look at the pads through the small openings at the bottom of the caliper and note whether the pads are worn down to the wear indicator marks parallel to the pad backing plates

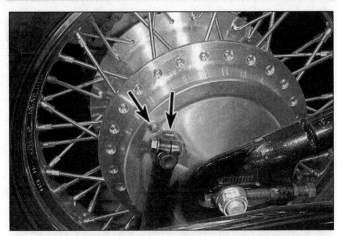

5.3 To check the rear brake shoe thickness, firmly depress the brake pedal; if the pointer on the brake arm points at or near the mark on the brake panel (arrows), replace the brake shoes

6.6a The VT600 rear brake light switch (arrow) is located on the right side, below the right passenger footpeg

the pads are worn down to the wear indicator marks which run parallel to the pad backing plates. If they are, replace the pads (see Chapter 7). If there are no wear indicator marks on the lower ends of the pads, look through the open part of the caliper facing toward the front of the machine and note the small rain grooves cut into each pad **(see illustration)**. If these grooves are still visible, the pads have some service life remaining. If the grooves are gone, replace the pads (see Chapter 7).

3   To check the rear brake shoes, press the brake pedal firmly while you look at the wear indicator mark on the brake panel **(see illustration)**. If the indicator pointer on the brake arm is close to or at the wear indicator mark, replace the shoes (see Chapter 7).

6 Brake system - general check

1   A routine general check of the brakes will ensure that any problems are discovered and remedied before the rider's safety is jeopardized.
2   Check the brake lever and pedal for loose connections, excessive play, bends, and other damage. Replace any damaged parts with new ones (see Chapter 7).

3   Make sure all brake fasteners are tight. Check the brake pads and shoes for wear (see Section 5) and make sure the fluid level in the front brake reservoir is correct (see Section 3). Look for leaks at the hose connections and check for cracks in the hose(s). If the lever or pedal is spongy, bleed the brakes (see Chapter 7).
4   Make sure the brake light operates when the brake lever is depressed.
5   Make sure the brake light is activated just before the rear brake takes effect.
6   If adjustment is necessary, hold the switch so it won't rotate and turn the adjusting nut on the switch body **(see illustrations)** until the brake light is activated when required. If the switch doesn't operate the brake lights, check the switch and circuit (see Chapter 9).
7   The front brake light switch is not adjustable. If it fails to operate properly, replace it (see Chapter 9).

7 Rear brake pedal height and freeplay - check and adjustment

1   The rear brake pedal height, measured from the top of the footpeg to the top of the pedal **(see illustration)**, should be at the

6.6b The VT750 rear brake light switch (arrow) is located on the right side, in front of the engine, near the brake pedal linkage

height listed in this Chapter's Specifications. If it isn't, adjust the pedal height. Loosen the locknut **(see illustration)**, turn the adjuster bolt to set the pedal height and tighten the locknut.

7.1b To adjust brake pedal height, loosen the locknut (arrow) and turn the adjustment bolt until pedal height is correct, then tighten the locknut

7.1a Brake pedal height (A) and freeplay (B)

7.2 To adjust brake pedal freeplay, turn this adjusting nut until the pedal freeplay is correct

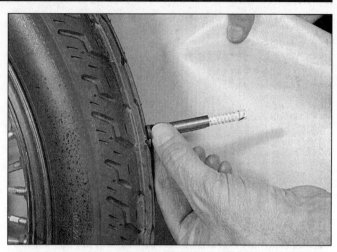

8.2 Measure tread depth at the center of the tire (tread depth gauges are available at most dealerships and motorcycle accessory shops)

2   Check pedal freeplay (the distance the pedal travels downward before the brake shoes contact the drum) and compare it to the value listed in this Chapter's Specifications. If the pedal freeplay isn't within this dimension, adjust it by turning the nut at the rear end of the brake rod **(see illustration)**.

3   If necessary, adjust the brake light switch (see Section 6).

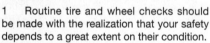

8   Tires/wheels - general check

1   Routine tire and wheel checks should be made with the realization that your safety depends to a great extent on their condition.

2   Check the tires carefully for cuts, tears, embedded nails or other sharp objects and excessive wear. Operation of the motorcycle with excessively worn tires is extremely hazardous, as traction and handling are directly affected. Measure the tread depth at the center of the tire **(see illustration)** and replace worn tires with new ones when the tread depth is less than specified.

3   Repair or replace punctured tires as soon as damage is noted. Do not try to patch a torn tire, as wheel balance and tire reliability may be impaired.

4   Check the tire pressures when the tires are cold and keep them properly inflated **(see illustration)**. Proper air pressure will increase tire life and provide maximum stability and ride comfort. Keep in mind that low tire pressures may cause the tire to slip on the rim or come off, while high tire pressures will cause abnormal tread wear and unsafe handling.

5   Make sure the valve stem locknuts **(see illustration)** are tight. Also, make sure the valve stem cap is tight. If it is missing, install a new one made of metal or hard plastic.

9   Throttle cable and choke operation - check and adjustment

Throttle cable

1   Make sure the throttle grip rotates easily from fully closed to fully open with the front wheel turned at various angles. The grip should return automatically from fully open to fully closed when released. If the throttle sticks, check the throttle cables for cracks or kinks in the housings and make sure the inner cables are clean and well-lubricated.

2   Start the engine and warm it up. With the engine idling, turn the handlebars all the way to the left, then all the way to the right. The idle speed should not increase. If it does, check throttle grip freeplay.

3   Throttle grip freeplay is the distance the throttle grip can be rotated before resistance is felt, i.e. the point at which the throttle cable begins to open the carburetor throttle plates. Measure the throttle grip freeplay **(see illus-**

tration) and compare your measurement to the value listed in this Chapter's Specifications.

4   There are actually two throttle cables - an "accelerator" cable and a "decelerator" cable. The accelerator cable opens the throttle plates; the decelerator cable closes them. If the throttle grip freeplay must be adjusted, it can be adjusted at either end of the accelerator cable, but only at the lower end of the decelerator cable. The upper adjuster at the throttle grip is used to make fine adjustments to the accelerator cable; throttle grip freeplay is usually adjusted here. The lower adjusters at the carburetors are only used to make major adjustments to the cables. Both cables can be adjusted at the carburetors, but the accelerator cable is the one that is adjusted to achieve correct throttle grip freeplay; the decelerator cable is adjusted only to compensate for the amount of freeplay that's added or subtracted from the accelerator cable. There should be no freeplay in the decelerator cable.

5   To adjust freeplay at the throttle grip,

8.4 Check tire pressures with an accurate gauge

8.5 Make sure the tire valve locknut (arrow) is snug and the valve cap is tight

9.3 Rotate the throttle grip to check freeplay; loosen the locknut and turn the adjuster (arrows) to change it (VT750 shown)

9.6 Lower locknuts and adjusters for accelerator cable (lower arrows) and decelerator cable (upper arrows)

loosen the locknut and turn the adjuster until the freeplay is within the specified distance. Tighten the locknut.

6 To adjust freeplay at the carburetors, loosen the cable adjuster locknuts **(see illustration)**, turn the adjuster nut on the decelerator cable to set freeplay to zero, tighten the decelerator cable adjuster locknut, then turn the accelerator cable adjuster nut to bring freeplay at the throttle grip within the range listed in this Chapter's Specifications. Once freeplay is correct, tighten the accelerator cable adjuster locknut.

7 Make sure the throttle grip is now in the fully-closed position.

8 Make sure the throttle linkage lever still contacts the idle adjusting screw when the throttle grip is in the fully-closed position.

9 Again, turn the handlebars all the way through their travel with the engine idling. Idle speed should not change. If it does, either the cables are incorrectly routed or freeplay is still insufficient.

 Warning: Correct this condition before riding the bike.

Choke

10 The choke system consists of a pair of starting enrichment (SE) valves - one per carburetor - which control the fuel enrichment circuits in the carburetors. When the choke knob on the left side of the engine is pulled out, the cable-actuated SE valves open the fuel enrichment circuits in the carburetors.

11 Make sure that the choke knob operates smoothly. If the knob is hard to pull out or push in, pull it out and lubricate its sliding surface with cable lubricant or a lightweight oil.

12 If the choke knob is still difficult to pull out or push in, pull back the rubber cover and back off the friction adjuster **(see illustration)**.

13 If adjusting the friction doesn't help, the SE valve cables need to be lubricated (see Chapter 4).

14 If the engine is hard to start when it's cold - but easy to start when it's warmed up - the SE valves are not opening completely. If the idle speed "wanders" up and down, even after the engine is warmed up, the SE valves are not closing completely. In either case, the SE valves should be removed and cleaned, and the valves and valve seats should be inspected (see Chapter 4).

10 Clutch - check and adjustment

1 Correct clutch freeplay is necessary to ensure proper clutch operation and reasonable clutch service life. Freeplay normally changes because of cable stretch and clutch wear, so it should be checked and adjusted periodically.

2 Clutch cable freeplay is checked at the lever on the handlebar. Slowly pull in on the lever until resistance is felt, measure this distance **(see illustration)** and compare it with

9.12 To adjust the amount of force required to pull out and push in the choke knob, pull back the rubber cover (right arrow) and rotate the friction adjuster (left arrow)

10.2 Clutch lever freeplay is the distance from the released position to the point at which you feel resistance

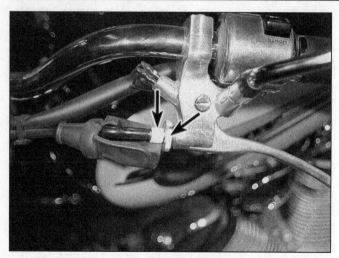

10.3 Normal clutch cable adjustments are made at the handlebar - loosen the clutch cable lockwheel (right arrow) and turn the adjuster (left arrow); tighten the lockwheel after adjustment

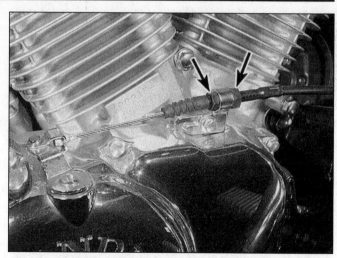

10.5 The clutch cable can also be adjusted at this bracket on the right side of the engine; loosen the locknut (left arrow) and turn the adjusting nut (right arrow) until clutch lever freeplay is correct (on pre-1995 models, the adjuster nut and locknut are on the same side of the bracket)

the value listed in this Chapter's Specifications. Too little freeplay might result in the clutch not engaging completely. If there is too much freeplay, the clutch might not release fully.

3   Normal freeplay adjustments are made at the clutch lever by loosening the lockwheel and turning the adjuster until the desired freeplay is obtained **(see illustration)**. Always retighten the lockwheel once the adjustment is complete.

4   If freeplay can't be adjusted at the handlebar, major adjustments can be made on the right side of the engine.

5   Loosen the locknuts at the clutch cable bracket on the engine **(see illustration)**. Turn the nuts to achieve the correct freeplay, then tighten them.

6   Recheck freeplay at the clutch lever and make further adjustments (if necessary) with the adjuster at the lever. If freeplay still can't

be adjusted within the Specifications, the cable may be stretched or the clutch may be worn. Inspect the clutch cable and the clutch (see Chapter 2).

11 Drive chain and sprockets - check, adjustment and lubrication

Check

1   Make sure the ignition switch is off. Shift the transmission into Neutral and place the bike on its sidestand.

2   Push up on the bottom run of the chain and measure the slack at a point about halfway between the two sprockets **(see illustration)**. Compare your measurement to the value listed in this Chapter's Specifications and, if necessary, adjust the chain.

3   The chain should be replaced at the specified mileage interval (see Chapter 5).

Adjustment

4   Loosen the rear axle nut **(see illustration)**.

5   Loosen and back off the locknuts on both axle adjuster bolts **(see illustration)**.

6   On VT600 models, there is a single index mark on each of the adjusters and a series of marks on each side of the swingarm **(see illustration 11.5)**; on VT750 models, there is a single mark on each side of the swingarm and a series of notches on the adjusters **(see illustration)**.

7   Turn the adjusting nuts on both sides of the swingarm until the proper chain tension is obtained (get the adjuster on the chain side close, then set the adjuster on the opposite side). Be sure to turn the adjusting nuts evenly to keep the rear wheel in alignment. If

11.2 Measure chain slack at a point about halfway between the two sprockets on the bottom run

11.4 Always loosen the axle nut before adjusting the chain slack

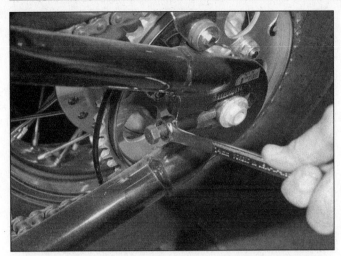

11.5 Loosen both chain adjuster locknuts before turning the adjuster bolts; on VT600 models (shown), note the pointer on top of the adjuster and the adjustment marks on the swingarm

11.6 On VT750 models, there's a single indicator mark (arrow) on each side of the swingarm, and notches in the adjusters themselves

the index mark on the left adjuster reaches the red zone of the chain wear label on the left side of the swingarm on VT600 models **(see illustration)**, or the red zone on the left adjuster reaches the index mark on the left side of the swingarm on VT750 models, the chain is worn out and must be replaced (see Chapter 7).

8   When the chain has the correct amount of slack, make sure the marks on the adjusters correspond to the same relative marks on each side of the swingarm (VT600 models) or the marks on each side of the swingarm correspond to the same relative notches on the adjusters (VT750 models).

9   Tighten the axle nut to the torque listed in this Chapter's Specifications.

10   Tighten the chain adjuster locknuts securely.

Lubrication

11   Lubricate the chain right after the motorcycle has been ridden. The chain is still warm, so chain lube will penetrate the joints between the side plates, pins, bushings and rollers and reach the internal load bearing surfaces. Use a good quality chain lubricant designed for O-ring type chains. Apply it to the areas where the side plates overlap - not the middle of the rollers. Apply the lube to the top of the lower chain run, so that centrifugal force will work the oil into the chain the next time the bike is ridden. After applying chain lube, let it soak in a few minutes before wiping off any excess.

12   Check the sprockets for wear while lubricating the chain (see Chapter 7).

12 Engine oil/filter - change

1   Regular oil and filter changes are the single most important maintenance procedure you can perform on a motorcycle. The oil not only lubricates the internal parts of the engine, transmission and clutch, but it also acts as a coolant, a cleaner, a sealant, and a protectant. Because of these demands, the oil takes a terrific amount of abuse and

should be replaced often with new oil of the recommended grade and type. Saving a little money on the difference in cost between a good oil and a cheap oil won't pay off if the engine is damaged.

2   Before changing the oil and filter, warm up the engine so the oil will drain easily. Be careful when draining the oil; the exhaust pipes, the engine and the oil itself can cause severe burns.

3   Support the motorcycle securely over a clean drain pan. Remove the oil filler cap to vent the crankcase and act as a reminder that there is no oil in the engine.

4   Next, remove the drain plug from the lower left side of the engine **(see illustration)** and allow the oil to drain into the pan. Discard the sealing washer on the drain plug; it should be replaced every time the plug is removed. While the engine is draining, replace the oil filter.

5   The automotive style spin-on oil filter is located at the left lower rear part of the engine; with the bike leaned over to the left

11.7 When the pointer on the adjuster points at the red zone on the chain wear label on VT600 models, replace the chain (on VT750 models, the chain wear label is on the left adjuster; when it reaches the mark on the swingarm, replace the chain)

12.4 The oil drain plug (arrow) is on the lower left side of the engine, behind the water pump

12.5a The oil filter (arrow) is at the lower rear part of the engine; the easiest way to reach it is from the right side, with the bike on its sidestand

12.5b Use a filter wrench to remove the oil filter (if you don't have this type of filter wrench, use a pair of large water pump pliers)

on its sidestand, it's easier to access the filter from the right side (see illustration). Remove the filter from the engine with a filter wrench (see illustration). If you don't have this type of filter wrench, use a pair of large water pump pliers to loosen the filter.

6   Coat the threads of the new oil filter and the new filter O-ring with clean engine oil.

7   Install the new filter and tighten it by hand.

8   Check the condition of the drain plug threads and the sealing washer.

9   Slip a new sealing washer over the drain plug, then install and tighten it to the torque listed in this Chapter's Specifications. Avoid overtightening the drain plug, which can strip the threads in the aluminum engine case.

10   Before refilling the engine, check the old oil carefully. If the oil was drained into a clean pan, small pieces of metal or other material can be easily detected. If the oil is very metallic colored, then the engine is experi-

encing wear from break-in (new engine) or from insufficient lubrication. If there are flakes or chips of metal in the oil, then something is drastically wrong internally and the engine will have to be disassembled for inspection and repair.

11   If there are pieces of fiber-like material in the oil, the clutch is experiencing excessive wear and should be checked.

12   If the inspection of the oil turns up nothing unusual, refill the crankcase to the proper level with the recommended oil and install the filler cap. Start the engine and let it run for two or three minutes. Shut it off, wait a few minutes, then check the oil level. If necessary, add more oil to bring the level up to the Maximum mark. Check around the drain plug and filter housing for leaks.

13   The old oil drained from the engine cannot be reused in its present state and should be disposed of. Check with your local refuse disposal company, disposal facility or environmental agency to see whether they will

accept the used oil for recycling. Don't pour used oil into drains or onto the ground. After the oil has cooled, it can be drained into a suitable container (capped plastic jugs, topped bottles, milk cartons, etc.) for transport to one of these disposal sites.

13 Air filter element - servicing

1   Remove the air cleaner housing cover (see illustrations).

2   On VT600 models, remove the filter element holder (see illustration).

3   Lift out the filter element (see illustration).

4   Tap the filter element on a hard surface to shake out dirt. If compressed air is available, use it to clean the element by

13.1a To remove the air cleaner housing cover on VT600 models, remove this Allen screw . . .

13.1b . . . remove the cover and inspect the foam strip (arrow)

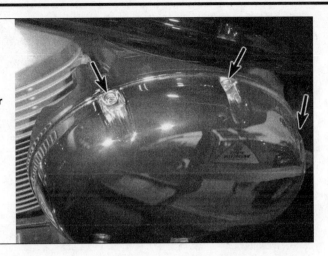

13.1c To remove the air cleaner housing cover on VT750 models, remove the six cover screws (three upper screws shown)

blowing from the inside out. If the element is extremely dirty or torn, or if dirt can't be blown or tapped out, replace the element.

5   Installation if the reverse of removal. Make sure the filter element is seated properly in the filter housing before installing the cover.

14 Cylinder compression - check

1   Among other things, poor engine performance may be caused by leaking valves, incorrect valve clearances, a leaking head gasket, or worn pistons, rings and/or cylinder walls. A cylinder compression check will help pinpoint these conditions and can also indicate the presence of excessive carbon deposits in the cylinder heads.

2   The only tools required are a compression gauge and a spark plug wrench. Depending on the outcome of the initial test, a squirt-type oil can may also be needed.

3   Start the engine and allow it to reach normal operating temperature.

4   Support the bike securely so it can't be knocked over during this procedure.

5   Remove one spark plug from each cylinder (see Section 15). Work carefully - don't strip the spark plug hole threads and don't burn your hands.

6   Disable the ignition by unplugging the primary wires from the coils (see Chapter 5). Be sure to mark the locations of the wires before detaching them.

7   Install the compression gauge in one of the spark plug holes.

8   Hold or block the throttle wide open.

9   Crank the engine over a minimum of four or five revolutions (or until the gauge reading stops increasing) and observe the initial movement of the compression gauge needle as well as the final total gauge reading. Repeat the procedure for the other cylinder and compare the results to the value listed in this Chapter's Specifications.

10   If the compression in both cylinders built up quickly and evenly to the specified amount, you can assume the engine upper end is in reasonably good mechanical condi-

tion. Worn or sticking piston rings and worn cylinders will produce very little initial movement of the gauge needle, but compression will tend to build up gradually as the engine spins over. Valve and valve seat leakage, or head gasket leakage, is indicated by low initial compression which does not tend to build up.

11   To further confirm your findings, add a small amount of engine oil to each cylinder by inserting the nozzle of a squirt-type oil can through the spark plug holes. The oil will tend to seal the piston rings if they are leaking. Repeat the test for the other cylinder.

12   If the compression increases significantly after the addition of the oil, the piston rings and/or cylinders are definitely worn. If the compression does not increase, the pressure is leaking past the valves or the head gasket. Leakage past the valves may be due to insufficient valve clearances, burned, warped or cracked valves or valve seats or valves that are hanging up in the guides.

13   If compression readings are considerably higher than specified, the combustion chambers are probably coated with excessive carbon deposits. It is possible (but not very likely) for carbon deposits to raise the compression enough to compensate for the effects of leakage past rings or valves. Remove the cylinder head and carefully decarbonize the combustion chambers (see Chapter 2).

15 Spark plugs - replacement

1   Make sure your spark plug socket is the correct size before attempting to remove the plugs.

2   Disconnect the spark plug caps from

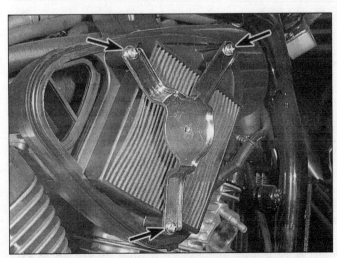

13.2 On VT600 models, remove the filter element holder screws (arrows) and remove the holder

13.3 Remove the filter element (VT600 shown; on VT750 models, simply pull the filter element off the air cleaner housing)

15.2a There are two spark plugs per cylinder; this is the spark plug cap for the left plug on the rear cylinder . . .

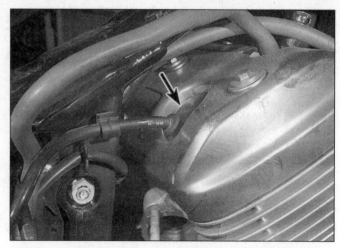

15.2b . . . and this is the cap (arrow) for the recessed right plug on the rear cylinder (fuel tank removed for clarity)

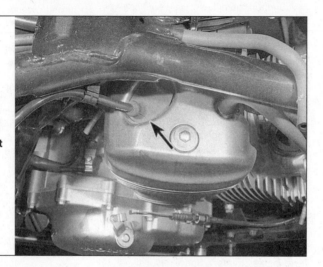

15.2c On the front cylinder, the open plug is on the right side and the recessed plug (arrow) is in the left front corner of the cylinder head cover (fuel tank removed for clarity)

the spark plugs **(see illustrations)**. Inspect the caps for damage and wear.

3   Using compressed air, blow any accumulated debris from around the spark plugs. No dirt or debris must be allowed into the combustion chamber. Remove the plugs with a spark plug socket.

4   Inspect the electrodes for wear. Both the center and side electrodes should have square edges and the side electrode should be of uniform thickness. Look for excessive deposits and evidence of a cracked or chipped insulator around the center electrode. Compare your spark plugs to the color spark plug reading chart. Check the threads, the washer and the ceramic insulator body for cracks and other damage.

5   If the electrodes are not excessively worn, and if the deposits can be easily removed with a wire brush, the plugs can be regapped and reused (if no cracks or chips are visible in the insulator). If in doubt concerning the condition of the plugs, replace them with new ones, as the expense is minimal.

6   Cleaning spark plugs by sandblasting is permitted, provided you clean the plugs with

a high flash-point solvent afterwards.

7   Before installing new plugs, make sure they are the correct type and heat range. Check the gap between the electrodes, as

they are not preset. For best results, use a wire-type gauge rather than a flat gauge to check the gap **(see illustration)**. If the gap must be adjusted, bend the side electrode only and be very careful not to chip or crack the insulator nose **(see illustration)**. Make sure the washer is in place before installing each plug.

8   Since the cylinder head is made of aluminum, which is soft and easily damaged, thread the plugs into the heads by hand. Since the plugs are recessed, slip a short length of hose over the end of the plug to use as a tool to thread it into place. The hose will grip the plug well enough to turn it, but will start to slip if the plug begins to cross-thread in the hole - this will prevent damaged threads and the accompanying repair costs.

9   Once the plugs are finger tight, the job can be finished with a socket. If a torque wrench is available, tighten the spark plugs to the torque listed in this Chapter's Specifications. If you do not have a torque wrench, tighten the plugs finger tight (until the wash-

15.7a Spark plug manufacturers recommend using a wire type gauge when checking the gap - if the wire doesn't slide between the electrodes with a slight drag, adjustment is required

15.7b To change the gap, bend the side electrode only, as indicated by the arrows, and be very careful not to crack or chip the ceramic insulator surrounding the center electrode

16.2a Lubricate the brake lever pivot (arrow) and clutch lever pivot (not shown, but similar)

16.2b Lubricate the shift lever pivot, the footpeg hinge and the sidestand pivot (arrows)

ers bottom on the cylinder head) then use a wrench to tighten them an additional 1/4 to 1/2 turn. Regardless of the method used, do not over-tighten them.
10   Reconnect the spark plug caps and reinstall the air ducts.

16 Lubrication - general

1   Since the controls, cables and various other components of a motorcycle are exposed to the elements, they should be lubricated regularly to ensure safe and trouble-free operation.
2   The clutch lever and brake lever pivots, the brake pedal, shift lever and sidestand pivots, the rear brake linkage, the shift linkage and the footpeg hinges should be lubricated frequently (see illustrations). In order for the lubricant to be applied where it will do the most good, the component should be disassembled. However, if chain and cable lubricant is being used, it can be applied

to the pivot joint gaps and will usually work its way into the areas where friction occurs. If motor oil or light grease is being used, apply it sparingly as it may attract dirt (which could cause the controls to bind or wear at an accelerated rate). **Note:** *One of the best lubricants for the control lever pivots is a dry-film lubricant (available from many sources by different names).*
3   To lubricate the throttle cables, disconnect them at the lower end, then lubricate them with a pressure lube adapter (see illustration). If you don't have one, disconnect both ends of the cable and use a funnel (see illustration). It's a good idea to remove and lubricate the throttle twist grip whenever the throttle cables are lubricated (see the handlebar switch removal section of Chapter 9).
4   The choke cables should be lubricated the same way as the throttle cables (see Chapter 4 for the choke cable removal procedure).
5   The speedometer cable should be removed from its housing and lubricated with motor oil or cable lubricant (see Chapter 9 for speedometer cable removal).
6   The swingarm pivot ball and needle

bearings should be lubricated with lithium-based multi-purpose grease (see Chapter 6 for the swingarm removal procedure).

17 Valve clearances - check and adjustment

1   The engine must be completely cool for this maintenance procedure, so let the machine sit overnight before beginning. Make sure the ignition switch is turned off and the kill switch is in the Off position.
2   Remove the fuel tank (see Chapter 4).
3   On VT600 models, remove the air cleaner housing cover, holder and filter element; on VT750 models, remove the air cleaner housing cover and filter element (see Section 13). On all models, remove the air

16.3a Lubing a cable with a pressure lube adapter is easier and less messy (they're available at most bike shops)

16.3b If you don't have a pressure lube adapter, make a funnel at one end of the cable with a small piece of plastic, tape it to the cable and carefully pour a small amount of oil into the funnel

17.5a Remove the two Allen bolts and remove the intake valve adjustment cover from the rear cylinder cover (VT600 models)

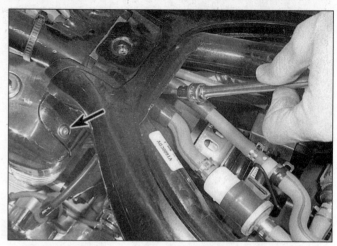

17.5b Remove the two Allen bolts (arrow indicates outer bolt; use a long Allen bit on the inner bolt) . . .

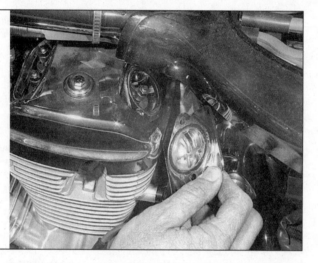

17.5c . . . and remove the exhaust valve adjustment cover from the rear cylinder cover (VT600 models)

first. Rotate the crankshaft counterclockwise with a socket (see illustration) until the FT mark on the flywheel is aligned with the index mark on the left crankcase cover. This places the front piston at top dead center (TDC). To verify that the front piston is on its compression stroke, wiggle the tip of each front cylinder rocker arm. If the front piston is at TDC, the valves will be fully closed; the rocker arms won't be pushing against the valves, so they should feel a little loose. If the rocker arms don't feel loose, the front piston is on its exhaust stroke. Rotate the crankshaft one full turn counterclockwise, so the FT mark again aligns with the index mark.

9 Insert a feeler gauge of the thickness listed in this Chapter's Specifications into the gap between the top of each valve stem and its rocker arm adjuster screw. Pull the feeler gauge out slowly - you should feel a slight drag. If there's no drag, the clearance is too loose. If there's a heavy drag, the clearance is too tight.

10 To adjust the clearance, loosen the rocker arm locknut with a box wrench. Turn

cleaner chamber and intake duct assembly (see Chapter 4).

4 Remove the spark plugs (see Section 15) so the crankshaft is easier to turn.

5 On VT600 models, remove the valve adjusting covers (see illustrations).

6 On VT750 models, remove the cylinder head covers (see Chapter 2).

7 Remove the crankshaft hole cap and the timing hole cap from the left side of the engine (see illustration).

8 Adjust the valves for the front cylinder

17.7 Remove the crankshaft and timing hole plugs

17.8 Rotate the crankshaft counterclockwise

17.12 To bring the rear piston to TDC, align the RT mark on the flywheel with the index mark on the edge of the timing hole

17.13 To measure the valve clearance, insert a feeler gauge of the specified thickness into the gap between each rocker arm and valve stem

the adjusting screw to adjust the clearance, then tighten the locknut.

11 Recheck the clearance with the feeler gauge to make sure it didn't change when you tightened the locknut. Readjust it if necessary.

12 Rotate the crankshaft counterclockwise again until the RT mark on the flywheel is aligned with the index mark on the crankcase cover **(see illustration)**. The rear piston should now be at TDC. Verify that it is by wiggling the rear cylinder rocker arms. With the engine in this position, the valves for the rear cylinder can be checked.

13 Referring to Step 9, insert a feeler gauge of the thickness listed in this Chapter's Specifications between each rocker arm and valve stem **(see illustration)**. Adjust the clearances if necessary as described in Step 10.

14 On VT600 models, inspect the O-rings on the valve adjustment covers. Replace them if they're cracked, torn, flattened or distorted. Install the valve adjustment covers and tighten the Allen bolts to the torque listed in this Chapter's Specifications.

15 On VT750 models, inspect the cylinder head cover O-rings. Replace them if they're

cracked, torn, flattened or distorted. Install the cylinder head covers and tighten the cover bolts to the torque listed in the Chapter 2 Specifications.

16 Install the spark plugs (see Section 15).

17 Inspect the O-rings for the crankshaft hole and timing hole plugs and replace them if necessary. Install the plugs and tighten them securely.

18 Install the air intake ducts and air chamber (see Chapter 4). Install the air cleaner filter element, holder (VT600 models) and air cleaner housing cover (see Section 13).

19 Install the fuel tank (see Chapter 4).

18 Idle speed - check and adjustment

1 The idle speed should be checked and adjusted before and after the carburetors are synchronized and whenever it is obviously high or low. Before adjusting the idle speed, make sure the valve clearances and spark plug gaps are correct. Also, turn the handlebars back-and-forth and see if the idle speed

changes as this is done. If it does, the throttle cables may not be correctly adjusted, or may be worn out. This is a dangerous condition that can cause loss of control of the bike. Be sure to correct this problem before proceeding.

2 The engine should be at normal operating temperature, which is usually reached after 10 to 15 minutes of stop and go riding. Put the transmission in Neutral and place the bike on its sidestand.

3 Turn the throttle stop screw **(see illustration)**, until the idle speed listed in this Chapter's Specifications is obtained.

4 Snap the throttle open and shut a few times, then recheck the idle speed. If necessary, repeat the adjustment procedure.

5 If a smooth, steady idle can't be achieved, the air/fuel mixture may be incorrect. Refer to Chapter 4 for additional carburetor information.

19 Carburetor synchronization - check and adjustment

18.3 Turn the throttle stop screw (arrow) to set idle speed (throttle link cover, throttle cables and choke knob removed for clarity)

⚠ *Warning: Gasoline is extremely flammable, so take extra precautions when you work on any part of the fuel system. Don't smoke or allow open flames or bare light bulbs near the work area, and don't work in a garage where a gas-type appliance (such as a water heater or clothes dryer) is present. Since gasoline is carcinogenic, wear latex gloves when there's a possibility of being exposed to fuel, and, if you get fuel on your skin, wash it off immediately with soap and water. Mop up any spills immediately and do not store fuel-soaked rags where they could ignite. When you perform any kind of work on the fuel system, wear safety glasses and have a class B type fire extinguisher (flammable liquids) on hand.*

19.7a Remove the vacuum screw (arrow) from the right side of the front cylinder intake port . . .

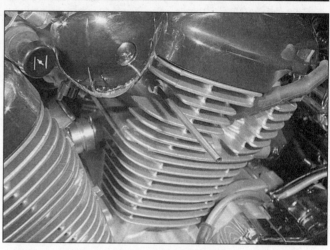

19.7b . . . remove the other vacuum screw from the left side of the rear cylinder intake port, then install an adapter tube in each vacuum port

1   Carburetor synchronization is simply the process of adjusting dual carburetors so they pass the same amount of fuel/air mixture to each cylinder. This is done by measuring the vacuum produced in each cylinder. Carburetors that are out of synchronization will result in decreased fuel mileage, increased engine temperature, less than ideal throttle response and higher vibration levels.

2   To properly synchronize the carburetors, you will need some sort of vacuum gauge setup, preferably with a gauge for each cylinder, or a mercury manometer, which is a calibrated tube arrangement that utilizes columns of mercury to indicate engine vacuum. You'll also need an auxiliary fuel tank, since the bike's fuel tank must be removed for access to the vacuum fittings and synchronizing screws.

3   A manometer can be purchased from a motorcycle dealer or accessory shop and should have the necessary rubber hoses supplied with it for hooking into the vacuum hose fittings on the carburetors.

4   A vacuum gauge setup can also be purchased from a dealer or fabricated from commonly available hardware and automotive vacuum gauges.

5   The manometer is the more reliable

and accurate instrument, and for that reason is preferred over the vacuum gauge setup; however, since the mercury used in the manometer is a liquid, and extremely toxic, extra precautions must be taken during use and storage of the instrument.

6   Because of the nature of the synchronization procedure and the need for special instruments, most owners leave the task to a dealer service department or a reputable motorcycle repair shop.

7   Remove the screws from the intake vacuum ports and install vacuum gauge adapters **(see illustrations)**. Connect the vacuum gauges or manometer to the adapters.

8   Start the engine and let it run until it reaches normal operating temperature.

9   Make sure there are no leaks in the vacuum gauge or manometer setup, as false readings will result.

10   Start the engine and make sure the idle speed is correct. If it isn't, adjust it (see Section 18).

11   The carburetor for the rear cylinder is the "base" carburetor. In other words, vacuum at the front carburetor should be compared to vacuum at the rear carburetor. The vacuum readings for both of the cylinders should be within the allowable deviation

listed in this Chapter's Specifications. If the variance in vacuum between the two carburetors exceeds the allowable deviation, synchronize the carburetors.

12   To perform the adjustment, synchronize the carburetors by turning the synchronizing screw **(see illustration)** until the vacuum is identical or within the allowable deviation for both cylinders.

13   Snap the throttle open and shut two or three times, then recheck synchronization and readjust if necessary.

14   When the adjustment is complete, recheck the vacuum readings and idle speed, then stop the engine. Remove the vacuum gauge or manometer and install the intake port screws.

20 Cooling system - check

 Warning: The engine must be cool before beginning this procedure.

Note: *Check the coolant level before checking the cooling system (see Section 3).*

1   The cooling system should be checked carefully at the recommended intervals. Look for evidence of leaks, check the condition of the coolant, check the radiator for clogged fins and damage. Make sure the radiator cooling fan operates when the coolant gets hot. If it doesn't, either the fan motor, the fan switch or the circuit is defective (see Chapter 3).

2   Inspect the condition of the coolant hoses. Look for cracks, abrasions and any other damage that might cause a leak. Squeeze the hoses. They should feel firm yet pliable, and should return to their original shape when released. If they feel hard or stiff, replace them.

19.12 The carburetor synchronization screw (arrow) is located between the carburetors and can be accessed (with the fuel tank removed) through the space between the intake ducts (carburetors removed for clarity)

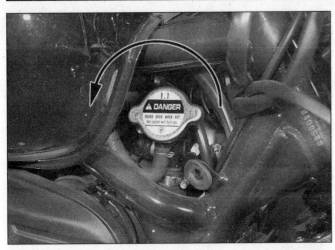

20.7 To remove the radiator cap, turn it counterclockwise to the first stop, let any residual pressure escape, then resume turning the cap counterclockwise until it's free and pull it off

20.8 An antifreeze hydrometer is helpful for determining the condition of the coolant

3   Look for signs of leaks at every cooling system joint (where the hoses are clamped to the radiator, thermostat and water pump). If a hose is leaking at one of these components, tighten the hose clamp. Of course, if a hose is in poor condition, tightening a hose clamp can tear the hose, making the leak worse. Such hoses must be replaced.

4   Inspect the radiator for signs of leaks and other damage. Leaks in the radiator leave tell-tale scale deposits or coolant stains on the outside of the core below the leak. If leaks are noted, remove the radiator and have it repaired or replace it (see Chapter 3). Do not use a liquid leak-stopping additive to try to repair leaks.

5   Inspect the radiator fins for any debris - mud, dirt, insects, etc. - which impedes the flow of air through the radiator. If the fins are dirty, force water or low pressure compressed air through the fins from the backside. If the fins are bent or distorted, carefully straighten them with a small flat-blade screwdriver.

6   Remove the fuel tank (see Chapter 4) and the steering covers (see Chapter 8).

7   Remove the radiator cap **(see illustration)** by turning it counterclockwise until it reaches a stop. If you hear a hissing sound, there's still pressure in the system. Wait until it stops. Then press down on the cap and continue turning it counterclockwise and remove it. Inspect the condition of the coolant in the radiator. If it's rust-colored, or if scale has accumulated inside the radiator, drain, flush and refill the system with a new 50/50 mixture of distilled water and ethylene glycol. Inspect the cap gasket for cracks and any other damage. If any damage is evident, have the cap pressure-tested by a dealer service department or replace it. Install the cap by turning it clockwise until it reaches the first stop, then push it down and continue turning it clockwise until it stops.

8   Check the antifreeze content of the coolant with an antifreeze hydrometer **(see illustration)**. Coolant might appear to be in good condition but might be too weak to offer adequate protection. If the hydrometer indicates a weak mixture, drain, flush and refill the cooling system (see Section 21).

9   Start the engine and let it reach normal operating temperature, then check for leaks again. As the coolant temperature reaches its upper operating temperature, the fan should come on automatically and the coolant temperature should begin to come back down. If the fan doesn't come on, inspect the fan, the fan switch and the circuit (see Chapter 3).

10   If the coolant level is constantly low, and no evidence of leaks can be found, have the cooling system pressure checked by a Honda dealer service department or by a motorcycle repair shop.

21 Cooling system - draining, flushing and refilling

⚠ *Warning: Allow the engine to cool completely before performing this maintenance operation. Also, don't allow antifreeze to come into contact with your skin or painted surfaces of the vehicle. Rinse off spills immediately with plenty of water. Antifreeze is highly toxic if ingested. Never leave antifreeze lying around in an open container or in puddles on the floor; children and pets are attracted by its sweet smell and may drink it. Check with local authorities about disposing used antifreeze. Many communities have collection centers that can dispose of antifreeze safely. Antifreeze is also combustible, so don't store it or use it near open flames.*

Draining

1   Remove the fuel tank (see Chapter 4) and the steering covers (see Chapter 8).

2   Remove the radiator cap (see Section 20).

3   To drain the cooling system, remove the drain bolts from the water pump and from the rear side of the rear cylinder, right above the starter motor **(see illustrations)**. Discard

21.3a There are two cooling system drain bolts: this one (arrow) is on the water pump . . .

21.3b . . . the other drain bolt is on the rear side of the rear cylinder, above the starter motor

22.3 Inspect the condition of the hoses connecting the various EVAP system components (late-model VT600 shown; refer to the vacuum hose routing diagram on the inside of the left side cover for a schematic of the system on your machine)

22.4 The EVAP canister is located down low, directly behind the engine, below the swingarm pivot; inspect the condition of the canister and make sure that the hoses and clamps are tight (VT600 model shown; on VT750 models, the canister is in the same location, but is installed transversely instead of longitudinally)

the drain bolt sealing washers. Use a funnel to direct the coolant from the rear cylinder drain hole away from the starter; make sure that no coolant is allowed to spill onto the starter. **Note:** *The coolant will rush out with some force, so be sure to position your drain pan(s) accordingly.*

4   Remove the reservoir (see Chapter 3). Drain the reservoir into the drain pan and wash out the reservoir with clean water. Install the reservoir.

Flushing

5   Flush the system with clean tap water by inserting a garden hose into the radiator filler neck. Allow the water to run through the system until clear water comes out the drain hole. If the radiator is extremely corroded, remove it by referring to Chapter 3 and have it cleaned at a radiator shop.

6   Clean the drain bolt holes and install the drain bolts with new sealing washers. Tighten the drain bolts to the torque listed in this Chapter's Specifications.

7   Fill the cooling system with a mixture of clean water and flushing compound. Make sure that the flushing compound is compatible with aluminum components and follow the manufacturer's instructions carefully.

8   Install the radiator cap (see Section 21), start the engine and allow it to reach normal operating temperature. Let it run for about ten minutes.

9   Stop the engine. Let the machine cool for awhile, then cover the radiator cap with a heavy rag and turn it counterclockwise to the first stop, wait for it to release any pressure in the system, then push down on the cap and remove it.

10   Drain the system again.

11   Fill the system with clean water, then repeat Steps 8, 9 and 10.

Refilling

12   Fill the system with a 50/50 mixture of distilled water and ethylene glycol. When the system is full (all the way up to the top of the radiator filler neck).

13   Remove the cap from the cooling system reservoir (see Section 3) and fill the reservoir.

14   To bleed the cooling system of air, place the fuel tank in position (it's not necessary to bolt it down), hook up the fuel lines to the carburetors, put the transmission in Neutral, start the engine and let it idle for two to three minutes. Snap the throttle three or four times. Stop the engine and add coolant up to the top of the filler neck again. Install radiator cap. Check the coolant level in the reservoir and, if necessary, fill it to the upper mark. Install the reservoir filler neck cap.

15   Install the steering head covers (see Chapter 8) and the fuel tank (see Chapter 4).

22 Evaporative emission control system (California models only) - inspection

1   Remove the fuel tank (see Chapter 4).

2   Remove the left side cover (see Chapter 8) and study the Vacuum Hose Routing Diagram on the inside of the side cover. You can order a new diagram from a Honda dealer if the old one is missing or illegible.

3   Inspect the hoses that connect the fuel tank, the EVAP canister, the EVAP purge control valve and the carburetors **(see illustration)**. Look for loose or detached hoses and weak or missing clamps. Note the condition of the hoses themselves. There should be no cracks, tears or general deterioration. Make sure that none of the hoses are kinked or twisted, which will obstruct the passage

of crankcase and fuel system emissions through the system. If any hose is damaged, replace it (see Chapter 4).

4   Lean the bike over to the left on its sidestand and inspect the EVAP canister **(see illustration)**, which is located underneath the machine, between the engine and the rear wheel, below the swingarm pivot.

5   Install the left side cover and the fuel tank.

23 Exhaust system - check

1   Periodically check all of the exhaust system joints for leaks and loose fasteners. If tightening the clamp bolts fails to stop any leaks, replace the gaskets with new ones (see Chapter 4).

2   The exhaust pipe flange nuts at the cylinder heads are especially prone to loosening, which could cause damage to the head. Check them frequently and keep them tight.

24 Steering head bearings - check, adjustment and lubrication

1   Steering head bearings can become dented, rough or loose as the machine ages. In extreme cases, worn or loose steering head bearings can cause steering wobble that is potentially dangerous.

Check

2   To check the steering hear bearings, support the motorcycle securely and block the machine so the front wheel is in the air.

24.7 You'll need the right socket to torque the steering head bearing adjustment nut (Honda tool 07916-3710100, or equivalent, available at Honda parts departments)

3   Point the wheel straight ahead and slowly move the handlebars from side-to-side. If there are any dents or rough spots in the bearing races, the front end will feel "rough" as the bearings roll over these spots when the handlebars are turned from side-to-side. If the front end feels rough, replace the steering head bearings and races (see Chapter 6).

4   Facing the bike from the front, grasp the fork legs firmly and try to move them forward and backward. If the steering head bearings are loose, you'll feel a "clunk" (freeplay) as the fork legs are moved back and forth. If there's freeplay in the steering head bearings, adjust the steering head as follows.

Adjustment

5   Remove the headlight (see Chapter 9).
6   Remove the handlebars, the upper triple clamp, the steering stem locknut and the lock washer (see Chapter 6).
7   Tighten the bearing adjustment nut **(see illustration)** to the torque listed in this Chapter's Specifications.
8   Turn the steering stem from lock to lock five or six times and check for binding.
9   If there is any binding in the steering stem, disassemble the steering stem assembly and inspect the bearings (see Chapter 6).
10   If the steering operates properly, verify that the adjustment nut is still tightened to the correct torque, then reassemble the front end.
11   Install the lock washer, locknut, upper triple clamp and handlebars (see Chapter 6).
12   Install the headlight (see Chapter 9).

Lubrication

13   Periodic cleaning and repacking of the steering head bearings is recommended by the manufacturer. Refer to Chapter 6 for steering head bearing lubrication and replacement procedures.

25 Fasteners - check

1   Since vibration of the machine tends to loosen fasteners, all nuts, bolts, screws, etc.

should be periodically checked for proper tightness.
2   Pay particular attention to the following:
     Brake caliper bolts and banjo bolts
     Spark plugs
     Engine oil drain plug
     Oil drain plug
     Cooling system drain plugs
     Gearshift pedal (and linkage, if
          equipped)
     Footpegs and sidestand
     Engine mounting bolts
     Shock absorber or rear suspension unit
     mounting bolts
     Front axle (or axle nut) and axle
          pinch bolt
     Rear axle nut
3   If a torque wrench is available, use it along with the torque specifications at the beginning of this and the other Chapters.

26 Fuel system - check and filter replacement

⚠️ **Warning: Gasoline is extremely flammable, so take extra precautions when you work on any part of the fuel system. Don't smoke or allow open flames or bare light bulbs near the work area, and**

don't work in a garage where a gas-type appliance (such as a water heater or clothes dryer) is present. Since gasoline is carcinogenic, wear latex gloves when there's a possibility of being exposed to fuel, and, if you get fuel on your skin, wash it off immediately with soap and water. Mop up any spills immediately and do not store fuel-soaked rags where they could ignite. When you perform any kind of work on the fuel system, wear safety glasses and have a class B type fire extinguisher (flammable liquids) on hand.

1   Remove the fuel tank (see Chapter 4).
2   Inspect the condition of the fuel tank, the fuel tap, the fuel lines and the carburetors. Look for leaks and signs of damage or wear (see Chapter 4).
3   If the fuel tap is leaking, note whether the fuel tap-to-fuel tank locknut is tight. If leakage persists, the tap should be removed from the fuel tank, disassembled, cleaned and inspected (see Chapter 4).
4   If the fuel lines are cracked or otherwise deteriorated, replace them.
5   If the carburetor gaskets are leaking, the carburetors should be disassembled and rebuilt (see Chapter 4).
6   Install the fuel tank.

Fuel filter replacement

7   Remove the fuel tank (see Chapter 4).
8   Disconnect the lines from the filter **(see illustration)** and remove the filter from its bracket.
9   Install the new filter with the directional arrow on the filter pointing toward the fuel pump.
10   Reconnect the lines. Make sure that the hoses fit tightly on the filter pipes and the clamps are snug.
11   Install the fuel tank.

27 Suspension - check

1   The suspension components must be maintained in top operating condition to ensure rider safety. Loose, worn or damaged

26.8 Install the fuel filter (left arrow) with its directional arrow pointing toward the fuel pump (right arrow)

27.3 Inspect each fork seal for oil leaks in the indicated areas (arrows); if oil is leaking past either side of the seal, replace the seal

28.2 To gain access to the spring preload adjuster on VT600 models, remove the left side cover, then use the pin spanner in the bike tool kit to turn the adjuster (arrow)

suspension parts decrease the vehicle's stability and control.

2   While standing alongside the motorcycle, lock the front brake and push on the handlebars to compress the forks several times. See if the fork tubes move up-and-down smoothly without binding. If the fork tubes stick in the sliders, disassemble and inspect the fork legs (see Chapter 6).

3   Carefully inspect the area around the fork seals for any signs of fork oil leakage **(see illustration)**. If leakage is evident, the seals must be replaced (see Chapter 6).

4   Check the tightness of all suspension nuts and bolts to be sure none have worked loose.

5   Inspect the shock absorber(s) for fluid leakage and tightness of the mounting nuts. If leakage is found, the shock(s) must be replaced.

6   Support the bike securely so it can't be knocked over during this procedure. Grab the swingarm on each side, just ahead of the axle. Rock the swingarm from side to side - there should be no discernible movement at the rear. If there's a little movement or a slight clicking can be heard, make sure the pivot bolt or shafts are tight. If they're tight but movement is still noticeable, remove the swingarm and replace the bearings (see Chapter 6).

7   Inspect the tightness of the rear suspension nuts and bolts (see Chapter 6).

28 Suspension adjustments

1   Rear spring preload can be adjusted on all models.

Warning: The rear shock absorber settings on VT750 models must be even to prevent unstable handling.

2   On VT600 models, remove the left side cover (see Chapter 8) and adjust rear spring preload with the special pin spanner and expansion bar provided in the tool kit. The pin spanner fits into the holes in the preload collar **(see illustration)**.

3   On VT750 models, adjust rear spring preload by turning the adjuster on the bottom of each shock absorber with the special pin spanner provided in the bike tool kit. The pin spanner fits into the holes in the lower part of the shock body **(see illustration)**.

4   The numerically lower settings are for lighter loads and smooth roads. The numerically higher settings are for heavier loads and rough roads. Position 2 is the standard position.

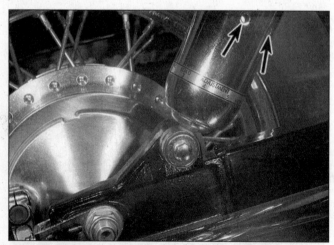

28.3 On VT750 models, insert the pin spanner included in the bike tool kit into the holes (arrows) in the shock body to adjust the spring preload

30.3 Here are the final drive housing check/fill plug (upper arrow) and drain plug (lower arrow)

29 Secondary air system (late VT600 models) - inspection

1   This system is used on 2004 and later California VT600 models and all 2005 and later VT600 models.
2   Remove the fuel tank (see Chapter 4).
3   Check the air hoses for cracks or deterioration. Make sure they're securely connected. If any problems are found, replace the hoses and test the air suction valve as described in Chapter 4.

30 Final drive oil - check and change

1   Final drive oil should be changed at the intervals specified in *Maintenance Schedule* at the beginning of this Chapter.

Check
2   Support the bike securely in a level position.

> ⚠ **Warning: When the bike is operated, the final drive unit gets hot enough to cause burns. If the machine has been ridden recently, make sure the final drive unit is cool to the touch before checking the oil level.**

3   Remove the filler plug from the final drive housing **(see illustration)**.
4   Look inside the hole and check the oil level. It should be even with the top of the hole.

Oil change
5   Ride the bike to warm the oil so it will drain completely.

> ⚠ **Warning: Be careful not to touch hot components (including the oil; they may be hot enough to cause burns.**

6   Remove the filler plug **(see illustration 30.3)**.
7   Remove the drain plug **(see illustration 30.3)** and let the oil drain for 10 to 15 minutes.
8   Clean the drain plug, reinstall it and tighten it to the torque listed in this Chapter's Specifications.
9   Fill the final drive unit to the correct level with the oil listed in this Chapter's Specifications.
10   Install the filler plug and tighten it to the torque listed in this Chapter's Specifications.

Notes

Chapter 2
Engine, clutch and transmission

Contents

Degrees of difficulty

Easy, suitable for novice with little experience	**Fairly easy,** suitable for beginner with some experience	**Fairly difficult,** suitable for competent DIY mechanic	**Difficult,** suitable for experienced DIY mechanic	**Very difficult,** suitable for expert DIY or professional

Specifications

VT600 models

General

Bore x stroke	75.0 x 66.0 mm (2.95 x 2.60 inches)
Displacement...	583 cc (35.5 cubic inches)
Compression ratio	9.2 to 1

VT600 models (continued)

Camshafts

Bearing oil clearance
  Standard .... 0.050 to 0.111 mm (0.0020 to 0.0044 inch)
  Limit .... 0.130 (0.0051 inch)
Camshaft journal diameter
  Standard .... 21.959 to 21.980 mm (0.8645 to 0.8654 inch)
  Limit .... 21.90 mm (0.862 inch)
Camshaft runout limit .... 0.05 mm (0.002 inch)
Camshaft lobe height
  Intake
    Standard .... 37.930 mm (1.4933 inches)
    Limit .... 37.730 mm (1.4854 inches)
  Exhaust
    Standard .... 37.950 mm (1.4941 inches)
    Limit .... 37.750 mm (1.4862 inches)
Cam chain tensioner wedge height limit .... No more than 0.6 mm (0.24 inch)

Rocker arms

Rocker arm inside diameter
  Standard .... 12.000 to 12.018 mm (0.4724 to 0.4731 inch)
  Limit .... 12.03 mm (0.474 inch)
Rocker arm shaft diameter
  Standard .... 11.966 to 11.984 mm (0.4711 to 0.4718 inch)
Rocker arm shaft diameter
  Limit
    1988 and 1989, 1991 through 1996 .... 11.83 mm (0.466 inch)
    1997 on .... 11.96 mm (0.471 inch)
Rocker arm-to-rocker shaft clearance
  Standard .... 0.016 to 0.052 mm (0.0006 to 0.0020 inch)
  Limit
    1988 and 1989, 1991 through 1996 .... 0.20 mm (0.008 inch)
    1997 on .... 0.07 mm (0.003 inch)

Cylinder head, valves and valve springs

Cylinder head warpage limit.. 0.10 mm (0.004 inch)
Valve stem diameter
  Intake
    Standard .... 5.475 to 5.490 mm (0.2156 to 0.2161 inch)
    Limit .... 5.45 mm (0.215 inch)
  Exhaust
    Standard .... 6.555 to 6.570 mm (0.2580 to 0.2587 inch)
    Limit .... 6.55 mm (0.258 inch)
Valve guide inside diameter
  Intake
    Standard .... 5.500 to 5.512 mm (0.2165 to 0.2170 inch)
    Limit .... 5.56 mm (0.219 inch)
  Exhaust
    Standard .... 6.600 to 6.615 mm (0.2598 to 0.2604 inch)
    Limit .... 6.65 mm (0.262 mm)
Stem-to-guide clearance
  Intake
    Standard .... 0.010 to 0.037 mm (0.0004 to 0.0015 inch)
    Limit .... 0.10 mm (0.004 inch)
  Exhaust
    Standard .... 0.030 to 0.060 mm (0.0012 to 0.0024 inch)
    Limit .... 0.11 (0.004 inch)
Valve seat width (intake and exhaust)
  Standard .... 0.90 to 1.10 mm (0.035 to 0.043 inch)
  Limit .... 1.50 mm (0.06 inch)
Valve guide projection height
  Intake .... 19.4 to 19.6 mm (0.76 to 0.77 inch)
  Exhaust .... 17.9 to 18.1 mm (0.70 to 0.71 inch)
Valve spring free length
  Outer spring
    Intake
      Standard.. 42.14 mm (1.659 inch)
      Limit.. 40.58 mm (1.598 inch)

Exhaust
    Standard... 42.83 mm (1.686 inch)
    Limit... 41.25 mm (1.624 inch)
Inner spring
  Intake
    Standard... 38.11 mm (1.500 inch)
    Limit... 36.47 mm (1.436 inch)
  Exhaust
    Standard... 38.81 mm (1.528 inch)
    Limit... 37.51 mm (1.477 inch)

Cylinders

Bore diameter
  Standard .... 75.000 to 75.015 mm (2.9528 to 2.9533 inches)
  Limit .... 75.10 mm (2.957 inches)
Warpage (across top of cylinder)... 0.10 (0.004 inch)
Taper and out-of-round limit.. 0.06 mm (0.002 inch)

Pistons

Piston diameter
  Standard .... 74.965 to 74.990 mm (2.9514 to 2.9524 inches)
  Limit .... 74.90 mm (2.949 inches)
Piston-to-cylinder clearance
  Standard .... 0.010 to 0.050 mm (0.0004 to 0.0020 inch)
  Limit .... 0.10 mm (0.004 inch)
Ring side clearance (top and second rings)
  Standard .... 0.015 to 0.045 mm (0.006 to 0.0018 inch)
  Limit .... 0.10 mm (0.004 inch)
Ring end gap
  Top and second rings
    Standard .... 0.10 to 0.30 mm (0.004 to 0.012 inch)
    Limit .... 0.50 mm (0.020 inch)
  Oil ring
    Standard .... 0.20 to 0.70 mm (0.008 to 0.028 inch)
    Limit .... 0.90 mm (0.035 inch)
Piston pin bore
  Standard .... 18.002 to 18.008 mm (0.7087 to 0.7090 inch)
  Limit .... 18.05 mm (0.711 inch)
Piston pin diameter
  Standard .... 17.994 to 18.000 mm (0.7084 to 0.7087 inch)
  Limit .... 17.98 mm (0.708 inch)
Piston-to-piston pin clearance
  Standard .... 0.002 to 0.014 mm (0.0001 to 0.0006 inch)
  Limit .... 0.040 mm (0.0016 inch)
Piston pin-to-connecting rod small end clearance
  Standard .... 0.016 to 0.040 mm (0.0006 to 0.0016 inch)
  Limit .... 0.060 mm (0.0024 inch)

Crankshaft, connecting rods and bearings

Connecting rod small end I.D.
  Standard .... 18.016 to 18.034 mm (0.7093 to 0.7100 inch)
  Limit .... 18.07 mm (0.711 inch)
Main bearing oil clearance
  Standard .... 0.025 to 0.041 mm (0.0010 to 0.0016 inch)
  Limit .... 0.06 mm (0.002 inch)
Connecting rod side clearance
  Standard .... 0.05 to 0.20 mm (0.002 to 0.008 inch)
  Limit .... 0.30 mm (0.001 inch)
Connecting rod bearing oil clearance
  Standard.. .... 0.028 to 0.052 mm (0.0011 to 0.0020 inch)
  Limit .... 0.07 mm (0.003 inch)
Crankshaft runout limit .... 0.05 mm (0.002 inch)

Oil pump

Rotor tip clearance
  Standard .... 0.15 mm (0.006 inch)
  Limit .... 0.20 mm (0.008 inch)
Pump body clearance
  Standard .... 0.15 to 0.22 mm (0.006 to 0.009 inch)
  Limit .... 0.35 mm (0.014 inch)

VT600 models

Oil pump (continued)

Rotor-to-pump body end clearance
    Standard .... 0.02 to 0.07 mm (0.001 to 0.003 inch)
    Limit .... 0.10 mm (0.004 inch)
Oil pump drive sprocket inside diameter
    Standard .... 32.000 to 32.025 mm (1.2598 to 1.2608 inches)
    Limit .... 32.10 mm (1.264 inches)

Clutch

Friction disc thickness
  Plate A
    Standard .... 2.62 to 2.78 mm (0.103 to 0.107 inch)
    Minimum .... 2.30 mm (0.090 inch)
  Plate B
    Standard .... 2.92 to 3.08 mm (0.115 to 0.121 inch)
    Minimum .... 2.60 mm (0.102 inch)
Steel plate warpage limit .... 0.30 mm (0.012 inch)
Spring free length
  1988
    Standard .... 39.0 mm (1.54 inches)
    Minimum .... 37.4 mm (1.47 inches)
  1989 on
    Standard .... 43.2 mm (1.70 inches)
    Minimum .... 41.6 mm (1.64 inches)
Mainshaft diameter (at clutch outer guide)
    Standard .... 21.967 to 21.980 mm (0.8648 to 0.8654 inch)
    Minimum .... 21.92 mm (0.863 inch)
Clutch outer guide
  Inside diameter
    Standard .... 21.991 to 22.016 mm (0.8658 to 0.8668 inch)
    Limit .... 22.09 mm (0.870 inch)
  Outside diameter
    Standard .... 31.959 to 31.025 mm (1.258 to 1.2589 inches)
    Limit .... 31.98 mm (1.259 inches)

Transmission

Gear inside diameter
  C1
    Standard .... 24.000 to 24.021 mm (0.9449 to 0.9457 inch)
    Limit .... 23.94 mm (0.943 inch)
  C3, M2, M4
    Standard .... 28.000 to 28.021 mm (1.1024 to 1.1032 inches)
    Limit .... 28.04 mm (1.104 inches)
Gear bushing
  Outside diameter
    C1
      Standard .... 23.959 to 23.980 mm (0.9433 to 0.9441 inch)
      Limit .... 24.94 mm (0.982 inch)
    C3, M2, M4
      Standard .... 27.959 to 27.980 mm (1.1007 to 1.1016 inches)
      Limit .... 27.94 mm (1.100 inches)
  Inside diameter
    C1
      Standard .... 20.016 to 20.037 mm (0.7880 to 0.7889 inch)
      Limit .... 20.06 mm (0.790 inch)
    M2
      Standard .... 25.000 to 25.021 mm (0.9843 to 0.9851 inch)
      Limit .... 25.04 mm (0.986 inch)
Bushing-to-shaft clearance
  C1
    Standard .... 0.023 to 0.057 mm (0.0009 to 0.022 inch)
    Limit .... 0.10 mm (0.004 inch)
  M2
    Standard .... 0.020 to 0.062 mm (0.0008 to 0.0024 inch)
    Limit .... 0.10 mm (0.004 inch)
Gear-to-bushing clearance (C1, C3, M2, M4)
    Standard .... 0.020 to 0.062 mm (0.0008 to 0.0024 inch)
    Limit .... 0.10 mm (0.004 inch)

Countershaft diameter (C1 bushing)
    Standard .... 19.980 to 19.993 mm (0.7866 to 0.7871 inch)
    Limit .... 19.96 mm (0.786 inch)
Mainshaft diameter (M2 bushing)
    Standard .... 24.959 to 24.980 mm (0.9835 to 0.9826 inch)
    Limit .... 24.94 mm (0.982 inch)
Backlash
    1st, 2nd, 3rd .... 1.021 to 0.110 mm (0.0008 to 0.0043 inch)
    4th .... 1.023 to 0.117 mm (0.0009 to 0.0046 inch)

Shift fork/shift fork shaft/shift drum
Shift fork tip thickness
    Standard .... 5.93 to 6.00 mm (0.233 to 0.236 inch)
    Limit .... 5.63 mm (0.222 inch)
Shift fork shaft bore inside diameter
    Standard .... 13.000 to 13.018 mm (0.5118 to 0.5125 inch)
    Limit .... 13.04 mm (0.513 inch)
Shift fork shaft diameter
    Standard .... 12.966 to 12.984 mm (0.5105 to 0.5112 inch)
    Limit .... 12.90 mm (0.508 inch)
Left shift drum journal diameter
    Standard .... 11.966 to 11.984 mm (0.4711 to 0.4718 inch)
    Limit .... 11.94 mm (0.470 inch)

Torque specifications
Cam chain tensioner bolt .... 10 Nm (88 in-lbs)
Cam chain tensioner set plate bolt .... 12 Nm (106 in-lbs)
Camshaft end holder bolt
    1988 through 1998 .... 9 Nm (78 in-lbs)
    1999 on .... 10 Nm (84 in-lbs)
Camshaft holder
    8 mm bolts and nuts .... 23 Nm (17 ft-lbs)
    6 mm bolts (pre-1997 only) .... 10 Nm (88 in-lbs)
Camshaft sprocket bolt .... 23 Nm (17 ft-lbs)
Clutch center locknut
    1988 through 1998 .... 127 Nm (94 ft-lbs)
    1999 on .... 128 Nm (95 ft-lbs)
Clutch lifter plate bolt .... 12 Nm (106 in-lbs)
Clutch lock nut .... 130 Nm (96 ft-lbs)
Connecting rod bearing cap nuts .... 34 Nm (25 ft-lbs)
Countershaft bearing set plate bolt .... 9 Nm (80 in-lbs)
Crankcase bolts
    1988 and 1989, 1991 through 1996
        8 mm stud bolts .... 20 to 30 Nm (15 to 22 ft-lbs)
        10 mm stud bolts .... 20 to 50 Nm (15 to 37 ft-lbs)
    1997 on
        6 mm bolts (1997 and 1998) .... 9 Nm (80 in-lbs)
        6 mm bolts (1999 on) .... 12 Nm (108 in-lbs)
        8 mm bolts .... 23 Nm (17 ft-lbs)
Cylinder head
    6 mm bolts
        1989 and 1990, 1991 through 1996 .... 10 Nm (88 in-lbs)
        1997 on .... 12 Nm (106 in-lbs)
    8 mm bolts .... 23 Nm (17 ft-lbs)
    8 mm nuts .... 23 Nm (17 ft-lbs)
    10 mm nuts .... 47 Nm (35 ft-lbs)
Cylinder head cover bolt .... 10 Nm (88 in-lbs)
Drum stopper plate bolt .... 12 Nm (106 in-lbs)
Flywheel bolt .... 127 Nm (94 ft-lbs)
Gearshift cam plate bolt .... 12 Nm (106 in-lbs)
Gearshift lever pinch bolt .... 12 Nm (106 in-lbs)
Gearshift drum stopper bolt .... 23 Nm (17 ft-lbs)
Left crankcase cover bolts .... 12 Nm (106 in-lbs)
Mainshaft bearing set plate bolt .... 12 Nm (106 in-lbs)
Oil pipe banjo bolt (1988 and 1989) .... 23 Nm (17 ft-lbs)
Oil pump driven sprocket bolt .... 15 Nm (132 in-lbs)
Primary drive gear bolt .... 88 Nm (65 ft-lbs)
Right crankcase cover bolts .... 12 Nm (106 in-lbs)
Starter clutch torx bolts .... 30 Nm (22 ft-lbs)
Stator socket mounting bolt .... 12 Nm (106 in-lbs)

VT750 models

General
Bore x stroke .... 79.0 x 76.0 mm (3.11 x 2.99 inches)
Displacement.. 745 cc (45.4 cubic inches)
Compression ratio
    2003 and earlier .... 9.0 to 1
    2004 and later .... 9.6 to 1

Camshafts
Bearing oil clearance
    2003 and earlier
        Standard .... 0.050 to 0.111 mm (0.0020 to 0.0044 inch)
        Limit .... 0.13 (0.005 inch)
    2004 and later
        Standard .... 0.020 to 0.141 mm (0.0008 to 0.0056 inch)
        Limit .... 0.16 mm (0.006 inch)
Camshaft journal diameter
    Standard .... 21.959 to 21.980 mm (0.8645 to 0.8654 inch)
    Limit .... 21.90 mm (0.862 inch)
Camshaft runout (VT750C/CD ACE)
    Standard .... 0.030 mm (0.012 inch)
    Limit .... 0.05 mm (0.002 inch)
Camshaft runout (VT750DC Spirit, VT750C Aero, VT750C2 Spirit)
    Standard .... Not specified
    Limit .... 0.03 mm (0.012 inch)
Camshaft lobe height
    Intake
        Standard .... 38.381 mm (1.5111 inches)
        Limit .... 38.10 mm (1.500 inches)
    Exhaust
        Standard .... 38.407 mm (1.5121 inches)
        Limit .... 38.20 mm (1.504 inches)
Camshaft lobe height (VT750DC Spirit, VT750C Aero, VT750C2 Spirit)
    Intake
        Standard .... 37.188 to 37.348 mm (1.4641 to 1.4704 inches)
        Limit .... 37.16 mm (1.463 inches)
    Exhaust
        Standard .... 37.605 to 37.765 mm (1.4805 to 1.4868 inches)
        Limit .... 37.58 mm (1.480 inches)
Cam chain tensioner wedge height limit .... No more than 6.0 mm (0.24 inch)

Rocker arms
Rocker arm inside diameter
    Standard .... 12.000 to 12.018 mm (0.4724 to 0.4731 inch)
    Limit .... 12.05 mm (0.474 inch)
Rocker arm shaft diameter
    Standard .... 11.966 to 11.984 mm (0.4711 to 0.4718 inch)
    Limit .... 11.83 mm (0.466 inch)
Rocker arm-to-rocker shaft clearance
    Standard .... 0.016 to 0.052 mm (0.0006 to 0.0020 inch)
    Limit .... 0.07 mm (0.003 inch)

Cylinder head, valves and valve springs
Cylinder head warpage limit.. 0.10 mm (0.004 inch)
Valve stem diameter
    Intake
        Standard .... 5.475 to 5.490 mm (0.2156 to 0.2161 inch)
        Limit .... 5.45 mm (0.215 inch)
    Exhaust (VT750C/DC ACE)
        Standard .... 6.555 to 6.570 mm (0.2580 to 0.2587 inch)
        Limit .... 6.55 mm (0.258 inch)
    Exhaust (VT750DC Spirit)
        Standard .... 6.600 to 6.615 mm (0.2598 to 0.2604 inch)
        Limit .... 6.55 mm (0.258 inch)
    Exhaust (VT750C Aero, VT750C2 Spirit)
        Standard .... 5.455 to 5.470 mm (0.2148 to 0.2154 inch)
        Limit .... 5.41 mm (0.213 inch)

Valve guide inside diameter
  Intake
    Standard .... 5.500 to 5.512 mm (0.2165 to 0.2170 inch)
    Limit .... 5.56 mm (0.219 inch)
  Exhaust
    Standard .... 6.600 to 6.615 mm (0.2598 to 0.2604 inch)
    Limit .... 6.65 mm (0.262 mm)
Stem-to-guide clearance
  2003 and earlier
    Intake
      Standard .... 0.010 to 0.037 mm (0.0004 to 0.0015 inch)
      Limit .... 0.10 mm (0.004 inch)
    Exhaust
      Standard .... 0.030 to 0.060 mm (0.0012 to 0.0024 inch)
      Limit .... 0.11 (0.004 inch)
  2004 and later
    Intake
      Standard .... 0.010 to 0.35 mm (0.0004 to 0.0014 inch)
      Limit .... 0.10 mm (0.004 inch)
    Exhaust
      Standard .... 0.030 to 0.057 mm (0.0012 to 0.0022 inch)
      Limit .... 0.11 mm (0.004 inch)
Valve seat width (intake and exhaust)
  Standard .... 0.90 to 1.10 mm (0.035 to 0.043 inch)
  Limit .... 1.50 mm (0.06 inch)
Valve guide projection height
  2003 and earlier
    Intake .... 18.0 mm (0.71 inch)
    Exhaust .... 19.5 mm (0.77 inch)
  2004 and later
    Intake .... 17.2 to 17.4 mm (0.68 to 0.69 inch)
    Exhaust .... 18.7 to 18.9 mm (0.736 to 0.744 inch)
Valve spring free length
  Intake
    Standard .... 42.14 mm (1.659 inches)
    Limit .... 40.58 mm (1.598 inches)
  Exhaust
    2003 and earlier
      Standard .... 42.83 mm (1.686 inches)
      Limit .... 41.25 mm (1.624 inches)
    2004 and later
      Standard .... 46.11 mm (1.815 inches)
      Limit .... 44.72 mm (1.761 inches)

Cylinders

Bore diameter
  Standard .... 79.000 to 79.015 mm (3.1102 to 3.1108 inches)
  Limit .... 79.10 mm (3.114 inches)
Warpage (across top of cylinder) .... 0.10 (0.004 inch)
Taper and out-of-round limit .... 0.06 mm (0.002 inch)

Pistons

Piston diameter
  Standard .... 78.97 to 78.99 mm (3.109 to 3.110 inches)
  Limit .... 78.90 mm (3.106 inches)
Piston-to-cylinder clearance
  Standard .... 0.010 to 0.045 mm (0.0004 to 0.0018 inch)
  Limit .... 0.10 mm (0.004 inch)
Ring side clearance
  Top ring
    Standard .... 0.025 to 0.055 mm (0.0010 to 0.0022 inch)
    Limit .... 0.08 mm (0.003 inch)
  Second ring
    Standard .... 0.015 to 0.045 mm (0.006 to 0.0018 inch)
    Limit .... 0.07 mm (0.003 inch)
Ring end gap
  Top ring (VT750C/CD ACE, 1998 through 2000)
    Standard .... 0.20 to 0.35 mm (0.008 to 0.014 inch)
    Limit .... 0.5 mm (0.02 inch)

VT750 models

Pistons (continued)

Top ring (VT750C/CD ACE, 2001 on)
Standard .... 0.025 to 0.055 mm (0.0010 to 0.0022 inch)
Limit .... 0.08 mm (0.003 inch)
Top ring (VT750DC Spirit)
Standard .... 0.025 to 0.055 mm (0.0010 to 0.0022 inch)
Limit .... 0.08 mm (0.003 inch)
Top ring (VT750C Aero, VT750C2 Spirit, 2004 and later)
Standard .... 0.15 to 0.25 mm (0.006 to 0.010 inch)
Limit .... 0.04 mm (0.020 inch)
Second ring (VT750C/CD ACE, 1998 through 2000)
Standard .... 0.35 to 0.50 mm (0.014 to 0.020 inch)
Limit .... 0.7 (0.03 inch)
Second ring (VT750C/CD, 2001 on)
Standard .... 0.015 to 0.025 mm (0.006 to 0.010 inch)
Limit .... 0.4 mm (0.020 inch)
Second ring (VT750DC Spirit, VT750C Aero, VT750C2 Spirit)
Standard .... 0.025 to 0.040 mm (0.0010 to 0.0016 inch)
Limit .... 0.50 mm (0.020 inch)
Oil ring
Standard .... 0.20 to 0.80 mm (0.008 to 0.031 inch)
Limit .... 1.0 mm (0.04 inch)
Piston pin bore
Standard .... 18.002 to 18.008 mm (0.7087 to 0.7090 inch)
Limit .... 18.05 mm (0.711 inch)
Piston pin diameter
Standard .... 17.994 to 18.000 mm (0.7084 to 0.7087 inch)
Limit .... 17.98 mm (0.708 inch)
Piston-to-piston pin clearance
Standard .... 0.002 to 0.014 mm (0.0001 to 0.0006 inch)
Limit .... 0.04 mm (0.002 inch)
Piston pin-to-connecting rod small end clearance
Standard .... 0.016 to 0.040 mm (0.0006 to 0.0016 inch)
Limit .... 0.06 mm (0.002 inch)

Crankshaft, connecting rods and bearings

Connecting rod small end I.D.
Standard .... 18.016 to 18.034 mm (0.7093 to 0.7100 inch)
Limit .... 18.07 mm (0.711 inch)
Main bearing oil clearance
2003 and earlier
Standard .... 0.030 to 0.046 mm (0.0012 to 0.0018 inch)
Limit .... 0.07 mm (0.003 inch)
2004 and later
Standard .... 0.020 to 0.38 mm (0.0008 to 0.0035 inch)
Limit .... 0.07 mm (0.003 inch)
Connecting rod side clearance
Standard .... 0.05 to 0.20 mm (0.002 to 0.008 inch)
Limit .... 0.30 mm (0.001 inch)
Connecting rod bearing oil clearance
Standard.. .... 0.028 to 0.052 mm (0.0011 to 0.0020 inch)
Limit .... 0.07 mm (0.003 inch)
Crankshaft runout limit .... 0.03 mm (0.001 inch)

Oil pump

Rotor tip clearance
Standard .... 0.15 mm (0.006 inch)
Limit .... 0.20 mm (0.008 inch)
Pump body clearance
Standard .... 0.15 to 0.22 mm (0.006 to 0.009 inch)
Limit .... 0.35 mm (0.014 inch)
Rotor-to-pump body end clearance
Standard .... 0.02 to 0.07 mm (0.001 to 0.003 inch)
Limit .... 0.10 mm (0.004 inch)
Oil pump drive sprocket inside diameter
Standard .... 30.025 to 30.145 mm (1.1821 to 1.1861 inches)
Limit .... 30.15 mm (1.187 inches)

Clutch

Friction plate thickness
  Plate A
    Standard..2.62 to 2.78 mm (0.103 to 0.107 inch)
    Minimum..2.3 mm (0.09 inch)
  Plate B
    Standard..2.92 to 3.08 mm (0.115 to 0.121 inch)
    Minimum..2.6 mm (0.10 inch)
Steel plate warpage limit...0.30 mm (0.012 inch)
Spring free length
  Standard..45.5 mm (1.79 inches)
  Minimum..43.9 mm (1.73 inches)
Mainshaft diameter (at clutch outer guide)
  Standard..21.967 to 21.980 mm (0.8648 to 0.8654 inch)
  Minimum..21.95 mm (0.864 inch)
Clutch outer guide
  Inside diameter
    Standard..21.991 to 22.016 mm (0.8658 to 0.8668 inch)
    Limit..22.03 mm (0.867 inch)
  Outside diameter
    2003 and earlier
      Standard..29.994 to 30.007 mm (1.1089 to 1.1814 inches)
      Limit..29.98 mm (1.180 inches)
    2004 and later
      Standard..32.000 to 32.025 mm (1.2598 to 1.2608 inches)
      Limit..32.09 mm (1.263 inches)

Transmission

Gear inside diameter
  C1, C4
    Standard..31.000 to 31.025 mm (1.2204 to 1.2215 inches)
    Limit..31.05 mm (1.222 inches)
  C2
    2003 and earlier
      Standard..31.000 to 31.025 mm (1.2204 to 1.215 inches)
      Limit..31.05 mm (1.222 inches)
    2004 and later
      Standard..24.000 to 24.021 mm (0.9449 to 0.9457 inch)
      Limit..24.04 mm (0.946 inch)
  M3, M5
    Standard..28.000 to 28.021 mm (1.1024 to 1.1032 inches)
    Limit..28.04 mm (1.104 inch)
Gear bushing
  Outside diameter
    C1, C4
      Standard..30.950 to 30.975 mm (1.2185 to 1.2195 inches)
      Limit..30.93 mm (1.218 inches)
    C2
      2003 and earlier
        Standard..30.950 to 30.975 mm (1.2185 to 1.2195 inches)
        Limit..30.93 mm (1.218 inches)
      2004 and later
        Standard..23.959 to 23.980 mm (0.9433 to 0.9441 inch)
    M3, M5
      Standard..27.959 to 27.980 mm (1.1007 to 1.1016 inches)
      Limit..27.94 mm (1.100 inches)
  Inside diameter
    C2
      2003 and earlier
        Standard..27.995 to 28.016 mm (1.1021 to 1.1030 inches)
        Limit..28.04 mm (1.104 inches)
      2004 and later
        Standard..20.000 to 20.021 mm (0.7874 to 0.7882 inch)
        Limit..20.04 mm (0.789 inch)
    M3
      Standard..25.000 to 25.021 mm (0.9843 to 0.9851 inch)
      Limit..25.04 mm (0.986 inch)

VT750 models

Transmission (continued)

Bushing-to-shaft clearance
  2003 and earlier
    C2
      Standard... 0.015 to 0.049 mm (0.0006 to 0.0119 inch)
      Limit.. 0.08 mm (0.003 inch)
    M3
      Standard... 0.007 to 0.0049 mm (0.0003 to 0.0019 inch)
      Limit.. 0.08 mm (0.003 inch)
  2004 and later
    C2
      Standard... 0.007 to 0.041 mm (0.0003 to 0.0016 inch)
      Limit.. 0.07 mm (0.003 inch)
    M3
      Standard... 0.020 to 0.062 mm (0.0008 to 0.0024 inch)
      Limit.. 0.10 mm (0.004 inch)
Gear-to-bushing clearance
  C1, C2 (2003 and earlier), C4
    Standard... 0.025 to 0.075 mm (0.0010 to 0.0030 inch)
    Limit.. 0.11 mm (0.004 inch)
  M3, C2 (2004 and later), M5
    Standard... 0.020 to 0.062 mm (0.0008 to 0.0024 inch)
    Limit.. 0.10 mm (0.004 inch)
Countershaft diameter
  At C2 bushing
    2003 and earlier
      Standard... 27.967 to 27.980 mm (1.1011 to 1.1016 inches)
      Limit.. 27.95 mm (1.100 inches)
    2004 and later
      Standard... 19.980 to 19.993 mm (0.7866 to 0.7871 inch)
      Limit.. 19.96 mm (0.786 inch)
  At case journal A (2003 and earlier only)
    Standard... 27.972 to 27.990 mm (1.1013 to 1.1020 inches)
    Limit.. 27.95 mm (1.100 inches)
  At case journal B (2003 and earlier only)
    Standard... 19.980 to 19.993 mm (0.7866 to 0.7871 inch)
    Limit.. 19.96 mm (0.786 inch)
Mainshaft diameter
  At M3 bushing
    2003 and earlier
      Standard... 24.972 to 24.993 mm (0.9831 to 0.9840 inch)
      Limit.. 24.95 mm (0.982 inch)
    2004 and later
      Standard... 24.959 to 24.980 mm (0.9826 to 0.9835 inch)
      Limit.. 24.94 mm (0.982 inch)
  At case journal A (2003 and earlier only)
    Standard... 19.980 to 19.993 mm (0.7866 to 0.7871 inch)
    Limit.. 19.96 mm (0.786 inch)
  At case journal B (2003 and earlier only)
    Standard... 21.967 to 21.980 mm (0.8648 to 0.8654 inch)
    Limit.. 21.94 mm (0.864 inch)

Output gear assembly (shaft drive)

Output gear bushing (shaft drive models)
  Inside diameter
    Standard... 20.020 to 20.041 mm (0.7882 to 0.7890 inch)
    Limit.. 20.06 mm (0.790 inch)
  Outside diameter
    Standard... 23.959 to 23.980 mm (0.9433 to 0.9441 inch)
    Limit.. 23.70 mm (0.933 inch)
Output gear diameter (shaft drive models)
  Standard... 24.000 to 24.021 mm(0.9449 to 0.9457 inch)
  Limit .... 24.04 mm (0.946 inch)
Output drive gear shaft diameter
  Standard .... 19.979 to 20.000 mm (0.7866 to 0.7874 inch)
  Limit .... 19.97 mm (0.786 inch)

Gear-to-bushing clearance
  Standard .... 0.020 to 0.062 mm (0.0008 to 0.0024 inch)
  Limit .... 0.082 mm (0.0032 inch)
Bushing-to-shaft clearance
  Standard .... 0.020 to 0.062 mm (0.0008 to 0.0024 inch)
  Limit .... 0.082 mm (0.0032 inch)
Drive gear backlash
  Standard .... 0.08 to 0.23 mm (0.003 to 0.009 inch)
  Limit .... 0.40 mm (0.016 inch)

Shift fork shaft/shift fork/shift drum

Shift fork tip thickness
  Standard .... 5.93 to 6.00 mm (0.233 to 0.236 inch)
  Limit .... 5.6 mm (0.22 inch)
Shift fork shaft bore inside diameter
  Standard .... 13.000 to 13.021 mm (0.5118 to 0.5126 inch)
  Limit .... 13.04 mm (0.513 inch)
Shift fork shaft diameter
  Standard .... 12.966 to 12.984 mm (0.5105 to 0.5112 inch)
  Limit .... 12.90 mm (0.508 inch)
Left shift drum journal diameter
  Standard .... 11.966 to 11.984 mm (0.4711 to 0.4718 inch)
  Limit .... 11.94 mm (0.470 inch)

Torque specifications

Cam chain tensioner bolt .... 10 Nm (88 in-lbs)
Cam chain tensioner set plate bolt.................................... 12 Nm (106 in-lbs)
Camshaft end holder bolt .... 10 Nm (88 in-lbs)
Camshaft holder... 23 Nm (17 ft-lbs)
Camshaft sprocket bolt.. 23 Nm (17 ft-lbs)
Clutch center locknut .... 127 Nm (94 ft-lbs)
Clutch lifter plate bolts .... 12 Nm (106 in-lbs)
Connecting rod bearing cap nuts .... 34 Nm (25 ft-lbs)
Countershaft bearing set plate bolt.................................... 9 Nm (80 in-lbs)
Crankcase bolts
  6 mm bolts .... 9 Nm (80 in-lbs)
  8 mm bolts .... 23 Nm (17 ft-lbs)
Crankcase breather case cover bolt .... 12 Nm (106 in-lbs)
Cylinder head
  6 mm bolts .... 12 Nm (106 in-lbs)
  8 mm bolts .... 23 Nm (17 ft-lbs)
  8 mm nuts .... 23 Nm (17 ft-lbs)
  10 mm nuts .... 47 Nm (35 ft-lbs)
Cylinder head cover bolt.. 10 Nm (88 in-lbs)
Cylinder fin socket bolts (2003 and earlier) .... 10 Nm (88 in-lbs)
Drum stopper plate bolt .... 12 Nm (106 in-lbs)
Flywheel bolt .... 127 Nm (94 ft-lbs)
Gearshift cam plate bolt .... 12 Nm (106 in-lbs)
Gearshift lever pinch bolt .... 12 Nm (106 in-lbs)
Gearshift drum stopper bolt .... 23 Nm (17 ft-lbs)
Left crankcase cover bolts .... 12 Nm (106 in-lbs)
Gearshift spindle stopper plate bolt (2005 and later)............ 13 Nm (120 inch-lbs)
Mainshaft bearing set plate bolt.. 12 Nm (106 in-lbs)
Oil pump driven sprocket bolt.. 15 Nm (132 in-lbs)
Primary drive gear bolt .... 88 Nm (65 ft-lbs)
Right crankcase cover bolts... 12 Nm (106 in-lbs)
Starter clutch torx bolts... 30 Nm (22 ft-lbs)
Stator socket mounting bolt.. 12 Nm (106 in-lbs)
Output gearcase bolts.. 31 Nm (23 ft-lbs) (1)

1 Apply non-hardening sealant to the bolt threads.

1 General information

The engine/transmission unit is a water-cooled V-twin. The valves are operated by overhead camshafts which are chain driven off the crankshaft. All models have three-valve heads (two intake and one exhaust valve per cylinder). The engine/transmission assembly is constructed from aluminum alloy. The crankcase is divided vertically.

The crankcase incorporates a wet sump, pressure-fed lubrication system which uses a gear-driven oil pump and an oil filter mounted on the rear of the crankcase.

Power from the crankshaft is routed to the transmission via a coil-spring, wet multi-plate type clutch, which is gear-driven off the crankshaft. The transmission on VT600 models is a four-speed, constant-mesh unit; the transmission on VT750 models is a five-speed, constant-mesh unit.

2 Operations possible with the engine in the frame

The following components and assemblies can be serviced with the engine in the frame:

Alternator/flywheel
Camshafts/cam sprockets/cam chains
Carburetors
Front cylinder head/cylinder/piston
Clutch
Gearshift linkage
Ignition pulse generator(s)
Primary drive gear
Starter clutch
Starter motor

3 Operations requiring engine removal

The engine/transmission assembly must be removed from the frame to gain access to the following components:

Rear cylinder head/cylinder/piston
Water pump body

The crankcase halves must be separated to gain access to the following components:

Crankshaft, connecting rods and bearings
Oil pump
Transmission
Shift drum and shift forks

5.12 Drive chain sprocket bolts (chain drive) (left arrows) and gearshift linkage pinch bolt (all models) (right arrow)

4 Major engine repair - general note

1　It is not always easy to determine when or if an engine should be completely overhauled, as a number of factors must be considered.
2　High mileage is not necessarily an indication that an overhaul is needed, while low mileage, on the other hand, does not preclude the need for an overhaul. Frequency of servicing is probably the single most important consideration. An engine that has regular and frequent oil and filter changes, as well as other required maintenance, will most likely give many miles of reliable service. Conversely, a neglected engine, or one which has not been broken in properly, may require an overhaul very early in its life.
3　Exhaust smoke and excessive oil consumption are both indications that piston rings and/or valve guides are in need of attention. Make sure oil leaks are not responsible before deciding that the rings and guides are bad. Refer to Chapter 1 and perform a cylinder compression check to determine for certain the nature and extent of the work required.
4　If the engine is making obvious knocking or rumbling noises, the connecting rod and/or main bearings are probably at fault.
5　Loss of power, rough running, excessive valve train noise and high fuel consumption rates may also point to the need for an overhaul, especially if they are all present at the same time. If a complete tune-up does not remedy the situation, major mechanical work is the only solution.
6　An engine overhaul generally involves restoring the internal parts to the specifications of a new engine. During an overhaul the piston rings are replaced and the cylinder walls are bored and/or honed. If a rebore is done, then new pistons are also required. The main and connecting rod bearings are generally replaced with new ones and, if necessary, the crankshaft is also replaced. Generally the valves are serviced as well, since

they are usually in less than perfect condition at this point. While the engine is being overhauled, other components such as the carburetors and the starter motor can be rebuilt also. The end result should be a like-new engine that will give as many trouble free miles as the original.
7　Before beginning the engine overhaul, read through all of the related procedures to familiarize yourself with the scope and requirements of the job. Overhauling an engine is not all that difficult, but it is time consuming. Plan on the motorcycle being tied up for a minimum of two weeks. Check on the availability of parts and make sure that any necessary special tools, equipment and supplies are obtained in advance.
8　Most work can be done with typical shop hand tools, although a number of precision measuring tools are required for inspecting parts to determine if they must be replaced. Often a dealer service department or motorcycle repair shop will handle the inspection of parts and offer advice concerning reconditioning and replacement. As a general rule, time is the primary cost of an overhaul so it doesn't pay to install worn or substandard parts.
9　As a final note, to ensure maximum life and minimum trouble from a rebuilt engine, everything must be assembled with care in a spotlessly clean environment.

5 Engine - removal and installation

Note: *Engine removal and installation should be done with the aid of an assistant to avoid damage or injury that could occur if the engine is dropped. A hydraulic floor jack should be used to support and lower the engine if possible (they can be rented at low cost).*

Removal

1　Support the bike securely so it can't be knocked over during this procedure. Place

5.23a To detach the front of the engine from the frame, remove
these nuts and bolts (arrows) from the right side . . .

5.23b . . . and this bolt (arrow) from the left side

a support under the swingarm pivot and be sure the motorcycle is safely braced.

2   Drain the engine oil and remove the oil filter (see Chapter 1).

3   Drain the coolant (see Chapter 1).

4   Remove the seat and side covers (see Chapter 8).

5   Disconnect the cable from the negative battery terminal (see Chapter 9).

6   Remove the fuel tank (see Chapter 4). If the bike has a PAIR system, disconnect the hoses from the reed valves on the valve covers.

7   Remove the air cleaner housing cover and the filter element (see Chapter 1).

8   Remove the air cleaner chamber and the carburetors (see Chapter 4).

9   Disconnect all four spark plug caps and set the spark plug leads aside.

10   Remove the exhaust pipe protectors and the exhaust pipes (see Chapter 4).

11   Remove the left rear engine cover (see Chapter 7).

12   Detach the gearshift arm from the gearshift spindle (see illustration).

13   If the bike has chain drive, remove the countershaft sprocket and drive chain. If it has shaft drive, remove the driveshaft (see Chapter 7).

14   Disconnect the electrical leads from the oil pressure and neutral switches (see Chapter 9). Detach the switch leads from all clamps on the engine and frame and set the leads safely aside.

15   Disconnect the starter motor cable and ground cable from the starter motor (see Chapter 9).

16   Detach the clutch cable bracket from the engine and disconnect the cable from the clutch lifter arm (see Section 17).

17   Detach the right footpeg, footpeg bracket and brake pedal from the frame (see Chapter 8). Disconnect and remove the middle brake rod (see Chapter 7).

18   Disconnect the electrical connector for the ignition pulse generator(s) (see Chapter 5) and detach the wire harness from the engine and frame.

19   Disconnect the electrical connector for the alternator (see Chapter 9) and detach the

wire harness from the engine and frame.

20   Disconnect and remove the coolant hoses between the radiator and the water pump, and the hoses between the thermostat and the cylinder heads (see Chapter 3).

21   Place a floor jack or a special motorcycle lift beneath the engine. Be sure to place a block of wood between the jack and the engine to protect the aluminum crankcase.

22   On 1988 and 1989 and 1991 through 1996 VT600 models, remove the rear wheel .(see Chapter 7) and the swingarm (see Chapter 6).

23   Remove the nuts and bolts from the upper and lower front engine mounting brackets (see illustrations) and remove the upper and lower front engine mounting brackets.

24   Remove the nut and bolt that attaches the rear engine mounting bracket to the frame and remove the two bolts that attach the rear mounting bracket to the engine (see illustrations) and remove the rear mounting bracket.

5.24a To detach the rear of the engine from the frame, remove
this bolt (arrow) and nut (not visible) . . .

5.24b . . . remove these two bolts (one bolt hidden) and the rear
mounting bracket

6.2a A selection of brushes is required for cleaning holes and passages in the engine components

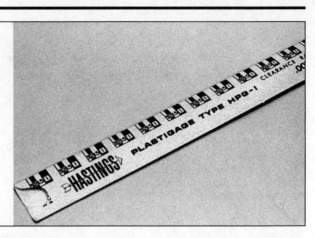

6.2b Type HPG-1 Plastigage is needed to check the connecting rod oil clearances

25 On 1997 and later VT600 and 1998 and later VT750 models, remove the swingarm pivot cap and remove the swingarm pivot nut, locknut, pivot bolt and collars (see Chapter 6).

26 Remove the engine from the right side of the frame. Protect the frame rails from scratches with duct tape.

Installation

27 Installation is the reverse of removal. Note the following points:

a) *Don't tighten any of the engine mounting bracket nuts and bolts until all of them have been installed.*

b) *Use new gaskets at all exhaust pipe connections.*

c) *Tighten the engine mounting bracket nuts and bolts securely.*

d) *Adjust the rear brake pedal height and freeplay, adjust the clutch cable freeplay and adjust the throttle cable freeplay (see Chapter 1).*

e) *Be sure to add engine oil and coolant (see Chapter 1) before starting the engine.*

6 Engine disassembly and reassembly - general information

1 Before disassembling the engine, clean the exterior with a degreaser and rinse it with water. A clean engine will make the job easier and prevent the possibility of getting dirt into the internal areas of the engine.

2 In addition to the precision measuring tools mentioned earlier, you will need a torque wrench, a valve spring compressor, oil gallery brushes, a piston ring removal and installation tool, a piston ring compressor and a clutch holder tool (which is described in Section 16). Some new, clean engine oil of the correct grade and type, some engine assembly lube or moly-based grease, and a tube of RTV (silicone) sealant will also be required. Plastigage (type HPG-1) should be used for checking bearing oil clearances **(see illustrations)**.

3 An engine support stand made from short lengths of lumber bolted together will facilitate the disassembly and reassembly procedures **(see illustration)**. The perimeter of the mount should be just big enough to accommodate the crankcase when it's laid on its side for removal of the crankshaft and transmission components. If you have an automotive-type engine stand, an adapter plate can be made from a piece of plate, some angle iron and some nuts and bolts.

The adapter plate can be attached to the engine mounting bolt holes.

4 When disassembling the engine, keep "mated" parts together (including gears, cylinders, pistons, etc.) that have been in contact with each other during engine operation. These "mated" parts must be reused or replaced as an assembly.

5 Engine/transmission disassembly should be done in the following general order with reference to the appropriate Sections:

> *Remove the cylinder head covers*
> *Remove the rocker arm assemblies*
> *Remove the camshafts and timing chain sprockets*
> *Remove the cylinder heads*
> *Remove the timing chain tensioners*
> *Remove the cylinders*
> *Remove the pistons*
> *Remove the flywheel and starter clutch assembly*
> *Remove the clutch assembly*
> *Remove the primary drive gear*
> *Remove the external gearshift mechanism*
> *Separate the crankcase halves*
> *Remove the crankshaft and connecting rods*
> *Remove the shift drum and forks*
> *Remove the transmission shafts and gears*
> *Remove the oil pump*

6 Reassembly is accomplished by reversing the general disassembly sequence.

6.3 An engine stand can be made from short lengths of lumber and lag bolts or nails

7 Cylinder head cover - removal and installation

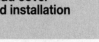

1 Drain the coolant (see Chapter 1).

2 Remove the fuel tank (see Chapter 4).

3 Remove the steering head covers (see Chapter 8).

4 Remove the air cleaner housing cover and filter element (see Chapter 1).

5 Remove the air cleaner chamber and the carburetors (see Chapter 4).

6 Detach the spark plug caps from the spark plugs (see Chapter 1) and set the high tension leads aside.

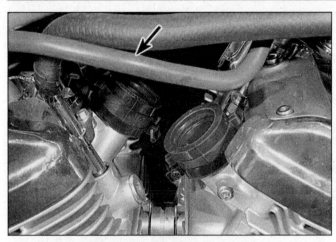

7.7 Detach the breather hose (arrow) from the cylinder head cover (VT600 models)

7.8 Remove the coolant hose and cylinder head cover bolts (arrows) (VT600 models)

7.9a To detach a coolant pipe from the cylinder head, remove the hold-down bolt (arrows) . . .

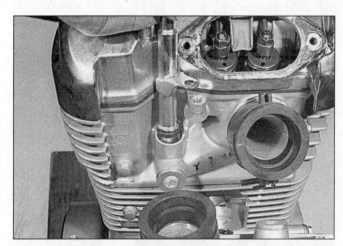

7.9b . . . and pull the pipe straight up (engine removed for clarity) (VT600 models)

VT600 models

7   Detach the breather hose from the front or rear cylinder head cover (see illustration).

8   Detach the coolant hose from the cylinder head (see illustration).

9   Remove the coolant pipe (see illustrations).

10   If you're removing the rear cylinder head cover on a 1995 or later model, remove the exhaust valve adjusting cover (see Section 17 in Chapter 1).

11   If you're removing the rear cylinder head cover on a pre-1995 model, unclamp the wiring harness above the cover and push it aside to provide sufficient clearance for cover removal. If you're removing the rear cover on a 1995 or later model, align the wire harness above the cover with the valve adjustment hole.

VT750 models

12   If you're removing the front cylinder head cover, remove the sub-air cleaner housing (see Chapter 4); if you're removing the rear cylinder head cover, remove the three

7.14a On VT750 models, the cylinder fins are attached to the cylinder head by four Allen bolts per side, two inner bolts (arrows) (left side of cylinders shown) . . .

breather cover bolts and remove the breather cover.

13   Remove the two cylinder head cover outer cover bolts and remove the outer cover.

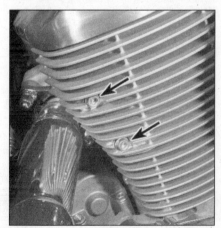

7.14b . . . and two outer bolts (arrows) (right side of rear cylinder shown)

If you're removing the outer cover from the rear cylinder head cover, don't lose the cable guide attached to the right bolt.

14   Remove the cylinder fins from both sides of the cylinder head (see illustrations).

15   If you're removing the front cylinder

7.16a Try simply lifting the cylinder head cover from the head with your hands (VT600 shown)

head cover, remove the thermostat housing mounting bolt (see Chapter 3) and push the thermostat housing up to provide clearance.

All models

16   Remove the cylinder head cover bolts **(see illustration 7.8)**. Remove the cylinder head cover and gasket **(see illustration)**. If the cover sticks, gently pry it loose at the prying points **(see illustration)**.
Caution: Do NOT pry the cylinder head cover anywhere except the prying points or you may damage the cover, the head or the gasket. Once the cover has been removed, don't drop anything into the cam chain tunnel (the opening below the camshaft sprocket). If you do, it might end up in the crankcase and you might have to split the cases to get it out! Stuff clean shop towels into the cam chain tunnel so nothing accidentally falls into the engine.
17   Pull the old gasket out of its groove in the cylinder head cover and discard it. Clean out the gasket groove, apply a thin coat of Honda Bond A, or a similar contact cement, and install the new gasket into the groove. Apply a thin coat of sealant to the gasket.
18   Separate the rubber grommets from the cylinder head cover bolts and washers and inspect the grommets. Replace them if

they're dried out, cracked or torn, or otherwise damaged.
19   Install the cylinder head cover. Make *sure* that the gasket is not pinched, kinked or otherwise distorted. If it is, the cylinder head cover will leak. Install the cylinder head cover bolts and washers and tighten the bolts to the torque listed in this Chapter's Specifications.
20   The remainder of installation is the reverse of removal.

---

8   Camshaft, sprocket and rocker arms - removal, inspection and installation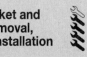

Note: *The following procedure applies to the front and rear camshaft and rocker arm assemblies.*

Removal

1   Remove the cylinder head cover (see Section 7).
2   Remove the crankshaft hole cap and the timing hole cap (see Section 17 in Chapter 1).
3   Rotate the crankshaft counterclockwise with a socket until the FT mark on the flywheel is aligned with the index mark on the

left crankcase cover. This places the front piston at top dead center (TDC) *on its compression stroke*. To verify that the front piston is at TDC on its compression stroke, wiggle the tip of each rocker arm. If the front piston *is* at TDC on its compression stroke, the valves are fully closed, so the rocker arms are not pushing against the valves, so they should feel a little loose. If the front piston is not at TDC on its compression stroke, rotate the crankshaft counterclockwise another 360 degrees and re-align the FT mark on the flywheel with the index mark on the left crankcase cover.
4   Before proceeding, determine cam chain wear as follows. There are two wedges, one behind the other, at the upper end of the cam chain tensioner: a thicker wedge adjacent to the chain and a thinner wedge next to the head **(see illustration)**. To determine whether the cam chain should be replaced, measure the height that the wedge near the chain projects above the top of the tensioner **(see illustration)** and compare your measurement to the maximum allowable height

8.4a There are two wedges (arrow) at the upper end of the cam chain tensioner: the thinner wedge is next to the head, the thicker one is nearer the cam chain

8.4b To determine whether the cam chain should be replaced, measure how far the thick wedge projects above the top of the chain tensioner

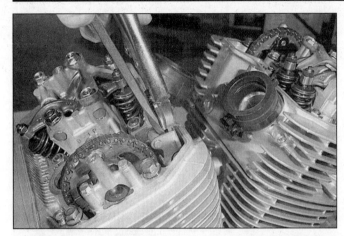

8.5a Before removing the camshaft, pull up the thin wedge . . .

8.5b . . . and insert a paper clip through the hole in the wedge to keep it up

8.6a Remove the camshaft end holder bolts (arrows) . . .

8.6b . . . then remove the end holder and dowel pins (arrows)

listed in this Chapter's Specifications. If the indicated height exceeds the specified maximum height, replace the cam chain (see Section 21).

5   Holding down the thicker cam chain tensioner wedge with a screwdriver, pull up the thinner cam chain tensioner wedge with a pair of pliers **(see illustrations)** and insert

a paper clip through the hole in the thinner wedge to keep it up **(see illustration)**.

6   Remove the bolts from the camshaft end holder (the smaller holder at the sprocket end of the cam), remove the end holder and remove the dowel pins **(see illustrations)**. Put the dowel pins in a plastic bag so you don't misplace them.

7   Remove the camshaft sprocket bolts **(see illustration 8.6b)**. After removing the first bolt, rotate the crankshaft 360 degrees to access the other bolt (the camshaft will rotate 1/2 turn for each full turn of the crankshaft).

8   Remove the camshaft holder bolts and nut, the oil guide plate, the camshaft holder and the dowel pins **(see illustrations)**.

8.8a Remove the nut and three bolts (arrows), remove the oil guide plate . . .

8.8b . . . remove the camshaft holder/ rocker arm assembly . . .

8.8c . . . and remove the dowel pins (arrows)

8.9a Remove the camshaft . . .

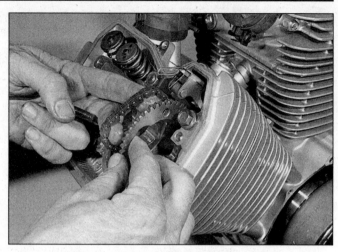

8.9b . . . and remove the camshaft sprocket

8.10 Inspect the camshaft bearing surfaces (arrows) in the cylinder head (and their corresponding upper surfaces in the camshaft holder and end holder) for signs of scoring or spalling

9   Remove the camshaft and the camshaft sprocket **(see illustrations)**. Secure the cam chain with a piece of wire or string to prevent it from falling into the crankcase.
Caution: Do NOT rotate the crankshaft while either or both camshafts are removed.

Inspection
Camshaft
Note: *Before replacing camshafts because of damage, check with local machine shops specializing in motorcycle engine work. A*

machine shop might be able to weld, regrind and harden the cam lobes for less than the price of a new camshaft.
10   Inspect the cam bearing surfaces in the camshaft holder, the cam end holder and the cylinder head **(see illustration)**. Look for signs of scoring (scratches or grooves in the bearing surfaces) and spalling (a pitted appearance), both of which are usually caused by dirty or insufficient oil. If either holder is damaged or worn, replace it; if the cylinder head is worn or damaged, replace it (see Section 10).
11   Support the camshaft on V-blocks and measure the camshaft runout with a dial indicator and compare your measurement to the runout listed in this Chapter's Specifications.
12   Check the camshaft lobes for heat discoloration (blue appearance), score marks, chipped areas, flat spots and spalling **(see illustration)**. Measure the height of each lobe with a micrometer **(see illustration)** and compare the results to the minimum lobe height listed in this Chapter's Specifications.

8.12a Inspect the lobes of the camshaft for wear; here's a good example of damage that will require replacement or repair of the camshaft

8.12b Measure the height of the cam lobes with a micrometer

8.14 Lay a strip of Plastigage along each camshaft journal, parallel with the centerline but not across an oil hole

17 Inspect the visible portion of the cam chain for obvious wear or damage. Except in cases of oil starvation, the chain wears very little. If the chain has stretched excessively, the tensioner cannot maintain correct chain tension; replace the chain (see Section 21).

18 Inspect the cam sprocket for wear, cracks and other damage. If any damage or wear is evident, replace the sprocket. If the sprocket is severely worn, the cam chain is probably worn too (see Section 21).

19 Using a flashlight, inspect the condition of the cam chain tensioner and the cam chain guide. If either of them looks worn or damaged, remove it for a better look (tensioner, see Section 9; guide, see Section 13).

Camshaft holder/rocker arm assembly

20 To disassemble the camshaft holder/rocker arm assembly, tap the rocker arm shafts with a soft hammer, separate the shafts from the holders, and remove the rocker arms and wave washers from the shafts **(see illustration)**. Note the location of the wave washers on the shafts; they must be reassembled in this exact order.

If damage is noted or wear is excessive, replace the camshaft.

13 Measure the camshaft bearing oil clearances. Clean the camshaft, the bearing surfaces in the cylinder head, and the cam holder and end holder, with a clean lint-free cloth, then lay the cam in place in the cylinder head. Secure the cam by installing the cam sprocket and chain so the camshaft doesn't turn as the holder nut and bolts are tightened.

14 Cut strips of Plastigage (type HPG-1) and lay one piece on each bearing journal, parallel with the camshaft centerline **(see illustration)**. Make sure that no oil hole in any journal is facing up; if Plastigage is laid across an oil hole, it will not produce an accurate representation of the actual clearance. Install the cam holder and the end holder in their proper positions and install the nut and bolts. Tighten the nut and bolts evenly in a criss-cross pattern until the specified torque is reached. While doing this, don't let the camshaft rotate.

15 Now unscrew the nut and bolts a little at a time, and carefully lift off the cam holder and end holder.

16 To determine the oil clearance, compare the crushed Plastigage (at its widest point) on each journal to the scale printed on the Plastigage container **(see illustration)**. Compare the results to this Chapter's Specifications. If the oil clearance is greater than specified, measure the diameter of the cam bearing journal with a micrometer **(see illustration)**. If the journal diameter is less than the specified limit, replace the camshaft and recheck the clearance. If the clearance is still excessive, replace the cylinder head and holders.

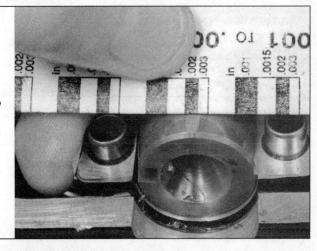

8.16a To calculate the clearance, compare the width of the crushed Plastigage to the scale printed on the Plastigage container

8.16b If cam journal diameter is less than the specified minimum, replace the camshaft

8.20 To disassemble the camshaft holder/rocker arm assembly, tap out the rocker shafts (arrows) with a soft hammer

21   Clean the rocker arm components with solvent and dry them off. Blow through the oil passages in the rocker arms with compressed air. Inspect the rocker arm slipper faces (the friction surfaces that ride on the cam lobes) for pits, spalling, score marks and rough spots. Check the rocker arm-to-shaft contact areas and the adjusting screws. Look for cracks in each rocker arm. If the slipper faces are damaged, the rocker arms and the shafts should be replaced as a set. If the slipper faces are worn or damaged, look closely at the corresponding cam lobes; they're probably also worn and they may be damaged.

22   Measure the inside diameter of each rocker arm, then measure the diameter of the rocker arm shafts in the area where each rocker arm rides. Calculate the difference between the inside diameter of each rocker arm and the diameter of the shaft where it rides. The difference is the oil clearance. Compare your measurements with the oil clearance listed in this Chapter's Specifications. If the clearance is beyond the specified limits, replace the rocker arms and shafts as a set.

23   Apply a coat of molybdenum disulfide oil to the rocker arm shafts and install the rocker arm shafts, rocker arms and wave washers in the camshaft holder. Don't mix up the rocker arms: The exhaust rocker arm has a larger slipper face than the intake rocker arms. Don't switch the two rocker arm shafts; they're not interchangeable. The intake rocker shaft has a hole in each end for the cam holder bolts; the exhaust rocker shaft has notches, instead of holes, for the holder bolts **(see illustration)**. The washers for the intake rocker arms go between the rocker arms and the middle boss of the camshaft holder; the washer for the exhaust rocker goes between the right side of the rocker (with the exhaust rocker arm and shaft facing toward you) and the right holder boss (which is marked by a D.) Position the grooves in the rocker arm shafts vertically to align the holes in the intake rocker shaft and the notches in the exhaust rocker shaft (*look* through the bolt holes in the holder to

8.23 Camshaft holder/rocker arm assembly details

1   *Camshaft holder*
2   *Intake rocker arm shaft*
3   *Intake rocker arm*
4   *Wave washer*
5   *Wave washer*
6   *Intake rocker arm*
7   *Exhaust rocker arm shaft*
8   *Exhaust rocker arm*
9   *Wave washer*

verify that the notches on the exhaust shaft are aligned; if they aren't, rotate the exhaust shaft 180 degrees).

Valve timing and camshaft installation

24   Remove the crankshaft and timing hole caps.

Valve timing

Both camshafts removed

25   If both camshafts were removed, install the front cylinder camshaft first.
26   The camshafts are not interchangeable. Look for the "F" (front cylinder camshaft) or "R" (rear cylinder cam) on the sprocket end of each cam **(see illustration)**. The index notch on the camshaft (directly above the F or R) indicates TDC.
27   Turn the crankshaft counterclockwise, align the FT mark on the flywheel with the index mark on the crankcase cover (see Section 17 in Chapter 1) and verify that the front cylinder piston is at TDC.
28   Install the front cylinder camshaft (go to Step 43).
29   Turn the crankshaft counterclockwise 232 degrees and align the RT mark on the flywheel with the index mark on the crankcase cover (see Section 17 in Chapter 1).

30   Install the rear cylinder camshaft (go to Step 43).

Rear camshaft only removed

31   If the rear cylinder camshaft was removed, but the front cam wasn't, remove the front cylinder head cover (see Section 7) and verify that the front cylinder camshaft is correctly positioned as follows. The front cylinder camshaft will be used as a reference for correct installation of the rear cylinder camshaft.
32   Remove the front cylinder camshaft end holder (see Step 6).
33   Turn the crankshaft counterclockwise, align the FT mark on the flywheel with the index mark on the crankcase cover (see Section 17 in Chapter 1) and verify that the camshaft TDC mark is facing up **(see illustration 8.26)**.
34   If the TDC mark is facing up, turn the crankshaft counterclockwise 232 degrees and align the RT mark on the flywheel with the index mark on the crankcase cover.
35   If the TDC mark is facing down, turn the crankshaft counterclockwise 592 degrees (360 degrees + 232 degrees) and align the RT mark on the flywheel with the index mark on the crankcase cover.
36   Install the rear cylinder camshaft (go to Step 43).

Front camshaft only removed

37   If the front cylinder camshaft was removed, but the rear cam wasn't, remove the rear cylinder head cover (see Section 7). Verify that the rear cylinder camshaft is correctly positioned as follows. The rear cylinder camshaft will be used as a reference for correct installation of the front cylinder camshaft.
38   Remove the front cylinder camshaft end holder (see Step 6).
39   Turn the crankshaft counterclockwise, align the RT mark on the flywheel with the index mark on the crankcase cover (see Section 17 in Chapter 1) and verify that the camshaft TDC mark is facing up **(see illustration 8.26)**.
40   If the TDC mark is facing up, turn the crankshaft counterclockwise 488 degrees (360 degrees + 128 degrees) and align the FT

8.26 The front and rear camshafts are identified by an "F" (shown) or "R;" the notch above the F or R indicates TDC when it's upward

8.43 Install the camshaft sprocket with the "IN" facing toward the valve springs and the timing marks (arrows) aligned with the gasket mating surface

8.45 Make sure the timing marks on the sprocket are still aligned with the gasket mating surface after bolting the sprocket to the camshaft

mark on the flywheel with the index mark on the crankcase cover.

41 If the TDC mark is facing down, turn the crankshaft counterclockwise 128 degrees and align the FT mark on the flywheel with the index mark on the crankcase cover.

42 Install the camshaft (go to Step 43).

Camshaft installation

43 Place the camshaft sprocket in position with the "IN" mark **(see illustration)** facing toward the valve springs and align the timing marks on the sprocket with the gasket mating surface of the cylinder head.

44 Install the camshaft with the TDC mark facing up **(see illustration 8.26)**. Install the camshaft holder dowel pins. Lubricate each rocker arm slipper face with molybdenum oil and install the camshaft holder/rocker arm assembly. Install the oil guide plate. Install the camshaft holder bolts and nut and tighten them to the torque listed in this Chapter's Specifications.

45 Install the camshaft sprocket on the

camshaft flange and verify that the timing marks are still aligned with the gasket mating surface of the head **(see illustration)**.

46 Clean the threads of the sprocket bolts, coat them with a thread-locking agent, align the holes in the cam sprocket with the holes in the camshaft sprocket flange and install the upper bolt.

47 Rotate the crankshaft counterclockwise 360 degrees and install the other sprocket bolt. Tighten the second bolt to the torque listed in this Chapter's Specifications.

48 Rotate the crankshaft counterclockwise 360 degrees and tighten the first bolt to the torque listed in this Chapter's Specifications.

49 Remove the paper clip from the cam chain tensioner. Don't drop the paper clip into the cam chain tunnel!

50 Install the dowel pins, the camshaft end holder and the end holder bolts. Tighten the end holder bolts to the torque listed in this Chapter's Specifications.

51 Adjust the valve clearances (see Chapter 1).

52 Install the cylinder head cover (see Section 7).

53 If you removed both camshafts, return to Step 29 to install the remaining camshaft.

9 Cam chain tensioner - removal, inspection and installation

Note: *The following procedure applies to the front and rear cam chain tensioners.*

1 Remove the cylinder head cover (see Section 7).

2 Remove the camshaft, sprocket and rocker arms (see Section 8).

3 Remove the cam chain tensioner mounting bolts **(see illustration)** and discard the sealing washers.

4 Remove the cam chain tensioner **(see illustration)**.

5 Clean the chain tensioner in solvent and blow dry it with compressed air. Inspect the

9.3 To remove the chain tensioner, remove these two bolts; discard the old sealing washers

9.4 Remove the chain tensioner from the cam chain tunnel

9.5 Replace the chain tensioner if the friction surface is scored or worn

10.6 To detach the cylinder head, remove these four nuts and three bolts (arrows) gradually and evenly, in a criss-cross pattern

friction surface of the tensioner **(see illustration)** for wear and damage. If the friction surface is worn or damaged, replace the tensioner.

6   Install the chain tensioner. Using new sealing washers, install the chain tensioner mounting bolts and tighten them to the torque listed in this Chapter's Specifications.

7   Install the camshaft, sprocket and rocker arms (see Section 8).

8   Install the cylinder head cover (see Section 7).

10 Cylinder head - removal and installation

Note: *The following procedure applies to the front and rear cylinder heads. However, if the rear cylinder is to be removed, the engine must be removed from the frame.*

Removal

1   Detach the exhaust pipe from the cylinder head (see Chapter 4).

2   If you are removing the rear cylinder head, remove the engine (see Section 5).

3   Remove the cylinder head cover (see Section 7).

4   Remove the camshaft, sprocket and rocker arms (see Section 8).

5   Remove the cam chain tensioner (see Section 9). Secure the chain so it can't fall into the crankcase.

6   Loosen the cylinder head nuts and bolts evenly in several stages **(see illustration).** Remove the nuts, bolts and washers.

7   Lift the cylinder head off the studs **(see illustration).** If it's stuck, tap it gently with a rubber or plastic mallet, being careful not to break the cooling fins. Don't pry against the gasket surfaces or they will be gouged.

8   Remove the dowel pins **(see illustration)** and the old gasket.

9   Inspect the cylinder head gasket and the mating surfaces on the cylinder head and the cylinder for leakage, which could indicate

warpage. Measure the flatness of the cylinder head (see Section 12).

10   Clean all traces of old gasket material from the cylinder head and block. Stuff clean shop rags into the cylinder bore and the cam chain tunnel to prevent gasket material from falling into the engine. Be careful not to let any debris fall into the crankcase, the cylinder bore or the oil passages.

11   Remove and inspect the cam chain guide (see Section 13).

12   Loosen the hose clamp screw and remove the carburetor insulator from the head.

Installation

13   Make sure that all old gasket material is removed from the cylinder head-to-cylinder mating surfaces.

14   Install the cam chain guide (see Section 13).

15   Install the dowel pins and the new cylinder head gasket.

16   Install the carburetor insulator on the head and tighten the hose clamp screw securely. Make sure the slot on the insula-

tor is correctly engaged with the boss on the head. On 1991 and later California VT600 models, make sure that the pin on the outer clamp (the one nearer the carburetor) is aligned with the slot on the insulator. Tighten the clamp screws securely.

17   If you removed both cylinder heads, note the identification mark on the heads: the front cylinder head is marked with an "F" **(see illustration 10.6)** and the rear cylinder head is marked with an "R."

18   Install the cylinder head. Install the cylinder head mounting washers, nuts and bolts and hand tighten them. Then tighten them gradually and evenly, in a criss-cross fashion, to the torque listed in this Chapter's Specifications.

19   Install the cam chain tensioner (see Section 9).

20   Install the camshaft, sprocket and rocker arms (see Section 8).

21   Install the cylinder head cover (see Section 7).

22   Install the engine, if removed (see Section 5).

23   Install the exhaust pipe (see Chapter 4).

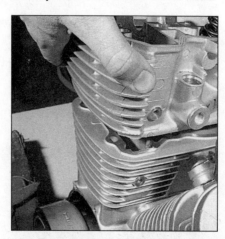

10.7 Try to remove the cylinder head with your hands; if it's stuck, tap it loose with a small plastic or rubber mallet

10.8 Remove the dowel pins (arrows) and the cylinder head gasket; if some of the gasket material sticks to the cylinder, carefully scrape it off

12.7a Compress the valve springs and remove the keepers, release the spring compressor . . .

12.7b . . . remove the spring retainer and the spring(s) . . .

12.7c . . . push on the valve stem . . .

11 Valves/valve seats/valve guides - servicing

1   Because of the complex nature of this job and the special tools and equipment required, servicing of the valves, the valve seats and the valve guides (commonly known as a valve job) is best left to a professional.

2   The home mechanic can, however, remove and disassemble the head, do the initial cleaning and inspection, then reassemble and deliver the head to a dealer service department or properly equipped motorcycle repair shop for the actual valve servicing.

3   The dealer service department will remove the valves and springs, recondition or replace the valves and valve seats, replace the valve guides, check and, if necessary, replace the valve springs, spring retainers and keepers, install new valve seals and reassemble the valve components.

4   After the valve job has been performed, the head will be in like-new condition. When the head is returned, be sure to clean it again very thoroughly before installation on the engine to remove any metal particles or abrasive grit that may still be present from the valve service operations. Use compressed air, if available, to blow out all the holes and passages.

12 Cylinder head and valves - disassembly, inspection and reassembly

Note: *If the bearing surfaces in the cylinder head are damaged, a shop might be able to repair them. A new cylinder head is expensive, so explore your options before discarding the old head.*

1   Valve servicing and valve guide replacement should be done by a dealer service department or motorcycle repair shop (see Section 11). However, disassembly, cleaning

and inspection of the cylinder head and valves can be done at home, with the right tools.

2   To disassemble the valve components safely, a valve spring compressor is absolutely necessary. If you don't own a valve spring compressor, you should be able to rent one at a local tool rental yard. If you're unable to obtain a valve spring compressor, leave the following procedure to a dealer service department or motorcycle repair shop.

Disassembly

3   Remove the cylinder head (see Section 10).

4   Before the valves are removed, scrape away any traces of gasket material from the head gasket sealing surface. Work slowly and do not nick or gouge the soft aluminum of the head. Gasket removing solvents, which work very well, are available at most motorcycle shops and auto parts stores.

5   Carefully scrape all carbon deposits out of the combustion chamber area. A hand held wire brush or a piece of fine emery cloth can be used once the majority of deposits have been scraped away. Do not use a wire

brush mounted in a drill motor, or one with extremely stiff bristles, as the head material is soft and may be eroded away or scratched by the wire brush.

6   Label three plastic bags, one for each valve spring/valve assembly, so it can be installed in the same valve guide from which it's removed.

7   Compress each valve spring assembly with a spring compressor **(see illustration)** and remove the keepers. Do not compress the spring any more than is absolutely necessary. If the keepers stick to the groove in the valve stem, use a magnet or a pair of tweezers to pull them off. Carefully release the valve spring compressor and remove the retainer **(see illustration)** and the spring(s) (VT600 models have an inner and an outer spring; VT750 models use a single spring). Push on the valve stem **(see illustration)**, pull on the valve head **(see illustration)** and remove the valve from the head. If the valve binds in the guide, push it back into the head and deburr the area around the keeper groove with a very fine file or whetstone **(see illustration)**.

12.7d . . . pull on the valve head and remove the valve from the cylinder head

12.7e If the valve binds in the guide, deburr the area above the keeper groove

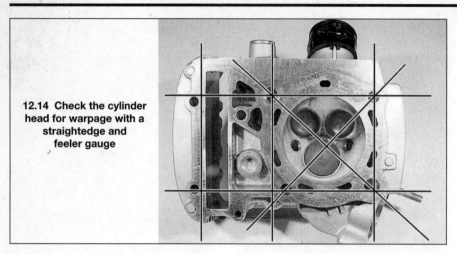

12.14 Check the cylinder head for warpage with a straightedge and feeler gauge

12.16 Measure the valve guide inside diameter with a small hole gauge, then measure the hole gauge with a micrometer

8   Once the valve and valve spring assembly have been removed, labeled and stored, pull off the valve stem seal and discard it (the old seals should never be reused), then remove the lower spring seat and store it with the other valve spring parts.

9   Repeat the previous two Steps for the other two valves. Be sure to keep the parts for each valve assembly in separate plastic bags so they won't be mixed up.

10   Clean the cylinder head with solvent and dry it thoroughly. Compressed air will speed the drying process and ensure that all holes and recessed areas are clean.

11   Clean all of the valve springs, keepers, retainers and spring seats with solvent and dry them thoroughly. Do one valve assembly to keep the original parts together.

12   Scrape off any deposits that may have formed on the valve, then use a motorized wire brush to remove deposits from the valve heads and stems. Again, make sure the valves do not get mixed up.

Inspection

13   Inspect the head very carefully for cracks and other damage. If cracks are found, a new head will be required. Inspect the cam bearing surfaces for wear and evidence of seizure. Check the camshaft and rocker arms for wear as well (see Section 8).

14   Using a precision straightedge and a feeler gauge, check the head gasket mating surface for warpage **(see illustration)**. Lay the straightedge lengthwise, across the head and diagonally (corner-to-corner), intersecting the head bolt holes, and try to slip a feeler gauge under it, on either side of each combustion chamber. The gauge should be the same thickness as the cylinder head warp limit listed in this Chapter's Specifications. If the feeler gauge can be inserted between the head and the straightedge, the head is warped and must either be machined or, if warpage is excessive, replaced with a new one. Minor surface imperfections can be cleaned up by sanding on a surface plate in a figure-eight pattern with 400 or 600 grit wet or dry sandpaper. Be sure to rotate the head every few strokes to avoid removing material unevenly.

15   Examine the valve seats in each of the combustion chambers. If they are pitted, cracked or burned, the head will require valve service that's beyond the scope of the home mechanic. Measure the valve seat width and compare it to the seat width listed this Chapter's Specifications. If it is not within the specified range, or if it varies around its circumference, valve service work is required.

16   Clean the valve guides to remove any carbon buildup, then measure the inside

diameters of the guides (at both ends and the center of the guide) with a small hole gauge and a 0-to-1-inch micrometer **(see illustration)**. Record the measurements for future reference. These measurements, along with the valve stem diameter measurements, will enable you to compute the valve stem-to-guide clearance. This clearance, when compared to the Specifications, will be one factor that will determine the extent of the valve service work required. The guides are measured at the ends and at the center to determine if they are worn in a bell-mouth pattern (more wear at the ends). If they are, guide replacement is an absolute must.

17   Carefully inspect each valve face for cracks, pits and burned spots. Check the valve stem and the keeper groove area for cracks **(see illustration)**. Rotate the valve and check for any obvious indication that it is bent. Check the end of the stem for pitting and excessive wear and make sure the bevel isn't worn away. The presence of any of the above conditions indicates the need for valve servicing.

18   Measure the valve stem diameter **(see illustration)**. By subtracting the stem diam-

12.17 Check the valve face (A), stem (B) and keeper groove (C) for signs of wear and damage

12.18 Measure the valve stem diameter with a micrometer

12.19a Measure the free length of the valve springs

12.19b Check the valve springs for squareness

eter from the valve guide diameter, the valve stem-to-guide clearance is obtained. If the stem-to-guide clearance is greater than listed in this Chapter's Specifications, the guides and valves will have to be replaced with new ones.

19   Check the end of each valve spring for wear and pitting. Measure the free length **(see illustration)** and compare it to this Chapter's Specifications. Any springs that are shorter than specified have sagged and should not be reused. Stand the spring on a flat surface and check it for squareness **(see illustration)**.

20   Check the spring retainers and keepers for obvious wear and cracks. Any questionable parts should not be reused, as extensive damage will occur in the event of failure during engine operation.

21   If the inspection indicates that no service work is required, the valve components can be reinstalled in the head.

Reassembly

22   Before installing the valves in the head, they should be lapped to ensure a positive seal between the valves and seats. This procedure requires coarse and fine valve lapping compound (available at auto parts stores) and a valve lapping tool. If a lapping tool is not available, a piece of rubber or plastic hose can be slipped over the valve stem (after the valve has been installed in the guide) and used to turn the valve.

23   Apply a small amount of coarse lapping compound to the valve face **(see illustration)**, then slip the valve into the guide. **Note:** *Make sure the valve is installed in the correct guide and be careful not to get any lapping compound on the valve stem.*

24   Attach the lapping tool (or hose) to the valve and rotate the tool between the palms of your hands. Use a back-and-forth motion rather than a circular motion. Lift the valve off the seat and turn it at regular intervals to distribute the lapping compound properly. Continue the lapping procedure until the valve face and seat contact area is of uniform width and unbroken around the entire circumference of the valve face and seat **(see illustration)**.

25   Carefully remove the valve from the guide and wipe off all traces of lapping compound. Use solvent to clean the valve and wipe the seat area thoroughly with a solvent soaked cloth.

26   Repeat the procedure with fine valve lapping compound, then repeat the entire procedure for the remaining valves.

27   Lay the spring seats in place in the cylinder head, then install new valve stem seals on each of the guides **(see illustration 12.7c)**. Use an appropriate size deep socket to push the seals into place until they are properly seated. Don't twist or cock them, or they will not seal properly against the valve stems. Also, don't remove them again or they will be damaged.

28   Coat the valve stems with assembly lube or moly-based grease, then install one of them into its guide. Next, install the springs and retainers, compress the springs and install the keepers. **Note:** *Install the springs with the tightly wound coils at the bottom (next to the spring seat).* When compressing the springs with the valve spring compressor, depress them only as far as is absolutely necessary to slip the keepers into

12.23 Apply the lapping compound very sparingly, in small dabs, to the valve face only

12.24 After lapping, the valve face should have a uniform, unbroken contact pattern (arrow)

12.28a A small dab of grease will hold the keepers in place on the valve while the spring is released

12.28b The small ridge near the top of each keeper locks the keeper into the groove in the valve stem (valve springs removed for clarity)

13.5 Remove the cam chain guide from the cam chain tunnel and inspect it for wear and damage

place. Apply a small amount of grease to the keepers (see illustration) to help hold them in place as the pressure is released from the springs. Make certain that the keeper ridges are securely locked in the retaining groove in the valve stem (see illustration).

29 Support the cylinder head on blocks so the valves can't contact the workbench top, then very gently tap each of the valve stems with a soft-faced hammer. This will help seat the keepers in their grooves.

30 Once all of the valves have been installed in the head, check for proper valve sealing by pouring a small amount of solvent into each of the valve ports. If the solvent leaks past the valve(s) into the combustion chamber area, disassemble the valve(s) and repeat the lapping procedure, then reinstall the valve(s) and repeat the check. Repeat the procedure until a satisfactory seal is obtained.

13 Cam chain guide - removal, inspection and installation

Note: The following procedure applies to the front and rear cam chain guides.

1　Remove the cylinder head cover (see Section 7).
2　Remove the camshaft, sprocket and rocker arms (see Section 8).
3　Remove the cam chain tensioner (see Section 9).
4　Remove the cylinder head (see Section 10).
5　Remove the cam chain guide (see illustration).
6　Inspect the cam chain guide for wear and damage. Replace the guide if it's worn or damaged.
7　Install the guide in the cam chain tunnel. Make sure that the guide mounting tabs

are correctly seated in the grooves in the cylinder (see illustration) and the lower end of the guide is correctly seated against the lower guide stop in the crankcase (see illustration).
8　Install the cylinder head (see Section 10).
9　Install the cam chain tensioner (see Section 9).
10　Install the camshaft, sprocket and rocker arms (see Section 8).
11　Install the cylinder head cover (see Section 7).

14 Cylinder - removal, inspection and installation

Note: The following procedure applies to the front and rear cylinders. However, the engine must be removed from the frame before the rear cylinder can be removed.

13.7a Make sure that the cam chain guide tabs are correctly seated in the cylinder . . .

13.7b . . . and that the lower end of the guide is correctly seated against its stop on the crankcase (front cam chain guide shown; rear similar)

14.5a These two retaining clips (arrows) lock the coolant pipe collar (lower arrow) in position

14.5b To unlock the collar, remove the two retaining clips . . .

Removal

1   Remove the cylinder head cover (see Section 7).

2   Remove the camshaft, sprocket and rocker arms (see Section 8).

3   Remove the cam chain tensioner (see Section 9).

4   Remove the cylinder head (see Section 10) and the cam chain guide (see Section 13).

5   Coolant passes from the front cylinder to the rear cylinder through a pair of pipes, one on each cylinder, which are connected by a sliding collar locked into position by a pair of retaining clips (see illustration). Remove the retaining clips (see illustration) and slide the collar away from the cylinder you're removing, far enough to expose the O-ring and the end of the coolant pipe (see illustration).

6   If you're removing the front cylinder, detach the coolant hose adapter (see illustration).

7   Lift the cylinder straight up to remove it (see illustration). If it's stuck, tap around

14.5c . . . and slide the collar away from the cylinder you're removing, until the coolant pipe and O-ring are exposed

its perimeter with a soft-faced hammer, taking care not to break the cooling fins. Don't attempt to pry between the cylinder and the

14.6 If you're removing the front cylinder, remove these two bolts (arrows) and detach the coolant hose adapter from the cylinder

crankcase, as you will ruin the sealing surfaces. Remove the old base gasket and dis-

14.7a Lift the cylinder straight up off the studs

14.7b Note the locations of the dowel pins (arrows), then remove them

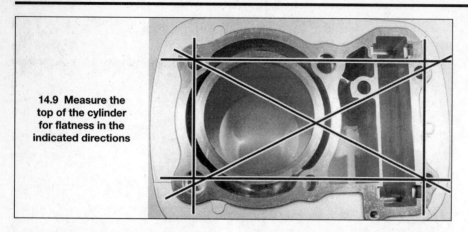

14.9 Measure the top of the cylinder for flatness in the indicated directions

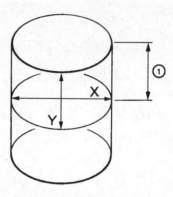

14.10 Measure the cylinder bore at the specified distance from the top of the cylinder (1); measure parallel to the crankshaft centerline, then at right angles to it

card it. Note the location of the dowel pins **(see illustration)**, then remove them. Be careful not to let the dowels drop into the engine.

8   Stuff clean shop towels into the cavity beneath the piston and carefully remove all traces of old gasket material from the mating surfaces of the cylinder and crankcase. Don't allow any gasket material to fall into the crankcase.

Inspection

Note: *If the following inspection indicates that a cylinder is warped, it can be resurfaced or replaced independently of the other cylinder. However, if a rebore is indicated for either cylinder, that cylinder will require an oversize piston, so BOTH cylinders must be rebored to accept the same size pistons, in order to maintain correct balance.*

9   Measure the top of the cylinder for flatness **(see illustration)** and compare your measurements to the allowable warpage listed in this Chapter's Specifications.

10   Inspect the cylinder wall thoroughly for scratches and score marks. Using a cylinder bore gauge or a telescoping snap-gauge and micrometer, measure the cylinder diameter. Make three pairs of measurements (six in all), parallel and perpendicular to the crankshaft axis, at the top, middle and bottom of the cylinder **(see illustration)**. First, deter-

mine cylinder bore diameter. Take the largest measurement and compare it to the cylinder bore diameter listed in this Chapter's Specifications. Next, determine whether the cylinder is round. Compare the readings in one direction to the readings in the other direction, subtract the smaller readings from the larger readings and compare any differences to the allowable out-of-round listed in this Chapter's Specifications. Finally, determine whether the cylinder is tapered. Compare the largest reading to the smallest reading in each direction, subtract the two and compare the difference to the allowable taper listed in this Chapter's Specifications. **Note:** *If you do not have access to a cylinder bore gauge or a three-inch telescoping snap-gauge and three-inch micrometer, have a dealer service department or motorcycle repair shop measure the cylinder(s).*

11   If the cylinder walls are worn, out-of-round or tapered beyond their specified limits, or badly scuffed or scored, have the cylinder rebored and honed by a dealer service department or a motorcycle repair shop. Remember, even if only one cylinder *must* be rebored, the other cylinder will also have to be rebored to the same diameter, so that both cylinders have the same oversize pistons, to maintain balance.

12   If the cylinder is in reasonably good condition and not worn beyond the limits, and if the piston-to-cylinder bore clearance (see Section 15) is still within the allowable range, then the cylinder does not have to be rebored; honing is all that is necessary.

13   To hone the cylinder, you will need the proper size flexible hone with fine stones, or a "bottle brush" type hone, plenty of light oil or honing oil, some shop towels and an electric drill motor. Hold the cylinder block in a vise (cushioned with soft jaws or wood blocks) when performing the honing operation. Mount the hone in the drill motor, compress the stones and slip the hone into the cylinder. Lubricate the cylinder thoroughly, turn on the drill and move the hone up and down in the cylinder at a pace which will produce a fine crosshatch pattern on the cylinder wall with the crosshatch lines intersecting at approximately a 60-degree angle **(see illustration)**. Be sure to use plenty of lubricant and do not take off any more material than is absolutely

necessary to produce the desired effect. Do not withdraw the hone from the cylinder while it is running. Instead, shut off the drill and continue moving the hone up and down in the cylinder until it comes to a complete stop, then compress the stones and withdraw the hone. Wipe the oil out of the cylinder and repeat the procedure on the remaining cylinder. Remember, do not remove too much material from the cylinder wall. If you do not have the tools, or do not desire to perform the honing operation, a dealer service department or motorcycle repair shop will generally do it for a reasonable fee.

14   Wash the cylinders thoroughly with warm soapy water to remove all traces of the abrasive grit produced during the honing operation. Be sure to run a brush through the bolt holes and flush them with running water. After rinsing, dry the cylinders thoroughly and apply a coat of light, rust-preventative oil to all machined surfaces.

Installation

15   Lubricate the cylinder bore and piston with plenty of clean engine oil. If both cylinders were removed, look for the F or R mark that indicates front or rear cylinder **(see illustration 7.16b)**.

16   Place a new cylinder base gasket on the crankcase. Make sure the two dowel pins are in position **(see illustration 14.7b)**.

17   Attach a piston ring compressor to the piston and compress the piston rings. Or use a large hose clamp; make sure it doesn't scratch the piston and don't tighten it too much.

18   Install the cylinder over the piston and carefully lower it down until the piston crown fits into the cylinder liner. While doing this, pull the camshaft chain up, using a hooked tool or a piece of coat hanger. Also keep an eye on the cam chain guide to make sure it doesn't wedge against the cylinder. Push down on the cylinder, making sure the piston doesn't get cocked sideways, until the

14.13 Move the hone rapidly up-and-down without stopping

15.3a The IN mark on the piston must be on the intake side of the cylinder

15.3b Wear eye protection when pulling out the circlips; they can pop out of the piston with sufficient force to cause an injury if they hit your eye

15.4a Push the piston pin partway out, then pull it out the rest of the way

bottom of the cylinder liner slides down past the piston rings. A wood or plastic hammer handle can be used to gently tap the cylinder down, but don't use too much force or the piston will be damaged.

19   Remove the piston ring compressor or hose clamp, being careful not to scratch the piston.

20   Install a new O-ring on the coolant pipe, lubricate the O-ring with coolant to allow the collar to slide over it without damaging it. Position the collar in the middle (covering the O-rings of both coolant pipes) and install the retaining clips.

21   If you're installing the front cylinder, install a new O-ring in the groove inside the coolant hose adapter, install the adapter and tighten the adapter bolts securely. If the coolant hose was detached from the adapter, reattach the hose and tighten the hose clamp securely.

22   Install the cam chain guide (see Section 13).

23   Install the cylinder head (see Section 10).

24   Install the cam chain tensioner (see Section 9).

25   Install the camshaft, sprocket and rocker arms (see Section 8).

26   Install the cylinder head cover (see Section 7).

15 Piston - removal, inspection and installation

Note: *The following procedure applies to the front and rear pistons.*

1   The pistons are attached to the connecting rods with piston pins that are a slip fit in the pistons and rods.

2   Before removing the pistons from the rods, stuff a clean shop towel into each crankcase hole, around the connecting rods. This will prevent the circlips from falling into the crankcase if they are inadvertently dropped.

Removal

3   Using a sharp scribe, scratch the location of each piston (front or rear cylinder) into its crown (or use a felt pen if the piston is clean enough). Each piston should also have an IN mark on its crown; this mark faces the intake side of the cylinder when the piston is installed **(see illustration)**. If not, scribe an arrow into the piston crown before removal. Support the first piston, grasp the circlip with a pointed tool or needle-nose pliers **(see illustration)** and remove it from the groove.

4   Push the piston pin out from the opposite end to free the piston from the rod, then pull it out **(see illustration)**; if it's too slippery, jam a pair of snap-ring or needle-nose pliers into the pin and pull it out **(see illustration)**. You may have to deburr the area around the groove for the circlip to allow the pin to slide out (use a triangular file for this procedure). If the pin won't come out, remove the other circlip. Fabricate a piston pin removal tool from threaded stock, nuts, washers and a piece of pipe **(see illustration)**.

15.4b If the piston pin is slippery or difficult to pull out, insert a pair of needle nose pliers into the pin and work it out of the piston with a back-and-forth twisting motion

15.4c The piston pins should come out with hand pressure - if they don't, this removal tool can be fabricated from readily available parts

1)	Bolt	5)	Piston
2)	Washer	6)	Washer (B)
3)	Pipe (A)	7)	Nut (B)
4)	Padding (A)		

A   Large enough for piston pin to fit inside

B   Small enough to fit through piston pin bore

15.5a There's an oil jet (arrow) for each cylinder inside the crankcase

15.5b To remove an oil jet, pull it straight up; remove and discard the old O-ring and blow out the oil passage in the jet; install the jet with a new O-ring

15.6 Remove the piston rings with a ring removal and installation tool

15.11 Check the piston pin bore and the piston skirt for wear, and make sure the internal holes are clear (arrows)

5   Remove the oil jet **(see illustration)**. Pull it straight up **(see illustration)** and discard the old O-ring.

Inspection

6   Using a piston ring installation tool, carefully remove the rings from the pistons **(see illustration)**. Do not nick or gouge the

15.13 Measure ring side clearance with a feeler gauge

pistons in the process.

7   Clean the piston thoroughly. Scrape all traces of carbon from the top of the piston. A hand-held wire brush or a piece of fine emery cloth can be used once most of the deposits have been scraped away. Do not, under any circumstances, use a wire brush mounted in a drill motor to remove deposits from the piston; the piston material is soft and will be eroded away by the wire brush.

8   Use a piston ring groove cleaning tool to remove any carbon deposits from the ring grooves. If a tool is not available, a piece broken off the old ring will do the job. Be very careful to remove only the carbon deposits. Do not remove any metal and do not nick or gouge the sides of the ring grooves.

9   Once the deposits have been removed, clean the pistons with solvent and dry them thoroughly. Make sure the oil return holes below the oil ring grooves are clear.

10   If the pistons are not damaged or worn excessively and if the cylinders are not rebored, new pistons will not be necessary. Normal piston wear appears as even, vertical wear on the thrust surfaces of the piston and slight looseness of the top ring in its groove. New piston rings, on the other hand, should

always be used when an engine is rebuilt.

11   Carefully inspect each piston for cracks around the skirt, at the pin bosses and at the ring lands **(see illustration)**.

12   Look for scoring and scuffing on the thrust faces of the skirt, holes in the piston crown and burned areas at the edge of the crown. If the skirt is scored or scuffed, the engine may have been suffering from overheating and/or abnormal combustion, which caused excessively high operating temperatures. The oil pump should be checked thoroughly. A hole in the piston crown, an extreme to be sure, is an indication that abnormal combustion (pre-ignition) was occurring. Burned areas at the edge of the piston crown are usually evidence of spark knock (detonation). If any of the above problems exist, the causes must be corrected or the damage will occur again.

13   Measure the piston ring-to-groove clearance by laying a new piston ring in the ring groove and slipping a feeler gauge in beside it **(see illustration)**. Check the clearance at three or four locations around the groove. Be

15.14 Measure the piston diameter with a micrometer

A *Specified distance from bottom of piston*
B *Piston diameter*

15.15 Slip the pin into the piston and try to wiggle it back-and-forth; if it's loose, replace the piston and pin

sure to use the correct ring for each groove; they are different. If the clearance is greater than specified, new pistons will have to be used when the engine is reassembled.

14   Check the piston-to-bore clearance by measuring the cylinder bore (see Section 14) and the piston diameter. Make sure that the pistons and cylinders are correctly matched. Measure the piston across the skirt on the thrust faces at a 90-degree angle to the piston pin, at the distance from the bottom of the skirt listed in this Chapter's Specifications **(see illustration)**. Subtract the piston diameter from the bore diameter to obtain the clearance. If it is greater than specified, the cylinders will have to be rebored and new oversized pistons and rings installed. If the appropriate precision measuring tools are not available, the piston-to-cylinder clearances can be obtained, though not quite as accurately, using feeler gauge stock. Feeler gauge stock comes in 12-inch lengths and various thicknesses and is generally available at auto parts stores. To check the clearance, select a feeler gauge of the same thickness as the piston clearance listed in this Chapter's Specifications and slip it into the cylinder along with the appropriate piston. The cylinder should be upside down and the piston must be positioned exactly as it normally would be. Place the feeler gauge between the piston and cylinder on one of the thrust

faces (90-degrees to the piston pin bore). The piston should slip through the cylinder (with the feeler gauge in place) with moderate pressure. If it falls through, or slides through easily, the clearance is excessive and a new piston will be required. If the piston binds at the lower end of the cylinder and is loose toward the top, the cylinder is tapered, and if tight spots are encountered as the feeler gauge is placed at different points around the cylinder, the cylinder is out-of-round. Repeat the procedure for the remaining pistons and cylinders. Be sure to have the cylinders and pistons checked by a dealer service department or a motorcycle repair shop to confirm your findings before purchasing new parts.

15   Apply clean engine oil to the pin, insert it into the piston and check for freeplay by rocking the pin back-and-forth **(see illustration)**. If the pin is loose, new pistons and pins must be installed. For a more precise assessment of piston/piston pin wear, measure the diameter of the piston pin and compare your measurement to the piston pin diameter listed in this Chapter's Specifications. Replace the pin if it's excessively worn. Next, measure the inside diameter of the piston pin holes in the piston, subtract the diameter of the piston pin and compare your measurement to the piston pin-to-piston clearance listed in this Chapter's Specifications. If the clearance exceeds the specified maximum, replace

the piston and/or the piston pin (depending on whether the pin diameter is acceptable). Finally, measure the inside diameter of the small end of the connecting rod, subtract the diameter of the piston pin and compare your measurement to the piston pin-to-connecting rod clearance listed in this Chapter's Specifications. If the clearance exceeds the specified maximum, replace the piston pin and/or the connecting rod (depending on whether the pin diameter is acceptable).

16   Install the rings on the piston (see Section 16).

Installation

17   Install a new O-ring on the oil jet and install the oil jet by pushing it firmly back into the crankcase until it's fully seated.

18   Install the piston with the IN mark pointing toward the intake side of the cylinder **(see illustration 15.3a)**. Lubricate the pins and the rod bores with clean engine oil. Install new circlips in the grooves on the inner sides of the pistons (don't reuse the old circlips). Push the pins into position from the opposite side and install new circlips. Compress the circlips only enough for them to fit in the piston. Make sure the circlips are correctly seated in the grooves **(see illustrations)**.

15.18a Slip the circlip into its bore with its gap away from the piston cutout . . .

15.18b . . . and push the circlip all the way into its groove; make sure it's securely seated

16.3 Measure ring end gap with a feeler gauge

16.5 If the end gap is too small, clamp a file in a vise and file the ring ends (from the outside in only) to enlarge the gap slightly

16.9a Install the oil ring expander first

16.9b Installing an oil ring side rail - don't use a ring installation tool to do this

16.11a Install the middle ring with its identification mark up

16 Piston rings - installation

1   Before installing the new piston rings, the ring end gaps must be checked.
2   Lay out the pistons and the new ring sets so the rings will be matched with the same piston and cylinder during the end gap measurement procedure and engine assembly.
3   Insert the top (No. 1) ring into the bottom of the first cylinder and square it up with the cylinder walls by pushing it in with the top of the piston (see illustration). The ring should be about one inch above the bottom edge of the cylinder. To measure the end gap, slip a feeler gauge between the ends of the ring and compare the measurement to this Chapter's Specifications.
4   If the gap is larger or smaller than specified, double check to make sure that you have the correct rings before proceeding.
5   If the gap is too small, it must be enlarged or the ring ends may come in contact with each other during engine operation, which can cause serious damage. The end gap can be increased by filing the ring ends

very carefully with a fine file (see illustration). When performing this operation, file only from the outside in.
6   Excess end gap is not critical unless it is greater than 0.040 in. (1 mm). Again, double check to make sure you have the correct rings for your engine.
7   Repeat the procedure for each ring that will be installed in the first cylinder and for each ring in the remaining cylinder. Remember to keep the rings, pistons and cylinders matched up.
8   Once the ring end gaps have been checked/corrected, the rings can be installed on the pistons.
9   The oil control ring (lowest on the piston) is installed first. It is composed of three separate components. Slip the expander into the groove, then install the upper side rail (see illustrations). Do not use a piston ring installation tool on the oil ring side rails as they may be damaged. Instead, place one end of the side rail into the groove between the spacer expander and the ring land. Hold it firmly in place and slide a finger around the piston while pushing the rail into the groove. Next, install the lower side rail in the same manner.
10   After the three oil ring components have

been installed, check to make sure that both the upper and lower side rails can be turned smoothly in the ring groove.
11   Install the second (middle) ring next (see illustration). Do not mix the top and middle rings. They can be identified by their profiles (see illustration), as well as the fact that the top ring is thinner than the middle ring.

TOP RING

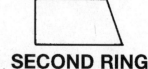

SECOND RING

16.11b The top and middle rings can be identified by their profiles

16.12 The top and middle rings have identification marks (arrows); these must be up when the rings are installed

16.15 Arrange the ring gaps like this

1) Top compression ring
2) Oil ring lower rail
3) Oil ring upper rail
4) Second compression ring

12   To avoid breaking the ring, use a piston ring installation tool and make sure that the identification mark is facing up **(see illustration)**. Fit the ring into the middle groove on the piston. Do not expand the ring any more than is necessary to slide it into place.
13   Finally, install the top ring in the same manner. Make sure the identifying mark is facing up.
14   Repeat the procedure for the remaining piston and rings. Be very careful not to confuse the top and second rings.
15   Once the rings have been properly installed, stagger the end gaps, including those of the oil ring side rails **(see illustration)**.

---

17 Clutch cable - replacement

1   Push the clutch lifter arm forward and disengage the clutch cable from the lifter arm clevis **(see illustration)**. **Note:** *If necessary,*

pry open the lifter arm gap slightly with a screwdriver so the cable can pass through it.
2   Loosen the locknut and adjustment nut **(see illustration)** and disengage the cable from the bracket on the engine.
3   Up at the handlebars, pull back the cable rubber dust boot, back off the locknut and adjuster **(see illustration)** and disengage

the cable from the clutch lever.
4   Note the routing of the cable and remove it.
5   Installation is the reverse of removal. Make sure the cable is routed correctly, with no kinks.
6   Adjust the clutch cable freeplay (see Chapter 1).

17.1 Push the clutch lifter arm forward and disengage the clutch cable; widen the gap if necessary with a screwdriver

17.2 Loosen the cable locknut and adjuster nut (arrows) and disengage the clutch cable from the bracket

17.3 Peel back the dust boot, back off the locknut (middle arrow), turn the adjuster (left arrow) all the way in (toward the lever), align the slots in the adjuster and locknut with the cable, pull out the cable and disengage the cable plug from the slot in the lever

18.4a To separate the right crankcase cover from the engine, loosen the bolts (arrows), 1/4-turn at a time, in a criss-cross pattern; one upper bolt secures the bracket for the clutch cable

18.4b If the clutch cover sticks to the crankcase, carefully tap it loose at the bosses provided for that purpose; don't pry on the crankcase cover or you will damage the gasket mating surface

18 Clutch - removal, inspection and installation

Removal

1   Drain the engine oil (see Chapter 1).
2   Disengage the clutch cable from the clutch lifter arm (see Section 17).
3   On 1988 and 1989 VT600 models, remove the oil pipe bracket and remove the oil pipe banjo bolt and sealing washers from the right crankcase cover.
4   Loosen the right crankcase cover bolts **(see illustration)**. Once they're all loose, remove the bolts and take off the cover. If the cover is stuck, gently tap on one or more of the cover bosses provided for this purpose **(see illustration)**. Don't pry on the cover; prying will damage the gasket surface. Remove the dowel pins **(see illustration)** and store them in a plastic bag. Remove the old gasket and discard it. Carefully remove any gasket

18.4c Right crankcase dowel pin location

material that's stuck to the crankcase or the cover.
5   Remove the clutch lifter piece from the lifter arm **(see illustration)**. Remove the snap-ring and return spring from the lifter arm **(see illustration)**.

6   Pull the lifter arm out of the right crankcase cover and set aside the parts for the lifter arm assembly for later inspection. Store the lifter piece, snap-ring and return spring in a plastic bag so you don't misplace them.
7   If you're planning to remove the oil

18.5a Remove the clutch lifter piece from the lifter arm

18.5b Remove the snap-ring and return spring (arrow) from the lifter arm

18.7 Place a penny between the gear teeth of the clutch housing and the primary drive gear, then loosen the primary drive gear bolt and the oil pump driven sprocket bolt (arrow)

18.8 Remove the lifter plate bolts (arrows), gradually and evenly, in a criss-cross pattern

18.9a Remove the lifter plate and bearing . . .

18.9b . . . and remove the four clutch springs (arrows)

pump drive chain and sprockets (see Section 19) and/or the primary drive gear (see Section 20), put a penny between the clutch housing gear teeth and the primary drive gear teeth and loosen the primary drive gear bolt and/or the oil pump driven

sprocket bolt **(see illustration)**.
8   Remove the clutch lifter plate bolts **(see illustration)**, gradually and evenly, in a criss-cross pattern.
9   Remove the clutch lifter plate/bearing and the clutch springs **(see illustrations)**.

10   Unstake the clutch center locknut **(see illustration)**.
11   Using the factory clutch center holder tool or equivalent **(see illustration)**, loosen the clutch center locknut.

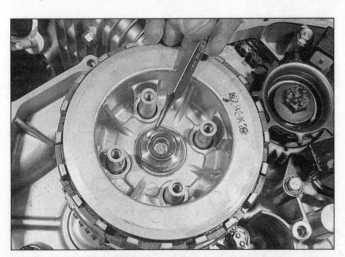

18.10 Unstake the clutch center locknut

18.11 To loosen the clutch center locknut, immobilize the center with the special Honda tool or a strap wrench

18.12a Remove the clutch center locknut and lockwasher (arrow); the OUT SIDE mark faces outward on installation. . .

18.12b . . . and remove the backup washer (if equipped)

18.13 Remove the pressure plate

12 Remove the clutch center locknut and the spring washer (**see illustrations**). Discard the old locknut and washer.

13 Remove the clutch center (**see illustration**).

14 Before disassembling the clutch pack, take a moment to study how it's assembled (**see illustration**). First, note that the tabs of the outer friction disc are not aligned with the tabs of the other friction discs, but are instead seated in their own cutouts in the clutch housing. Also note that the spring seat and judder spring fit within this outer friction disc, which has a slightly larger diameter than the other friction discs. (This outer friction disc is identified as friction disc "B" in the Specifications.) Remove the outer friction disc, the spring seat and the judder spring. Note that the concave face of the judder spring faces out, toward the spring seat and the clutch center. After removing the outer friction disc, the spring seat and the judder spring, you'll see the first steel plate (**see illustration**). After removing this steel plate,

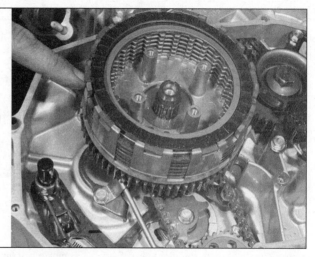

18.14a Remove the outer friction disc, judder spring and spring seat (the two narrow metal rings installed concentric with the outer friction disc) . . .

you'll see the first friction disc (**see illustration**). Remove all the steel plates and all the friction discs. On VT600 models, there are six steel plates and six friction discs (not count-

ing the outer friction disc described above); on VT750 models, there are eight steel plates and seven friction discs (not counting the outer friction disc).

18.14b . . . remove the first metal plate . . .

18.14c . . . then alternately, the remaining friction discs and metal plates

18.15a Remove the washer . . .

18.15b . . . and the clutch housing

18.17 Remove the clutch housing guide

18.19 The clutch lifter piece fits in this notch in the lifter arm

15   Remove the clutch housing washer and the clutch housing **(see illustrations)**.
16   Remove and inspect the oil pump drive chain and sprockets (see Section 19).
17   Remove the clutch housing guide **(see illustration)** from the mainshaft.
18   Remove and inspect the primary drive gear (see Section 20).

Inspection

19   Inspect the lifter arm and the clutch lifter piece **(see illustration)** for damage and wear. Make sure the lifter arm isn't bent. The clutch lifter piece should slide in and out of its bore in the right crankcase cover without binding. Inspect the return spring and snap-ring for fatigue and other damage. If any part of the lifter arm assembly is damaged, replace it.
20   Inspect the lifter arm seal **(see illustration)** in the right crankcase cover. If it's cracked, torn or worn, remove it and install a new seal.
21   Inspect the lifter plate bearing for wear and damage. Turn the bearing inner race with your finger; it should turn smoothly and qui-

18.20 Inspect the lifter arm seal for cracks, tears and excessive wear; if it's worn or damaged, pry it out with a screwdriver and drive a new seal into place with a socket

etly. Make sure that the bearing outer race fits tightly into the lifter plate. If the bearing is damaged or worn, replace the lifter plate and

18.22 Measure the clutch spring free length

bearing. (The bearing can be replaced separately but it's a good idea to replace the lifter plate and bearing as a set to maintain a tight fit between the two.)
22   Measure the free length of the clutch springs **(see illustration)**. Replace the

18.23 Inspect the splines on the clutch center; if any wear is evident, replace the center

18.24 Inspect the spring seat (left) and the judder spring (right) for distortion and wear; if either of them is damaged or worn, replace it

springs as a set if any one of them is not within the values listed in this Chapter's Specifications.

23 Examine the inner and outer splines on

18.25a Measure the thickness of the friction discs

the clutch center **(see illustration)**. If any wear is evident, replace the clutch center.

24 Inspect the judder spring and spring seat **(see illustration)** for distortion, wear and damage. Replace them if necessary.

25 If the lining material of the friction discs is burned or glazed, replace the friction discs. If the metal clutch plates are scored or discolored, replace them. Measure the thickness of each friction disc **(see illustrations)** and compare your measurements to this Chapter's Specifications. If any are near the wear limit, replace the friction discs as a set.

26 Lay the metal plates, one at a time, on a perfectly flat surface (such as a piece of plate glass) and check for warpage by trying to slip a gauge between the flat surface and the plate **(see illustration)**. The feeler gauge should be the same thickness as the warpage limit listed in this Chapter's Specifications. Do this at several places around the plate's circumference. If the feeler gauge can be slipped under the plate, it is warped and should be replaced with a new one.

27 Check the tabs on the friction discs for excessive wear and mushroomed edges. They can be cleaned up with a file if the deformation is not severe.

28 Check the edges of the slots in the clutch housing **(see illustration)** for indentations made by the friction plate tabs. If the indentations are deep they can prevent clutch release, so the housing should be replaced with a new one. If the indentations can be removed easily with a file, the life of the housing can be prolonged to an extent.

29 Check the primary driven gear teeth on the clutch housing **(see illustration 18.28)** for wear or damage. If the teeth are worn or damaged, replace the clutch housing. If the primary driven gear teeth are damaged, the primary drive gear teeth may also be damaged. Inspect the primary drive gear and, if necessary, replace it (see Section 20).

30 On VT600 models, inspect the bushing in the clutch housing hub. On VT750 models, inspect the needle bearing in the clutch housing hub. If the bushing or bearing is worn or

18.25b The friction disc around the judder spring (B) is narrower than the other friction discs (A)

18.26 Check the metal plates for warpage

18.28 Check for wear in the slots, driven gear teeth and center bushing or needle bearing

18.35 Be sure the teeth or pins on the oil pump drive sprocket align with the notches or holes in the clutch housing

damaged, have it replaced by a dealer or by a motorcycle machine shop.

31   Measure the inside and outside diameters of the clutch outer guide and compare your measurements to the dimensions listed in this Chapter's Specifications. If the guide inside or outside diameter is worn beyond the specified limit, replace the guide.

Installation

32   Lubricate the clutch outer guide with molybdenum disulfide grease and install the guide on the mainshaft.

33   Install the oil pump drive sprocket, chain and driven sprocket (see Section 19).

34   Install the primary drive gear (see Section 20).

35   Coat the clutch housing bearing surface with clean engine oil, slip the clutch housing onto the outer guide, align the clutch housing hub with the oil pump drive sprocket **(see illustration)** and push the clutch housing onto the outer guide.

36   Coat the thrust washer with clean engine oil and install it on the mainshaft.

37   Lay the clutch center face down, with the splines facing up, and install the spring seat, then the judder spring, in that order, on the clutch center; make sure that the concave face of the judder spring faces away from the spring seat, i.e. toward the other discs and plates, then install the outer friction disc.

38   Coat the friction discs and the steel plates with engine oil and install them on the clutch center, alternating between steel plates and friction discs. Start with a steel plate next to the outer friction disc, then install a friction disc, then a steel plate, then another friction disc, etc., and, finally, install the pressure plate. On VT600 models, there are six friction discs and six steel plates; on VT750 models, there are seven friction discs and eight steel plates (which means you will begin with a steel plate and end with one too).

39   Install the clutch pack assembly on the mainshaft. The tabs on all the clutch friction discs (except the outer friction disc) should

fit into the slots in the clutch housing (the tabs on the outer friction disc fit into their own cutouts between the slots).

40   Install the new spring washer with the OUTSIDE facing out.

41   Install the new clutch center locknut, install the clutch center holder and tighten the locknut to the torque listed in this Chapter's Specifications. Remove the holder and stake the locknut. Be careful not to damage the threads on the mainshaft.

42   Install the clutch springs, the lifter plate and the lifter plate bolts. Tighten the lifter plate bolts to the torque listed in this Chapter's Specifications.

43   If the oil pump driven sprocket or primary drive gear was removed, put a penny between the primary drive gear teeth and the primary driven gear teeth **(see illustration 18.7)** and tighten the sprocket retaining bolt and/or primary drive gear bolt to the torque listed in this Chapter's Specifications.

44   Clean all traces of old gasket material from the right crankcase cover and its mating surface on the crankcase. Install a new gasket on the crankcase and install the dowel pins **(see illustration 18.4c)**.

45   Install the right crankcase cover and install the 14 bolts finger tight. Don't forget to

reattach the clutch cable bracket.

46   Tighten the bolts in stages, using a criss-cross pattern, to the torque listed in this Chapter's Specifications.

47   On 1988 and 1989 VT600 models, install the oil pipe banjo bolt with new sealing washers and tighten the banjo bolt to the torque listed in this Chapter's Specifications. Install the oil pipe bracket.

48   Reattach the clutch cable to the clutch lifter arm (see Section 17) and adjust the clutch cable (see Chapter 1).

49   Fill the crankcase with the recommended type and amount of engine oil (see Chapter 1).

19 Oil pump drive chain and sprockets - removal, inspection and installation

Removal

1   Remove the clutch (see Section 18). When you get to Step 7 in Section 18, loosen the oil pump driven sprocket bolt **(see illustration 18.7)**.

2   Remove the oil pump driven sprocket bolt **(see illustration)**.

19.2 Remove the oil pump driven sprocket retaining bolt

19.3 Remove the oil pump drive sprocket, chain and driven sprocket as a set

20.3 Remove the primary drive gear retaining bolt and washer

3   Remove the oil pump drive sprocket, chain and driven sprocket **(see illustration)**.

Inspection

4   Inspect the drive chain rollers and side plates and the sprocket teeth for damage and wear. If the chain or either sprocket is damaged or worn, replace it. (It's a good idea to replace the sprockets and chain as a set.)
5   Measure the inside diameter of the drive sprocket and compare your measurement to the drive sprocket inside diameter listed in this Chapter's Specifications. If the inside diameter of the sprocket exceeds the limit, replace the drive sprocket. (Again, it's a good idea to replace the sprockets and chain as a set.)

Installation

6   Lubricate the clutch outer guide with clean engine oil, install the driven sprocket first, with the IN facing toward the engine, then slide the driven sprocket onto the guide. Install the driven sprocket retaining bolt and tighten it until the sprocket starts to turn.
7   Install the clutch (see Section 18).

When you get to Step 43, tighten the driven sprocket retaining bolt to the torque listed in this Chapter's Specifications. Finish the clutch installation procedure.

20 Primary drive gear - removal, inspection and installation

1   Remove the clutch (see Section 18). When you get to Step 7 in Section 18, loosen the primary drive gear bolt **(see illustration 18.7)**.
2   Remove the ignition pulse generator(s) (see Chapter 5).
3   Remove the primary drive gear bolt and washer **(see illustration)**.
4   Remove the ignition pulse generator rotor **(see illustration)**.
5   Remove the primary drive gear **(see illustration)**.
6   On VT600 models and 2004 and later VT750 models, inspect the teeth of the primary drive gear for wear and damage. If the

teeth are worn or damaged, replace the primary drive gear.
7   On 2003 and earlier VT750 models, disassemble the primary drive gear and the sub gear. Note the relationship of the parts to one another as you take the assembly apart. Inspect the teeth on both the primary drive gear and the sub-gear. Inspect the three primary drive gear springs and the friction spring (washer) for wear and damage. If anything is damaged or worn, replace the primary drive gear. Reassemble the primary drive gear and sub-gear. Make sure the three holes on the sub-gear and the primary drive gear are aligned.
8   On VT600 and 2004 and later VT750 models, install the primary drive gear with the OUT facing out; the gear will only go on one way because of the extra wide spline **(see illustration 20.5)**.
9   On 2003 and earlier VT750 models, install the primary drive gear with the sub-gear side facing out. The gear will only go on one way because of an extra wide spline.
10   Install the ignition pulse generator rotor. Again, the rotor will only go on one way because of the extra wide spline.
11   Install the primary drive gear bolt and washer. Install the clutch (see Section 18). When you get to Step 43, tighten the primary drive gear bolt to the torque listed in this Chapter's Specifications. Finish the clutch installation procedure.

21 Cam chains and rear cam chain drive sprocket - removal, inspection and installation

Note: *This procedure applies to the front and rear cam chains and to the rear cam chain drive sprocket on VT600 models (the front cylinder cam chain drive sprocket on VT600 models and both cam chain sprockets on VT750 models are part of the crankshaft.)*

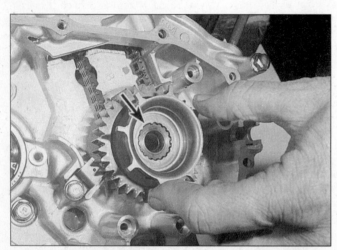

20.4 Remove the ignition pulse generator rotor; the extra wide spline (arrow) allows the rotor to be installed only one way

20.5 Remove the primary drive gear; note the OUT, which must face out when the primary drive gear is installed; and again, note the extra wide spline (arrow) which means the primary drive gear can only be installed one way

21.8 Loosen the cam chain tensioner set plate bolt (arrow) and swing the plate out of the way (set plate at left end of crank shown; right set plate similar)

21.9 Remove the cam chain from the drive sprocket and pull the chain up through the cam chain tunnel (front cylinder cam chain shown; rear cylinder cam chain similar)

Removal

1   Remove the cylinder head cover (see Section 7).

2   Remove the camshaft, sprocket and rocker arms (see Section 8).

3   Remove the cam chain tensioner (see Section 9).

4   Remove the cylinder head (see Section 10). If you're removing the rear cylinder head, remove the engine first (see Section 5).

5   Remove the chain guide (see Section 13).

6   If you're removing the front cylinder cam chain, remove the left crankcase cover and remove the alternator rotor (see Chapter 9).

7   If you're removing the rear cylinder cam chain, remove the right crankcase cover and the clutch (see Section 18) and remove the primary drive gear (see Section 20).

8   Remove the cam chain tensioner set plate **(see illustration)**.

9   Remove the cam chain from the drive sprocket **(see illustration)** and pull it up through the cam chain tunnel.

10   If you're removing the rear cam chain on a VT600 model, the drive sprocket should be removed from the crankshaft **(see illustration)** and inspected. (The front cam chain drive sprocket on VT600 models and both sprockets on VT750 models are not removable; they're part of the crank.)

Inspection

11   Clean the cam chain in solvent and dry it with compressed air. Inspect the rollers and side plates for wear. Replace the chain if it's worn or damaged.

12   If the cam chain is worn, inspect the drive sprocket on the crankshaft and the driven sprocket on the camshaft (see Section 8). If the drive sprocket for the rear cylinder cam chain on a VT600 is worn, replace it; if any other drive sprocket is worn, replace the crankshaft.

21.10 On VT600 models, the cam chain drive sprocket for the rear cylinder can be removed from the crankshaft (the drive sprocket for the front cylinder cam chain on VT600 models, and both sprockets on VT750 models, are not removable)

Installation

13   If you removed the drive sprocket for the rear cam chain on a VT600, install it on the crankshaft.

14   Drop the cam chain through the cam chain tunnel and install it on the drive sprocket at the crank. Wire up the cam chain so it can't fall back into the crankcase and install the parts and components removed.

15   If you're installing the front cylinder cam chain, install the alternator rotor and the left crankcase cover (see Chapter 9).

16   If you're installing the rear cylinder cam chain, install the primary drive gear (see Section 20) and the clutch and the right crankcase cover (see Section 18).

17   Install the chain guide (see Section 13).

18   Install the cylinder head (see Section 10).

19   If you removed the rear cylinder head, install the engine (see Section 5).

22.3 Check for alignment marks on the spindle and lever, then remove the pinch bolt (arrow) completely and pull the lever off the spindle

20   Install the cam chain tensioner (see Section 9).

21   Install the camshaft, sprocket and rocker arm assembly (see Section 8).

22   Install the cylinder head cover (see Section 7).

22 Gearshift linkage - removal, inspection and installation

Removal
Gearshift linkage

1   Support the bike securely so it can't be knocked over during this procedure.

2   Remove the left rear cover (see Chapter 7).

3   Look for the index marks on the gearshift lever and the end of the gearshift spindle **(see illustration)**. These marks must be

aligned when the shift lever is installed again. If you can't find any marks, make your own punch marks to ensure correct realignment during installation.

4   Remove the lever pinch bolt **(see illustration 22.3)**. Pull the lever off the spindle.

5   Unbolt the left footpeg assembly from the frame and remove the gearshift pedal, shift rod and shift lever as a single assembly **(see illustrations)**.

External shift mechanism

6   Disconnect the shift lever from the gearshift spindle (Steps 1 through 4).

7   Remove the right crankcase cover and the clutch (see Section 18) and the oil pump drive chain and sprockets (see Section 19).

8   Remove the oil pipe bracket and mainshaft bearing set plate bolts **(see illustration)**. Pull the oil pipe out of the mainshaft bearing set plate and out of the oil pump and remove the oil pipe and bearing set plate **(see illustration)**. Remove and discard the

22.5a To detach the footpeg bracket from the frame, remove these bolts (arrows) . . .

22.5b . . . and remove the footpeg/bracket/gearshift pedal, shift rod and shift lever as a single assembly

O-ring from the lower end of the oil pipe.

9   Unhook the shifter arm from the gearshift cam plate **(see illustration)** and pull the

gearshift spindle out of the crankcase **(see illustration)**.

22.8a To remove the oil pipe bolt, remove the mainshaft bearing set plate bolts (upper arrows) and the oil pipe bracket bolt (lower arrow) . . .

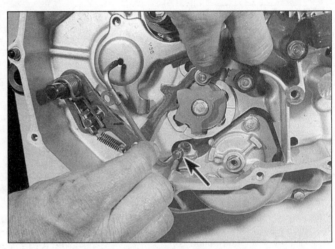

22.8b . . . separate the oil pipe from the set plate and from the oil pump, and remove the O-ring (arrow) from the lower end of the oil pipe

22.9a Unhook the shifter arm from the gearshift cam plate (note how the return spring pin on the crankcase is positioned between the two ends of the return spring) . . .

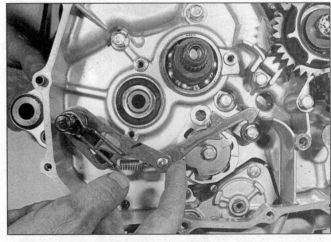

22.9b . . . and pull the gearshift spindle out of the crankcase

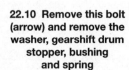

22.10 Remove this bolt (arrow) and remove the washer, gearshift drum stopper, bushing and spring

22.11a Remove this bolt (arrow) . . .

22.11b . . . and remove the gearshift cam plate; the dowel pin (upper arrow) drum and hole (lower arrow) must align when installed

22.12 Remove this bolt (arrow) and remove the gearshift pedal, bushing and dust seals

10   Remove the bolt, washer, gearshift drum stopper, bushing and spring **(see illustration)**.

11   Remove the bolt and gearshift cam plate **(see illustrations)**.

Inspection
Gearshift linkage
12   Unbolt the shift pedal from the footpeg bracket **(see illustration)**.
13   Disassemble the shift pedal assembly, wipe off all grease and dirt and inspect the dust seals and the bushing **(see illustration)** for wear and damage. If any of these parts are worn or damaged, replace them.
14   Inspect the shift rod. Make sure that the rod is straight and the locknuts at both ends are tight. If the shaft is bent, replace it.
15   Lubricate the bushing and the dust seal lips with multipurpose grease and reassemble the shift pedal assembly. Tighten the shift pedal bolt securely.

External shift mechanism
16   Inspect the gearshift spindle and return spring **(see illustration)**. If the spindle is damaged, replace the gearshift spindle assembly. If the spring is fatigued, replace it.

22.13 Clean and inspect the gearshift pedal assembly; if the dust seals or bushing are damaged or worn, replace them

1	Gearshift pedal pivot bolt	5	Gearshift pedal and shift rod
2	Dust seal	6	Footpeg bracket
3	Bushing		
4	Dust seal		

22.16 Inspect the gearshift spindle and return spring (arrows); make sure the spindle is straight and the spring isn't fatigued

22.17 Shift drum stopper details

1 Drum stopper bolt
2 Drum stopper
3 Bushing
4 Spring

22.18 Inspect the cam plate pin holes for wear or damage

17 Inspect the gearshift drum stopper, bushing and spring **(see illustration)**. If the stopper is worn where it contacts the gearshift cam plate, replace the stopper. If the spring is distorted, replace it.

18 Remove the three pins from the gearshift cam plate and inspect the pins and the holes for the pins in the cam plate **(see illustration)**. If the pins or holes are worn or damaged, replace the gearshift cam plate. Reassemble the gearshift cam plate assembly.

19 Inspect the gearshift spindle seal. If it's leaking, remove the countershaft sprocket (see Chapter 7), remove the countershaft bearing set plate **(see illustration)** and remove the seal **(see illustration)**. It's a good idea to replace the seal whenever the gearshift spindle is removed. To replace the seal, pry it out with a screwdriver or seal removal tool and tap a new seal into place with a deep socket.

Installation

20 Install the gearshift cam plate. Make sure the positioning hole on the cam plate is aligned with the dowel pin on the shift drum **(see illustration 22.11b)**.

21 Clean the bolt threads of the cam plate bolt, apply a thread locking agent to the threads, install the bolt and tighten it to the torque listed in this Chapter's Specifications.

22 Install the bushing, spring, gearshift drum stopper, washer and bolt. Tighten the gearshift drum stopper bolt to the torque listed in this Chapter's Specifications.

23 Install the gearshift spindle assembly. Make sure that the dowel pin on the crankcase fits between the two ends of the return spring **(see illustration 22.9a)**.

24 Apply clean engine oil to the new oil pipe O-ring and install the O-ring on the oil pipe. Install the mainshaft bearing set plate and the oil pipe, install the set plate and oil pipe bracket bolts and tighten them securely.

25 Install the gearshift pedal and foot-peg bracket and tighten the bracket bolts securely.

26 Install the shift lever on the gearshift spindle. Make sure the punch marks on the shift lever and the spindle are aligned. Install the shift lever pinch bolt and tighten it to the torque listed in this Chapter's Specifications.

27 Install the left rear engine cover (see Chapter 7).

23 Crankcase - disassembly and reassembly

1 To examine and repair or replace the oil pump, crankshaft, connecting rods, bearings, or transmission components, the crankcase must be split into two parts.

Disassembly

2 Remove the engine from the frame (see Section 5).

3 Remove the cylinder head covers (see Section 7).

4 Remove the camshafts, sprockets and rocker arms (see Section 8).

5 Remove the cam chain tensioners (see Section 9).

6 Remove the cylinder heads (see Section 10).

7 Remove the cam chain guides (see Section 13).

8 Remove the cylinders (see Section 14).

9 Remove the pistons (see Section 15).

10 Remove the left crankcase cover and the alternator (see Chapter 9). Remove all

22.19a Remove the retainer bolts (arrows) and replace the gearshift spindle seal if it's leaking

22.19b Gearshift spindle seal (right arrow) and countershaft seal (left arrow)

23.17 Remove these bolts (arrows) from the left crankcase half; loosen the two 6 mm bolts first, then loosen the other four (8 mm) bolts, gradually and evenly, in a criss-cross pattern

23.18 Remove these bolts (arrows) from the right crankcase half; loosen the three 6 mm bolts first, then loosen the other eight (8 mm) bolts, gradually and evenly, in a criss-cross pattern (two right-hand bolts hidden)

23.19a Locate the prying points (this one on the underside of the cases and two more on the front of the crankcase)

23.19b Once you've broken the seal, carefully separate the crankcase halves

23.20 Remove both dowel pins (arrows) from the left crankcase half (front dowel is missing in this photo; it came off with the other crankcase half) and store them in a plastic bag

electrical harnesses from the left side of the engine.

11   Remove the right crankcase cover and the clutch (see Section 18).

12   Remove the oil pump driven chain and sprockets (see Section 19).

13   Remove the ignition pulse generator(s) (see Chapter 5).

14   Remove the primary drive gear (see Section 20).

15   Remove the cam chains (see Section 21).

16   Remove the oil pipe, mainshaft bearing set plate, gearshift spindle, gearshift drum stopper, gearshift cam plate and countershaft bearing set plate (see Section 22).

17   Remove the bolts from the left crankcase half **(see illustration)**. First, loosen the two 6 mm bolts, then loosen the four 8 mm bolts. Working in a criss-cross pattern, loosen the bolts gradually and evenly.

18   Remove the bolts from the right crankcase half **(see illustration)**. First, loosen the three 6 mm bolts, then loosen the eight 8 mm bolts. Working in a criss-cross pattern, loosen the bolts gradually and evenly.

19   With the engine lying on its left crankcase half, carefully separate the crankcase halves by prying gently and evenly at the pry points around the crankcase seam **(see illustrations)**. Using a soft hammer, tap alternately on the transmission shafts and the engine mounting bosses. If the halves won't separate easily, double check to make sure that all fasteners have been removed. Don't pry against the crankcase mating surfaces or they'll leak.

20   Look for the dowels **(see illustration)**. If they're not in one of the crankcase halves, locate them.

25.3a To remove the oil relief pipe, remove its bolt (lower arrow) (the other two bolts are the oil pump mounting bolts) . . .

25.3b . . . and lift the pipe off

21 Remove all traces of sealant from the crankcase mating surfaces.
22 Refer to Sections 25 through 30 for information on servicing the internal components of the crankcase.

Reassembly

23 Make sure the oil pump, crankshaft and transmission shafts are correctly installed in the upper crankcase half (see Sections 25, 28 and 29, respectively).
24 Pour some engine oil over the transmission gears, the crankshaft main bearings and the shift drum. Also pour oil into the exposed internal oil passages. Don't get any oil on the crankcase mating surfaces.
25 Make sure the dowels are in place (see illustration 23.20).
26 Apply a thin, even bead of sealant to the crankcase mating surfaces.
Caution: Don't apply an excessive amount of sealant. Make sure that no sealant is applied to oil passages.
27 Carefully assemble the crankcase halves over the dowels.

Caution: The crankcase halves should fit together completely without being forced. If they're slightly apart, DO NOT force them together by tightening the crankcase bolts.
28 Install the right crankcase bolts in their holes (see illustration 23.18). Make sure you don't install a 6 mm bolt in an 8 mm hole, or vice versa. Tighten the bolts gradually and evenly, in a criss-cross fashion, to the torque listed in this Chapter's Specifications. **Note:** *There are different torque settings for the 8 mm bolts and the 6 mm bolts.*
29 Turn the engine over and install the left crankcase bolts in their holes (see illustration 23.17). Make sure you don't install a 6 mm bolt in an 8 mm hole, or vice versa. Tighten the bolts gradually and evenly, in a criss-cross fashion, to the torque listed in this Chapter's Specifications. **Note:** *There are different torque settings for the 8 mm bolts and the 6 mm bolts.*
30 Turn the crankshaft, the mainshaft and the countershaft to make sure they turn freely.
31 Install the gearshift cam plate (see Section 22). Rotate the shift cam by hand to make sure the transmission shifts into the

different gear positions.
32 The remainder of assembly is the reverse of disassembly.
33 Be sure to refill the engine oil (see Chapter 1).

24 Crankcase components - inspection and servicing

1 After the crankcases have been separated and the oil pump, the crankshaft, the shift drum and forks, and the transmission shafts have been removed, the crankcases should be cleaned thoroughly with new solvent and dried with compressed air.
2 Remove the oil jets (see illustrations 15.5a and 15.5b). All oil passages should be blown out with compressed air.
3 All traces of old gasket sealant should be removed from the mating surfaces. Minor damage to the mating surfaces can be cleaned up with a fine sharpening stone or grindstone.
Caution: Be very careful not to nick or gouge the crankcase mating surfaces or leaks will result.
Check both crankcase halves very carefully for cracks and other damage.
4 If any damage is found that can't be repaired, replace the crankcase halves as a set.

25 Oil pump - removal, inspection and installation

Removal

1 Remove the engine (see Section 5).
2 Disassemble the engine and separate the crankcase halves (see Section 23).
3 Remove the oil relief pipe bolt and remove the oil relief pipe (see illustrations).

25.4 Remove the oil pump from the crankcase

25.5 The collars, O-rings, and dowel (arrows) may stay in the engine or come out with the oil pump; be sure to remove and install all of them

25.6 If the O-ring isn't on the end of the pipe, it's in the pump passage (arrow)

25.7a Remove the cover bolts (arrows) . . .

25.7b . . . remove the pump cover . . .

25.7c . . . and locate the dowels

4   Remove the oil pump mounting bolts **(see illustration 25.3a)** and remove the pump **(see illustration)**.

5   Remove the oil pump collars, O-rings and dowels **(see illustration)**.

Disassembly

6   Remove the oil pipe and discard the old O-rings and seal **(see illustration)**.

7   Remove the pump cover bolts, lift off the cover and remove the dowel pins **(see illustrations)**.

8   Remove the washer, the driveshaft, the drive pin, the inner rotor and the outer rotor **(see illustration)** from the pump body.

9   Pull off the strainer **(see illustration)**. Discard the old O-ring.

25.8 Oil pump details

1   Pump cover
2   Washer
3   Driveshaft
4   Drive pin
5   Inner rotor
6   Outer rotor
7   Pump body

25.9 Pull off the strainer and discard the old O-ring

25.10a Pull out the pressure relief valve and discard the old O-ring

10   Pull out the pressure relief valve **(see illustration)**. Remove the snap-ring and remove the washer, spring and piston from the relief valve **(see illustrations)**. Discard the old O-ring.

Inspection

11   Wash the oil pump parts in solvent and dry them off.
12   Check the pump body and rotors for scoring and wear. If any damage or uneven or excessive wear is evident, replace the pump; (individual parts aren't available. (If you are rebuilding the engine, it's a good idea to install a new oil pump anyway.)
13   Measure the clearance between the inner and outer rotors and between the outer rotor and housing **(see illustrations)**. Replace the pump if the clearance is excessive.
14   Inspect the piston and the bore of the relief valve for scoring or other damage. Inspect the spring for fatigue. If any of the relief valve parts are worn or damaged, replace the oil pump.

Reassembly

15   If the pump is good, make sure all the parts are spotlessly clean, then lubricate everything with clean engine oil or assembly lube.
16   Install the inner and outer rotors in the pump body. Make sure the outer rotor is installed with the punch mark facing out, toward the cover **(see illustration)**.
17   Install the washer and driveshaft in the inner rotor. Make sure that the pin is centered in the driveshaft so it will align with the slot in the inner rotor **(see illustration)**.
18   Install the pump cover and tighten the cover bolts securely.
19   Install the piston, spring and washer in the pressure relief valve and secure them with the snap-ring. Using a new O-ring, install the pressure relief valve in the pump body.
20   Using a new O-ring, install the strainer in the pump body.

Installation

21   Make sure the dowel, collars and O-rings are in position **(see illustration 25.5)**.
22   Make sure that the T-shaped oil pipe has a new seal on the end that fits into the pump and new O-rings on the two ends that fit into the cases **(see illustrations)**. And make SURE that the old oil pipe seal and O-rings are not still in their respective bores in the pump body or the cases (which they sometimes are).

25.10b Remove the snap-ring from the pressure relief valve . . .

25.10c . . . and disassemble the pressure relief valve

1 Snap-ring	4 Piston
2 Washer	5 Pressure relief valve
3 Spring	

25.13a Measure the clearance between the outer rotor and pump body

25.13b Measure the clearance between the inner and outer rotors

25.13c Measure the clearance between rotors and the cover

23 Install the pump, install the mounting bolts and tighten them securely.
24 Install the oil relief pipe, install the oil relief pipe bolt and tighten it securely.
25 Installation is otherwise the reverse of removal.

26 Main and connecting rod bearings - general note

1 Even though main and connecting rod bearings are generally replaced with new ones during the engine overhaul, the old bearings should be retained for close examination as they may reveal valuable information about the condition of the engine.
2 Bearing failure occurs mainly because of lack of lubrication, the presence of dirt or other foreign particles, overloading the engine and/or corrosion. Regardless of the cause of bearing failure, it must be corrected before the engine is reassembled to prevent it from happening again.
3 When examining the bearings, remove the rod bearings from the connecting rods and caps and lay them out on a clean surface in the same general position as their location on the crankshaft journals. This will enable you to match any noted bearing problems with the corresponding side of the crankshaft journal. The main bearings are pressed into the crankcase halves and are only removed if they need to be replaced.
4 Dirt and other foreign particles get into the engine in a variety of ways. It may be left in the engine during assembly or it may pass through filters or breathers. It may get into the oil and from there into the bearings. Metal chips from machining operations and normal engine wear are often present. Abrasives are sometimes left in engine components after reconditioning operations such as cylinder honing, especially when parts are not thoroughly cleaned using the proper cleaning methods. Whatever the source, these foreign

25.16 Install the outer rotor with the punch mark (arrow) facing out (toward the cover)

25.17 Center the drive pin in the driveshaft, then push the driveshaft into the inner rotor until the drive pin is seated in the grooves in the inner rotor

objects often end up imbedded in the soft bearing material and are easily recognized. Large particles will not imbed in the bearing and will score or gouge the bearing and journal. The best prevention for this cause of bearing failure is to clean all parts thoroughly and keep everything spotlessly clean during engine reassembly. Frequent and regular oil and filter changes are also recommended.
5 Lack of lubrication or lubrication breakdown has a number of interrelated causes. Excessive heat (which thins the oil), overloading (which squeezes the oil from the bearing face) and oil leakage or throw off (from excessive bearing clearances, worn oil pump or high engine speeds) all contribute to lubrication breakdown. Blocked oil passages will also starve a bearing and destroy it. When lack of lubrication is the cause of bearing failure, the bearing material is wiped or extruded from the steel backing of the bearing. Temperatures may increase to the point where the steel backing and the journal turn blue from overheating.
6 Riding habits can have a definite effect on bearing life. Full throttle low speed operation, or lugging the engine, puts very high

loads on bearings, which tend to squeeze out the oil film. These loads cause the bearings to flex, which produces fine cracks in the bearing face (fatigue failure). Eventually the bearing material will loosen in pieces and tear away from the steel backing. Short trip driving leads to corrosion of bearings, as insufficient engine heat is produced to drive off the condensed water and corrosive gases produced. These products collect in the engine oil, forming acid and sludge. As the oil is carried to the engine bearings, the acid attacks and corrodes the bearing material.
7 Incorrect bearing installation during engine assembly will lead to bearing failure as well. Tight fitting bearings which leave insufficient bearing oil clearances result in oil starvation. Dirt or foreign particles trapped behind a bearing insert result in high spots on the bearing which lead to failure.
8 To avoid bearing problems, clean all parts thoroughly before reassembly, double check all bearing clearance measurements and lubricate the new bearings with engine assembly lube or moly-based grease during installation.

25.22a Install a new seal on the oil pipe before pushing the pipe into the pump body

25.22b Use new O-rings on the ends of the oil pipe which are seated in the cases

27.3 Measure the side clearance between the rods and the crankshaft weights

27.7 Slip the piston pin into the rod and rock it back-and-forth to check for looseness

27 Connecting rods and bearings - removal, inspection and installation

Removal

1   Separate the crankcase halves (see Section 23).
2   Lift the crankshaft out, together with the connecting rods, and set them on a clean surface.
3   Before removing the connecting rods from the crankshaft, measure the connecting rod side clearance. Insert a feeler gauge between each side of the big end of each connecting rod and the crankshaft **(see illustration)** and compare your measurements to the side clearance listed in this Chapter's Specifications. If the side clearance between either rod and the crank is greater than the specified side clearance, replace that rod.
4   Using a center punch or a laundry marker pen with indelible ink, mark the position of each rod and cap, relative to its posi-

tion on the crankshaft (left or right) to ensure that the same rod removed from each crankpin will be reinstalled on the same crankpin.
5   Unscrew the bearing cap nuts, separate the cap from the rod, then detach the rod from the crankshaft. If a rod cap is stuck, tap on the ends of the rod bolts with a soft-faced hammer to free it.
6   Roll the bearing inserts sideways to separate them from the rods and caps. Keep them in order so they can be reinstalled in their original locations. Wash the parts in solvent and dry them with compressed air, if available.

Inspection

7   Check the connecting rods for cracks and other obvious damage. Lubricate the piston pin for each rod, install it in the proper rod and check for play **(see illustration)**. If it wobbles, measure the outside diameter of the piston pin, the inside diameter of the connecting rod, and the inside diameter of the pin bore in the piston (see Section 15). Replace the piston (see Section 15), the pin

and/or the connecting rod (see Step 20) as necessary.
8   Examine the connecting rod bearing inserts. If they are scored, badly scuffed or appear to have been seized, new bearings must be installed. Always replace the bearings in the connecting rods as a set. If they are badly damaged, check the corresponding crankshaft journal. Evidence of extreme heat, such as discoloration, indicates lubrication failure. Be sure to inspect the oil pump and pressure relief valve (see Section 25) as well as all oil holes and passages before reassembling the engine.
9   Have the rods checked for twist and bending at a dealer service department or other motorcycle repair shop. If a rod must be replaced, refer to Step 20.
10   If the bearings and journals appear to be in good condition, check the oil clearances as follows:
11   Start with the rod for one cylinder. Wipe the bearing inserts and the connecting rod and cap clean, using a lint-free cloth.
12   Install the bearing inserts in the con-

27.12 Make sure the tab (arrow) on the bearing is aligned with the notch (arrow) in the rod or cap

27.13 Lay a strip of Plastigage on the journal, parallel to the crankshaft centerline

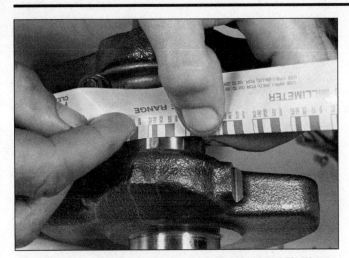

27.15 Place the Plastigage scale next to the flattened Plastigage to measure the bearing clearance

27.19a The number code on the connecting rod and the letter code on the crankshaft weight are used to determine the color (size) of the rod bearing insert; the code letter on the rod is used to determine the connecting rod weight

necting rod and cap. Make sure the tab on the bearing engages with the notch in the rod or cap (see illustration).

13   Wipe off the connecting rod journal with a lint-free cloth. Lay a strip of Plastigage (type HPG-1) across the top of the journal, parallel with the journal axis (see illustration).

14   Referring to the marks you made prior to disassembly, position the connecting rod on the correct journal, then install the rod cap and nuts. Tighten the nuts to the torque listed in this Chapter's Specifications, but don't allow the connecting rod to rotate at all.

15   Unscrew the nuts and remove the connecting rod and cap from the journal, being very careful not to disturb the Plastigage. Compare the width of the crushed Plastigage to the scale printed in the Plastigage envelope to determine the bearing oil clearance (see illustration).

16   If the clearance is within the range listed in this Chapter's Specifications and the bearings are in perfect condition, they can be reused. If the clearance is greater than the wear limit, replace the bearing inserts with new inserts that have the same color code, then check the clearance once again. Always replace all of the inserts at the same time.

17   If the clearance is greater than the maximum clearance listed in this Chapter's Specifications, measure the diameter of the connecting rod journal with a micrometer. To determine whether the journal is out-of-round, measure the diameter at a number of points around the journal's circumference. Take the measurement at each end of the journal to determine if the journal is tapered.

18   If any journal is tapered or out-of-round or bearing clearance is beyond the maximum listed in this Chapter's Specifications (with

new bearings), replace the crankshaft (see Section 28).

Connecting rod bearing selection

19   Each connecting rod has a "1" or "2" stamped on it (see illustration); this is the code for the connecting rod inside diameter. Next to that, on the crank weight, is an "A" or a "B;" this is the code for the crankpin outside diameter. The bearings are color-coded brown, black or blue. To determine the correct bearing color, match the connecting rod I.D. code (left column) to the crankpin O.D. code (upper row) and note the corresponding color code in the following chart. For example, a code 2 on the connecting rod and an A code on the crank weight would indicate a black color-coded rod bearing (see illustration). The color codes are painted on the edges of the bearings.

Crankpin O.D. code	Code "A" 39.982 to 39.990 mm (1.5741 to 1.5744 inches)	Code "B" 39.974 to 39.981 mm (1.5738 to 1.5741 inches)
Connecting rod I.D. code	Bearing insert thickness	Bearing insert thickness
Code "1" 43.000 to 43.007 mm (1.6929 to 1.6935 inches)	"C" (Brown) 1.487 to 1.491 mm (0.0585 to 0.0587 inch)	"B" (Black) 1.491 to 1.495 mm (0.0587 to 0.0589 inch)
Code "2" 43.008 to 43.016 mm (1.6932 to 1.6935 inches)	"B" (Black) 1.491 to 1.495 mm (0.0587 to 0.0589 inch)	"A" (Blue) 1.495 to 1.499 mm (0.0589 to 0.0590 inch)

27.19b Connecting rod bearing selection chart

27.21 Coat the bearings with assembly lube or moly-based grease

27.22 If the halves of the number stamped on the rod and cap don't fit together perfectly, the wrong cap is on the rod (or the cap is on backwards)

Matching the connecting rods to the crankshaft

20 The connecting rods and the crankshaft are "select fitted." If a connecting rod must be replaced, make sure you select a new rod with the same weight code as the rod being replaced. Each connecting rod has an "A," a "B" or a "C" stamped on the side of the rod **(see illustration 27.19a)**. This is the connecting rod weight code.

Installation

21 Wipe off the bearing inserts, connecting rods and caps. Install the inserts into the rods and caps, using your hands only, making sure the tabs on the inserts engage with the notches in the rods and caps **(see illustration 27.12)**. When all the inserts are installed, lubricate them with engine assembly lube or moly-based grease **(see illustration)**. Don't get any lubricant on the mating surfaces of the rod or cap.

22 Install each connecting rod on the correct journal, referring to the marks you made prior to disassembly. Make sure that the connecting rod code number stamped on the side of the rod across the rod/cap seam fits together perfectly when the rod and cap are assembled **(see illustration)**. If it doesn't, the wrong cap is on the rod. Fix this problem before proceeding.

23 When you're sure the rods are positioned correctly, lubricate the threads of the rod bolts and the surfaces of the nuts with molybdenum disulfide grease and tighten the nuts to the torque listed in this Chapter's Specifications. Snug both rod cap nuts evenly, then gradually and evenly tighten them to the specified torque in several steps.

24 Turn the rods on the crankshaft. If either of them feels tight, tap on the bottom of the connecting rod caps with a hammer - this should relieve stress and free them up. If it doesn't, recheck the bearing clearance.

25 As a final step, recheck the connecting rod side clearances (see Step 3). If the clearances aren't correct, find out why before proceeding with engine assembly.

---

28 Crankshaft and main bearings - removal, inspection and installation

Crankshaft removal

1 Separate the crankcase halves (see Section 23).

2 Lift out the crankshaft and connecting rods and set the assembly on a clean surface.

3 Mark, remove and inspect the connecting rods and rod bearings (see Section 27).

Inspection

4 Clean the crankshaft with solvent, using a rifle-cleaning brush to scrub out the oil passages. Dry off the crank with compressed air. Inspect the main and connecting rod journals for uneven wear, scoring and pits. Rub a copper coin across the journal several times

- if a journal picks up copper from the coin, it's too rough. Replace the crankshaft.

5 Inspect the teeth on the cam chain drive sprocket(s) on the crankshaft. If the sprocket teeth are damaged or worn, replace the crankshaft. (The rear cylinder cam chain sprocket on VT600 models is removable; the front cylinder cam chain sprocket on VT600 models and both sprockets on VT750 models are part of the crankshaft.) If there's sprocket wear or damage, inspect the cam chains too (see Section 21). Inspect the rest of the crankshaft for cracks and other damage. Have it magnafluxed by a dealer service department or motorcycle machine shop; magnafluxing will reveal any hidden cracks.

6 Set the crankshaft on V-blocks and measure the crank runout at the bearing surfaces with a dial indicator **(see illustration)**. Compare your measurement with the runout listed in this Chapter's Specifications. If the runout exceeds the limit, replace the crank.

Main bearing selection

7 Measure the diameter of the main bearing journals with a micrometer **(see illus-**

28.6 Place the crankshaft in V-blocks or a holding fixture and check for runout with a dial indicator

28.7a Measure journal diameter with a micrometer

28.7b Measure main bearing diameter with a hole gauge . . .

28.7c . . . then measure the gauge diameter with a micrometer

tration). Measure the inside diameter of the main bearings with a hole gauge and micrometer **(see illustrations)**. The difference between these two measurements is the bearing clearance. It should be within the range listed in this Chapter's Specifications.

8   If the clearance is greater than the service limit listed in this Chapter's Specifications but journal diameter is within specifications, press out the old bearings. If you do not have a hydraulic press and the correct bearing driver, have the main bearings replaced at a dealer service department or a motorcycle machine shop.

9   The main journal outside diameter code number, a "1" or a "2," is stamped on the crankshaft weights **(see illustration 27.19a)**.

10   Measure the inside diameter of the main bearing bores in the crankcase (with the bear-

ings removed). Record your measurements and compare them to the two crankcase I.D. size ranges listed in the accompanying chart to determine whether the crankcase I.D. is a code "A" or a code "B." Cross reference the crankcase I.D. code to the main journal O.D. code to select the correct main bearing color **(see illustration)**.

Matching the crankshaft to the connecting rods

11   The crankshaft and the connecting rods are "select fitted" (see Section 27).

12   Some crankshafts have an "L" or an "H" stamped on the outside face of the right crank weight; this is the crankshaft weight code.

13   If the front and rear connecting rods have an "A" stamped on them, select an "L"

crank; if the rods have a "C" on them, select an "H" crank. Aside from these two combinations, select a crank *with no weight code*. Select the correct crankshaft as follows:

a) *If both connecting rods have an "A" stamped on them, select an "L" crank.*
b) *If both connecting rods have a "C" on them, select an "H" crank.*
c) *If both connecting rods have a "B" on them, select a crank with no weight code.*
d) *If the two connecting rods have different letters, select a crank with no weight code.*

Matching the crankshaft to the crankcase

14   The crankshaft and the crankcase are also select fitted. There is a "1" or a "2"

Main journal O.D. code	Code "1" 44.992 to 45.000 mm (1.7713 to 1.7717 inches)	Code "2" 44.984 to 44.991 mm (1.7710 to 1.7713 inches)
Crankcase I.D. code	Bearing insert thickness	Bearing insert thickness
Code "A" 48.990 to 49.000 mm (1.9287 to 1.9291 inches)	"C" (Brown) 1.993 to 2.003 mm (0.0785 to 0.0789 inch)	"B" (Black) 1.998 to 2.008 mm (0.0787 to 0.0791 inch)
Code "B" 49.000 to 49.010 mm (1.9291 to 1.9295 inches)	"B" (Black) 1.998 to 2.008 mm (0.0787 to 0.0791 inch)	"A" (Blue) 2.003 to 2.013 mm (0.0789 to 0.0793 inch)

28.10 Main bearing selection chart

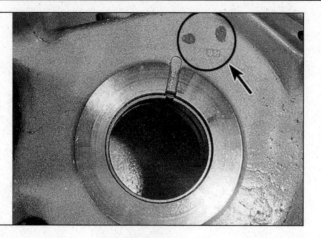

28.14 The main bearing I.D. code (arrow) is stamped into the left case half

stamped on the crank weights **(see illustration 27.19a)**; this is the main journal outside diameter code number. An "A" or a "B" is stamped into the case **(see illustration)**; this is the main bearing inside diameter code. A "1" crankshaft must be matched with an "A" crankcase; a "2" crankshaft must be matched with a "B" crankcase.

Installation

15   Install the connecting rods on the crankshaft (see Section 27).
16   Lubricate the main bearings with engine assembly lube or moly-based grease.
17   Carefully lower the crankshaft/connecting rod assembly into the left crankcase half. Align the connecting rods with the cylinders.

18   Assemble the crankcase halves (see Section 23) and check to make sure the crankshaft and the transmission shafts turn freely.

29 Transmission - removal, inspection and installation

Removal

1   Remove the engine (see Section 5) and separate the crankcase halves (see Section 23).
2   On 1988 and 1989 and 1991 through 1995 VT600 models, remove the mainshaft, countershaft, shift fork shaft and shift drum as a single assembly.
3   On 1996 and later VT600 models and on all VT750 models, remove the shift fork shaft from the shift fork **(see illustrations)**.
4   Remove the first gear washer and first gear from the countershaft **(see illustration)**.
5   Remove the shift drum **(see illustration)**.

29.3a Firmly grasp the end of the shift fork shaft . . .

29.3b . . . and carefully pull it out of the case and out of the shift forks

29.4 Remove the washer and 1st gear from the countershaft and set them aside

29.5 Remove the shift drum

29.6 Remove the mainshaft assembly

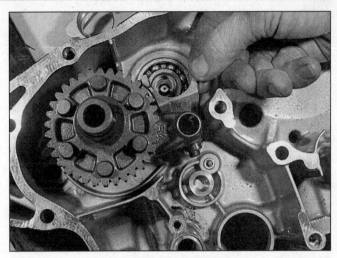

29.7 Remove the shift forks

6   Remove the mainshaft assembly **(see illustration)**.
7   Remove the shift forks **(see illustration)**.
8   Remove the countershaft assembly **(see illustration)**.

Inspection

9   Thoroughly wash the transmission components in clean solvent and dry them off with compressed air.

Shift drum, shift forks and shift fork shaft

10   Inspect the shift drum **(see illustration)** for evidence of insufficient lubrication and inspect the edges of the grooves in the shift drum for excessive wear. If the drum is worn or damaged, replace it. Measure the diameter of the left shift drum journal and compare your measurement to the journal diameter listed in this Chapter's Specifications. If it's smaller than the limit, replace the shift drum.

11   Inspect the shift forks for distortion and wear, especially the fork tips. If they're discolored or severely worn they are probably bent. If damage or wear is evident, check the shift fork groove in the corresponding sliding gear as well. Inspect the guide pins too. If the fork tips or the guide pins are worn or damaged, replace the forks. Measure the inside diameter of the shift fork shaft bore and the fork tip thickness of both forks and compare your measurements to the dimensions listed in this Chapter's Specifications. If the shift fork shaft bore is bigger than the limit or the tips are thinner than the limit, replace the shift fork(s).

12   Inspect the shift fork shaft for excessive wear, evidence of poor lubrication and straightness (roll it on a flat surface). See if the shift forks slide freely and smoothly on the shaft. Measure the diameter of the shaft and compare your measurement to the shift fork shaft diameter listed in this Chapter's Specifications.

Countershaft and mainshaft

13   Disassemble the transmission shafts. You'll need snap-ring pliers to remove some of the parts from the shafts. It's a good idea to discard all old snap-rings and install new ones when reassembling the transmission. Carefully study each part before removing it from the shaft; if the two sides of a part are not the same, make sure you know which side faces which way before removing that part. There are various ways to do this. One way to ensure that the parts retain their correct relationship to one another is to "stack" them on a long dowel, extension, etc. or to "thread" them on a piece of wire, as they're

29.8 Remove the countershaft assembly

29.10 Inspect the grooves in the shift drum and the tips and pin guides of the shift forks

| 1 | Shift drum | 3 | Shift fork |
| 2 | Shift fork | 4 | Shift fork shaft |

29.13 Transmission details (four-speed shown; five-speed similar)

A	Mainshaft	J	Mainshaft fourth gear
B	Thrust washer	K	Thrust washer
C	Mainshaft second gear	L	Countershaft first gear
D	Bushing	M	Countershaft second gear
E	Splined thrust washer	N	Countershaft third gear
F	Snap-ring	O	Lock washer and stop
G	Mainshaft third gear		washer
H	Snap-ring	P	Countershaft fourth gear
I	Splined thrust washer	Q	Countershaft

29.19 Inspect the bearings (arrows) for the shift drum, the mainshaft and the countershaft; if a bearing is rough or noisy or loose, replace it (or have it replaced by a dealer or by a machine shop)

removed. If you're still in doubt, label the bigger parts to indicate which side faces left or right. Once you're confident that you know how the transmission goes back together, carefully lay out the parts in the order in which they were removed **(see illustration)**.

14   Inspect the gears. Check the gear dogs, gear dog holes and gear teeth for cracks, excessive wear and other obvious damage. If a gear is obviously worn or damaged, replace it, and replace its corresponding gear on the other shaft too. Measure the inside diameter of each gear and compare your measurements to the inside diameters for the various gears listed in this Chapter's Specifications. If the inside diameter of a gear is excessive, replace the gear.

15   Inspect the gear bushings. Check the surface of the inner diameter of each bushing for scoring or heat discoloration or signs of poor lubrication. If a gear or bushing is obviously damaged or worn, replace it. Measure the inside and outside diameters of each bushing and compare your measurements to the I.D. and O.D. dimensions for the bushings listed in this Chapter's Specifications.

16   Inspect the mainshaft and countershaft. Check the splines and sliding surfaces for

wear and damage. If either shaft is worn or damaged, replace it. Measure the diameter of each shaft at the gear and bushing sliding surfaces. Compare your measurements to the mainshaft and countershaft diameters listed in this Chapter's Specifications. If either

shaft is worn below the limit, replace it.

17   To calculate the gear-to-mainshaft clearance, subtract the shaft diameter from the inside diameter of each gear. Compare your measurements to the gear-to-shaft clearances listed in this Chapter's Specifications. If the clearance is excessive, replace the gear and/or the shaft, depending on which part is causing the excessive clearance. Calculate the bushing-to-shaft clearances the same way and replace the bushing(s) and/or shaft accordingly.

18   Repeat Step 17 for the gear-to-countershaft clearance.

19   Inspect the bearings for the shift drum and the transmission shafts **(see illustration)**. Make sure they rotate smoothly and quietly. If they're rough or noisy or loose, press them out of the cases and press in new bearings, or have them replaced at a dealer service department or motorcycle machine shop.

20   Install the C4 gear on the countershaft **(see illustration)**.

21   Install the stopper ring on the countershaft **(see illustration)**.

29.20 Install the C4 gear on the countershaft

29.21 Install the stopper ring on the countershaft and seat it in its groove in the shaft adjacent to the C4 gear

29.22a Install the lock washer first, then the stop washer, on the countershaft

29.22b Position the lock washer and the stop washer so that the bigger tabs of the lock washer are aligned with the bigger grooves of the stop washer . . .

29.22c . . . and so that both washers are in their groove in the shaft

29.23a Install the stop washer first, then the lock washer, for the C3 gear . . .

22 Install the lock washer and stop washer on the countershaft **(see illustration)**. Position the lock washer and stop washer so that the bigger tabs of the lock washer are aligned with the bigger grooves of the stop washer and so that both washers are located at their

groove in the shaft **(see illustrations)**.
23 Install the stop washer, then the lock washer, for the C3 gear, and align them the same way you aligned the stop washer and lock washer for the C4 gear **(see illustrations)**.

24 Reassembly of the countershaft is otherwise the reverse of disassembly.
25 Reassembly of the mainshaft is the reverse of disassembly **(see illustration)**.
26 When you're done this is how the two

29.23b . . . and align them the same way you aligned the washers for the C4 gear

29.25 The mainshaft assembly should look like this when it's reassembled

29.26 The transmission assembly should look like this when it's reassembled

29.27 Install the transmission shafts in the left case half; before installing the other case half, make sure that the shift forks are correctly engaged with their respective shafts

assembled shafts should look **(see illustration)**.

Installation

27 Installation of the transmission in the left case half **(see illustration)** is the reverse of removal, noting the following points:

a) *Install a new countershaft seal in the left crankcase half* **(see illustration 22.19b)**.

b) *Lubricate all parts with engine oil before installing them.*

c) *Use the letters on the forks to position them correctly. The forks are identified by a "C" (center) or an "R" (right), starting from the left side of the engine. The letters face the right side of the engine when installed.*

d) *Engage the guide pin on each shift fork with the groove in the shift drum as you insert the shift fork shaft through the forks.*

e) *After reassembling the case halves, make sure that both shafts turn freely and the shift drum and shift forks function correctly.*

30 Output gear assembly (shaft drive models) - removal and installation

Removal

1 Remove the engine (see Section 5) and separate the crankcase halves (see Section 23).

2 Remove the output gear, bushing and thrust washer from the right crankcase **(see illustration)**.

3 Before the output gear assembly can be unbolted from the left half of the crankcase, the damper cam and spring must be removed from the output gear driveshaft. A special spring compressor (Honda part no.

07964-ME90000) is needed to remove the snap-ring from the output gear driveshaft. If you don't have the tool or an equivalent, take the left half of the crankcase to a Honda dealer and have the service department remove the snap-ring from the output drive gear shaft.

4 Remove the damper cam and spring from the output drive gear shaft **(see illustration)**.

5 Remove the output gear assembly retaining bolts **(see illustration)**.

6 Remove the oil orifice and O-rings **(see illustration)**. Remove and discard the O-rings.

Inspection

7 Inspect the condition of the teeth and the gear dog holes on the output gear. If they're damaged or excessively worn, replace the output gear. Measure the inside diameter of the output gear and compare your measurement to the output gear inside

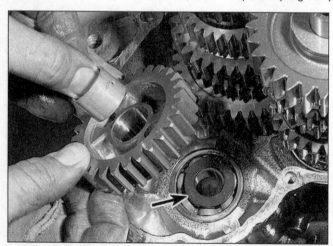

30.2 Remove the bushing, output gear and thrust washer (arrow)

30.4 After the snap-ring has been removed, remove the damper cam and spring (arrows) from the output gear driveshaft (output gear assembly removed for clarity)

30.5 To detach the output gear assembly from the left crankcase half, remove these three bolts (arrows)

30.6 Remove the oil orifice and discard the O-rings

diameter listed in this Chapter's Specifications. If the indicated I.D. exceeds the limit, replace the output gear.

8   Inspect the bushing and replace it if it's worn or damaged. Inspect the bushing inside and outside diameters and compare your measurements to the values listed in this Chapter's Specifications. If either measurement is outside the limit, replace the bushing.

9   Measure the diameter of the friction surface of the output drive gear shaft and compare your measurement to the output drive gear shaft diameter listed in this Chapter's Specifications. If the indicated diameter of the shaft is smaller than the shaft diameter limit, have a Honda dealer disassemble the output gear assembly and install a new shaft.

10   Measure the free length of the spring and compare your measurements to the spring free length listed in this Chapter's Specifications. If the measurement is less than the minimum, replace the spring.

11   Place the output gear assembly in a bench vise. Using a dial indicator and a suitable base, set the dial indicator next to the output gear assembly with the probe touching the output drive gear shaft **(see illustration)**. Install the shaft holder (Honda part no. 07923-6890101) or a suitable equivalent, rotate the output shaft driven gear back and forth and measure the amount of backlash. Make this measurement at three locations on the output drive gear shaft, average the measurements and compare the average to the backlash listed in this Chapter's Specifications. If the indicated backlash is outside the specified range, have the output gear assembly overhauled by a dealer service department or other qualified shop.

Installation

12   Installation is the reverse of the removal steps. Be sure to use new O-rings on the oil orifice and tighten the output gear assem-

bly retaining bolts to the torque listed in this Chapter's Specifications.

31 Initial start-up after overhaul

1   Make sure the engine oil level is correct, then remove the spark plugs from the engine. Place the engine kill switch in the Off position and unplug the primary (low tension) wires from the coils.

2   Turn on the key switch and crank the engine over with the starter several times to build up oil pressure. Reinstall the spark plugs, connect the wires and turn the switch to On.

3   Make sure there is fuel in the tank, then turn the fuel tap to the On position and operate the choke.

4   Start the engine and allow it to run at a moderately fast idle until it reaches operating temperature.

5   Check carefully for oil leaks and make sure the transmission and controls, espe-

cially the brakes, function properly before road testing the machine. Refer to Section 32 for the recommended break-in procedure.

6   Upon completion of the road test, and after the engine has cooled down completely, recheck the valve clearances (see Chapter 1).

32 Recommended break-in procedure

1   Any rebuilt engine needs time to break-in, even if parts have been installed in their original locations. For this reason, treat the machine gently for the first few miles to make sure oil has circulated throughout the engine and any new parts installed have started to seat.

2   Even greater care is necessary if the engine has been rebored or a new crankshaft has been installed. In the case of a rebore, the engine will have to be broken in as if the machine were new. This means greater use of the transmission and a restraining hand

30.11 Use a dial indicator to measure the output gear backlash

on the throttle until at least 500 miles have been covered. There's no point in keeping to any set speed limit - the main idea is to keep from lugging the engine and to gradually increase performance until the 500 mile mark is reached. These recommendations can be lessened to an extent when only a new crankshaft is installed. Experience is the best guide, since it's easy to tell when an engine is running freely. The following recommendations can be used as a guide:

a) *0 to 90 miles (0 to 150 km): Keep engine speed below 3,000 rpm. Turn off the engine after each hour of operation and let it cool for 5 to 10 minutes. Vary the engine speed and don't use full throttle.*

b) *90 to 300 miles (150 to 500 km): Don't run the engine for long periods above 4,000 rpm. Rev the engine freely through the gears, but don't use full throttle.*

c) *300 to 600 miles (500 to 1000 km): Don't use full throttle for prolonged periods and don't cruise at speeds above 5,000 rpm.*

d) *At 600 miles (1,000 km): Change the engine oil and filter. Full throttle can be used after this point.*

3   If a lubrication failure is suspected, stop the engine immediately and try to find the cause. If an engine is run without oil, even for a short period of time, severe damage will occur.

Chapter 3
Cooling system

Contents

Degrees of difficulty

Easy, suitable for novice with little experience		Fairly easy, suitable for beginner with some experience		Fairly difficult, suitable for competent DIY mechanic		Difficult, suitable for experienced DIY mechanic		Very difficult, suitable for expert DIY or professional	

Specifications

General

Coolant type..	See Chapter 1
Mixture ratio	See Chapter 1
Radiator cap pressure rating	
VT600..	88 to 127 kPa (0.9 to 1.3 kgf/cm², 12.8 to 18 psi)
VT750..	108 to 137 kPa (1.1 to 1.4 kgf/cm², 16 to 20 psi)
Thermostatic fan switch	
Closes circuit at	98 to 102 degrees C (208 to 216 degrees F)
Opens circuit at	93 to 97 degrees C (199 to 207 degrees F)
Coolant temperature sensor or switch resistance	
VT600 (1988 through 2000), VT750DC	
At 50 degrees C (122 degrees F)................................	130 to 180 ohms
At 80 degrees C (176 degrees F)................................	45 to 60 ohms
At 120 degrees C (248 degrees F)..............................	10 to 20 ohms
VT600 (2001 on), VT750C/CD	
112 to 118 degrees C (259 to 270 degrees F).............	Starts to close (continuity)
Below 108 degrees C (252 degrees F)	Starts to open (no continuity)

Thermostat rating

Valve opening temperature	80 to 84-degrees C (176 to 183-degrees F)
Valve fully open at	95-degrees C (203-degrees F)
Valve travel (when fully open)	Not less than 8 mm (5/16-inch)

Torque specifications

Coolant temperature sensor	10 Nm (84 in-lbs)
Filler neck flange-to-thermostat housing cover bolts	9 Nm (78 in-lbs)
Thermostat housing cover bolts	
VT600, 2004 and later VT750	10 Nm (84 in-lbs)
2003 and earlier VT750	9 Nm (78 in-lbs)
Thermostatic fan switch	
VT600, VT750DC	18 Nm (156 in-lbs)
VT750C/CD	8 Nm (70 in-lbs)
VT750C Aero, VT750C2 Spirit (2004 and later)	18 Nm (156 in-lbs)
Water pump cover bolts	13 Nm (108 in-lbs)

1 General information

The models covered by this manual are liquid-cooled. The liquid-cooling system uses a water/antifreeze mixture to carry away excess heat produced during the combustion process. The cylinders are surrounded by water jackets, through which the coolant is circulated by the water pump. The pump is mounted on the left side of the crankcase and is driven by the oil pump shaft. Coolant is pumped through a flexible hose into the front cylinder. There, it flows through the water jacket surrounding the front cylinder. Some coolant exits through a smaller diameter pipe in the head and goes to the thermostat housing; the rest exits the front cylinder through a connecting pipe to the rear cylinder, where it again flows through the rear cylinder water jacket, exits the rear cylinder through another pipe and flows through a flexible hose to the thermostat housing. From the thermostat housing, coolant flows down into the radiator (which is mounted behind the front wheel, on the front of the frame, to take advantage of maximum air flow), where it is cooled by the passing air, through another hose and back to the water pump, where the cycle is repeated.

An electric fan, mounted behind the radiator and automatically controlled by a thermostatic switch, provides a flow of cooling air through the radiator when the coolant temperature exceeds a an upper threshold.

The coolant temperature sending unit, threaded into the thermostat housing, senses the temperature of the coolant and turns on the coolant temperature warning light on the instrument cluster when the coolant temperature reaches a dangerous level.

The entire system is sealed and pressurized. The pressure is controlled by a valve which is part of the radiator cap. By pressurizing the coolant, the boiling point is raised, which prevents premature boiling of the coolant. An overflow hose, connected between the radiator and reservoir tank, directs coolant to the tank when the radiator cap valve is opened by excessive pressure. The coolant is automatically siphoned back to the radiator as the engine cools.

Many cooling system inspection and service procedures are considered part of routine maintenance and are included in Chapter 1.

 Warning 1: Do not allow antifreeze to come in contact with your skin or painted surfaces of the vehicle. Rinse off spills immediately with plenty of water. Antifreeze is highly toxic if ingested. Never leave antifreeze lying around in an open container or in puddles on the floor; children and pets are attracted by its sweet smell and may drink it. Check with local authorities about disposing of used antifreeze. Many communities have collection centers which will see that antifreeze is disposed of safely.

 Warning 2: Do not remove the radiator cap when the engine and radiator are hot. Scalding hot coolant and steam may be blown out under pressure, which could cause serious injury. To open the radiator cap, remove the rear screw from the right side panel on the inside of the fairing (if equipped). When the engine has cooled, lift up the panel and place a thick rag, like a towel, over the radiator cap; slowly rotate the cap counterclockwise to the first stop. This procedure allows any residual pressure to escape. When the steam has stopped escaping, press down on the cap while turning counterclockwise and remove it.

2 Radiator cap - check

If problems such as overheating and loss of coolant occur, check the entire system as described in Chapter 1. The radiator cap opening pressure should be checked by a dealer service department or service station equipped with the special tester required to do the job. If the cap is defective, replace it.

3.2 Loosen the hose clamp and detach the lower radiator hose from the water pump

3.4 The black two-pin connector (upper arrow) for the fan motor is on the left side, just behind the steering head (the lower arrow indicates the white turn signal connector)

3 Radiator - removal and installation

 Warning: The engine must be completely cool before beginning this procedure.

1   Set the bike on its side stand. Disconnect the cable from the negative terminal of the battery.

2   Place a drain pan under the water pump, loosen the lower radiator hose clamp at the pump, detach the hose from the pump **(see illustration)** and drain the coolant.

3   Remove the fuel tank (see Chapter 4) and the steering head covers (see Chapter 8).

4   Follow the wiring harness from the fan motor to the two-pin black electrical connector on the left side, right behind the steering head **(see illustration)**. Unplug this connector and carefully disentangle the fan motor harness so it doesn't snag other wiring when the radiator is removed.

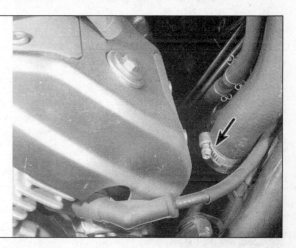

3.6 Loosen the upper radiator hose clamp and detach the upper hose from the radiator (VT600 model shown; on VT750 models, the upper hose is attached to the center of the upper backside of the radiator)

5   On VT600 models, disconnect the horn leads and remove the horn (see Chapter 9).

6   Loosen the hose clamp on the upper radiator hose **(see illustration)** and detach the hose. Loosen the hose clamp on the lower hose too, if you can. On some models, it's easier to remove the lower hose with

the radiator, because the hose clamp screw is not accessible until the radiator has been removed.

7   Remove the radiator mounting bolt from the bottom of the radiator on VT600 models or from the upper end on VT750 models **(see illustrations)**.

3.7a On VT600 models, the radiator mounting bolt is below the radiator

3.7b On VT750 models, the radiator mounting bolt is up top, directly above the radiator

3.10 On VT600 models, detach the lower radiator hose (A); remove the rubber insulators (B) if necessary

3.8 On VT600 models, seat the two rubber insulators on the upper backside of the radiator in their saddles on the frame when installing the radiator

8 Lift up the radiator and disengage the two rubber insulators on the underside of the radiator from the insulator bracket on the frame. On VT600 models, there are also two insulators located on the upper backside of the radiator **(see illustration)**.

9 Remove the radiator.

10 Detach the lower radiator hose from the radiator, if you were unable to do so earlier, and remove the grille from the radiator. On VT600 models, the radiator grille is secured to the radiator by a single screw at the upper end of the grille; on VT750 models, the grille is secured by the same bolt that attaches the radiator to the frame **(see illustration)**.

11 If the radiator is to be repaired or replaced, remove the insulators **(see illustration 3.10)** and remove the fan assembly and the thermostatic fan switch (see Section 4).

12 Carefully inspect the radiator for signs of leaks and any other damage. If repairs are necessary, take the radiator to a reputable radiator repair shop. If the radiator is clogged,

or if large amounts of rust or scale have formed, the repair shop will also do a thorough cleaning job.

13 Make sure the spaces between the cooling tubes and fins are clear. If necessary, use compressed air or running water to remove anything that may be clogging them. If the fins are bent or flattened, straighten them very carefully with a small screwdriver.

14 Inspect the radiator hoses for cracks, tears and other damage. Be sure to replace the hoses if they are damaged or deteriorated.

15 Installation is the reverse of the removal procedure.

16 Refill the cooling system with the recommended coolant (see Chapter 1).

4 Cooling fan and thermostatic fan switch - check and replacement

Check

1 If the engine is overheating and the cooling fan isn't coming on, remove the right

side cover (see Chapter 8) and check the 10A fan motor fuse (see Chapter 9). If the fuse is blown, check the fan motor circuit for a short to ground (see the *Wiring diagrams* at the end of this book). If the fuse is good, locate the fan switch at the lower right rear corner of the radiator on VT600 models **(see illustration)** or at the lower left side of the radiator on VT750 models. Warm up the engine, turn the ignition switch to OFF, unplug the electrical connector from the fan switch, ground the connector with a jumper wire, turn the ignition switch to ON and note whether the fan motor comes on. If the fan motor comes on, the fan switch is defective. If the fan motor still doesn't come on, inspect the wiring and the connectors (see *Wiring diagrams*), then check the fan motor itself.

2 To check the fan motor, remove the fuel tank (see Chapter 4), remove the steering head covers (see Chapter 8), unplug the two-wire black electrical connector **(see illustration 3.4)** and, using a pair of jumper wires connected to the battery terminals, apply battery voltage to the fan-motor side of the connector. If the fan doesn't come on, replace the fan motor. If it does come on, the problem is in the wiring on the switch side

4.1 The VT600 fan switch (arrow) is at the lower right rear corner of the radiator (radiator removed for clarity); the VT750 switch is at the lower left side of the radiator

4.3 Thermostatic fan switch test

4.6 These are the fan motor bracket bolts; one bolt secures a ground wire

4.7 Here are the fan-to-motor nut (center arrow) and the fan motor-to-bracket nuts (outer arrows)

of the connector, or the fan switch itself is defective.

3   To check the fan switch, remove the switch (see Steps 10 through 12), suspend it in a pan of water, heat the water and, using a cooking thermometer and an ohmmeter, test the switch as shown **(see illustration)**.

Warning: Antifreeze is poisonous. Don't use a cooking pan.

Note the temperature at which the switch closes the circuit and compare this to the temperature listed in this Chapter's Specifications. If the switch doesn't perform as described, replace it.

Replacement
Fan motor

Warning: The engine must be completely cool before beginning this procedure.

4   Disconnect the cable from the negative terminal of the battery.

5   Remove the radiator (see Section 8).

6   Remove the four bolts securing the fan bracket to the radiator **(see illustration)**. Note how the harnesses for the fan motor and fan switch are routed and how they're clamped to the fan bracket and to the radiator; they must be correctly rerouted before the radiator is installed. Separate the fan and bracket from the radiator.

7   Remove the nut that retains the fan to the motor shaft **(see illustration)** and remove the fan blade assembly from the motor.

8   Remove the three nuts that secure the fan motor to the bracket **(see illustration 4.7)** and detach the motor from the bracket.

9   Installation is the reverse of the removal procedure.

Thermostatic fan switch

Warning: The engine must be completely cool before beginning this procedure.

10   On VT750 models, remove the radiator (see Section 3).

11   Prepare the new switch by wrapping the threads with Teflon tape or by coating the threads with RTV sealant. Make sure there's a new O-ring on the switch.

12   Place a drain pan under the radiator and have some rags handy to soak up the coolant that will inevitably spill out. Unscrew the switch from the radiator **(see illustration 4.1)** and quickly install the new switch, tightening it to the torque listed in this Chapter's Specifications.

13   Plug the electrical connector into the switch.

14   Check and, if necessary, add coolant to the system (see Chapter 1).

---

5   Coolant temperature warning system - check and component replacement

Check
System

Note: *Before troubleshooting the coolant temperature warning system, make sure that the coolant is at the correct level (see Chapter 1) and there are no leaks in the system.*

1   The coolant temperature warning light comes on if the engine coolant exceeds its normal operating temperature. If the warning light, or the temperature sensor that turns it on, is defective, you will not know that the engine is overheating until it is too late. To determine whether the system is operating correctly, turn the ignition key to the ON position and watch the coolant temperature

warning light (located in the speedometer). It should come on for a few seconds, then go off. This verifies that the coolant temperature warning system is operating correctly on all except 2001 and later VT600 and VT750C/CD models.

2   If the coolant temperature warning light doesn't come on momentarily when the ignition key is turned to ON, or if it stays on all the time, check the system.

VT600 models (1988 through 2000)

3   Remove the fuel tank (see Chapter 4) and the left steering head cover (see Chapter 8).

4   If the coolant temperature warning light isn't coming on briefly when the ignition key is turned to ON, locate the electrical connectors for the black/brown wire and the green/black wire and unplug them. Turn the ignition key to ON and, using a voltmeter or test light, determine whether there's voltage between the black/brown wire and the green/black wires on the harness side of the connectors. If there is, replace the speedometer (see Chapter 9). If there isn't, inspect the harness side of the black/brown and green/black wiring for an open circuit or for loose connections.

5   If the temperature warning light stays on all the time, locate the electrical connector for the green/blue wire and unplug it. Using an ohmmeter, determine whether there is continuity between the harness side of the connector and ground. If there is, look for a short circuit in the green/blue wire. If there isn't, check the coolant temperature sensor.

VT600 and VT750C/CD models (2001 on)

6   Turn the ignition switch to the ON position. The temperature indicator lamp should not light. If it does, follow the wiring harness from the light to the thermosensor, checking for a break or bad connection. Make any necessary repairs and retest.

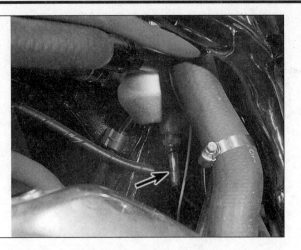

5.14 The coolant temperature sensor (arrow) is installed in the thermostat housing (VT600 shown; VT750 similar)

VT750 C/CD models (1998 through 2000), VT750DC models

7   Remove the headlight lens and reflector (see Chapter 9). (Don't remove the headlight housing, just remove the lens and reflector; the wiring for the coolant temperature sensor and the warning light is inside the headlight housing.)

8   If the coolant temperature warning light isn't coming on briefly when the ignition key is turned to ON, unplug the black six-pin electrical connector for the speedometer. Turn the ignition key to ON and, using a voltmeter or test light, determine whether there's voltage between the black/brown wire and the green/blue wires on the harness side of the connector. If there is, replace the speedometer (see Chapter 9). If there isn't, inspect the harness side of the black/brown and green/blue wires for an open circuit or for loose connections.

9   If the temperature warning light stays on all the time, unplug the black six-pin electrical connector for the speedometer. Using an ohmmeter, determine whether there is continuity between the harness side of the green/blue wire and ground. If there is, look for a short circuit in the green/blue wire. If there isn't, check the coolant temperature sensor.

Coolant temperature sensor

10   Remove the coolant temperature sensor (see Steps 12 through 14).

11   Suspend the temperature sensor in a pan of 50/50 antifreeze/water mixture (plain water will boil before it reaches the maximum test temperature). Heat the water and test the sensor with a cooking thermometer and an ohmmeter **(see illustration 4.3)**.

> ⚠ **Warning: Antifreeze is poisonous. Don't use the pan or thermometer for cooking after this test.**

Note the temperature at which the resistance changes and compare your observations to the sensor resistance listed in this Chapter's Specifications. If the sensor doesn't operate as specified, replace it.

Replacement

Coolant temperature sensor

> ⚠ **Warning: The engine must be completely cool before beginning this procedure.**

12   Drain the coolant (see Chapter 1).
13   Prepare the new coolant temperature

sensor by wrapping the threads with Teflon tape or by coating the threads with RTV sealant.

14   Unscrew the coolant temperature sensor **(see illustration)** from the thermostat housing.

15   Install the new sensor and tighten it to the torque listed in this Chapter's Specifications.

16   Reconnect the electrical connector to the sensor.

17   Refill the cooling system (see Chapter 1).

Speedometer

18   Refer to Chapter 9.

6   Thermostat - removal, check and installation

Removal

> ⚠ **Warning: The engine must be completely cool before beginning this procedure.**

1   If the thermostat is functioning correctly, the engine should warm up quickly, within a few minutes (unless the temperature is cold), and should not overheat (indicated by the coolant temperature warning light coming on). If the engine does not reach normal operating temperature quickly, or if it overheats, the thermostat should be removed, checked and, if necessary, replaced.

2   Remove the fuel tank (see Chapter 4) and the steering head covers (see Chapter 8).

3   On VT600 models, remove the air cleaner housing cover and filter element (see Chapter 1) and remove the air cleaner housing (see Chapter 4).

4   Drain the cooling system (see Chapter 1).

5   Detach the siphon tube **(see illustration)** from the radiator filler neck. Remove

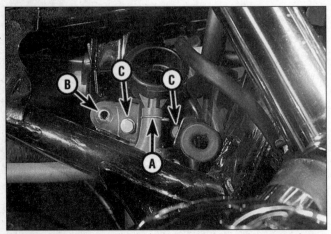

6.5a Remove the siphon tube (A), the filler neck-to-bracket bolt (B) and the flange-to-cover bolts (C) (one bolt hidden)

6.5b Detach the radiator filler neck flange from the thermostat housing and remove the O-ring (thermostat housing assembly removed for clarity)

6.6 Remove the thermostat housing cover bolts (arrows) and lift off the cover

6.7 Note how the thermostat is installed, then remove it and discard the old O-ring

the bolt that secures the filler neck flange to the filler neck bracket and the two bolts that secure the flange to the thermostat housing cover. Separate the filler neck flange from the housing cover **(see illustration)** and discard the old O-ring.

6 Remove the thermostat housing cover bolts **(see illustration)** and remove the cover.

7 Note how the thermostat is oriented in the thermostat housing **(see illustration)**, then remove it from the housing and discard the old O-ring.

Check

8 Remove any coolant deposits, then visually check the thermostat for corrosion, cracks and other damage. If it was open when it was removed, it is defective. Check the O-ring for cracks and other damage.

9 To check the thermostat's operation, submerge it in a container of water along with a thermometer **(see illustration)**.

 Warning: Antifreeze is poisonous. Don't use a cooking pan.

The thermostat should be suspended so it does not touch the container.

10 Gradually heat the water in the container with a hot plate or stove and check the temperature when the thermostat first starts to open. Continue heating the water and check the temperature when the thermostat is fully open.

11 Compare your results to the specified thermostat opening temperature range listed in this Chapter's Specifications.

12 If the thermostat does not open as described, replace it.

Installation

13 Install the thermostat into the housing, spring end first **(see illustration 6.7)**.

14 Install a new O-ring in the groove in the thermostat housing.

15 Place the cover on the housing, install the cover screws and tighten them to the torque listed in this Chapter's Specifications.

16 Install a new O-ring on the filler neck flange.

17 Attach the filler neck flange to the thermostat housing cover, install the flange-to-cover bolts and tighten them to the torque listed in this Chapter's Specifications.

18 Reattach the filler neck flange to the frame bracket and tighten the bolt securely.

19 Reattach the siphon tube to the radiator filler neck. If the wire retainer is fatigued, replace it.

20 On VT600 models, install the air cleaner housing (see Chapter 4), the filter element and the air cleaner housing cover (see Chapter 1).

21 Install the steering head covers (see Chapter 8) and the fuel tank (see Chapter 4).

22 Fill the cooling with the recommended coolant (see Chapter 1).

7 Thermostat housing - removal and installation

 Warning: The engine must be completely cool before beginning this procedure.

1 Remove the fuel tank (see Chapter 4) and the steering head covers (see Chapter 8).

2 On VT600 models, remove the air cleaner housing cover and filter element (see

6.9 Heat the thermostat in a pan of water and note the temperatures when it starts to open and when it's fully open

Must be completely submerged.

They must not touch the container sides or bottom

8.2 The VT600 coolant reservoir is under the swingarm, behind the engine; the lower hose (arrow) is the siphon tube . . .

8.6 . . . and the upper hose (arrow) is the overflow tube

8.7a On VT600 models, remove the filler neck retaining nut (arrow) . . .

8.7b . . . the reservoir retaining bolt (arrow) . . .

8.7c . . . and pull this positioning pin out of its grommet in the frame and remove the reservoir (engine removed for clarity)

Chapter 1) and remove the air cleaner housing (see Chapter 4).
3   Drain the cooling system (see Chapter 1).

4   Unplug the electrical lead from the coolant temperature sensor **(see illustration 5.13)**.
5   Detach the siphon tube from the radiator filler neck and remove the bolt that secures the filler neck flange to the filler neck bracket **(see illustration 6.5a)**.
6   Loosen the hose clamps and detach both hoses from the thermostat housing.
7   Remove the thermostat housing.
8   Installation is the reverse of removal.
9   Fill the cooling system with the recommended coolant (see Chapter 1).

8 Coolant reservoir - removal and installation

1   Drain the cooling system (see Chapter 1).
2   On VT600 models, the coolant reservoir **(see illustration)** is located behind the engine, below the swingarm pivot bolt and (on California models) in front of the evaporative

canister. Raise the motorcycle under the rear part of the frame and support it securely with jackstands.
3   On VT600 California models, remove the evaporative canister (see Chapter 4).
4   On VT750 models, the coolant reservoir is located ahead of the engine, behind and below the radiator.
5   On VT750 models, remove the radiator (see Section 3).
6   Place a container under the reservoir to catch spilled coolant. Detach the siphon tube **(see illustration 8.2)** and the overflow tube **(see illustration)**.
7   On VT600 models, remove the filler neck retaining nut **(see illustration)** and the reservoir retaining bolt **(see illustration)** and detach the reservoir position pin from the grommet in the frame **(see illustration)**.
8   On VT750 models, remove the reservoir retaining bolt and the filler neck retaining nut.
9   Remove the reservoir.
10   Installation is the reverse of removal. Be sure to fill the cooling system when you're done (see Chapter 1).

9.1 If coolant is leaking from the weep hole (arrow), replace the water pump

9.5 Remove the hold-down bolts (A) and cover bolts (B) and lift off the cover

9 Water pump - check, removal and installation

Check

Note: *The water pump on these models can't be overhauled - it must be replaced as a unit.*

1 Inspect the area around the water pump for coolant leaks. Try to determine whether the leak is simply the result of a loose hose clamp or deteriorated hose, or whether it's leaking from a damaged pump cover O-ring or from the "weep hole" (coolant drainage passage) in the underside of the pump body **(see illustration)**.

2 If the leak appears to be caused by a loose hose clamp, tighten the clamp, clean up the area, ride the bike and verify that the leak has been fixed. If the leak appears to be caused by a damaged hose, drain the coolant (see Chapter 1) and replace the hose. If the pump is leaking from a bad cover O-ring, replace the O-ring. If the pump is leaking from the weep hole, replace the pump.

3 If there is any sign of oil in the area

9.8 Locate the cover dowels (arrows); install a new O-ring if the old one is damaged

around the water pump, the pump housing O-ring may be damaged. Remove the pump and replace the pump housing O-ring.

Removal, inspection and O-ring replacement

4 Remove the engine (see Chapter 2).

5 To inspect the pump cover or the impeller, or to replace the pump cover O-ring,

remove the cover bolts **(see illustration)** and separate the cover from the water pump body.

6 Try to wiggle the water pump impeller back-and-forth and in-and-out. If you can feel movement, the water pump must be replaced.

7 Inspect the impeller blades for corrosion. If they are heavily corroded, replace the water pump and flush the system thoroughly (it would also be a good idea to check the internal condition of the radiator).

8 If the cause of the leak was a defective cover O-ring, remove the old O-ring **(see illustration)** and install a new one.

9 Install the pump cover and tighten the pump cover bolts to the torque listed in this Chapter's Specifications.

10 If the pump housing O-ring or the pump itself must be replaced, remove the pump from the engine by pulling it straight out **(see illustration)**.

Installation

11 Before installing the pump, smear a little engine oil on the pump housing O-ring.

9.10 Remove the pump hold-down bolts and pull the pump straight out; use a new O-ring (arrow) on installation

9.12a When installing the water pump, make sure that this slot in the pump shaft . . .

9.12b . . . is aligned with this ridge on the end of the oil pump shaft

12 The water pump is driven off the left end of the oil pump shaft. Make sure the slot in the pump shaft is engaged properly with the ridge on the end of the oil pump shaft **(see illustrations)**.

13 Install the engine (see Chapter 2).

14 Fill the cooling system with the recommended coolant (see Chapter 1), ride the bike and check for leaks.

Chapter 4
Fuel and exhaust systems

Contents

Degrees of difficulty

| **Easy,** suitable for novice with little experience | | **Fairly easy,** suitable for beginner with some experience | | **Fairly difficult,** suitable for competent DIY mechanic | | **Difficult,** suitable for experienced DIY mechanic | | **Very difficult,** suitable for expert DIY or professional | |

Specifications

Carburetors

VT600 models (1988 through 1998)

Type
    Except California... VDFDA
    California... VDFEA
Float level .... 7.0 mm (0.28 inch)
Main jet.. 115
Slow jet.. 40
Pilot screw adjustment
    Initial opening... 1-1/4 turns out
    Final opening... 1 turn out
    High altitude adjustment .... 1/2 turn in (from low altitude setting)

Carburetors (continued)

VT600 models (1999 on)

Type
  Except California... VE5AC
  California.. VE5AB
Float level .... 18.5 mm (0.73 inch)
Main jet 125
Slow jet 45
Pilot screw adjustment
  Initial opening
    Except California .... 3 turns out
    California.. 2-3/4 turns out
  Final opening .... 3/4 turn out

VT750C/CD models

Type
  1998
    49 states .... VDFFG
    California.. VDFEB
    Canada (VT750C/CD/CD2)... VDFFG
    Canada (VT750C3/CD3)... VDFFJ
  1999 on
    Except California .... VDFFJ
    California.. VDFEC
Float level .... 7.0 mm (0.28 inch)
Main jet
  Front carburetor 105
  Rear carburetor 110
Slow jet 40
Pilot screw adjustment
  Initial opening.. 2-1/4 turns out
  Final opening .... 1 turn out

VT750DC models

Type
  Except California... VDF2D
  California.. VDF2C
Float level .... 7.0 mm (0.28 inch)
Main jet
  Front carburetor 05
  Rear carburetor 108
Slow jet.. 40
Pilot screw adjustment
  Initial opening.. 2-3/8 turns out
  Final opening.. 1/2 turn out
  High altitude setting .... 1/2 turn in (from low altitude setting)

VT750C Aero (2004 and later)

Type
  Except California
    2004 through 2007 .... VE5BA
    2008.. VE5EA
  California
    2004 through 2007 .... VE5BB
    2008.. VE5EB
Float level .... 18.5 mm (0.73 inch)
Main jet
  Standard
    2004 through 2007 125
    2008.. 122
  High altitude
    2004 through 2007 122
    2008.. 120
Pilot screw adjustment
  Initial opening
    2004 through 2007 .... 2-3/4 turns out
    2008
      Except California.. 2 turns out
      California.. 2-1/8 turns out

Final opening
    2000 through 2007 .... 1/2 turn out from lean drop setting
    2008 .... 1/4 turn out from lean drop setting

VT750C2 Spirit (2007 and later)
Type
    Except California VE5EA
    California VE5EB
Float level .... 18.5 mm (0.73 inch)
Main jet
    Standard 122
    High altitude 120
Pilot screw adjustment
    Initial opening
        Except California .... 2 turns out
        California .... 2-1/8 turns out
    Final opening .... 1/4 turn out from lean drop setting

Fuel pump
Discharge volume (minimum)
    VT600 .... 800 cc (27.1 fl oz) per minute
    VT750 .... 900 cc (30.4 fl oz) per minute

Torque specifications
Fuel tank mounting bolt
    2003 and earlier .... 19 Nm (14 ft-lbs)
    2004 and later .... 27 Nm (20 ft-lbs)
Fuel valve nut
    VT600
        1988 through 1998 .... 23 Nm (17 ft-lbs)
        1999 on .... 35 Nm (26 ft-lbs)
    VT750 .... 34 Nm (25 ft-lbs)

2.3 Remove the fuel tank mounting bolt and bushing; inspect the rubber grommet and replace it if it's damaged

2.4 If you're planning to clean or replace the fuel tank on a VT600, remove the fuel valve knob retaining screw and remove the knob

1 General information

The fuel system consists of the fuel tank, the fuel valve, the fuel pump, the fuel filter, the carburetors, the hoses connecting these components, and the accelerator cables.

The carburetors used on these motorcycles are Keihins with butterfly-type throttle valves. All except 1999 and later VT600 models use twin carburetors. VT600 models from 1999 on use a single carburetor equipped with an accelerator pump. For cold starting, an enrichment circuit is actuated by a choke knob mounted on the left side of the bike.

The exhaust system routes the exhaust gases through a pair of exhaust pipes and mufflers on the right side of the bike.

Some of the fuel system service procedures are included in Chapter 1 as routine maintenance items.

2 Fuel tank - removal and installation

⚠ **Warning: Gasoline (petrol) is extremely flammable, so take extra precautions when you work on any part of the fuel system. Don't smoke or allow open flames or bare light bulbs near the work area, and don't work in a garage where a gas-type appliance (such as a water heater or clothes dryer) is present. If you spill any fuel on your skin, rinse it off immediately with soap and water. When you perform any kind of work on the fuel system, wear safety glasses and have a fire extinguisher suitable for class B fires (flammable liquids) on hand.**

2.5 Lift the tank slightly, back off the wire retainers and detach the fuel hoses from the fuel valve

1   Support the bike securely so it can't be knocked over during this procedure.
2   Remove the seat (see Chapter 8). If the motorcycle has a tank-mounted speedometer, remove it (see Chapter 9).
3   Remove the fuel tank hold-down bolt and bushing (see illustration). Inspect the rubber grommet. If it's cracked, torn or deteriorated, replace it.
4   If necessary, remove the fuel valve knob retaining screw (see illustration) and remove the knob.
5   Hold a pan under the fittings to catch drained fuel, lift up the tank and disconnect the fuel hoses from the fuel tap (see illustration).
6   Remove the tank from the bike.

⚠ **Warning: Pour the drained fuel into a safe fuel storage container. Don't leave it in the drain pan.**

7   If you're going to have the tank professionally cleaned, or if you're going to replace it, unscrew the fuel valve nut and remove the fuel valve, the O-ring and the strainer. Discard the old O-ring.
8   Clean the fuel strainer screen thoroughly and inspect it. If the strainer is clogged, torn or otherwise damaged, replace it.

9   Install the strainer, a new O-ring and the fuel valve in the tank and tighten the fuel valve nut securely.
10   Before installing the tank, inspect the fuel hoses and the rubber tank insulators on the frame (see illustration). If the hoses or insulators are cracked, hardened, or otherwise deteriorated, replace them.

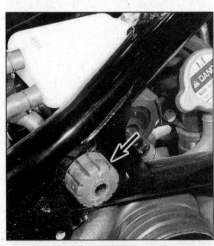

2.10 Inspect the rubber tank insulators; if they're damaged, replace them

2.11 The square hole in the fuel valve knob aligns with the square lug on the fuel valve shaft

2.12 If the fuel tank is correctly seated on the rubber insulators, the hole in the bracket for the hold-down bolt will be aligned with the bolt hole in the frame

11   If you removed the fuel valve knob on a VT600 model, install it and tighten the knob retaining screw securely. Make sure that the square hole in the knob is aligned with the square lug on the fuel valve shaft (see illustration).

12   Installation is the reverse of removal. Make sure the tank is correctly seated on the rubber insulators (see illustration) and make sure it doesn't pinch any control cables or wire harnesses.

3   Fuel tank - cleaning and repair

1   All repairs to the fuel tank should be carried out by a professional who has experience in this critical and potentially dangerous work. Even after cleaning and flushing of the fuel system, explosive fumes can remain and ignite during repair of the tank.

2   If the fuel tank is removed from the vehicle, it should not be placed in an area where sparks or open flames could ignite the fumes coming out of the tank. Be especially careful inside garages where a gas-type appliance is located, because it could cause an explosion.

4   Crankcase emission control system - description, check and component replacement

Description

1   The closed crankcase emission control system prevents crankcase emissions from escaping into the atmosphere by routing blow-by gas from the rear cylinder head through a hose into the crankcase breather separator (see illustration). Blow-by gas is routed from the separator through another hose to the air cleaner housing, where it's mixed with fresh intake air. Finally, the blow-by is drawn into the intake ducts, through the carburetors and into the combustion chamber, where it is burned.

Check

2   Inspect the condition of the system hoses (see illustration). Make sure that there are no cuts or tears in the hoses and all connections are tight. If the hoses are worn or damaged, replace them.

3   Inspect the condition of the crankcase breather separator (see illustration 4.1). If it's cracked, deteriorated or otherwise damaged, replace it.

4.1 VT600 emission control components (VT750 similar)

A   Crankcase breather separator
B   Carburetor air vent control valve (California models)
C   Purge control valve (California models)

4.2 Inspect the crankcase emission control system hoses from the rear cylinder head cover to the separator and from the separator to the air cleaner housing (arrows)

4.4 To detach the crankcase breather separator from the bike, remove this hold-down screw

4.5 Lift up the separator slightly and detach the drain tube (arrow) from the front of the separator

Component replacement

4 Remove the crankcase breather separator hold-down screw **(see illustration)** and lift up the separator.

5 Disconnect the drain tube from the separator **(see illustration)**.

6 Disconnect the inlet and outlet hoses from the separator **(see illustration)**.

7 Installation is the reverse of removal.

8 If you're replacing any of the three hoses, carefully note how they're routed before removing them and route the new hose(s) exactly the same way.

---

5 Evaporative emission control system (California models) - description, check and component replacement

Description

1 On California models, an evaporative emission control (EVAP) system captures raw hydrocarbon vapors from the carburetor float bowls and the fuel tank when the engine is not running. The vapors are stored in a canister located below the swingarm **(see illustration)**. When the engine is started, these vapors are routed from the canister into the combustion chambers and burned.

2 The EVAP system is controlled by the carburetor air vent (CAV) control valve and the purge control valve **(see illustration 4.1)**. When the engine is started, both valves are opened by intake vacuum. Vacuum from the front intake opens the carburetor air vent valve, venting the carburetor float bowls through the air vent valve to the canister; vacuum from the rear intake opens the purge control valve, drawing vapors from the canister through the purge control valve into the intakes. When the engine is turned off, intake vacuum is cut, closing the valves.

3 When the fuel inside the carburetor float bowls heats up, vapors from the float bowls are pushed into the canister. When fuel inside the fuel tank heats up, vapors from the fuel tank are pushed into the canister. These vapors are stored in the canister until the next time the engine is started.

4 Periodically, inspect the hoses connecting the canister, the carburetor air vent control valve and the purge control valve and the intakes.

Check and component replacement

5 Remove the fuel tank (see Section 2).

6 Remove the left side cover (see Chapter 8) and refer to the vacuum hose routing diagram on the inside of the cover for the following inspection and component tests.

7 Make sure that all the hose connections are tight, the hoses are in good condition and none of the hoses are kinked. If any of the hoses are torn, frayed or otherwise deteriorated, replace them.

Carburetor air vent control valve

Note: *You will need a vacuum pump/gauge and a pressure pump/gauge to do the following test. If you don't have these tools, have the carburetor air vent control valve checked by a dealer service department.*

8 Mark the four hoses attached to the carburetor air vent control valve to ensure correct reassembly, then disconnect all four

4.6 Detach the hoses from the rear of the separator

5.1 The evaporative emission control (EVAP) system canister (arrow) is located behind and below the engine

5.8a To detach the carburetor air vent control valve, detach the hose from the air vent port . . .

5.8b . . . lift up the valve, label the other hoses and detach them from the valve

AIR VENT PORT

No. 6 HOSE
(to air joint pipe at carburetor)

No. 4 HOSE
(to canister)

No. 10 HOSE
(to carburetor for front cylinder)

2312 4-5.9 HAYNES

5.9 The carburetor air vent control valve (California models)

hoses from the carburetor air vent control valve (see illustrations) and remove the valve.

9   Connect a hand-held vacuum pump/gauge to the port for the No. 10 hose (see illustration), which goes to the carburetor for the front cylinder. Apply 250 mm Hg (9.8 in-Hg) and verify that the valve holds vacuum. If it doesn't, replace the valve.

10   Connect the vacuum pump/gauge to the air vent port (on top of the valve), apply 250 mm Hg (9.8 in-Hg) and verify that the valve holds vacuum. If it doesn't, replace the valve.

11   Reconnect the vacuum pump/gauge to the port for the No. 10 hose and connect a pressure pump/gauge to the air vent port. Plug the port for the No. 4 hose (which goes to the canister), apply 250 mm Hg (9.8 in-Hg) vacuum to the No. 10 port, pump some air into the air vent port and verify that air exits from the port for the No. 6 hose (which goes to the air joint pipe at the carburetors). If it doesn't, replace the valve.

12   If the carburetor air vent control valve fails to perform as described, replace it. Make sure that the hoses are reattached to

the valve as indicated by the vacuum hose routing diagram label on the left side cover. Install the left side cover and the fuel tank.

Purge control valve

Note: *You will need a vacuum pump/gauge and a pressure pump/gauge to do the following tests. If you don't have these tools, have*

the purge control valve checked by a dealer service department.

13   Mark the three hoses attached to the purge control valve to ensure correct reassembly, then disconnect all three hoses from the purge control valve and remove the valve.

14   Connect a hand-held vacuum pump/gauge to the port for the No. 5 hose (see illustration), which goes to the three-way joint. Apply 250 mm Hg (9.8 in-Hg) vacuum and verify that the valve holds this vacuum. If it doesn't, replace the valve.

15   Disconnect the vacuum pump from the No. 5 port and connect it to the port for the No. 11 hose (which goes to the carburetor for the rear cylinder). Apply 250 mm Hg (9.8 in-Hg) vacuum and verify that the valve holds the vacuum. If it doesn't, replace the valve.

16   Connect a hand-held pressure pump/gauge to the port for the No. 4 hose (which goes to the canister). Apply 250 mm Hg (9.8 in-Hg) vacuum to the No. 11 port and pump air into the No. 4 port. Air should flow through the valve and out the No. 5 port for the three-way joint hose. If it doesn't, replace the valve.

No. 5 HOSE
(to 3-way joint at carburetors)

No. 4 HOSE
(to canister)

No. 11 HOSE
(to carburetor for rear cylinder)

2312 4-5.14 HAYNES

5.14 The purge control valve (California models)

6.3 To detach the air cleaner housing from the air intake chamber on a VT600 model, loosen this hose clamp (right arrow) that secures the housing to the air intake chamber and remove these two bolts (left arrows)

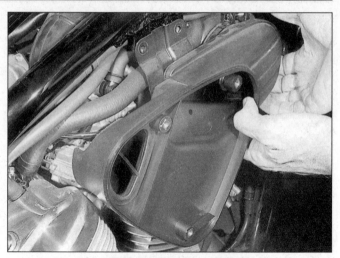

6.5a Pull off the air cleaner housing . . .

6.5b . . . and detach the crankcase breather separator hose from the backside of the housing (VT600 model shown)

7.1 Pull down this coolant hose to expose the sub-air cleaner cover, then detach the small hose from the carburetor and remove the cover retaining screw (arrows) (VT600 models)

17   If the purge control valve fails to perform as described, replace it. Make sure that the hoses are reattached to the valve as indicated by the vacuum hose routing diagram label on the left side cover. Install the left side cover and the fuel tank.

6   Air cleaner housing - removal and installation

1   Remove the fuel tank (see Section 2).
2   Remove the air cleaner housing cover and the air filter element (see Chapter 1). **Note:** *It's not necessary to remove the housing cover and filter element in order to remove the air cleaner housing. But if you're planning to disassemble the air cleaner housing assembly, it's easier to remove the cover*

and filter while the housing is still installed. Of course, if you're simply removing the air cleaner housing assembly in order to reach the sub-air cleaner element, the air cleaner chamber, the carburetors or the engine, then skip this step.
3   Remove the big hose clamp that secures the air cleaner housing to the air cleaner chamber **(see illustration)**.
4   Remove the air cleaner housing mounting bolts.
5   Pull the air cleaner housing away from the bike and detach the crankcase breather separator hose from the housing **(see illustrations)**.
6   Installation is the reverse of removal. Before reconnecting the air cleaner housing to the air intake chamber on VT600 models, apply a light coat of sealant to the area where the air cleaner housing fits onto the air intake

chamber. Before reconnecting the air cleaner housing to the air intake chamber on VT750 models, apply a little grease to the inside of the big hose clamp, and make sure that the positioning pin on the backside of the housing is correctly aligned with the grommet on the front cylinder head fin.

7   Sub-air cleaner element (dual-carburetor models) - removal and installation

1   If you're working on a VT600, remove the air cleaner housing (see Section 6). Detach the hose between the carburetor and the sub-air cleaner cover and remove the cover retaining screw **(see illustration)**.
2   If you're working on a VT750, remove the fuel tank (see Section 2).

7.3 Pull off the sub-air cleaner cover (VT600 shown; VT750 similar)

7.4 Remove the filter element from the sub-air cleaner cover (VT600 shown; VT750 similar)

8.4a On VT600 models, loosen the hose clamp screw for the left intake duct at the rear cylinder carburetor . . .

8.4b . . . loosen the hose clamp screw for the right intake duct at the front cylinder carburetor . . .

3   Remove the sub-air cleaner cover **(see illustration)**.
4   Remove the filter element from the sub-air cleaner cover **(see illustration)**.
5   Wash the element thoroughly in non-flammable or high-flash-point solvent, squeeze it out and allow it to dry thoroughly.
6   Soak the element in gear oil (SAE 80/90) and squeeze out the excess.
7   Installation is the reverse of removal.

8.4c . . . and loosen the hose clamp screw for the right intake duct at the air intake chamber

8   Air intake chamber and intake ducts - removal and installation

1   Remove the fuel tank (see Section 2).
2   Remove the air cleaner housing (see Section 6).

VT600 models (1988 through 1998)

3   Remove the sub-air cleaner element (see Section 7).
4   Loosen the three intake duct hose clamp screws **(see illustrations)**.
5   Detach the air intake chamber drain

8.5 On VT600 models, detach the air intake chamber drain tube from the frame

8.6 On VT600 models, detach this sub-air cleaner hose from the left carburetor to allow more clearance for removing the air intake chamber

8.7 To protect the hoses and wires from damage on VT600 models, remove the three air intake hose clamps before removing the air intake chamber

8.8 On VT600 models, detach the right air intake duct from the air intake chamber

tube from the frame (see illustration).

6   Disconnect the sub-air cleaner hose from the left carburetor to provide clearance for removing the left intake duct (see illustration).

7   Pull off the hose clamps so they don't cut any hoses or wires or snag on something when the air intake chamber is removed (see illustration).

8   Disconnect the right air intake duct from

the air intake chamber (see illustration).

9   Remove the air intake chamber and left duct (see illustration).

10   Installation is the reverse of removal. Make sure that the coolant hoses and the hoses for the crankcase emission control system, the evaporative emission control system (California models), the air cleaner housing and the sub-air cleaner element are correctly routed around the air intake chamber and intake ducts (see illustrations). Make sure that none of the hoses are kinked, pinched or pulled loose.

VT600 models (1999 on)

11   Remove the air cleaner housing (see Section 6).

12   Disconnect the front cylinder's spark plug wire (see Chapter 1 if necessary).

13   Detach the air cleaner chamber from the mounting boss and remove it from the left side of the frame.

8.9 On VT600 models, remove the air intake chamber from the left side

8.10a When installing the air intake chamber and air intake ducts on VT600 models, make sure that the coolant hoses . . .

8.10b . . . and emission hoses are routed as shown; make sure none of the hoses are kinked or pinched or accidentally disconnected

14   Installation is the reverse of the removal steps.

VT750 models

15   Loosen the two intake duct hose clamp screws.
16   Pull out the air intake chamber.
17   Disconnect the breather tube from the air intake chamber.
18   Remove the air intake chamber.
19   Installation is the reverse of removal.

9   Fuel pump system (dual-carburetor models) - check and component replacement

1   On VT600 models, remove the seat; on VT750 models, remove the right side cover (see Chapter 8).

System check

2   Make sure that the ignition switch is off before proceeding.
3   Locate the white three-pin fuel pump relay connector **(see illustration)**. On VT600 models, the fuel pump relay connector is located to the left of the fuel pump, behind the fuel filter; on VT750 models, it's on the right side of the bike, right above the coil. All fuel pump relay connectors have a black wire, a black/blue wire and either a yellow wire (1988 and 1989 VT600 models) or a yellow/blue wire (all other models). (Neither the yellow nor the yellow/blue wires are part of any of the following tests.)
4   Connect the positive lead of a voltmeter to the terminal for the black wire on the harness side of the fuel pump relay connector and connect the negative voltmeter lead to ground. Turn the ignition switch key to the On position and verify that there is battery voltage.

5   If there is no voltage, check the black wire for a loose connection or an open circuit.
6   If there is voltage, check the black/blue wire for continuity.
7   Connect the leads of an ohmmeter to the terminal for the black/blue wire on the harness side of the fuel pump relay connector and to ground and check for continuity between the black/blue wire and ground.
8   If there is continuity, replace the fuel pump relay.
9   If there is no continuity, jump the terminals for the black and the black/blue wires on the wire harness side of the fuel pump relay connector, unplug the white two-pin fuel pump connector **(see illustration)**. On VT600 models, this connector is located to the right of the fuel pump; on VT750 models, it's located on the right side of the bike (it's the inner connector of a bank of connectors, including a black connector and a green connector). Connect the leads of a voltmeter to

9.3 The VT600 fuel pump relay and connector (arrows) are located under the seat, to the left of the fuel pump

9.9 The VT600 fuel pump connector (white, two-pin) is located to the right of the fuel pump

9.15 Don't confuse the fuel pump inlet and outlet ports (VT600 shown; VT750 similar)

1 *Inlet port (marked by IN above port)*
2 *Outlet port*

the harness side of the fuel pump connector, turn the ignition switch to On and verify that there is voltage at the connector.
10   If there no voltage, check the black/blue wire and the green wire for a loose connection or an open circuit.
11   If there is voltage, replace the fuel pump.

Fuel pump discharge volume check

12   The fuel pump system may check out okay but still be delivering poor performance. If the engine lacks power or accelerates poorly, the fuel pump may be wearing out. Check the fuel pump discharge volume as follows.
13   Unplug the white three-pin fuel pump relay connector **(see illustration 9.3)**.
14   Jump the terminals for the black and the black/blue wires with a suitable jumper wire.
15   There are two fuel hoses attached to the fuel pump **(see illustration)**. Disconnect the *outlet* hose (NOT the hose between the fuel filter and the fuel pump, but the other hose).

16   Put this hose into a graduated beaker. Turn the ignition switch to On for five seconds then turn it Off. To determine the fuel pump discharge volume per minute, multiply by 12. Compare your measurement to the minimum fuel pump discharge volume listed in this Chapter's Specifications.
17   If the pump fails to deliver the minimum discharge volume, replace it.

Replacement

18   On VT600 models, remove the seat; on VT750 models, remove the right side cover (see Chapter 8).

Fuel pump relay

19   Locate the fuel pump relay. On VT600 models, it's to the left, and slightly to the rear, of the fuel pump **(see illustration 9.3)**. On VT750 models, it's on the right side of the bike, right above the coil for the rear cylinder.
20   Unplug the fuel pump relay electrical connector **(see illustration 9.3)**.
21   Remove the relay from its mounting bracket.
22   Installation is the reverse of removal.

Fuel pump

23   Unplug the fuel pump electrical connector **(see illustration 9.9)**.
24   Loosen the fuel line clamps and push the ends of the fuel lines off the pump fittings **(see illustration 9.15)**.
25   Disengage the fuel pump from its rubber mounting bracket **(see illustration)** and lift it up.
26   Disconnect the fuel pump tube from the pump and remove the pump.
27   Installation is the reverse of removal. Don't forget to reattach the fuel pump tube before installing the pump in its mounting bracket, and make sure that the hose between the fuel filter and the pump is attached to the inlet port, marked IN.

---

10 Throttle cables and grip - removal, installation and adjustment

Removal

1   Loosen the throttle cable adjuster (see Section 9 in Chapter 1).
2   Back off the throttle cable-to-switch housing locknuts **(see illustration)**.
3   Remove the handlebar switch retaining screws. Separate the halves of the handlebar switch and detach the throttle cables from the throttle grip pulley **(see illustrations)**.
4   On VT600 models, remove the throttle linkage cover **(see illustration)**.
5   On VT600 models, remove the bracket for the throttle linkage cover and detach the throttle cable bracket from the left carburetor **(see illustrations)**. It's not absolutely necessary to detach the throttle cable bracket to replace the cable(s), but it's easier to disengage the cables from the bracket after it's detached. Note also that the choke knob is attached to the throttle cable bracket. It's not

9.25 To disengage the VT600 fuel pump from its rubber mounting bracket, simply lift it up, then disconnect the fuel pump tube and remove the pump

10.2 Before opening up the switch housing, back off the throttle cable-to-switch housing locknuts (arrows) (VT600 shown, VT750 similar)

10.3a Remove the switch housing retaining screws from the underside of the lower half of the housing, then open up the switch housing

10.3b Disengage the upper ends of both cables from the throttle grip pulley

10.4 On VT600 models, remove the throttle linkage cover screw (arrow) and remove the cover

10.5a On VT600 models, remove the two throttle linkage cover screws, remove the bracket . . .

10.5b . . . remove the decelerator cable protector (small clear plastic tube) . . .

necessary to detach the choke knob from the bracket unless you're removing the carburetors (see Section 12) or servicing the starting

enrichment valves (see Section 13).
6   On VT750 models, remove the throttle cable bracket screws and detach the throttle

cable bracket from the left carburetor.
7   Detach the throttle cables from the throttle pulley at the carburetors **(see illustration)**.

10.5c . . . remove the accelerator cable bracket screws and remove the accelerator cable bracket

10.7 Disengage the lower ends of both cables from the throttle pulley

10.11 Make sure that the upper cable ends are correctly engaged with the throttle grip pulley

Note how the cables are routed, then remove them.

8   Slide the throttle grip off the handlebar.

Installation

9   Clean the end of the handlebar and the inside of the throttle grip, apply a light coat of multi-purpose grease to both surfaces and install the twist grip on the handlebar. Verify that it turns freely and smoothly with no binding or rough spots.

10   Route the cables exactly the same way they were routed prior to removal. Make sure they don't interfere with other components and are not kinked or sharply angled.

11   Lubricate the ends of the accelerator and decelerator cables with multi-purpose grease and connect them to the throttle pulleys at the carburetors and at the throttle grip. Make sure that the cable ends are correctly engaged with the pulleys **(see illustration)**.

12   On VT600 models, install the throttle cable bracket, the throttle linkage cover bracket and the throttle linkage cover. Tighten the screws securely.

13   On VT750 models, install the throttle cable bracket. Tighten the screws securely.

Adjustment

14   Adjust the throttle cables (see Section 9 in Chapter 1).

15   Turn the handlebars back and forth to make sure the cables don't cause the steering to bind. With the engine idling, turn the handlebars back and forth and make sure idle speed doesn't change. If it does, find and fix the cause before riding the motorcycle.

11 Carburetor overhaul - general information

1   Poor engine performance, hesitation, hard starting, stalling, flooding and backfiring are all signs that major carburetor maintenance may be required.

2   Keep in mind that many so-called carburetor problems are really not carburetor problems at all, but engine mechanical problems or ignition system malfunctions. Try to verify that the carburetors need to be serviced before beginning a major overhaul.

3   Before assuming that a carburetor overhaul is required, inspect the fuel filter; the fuel lines; the crankcase emission control system hoses; the evaporative emission control system hoses (California models); all vacuum hoses; the hose clamps and connections for the air intake chamber and intake ducts; the air filter element; the sub-air cleaner element; the cylinder compression; the spark plugs; the carburetor synchronization; and the fuel pump.

4   Most carburetor problems are caused by dirt particles, varnish and other deposits which accumulate in, and eventually clog, fuel and air passages. Also, gaskets and O-rings shrink or deteriorate, causing fuel and air leaks which lead to poor performance.

5   A carburetor overhaul consists of disassembly, cleaning, reassembly and adjustments. Completely disassemble both carburetors, clean all parts thoroughly with a carburetor cleaning solvent, then dry them with filtered, unlubricated, compressed air. Blow out the fuel and air passages with compressed air to force out any dirt that may have been loosened but not removed by the solvent. Finally, reassemble the carburetors, using new gaskets, O-rings and, if necessary, a new float valve and seat.

6   Before getting started, make sure that you have the correct carburetor rebuild kit with all the necessary O-rings and other parts, carburetor cleaner, some clean shop rags, an air compressor and a place to work. If you don't have a compressor, buy a couple of cans of compressed air (the type used for cleaning computer keyboards and electronic components, available at any office supply store).

7   Overhaul only one carburetor at a time to avoid mixing up parts.

8   We will show you how to separate the carburetors, but it isn't usually necessary to do so. Don't separate the carburetors unless one of the joints between them is leaking, or

one of the carburetors must be replaced. The vacuum chamber, the air cut-off diaphragm, the float assembly and the jets can be serviced without separating the carburetors. Achieving correct synchronization can be tricky after disconnecting and reconnecting the carburetors.

12 Carburetors - removal and installation

⚠ *Warning: Gasoline (petrol) is extremely flammable, so take extra precautions when you work on any part of the fuel system. Don't smoke or allow open flames or bare light bulbs near the work area, and don't work in a garage where a gas-type appliance (such as a water heater or clothes dryer) is present. If you spill any fuel on your skin, rinse it off immediately with soap and water. When you perform any kind of work on the fuel system, wear safety glasses and have an extinguisher suitable for class B fires (flammable liquids) on hand.*

Removal

VT600 (1988 through 1998) and VT750C/CD models

1   Remove the fuel tank (see Section 2).

2   Remove the drain screws from both float bowls and drain the carburetors into a suitable container.

3   Remove the air cleaner housing (see Section 6).

4   Remove the sub-air cleaner element (see Section 7).

5   Remove the air intake chamber and intake ducts (see Section 8).

6   Detach the fuel line from the T-fitting located behind the carburetors on VT600 models **(see illustration)** and below the carbs on VT750 models.

12.6 Detach the fuel hose from the T-fitting behind the carburetors on VT600 models (shown) or below the carbs on VT750 models

12.10a On VT600 models, back off the choke shaft locknut on the backside of the throttle cable bracket . . .

12.10b . . . and disengage the choke knob and shaft from the bracket

12.12a Loosen the insulator clamp screws . . .

7   On VT600 models, remove the throttle linkage cover and the cover bracket (see Section 10).

8   On VT750 models, remove the left side cover (see Chapter 8).

9   Detach the throttle cable bracket from the left carburetor and disengage the throttle cables from the pulley (see Section 10). Unless you're replacing the throttle cables, it's not necessary to detach them from the cable bracket; they can remain attached to the bracket.

10   On VT600 models, separate the choke knob and cable from the throttle cable bracket **(see illustrations)**.

11   On VT750 models, remove the cylinder fins from the left side of the rear cylinder (see Section 7 in Chapter 2), detach the choke knob bracket, then detach the choke knob from the bracket.

12   Loosen the carburetor insulator clamp screws **(see illustration)**, carefully work the carbs free from the insulators **(see illustration)**, with a big screwdriver if necessary, pull the carbs from the left side of the engine

(see illustration), detach the air hoses and remove the carburetors. (If you're planning to service the cylinder heads, you can also unbolt the insulators from the cylinder heads and remove the carburetor assembly and insulators together.)

13   After the carburetors have been removed, stuff clean rags into the insulators to prevent the entry of dirt or other objects.

14   Inspect the carburetor insulators. If they're cracked or brittle, replace them.

1999 and later VT600 models, 2004 and later VT750

15   Remove the air cleaner (see Section 6).

16   Loosen the float bowl drain screw and drain the carburetor into a suitable container.

17   Remove the fuel tank (see Section 2).

18   Remove the throttle linkage cover. Loosen the throttle cable adjusters, but don't remove the cables yet.

19   Remove the choke and idle speed knobs.

20   Label and disconnect the fuel line, vac-

uum hoses and coolant hoses. Plug or cap the coolant hoses so they don't drip.

21   Loosen the clamping band screws and work the carburetor out of the intake manifold. Pull the carburetor out, slip the throttle cables out of the brackets, then disconnect the cable ends from the throttle pulley.

VT750DC models

22   Remove the fuel tank and air cleaner housing (see Sections 2 and 6).

23   Free the fuel line from the retainer on top of the rear cylinder.

24   Remove one screw and take off the throttle cable cover. Working behind the cover, loosen the throttle cable adjuster locknuts, then remove the wiring harness retainer, cover bracket and throttle cable bracket.

25   Slip the throttle cables out of the brackets, then disconnect the cable ends from the throttle pulley.

26   Unbolt the choke cable bracket from the rear cylinder.

27   At the rear carburetor, disconnect the carburetor heater electrical connector,

12.12b . . . separate the carburetors from the insulators (if they're hard to pull out of the insulators, use a big screwdriver to gently pry them loose) . . .

12.12c . . . pull the carbs out from the left side of the engine, detach the air tubes (arrow) and remove the carbs

13.2a Carburetor hose routing (top view, as seen from the front)

1	Fuel hose	4	Choke cable/starting
2	Air hoses		enrichment valve
3	Air vent control valve	5	Sub-air cleaner hose
	hose	6	Purge valve hose

13.2b Carburetor hose routing (top view, as seen from the rear)

2	Air hoses
3	Air vent control valve hose
4	Choke cable/starting enrichment valve
5	Sub-air cleaner hose

detach the sub-air cleaner tube and loosen the clamping band screw at the cylinder.

28 Repeat Step 27 at the front carburetor.

29 Label and disconnect the vacuum hoses.

30 Work the carburetors and intake tubes free of the cylinders, then lift the assembly, disconnect the fuel line and take it out.

31 Pull back the choke plunger boots, unscrew the nuts and take the plungers out of the carburetors.

Installation

32 Place the carburetor assembly in position on the engine and connect the air intake tube(s), but don't tighten the clamping screws yet.

33 Reverse the removal steps to connect the throttle cables, fuel lines, coolant hoses (if equipped) and emission hoses.

34 Make sure the carburetor(s) and securely seated in the insulator(s), then tighten the clamping screws securely.

35 The remainder of installation is the reverse of the removal steps.

36 Check the idle speed (and carburetor synchronization on dual-carburetor models). Adjust if necessary (see Chapter 1).

13 Carburetors - disassembly, inspection, cleaning and reassembly

⚠ *Warning: Gasoline (petrol) is extremely flammable, so take extra precautions when you work on any part of the fuel system. Don't smoke or allow open flames or bare light bulbs near the work area, and don't work in a garage where a gas-type appliance (such as a water heater or clothes dryer) is present. If you*

13.2c Carburetor hose routing (front view)

1	Fuel hose
2	Air hose
6	Purge valve hose

13.2d Carburetor hose routing (rear view)

1	Fuel hose
2	Air hose
3	Air vent control valve hose
4	Choke cable/starting enrichment valve
6	Purge valve hose

13.2e Carburetor hose routing (left view)

1 Fuel hose
2 Air hose
3 Air vent control valve hose
4 Choke cable/starting enrichment valve

13.2f Carburetor hose routing (right view)

1 Fuel hose
2 Air hose
4 Choke cable/starting
    enrichment valve
5 Sub-air cleaner hose
6 Purge valve hose

13.3a To remove the starting enrichment valve, loosen it with a wrench . . .

13.3b . . . and pull out the valve

spill any fuel on your skin, rinse it off *immediately with soap and water. When you perform any kind of work on the fuel system, wear safety glasses and have a fire extinguisher suitable for class B type fires (flammable liquids) on hand.*

Note: *The following procedures are specific to dual carburetors, used on all except 1999 and later VT600 and 2004 and later VT750 models. Service procedures for the single carburetor used on these are similar in design to those for dual carburetors, but include an accelerator pump. If you're working on a single carburetor, ignore the steps which don't apply, and service the accelerator pump diaphragm in the same way as the air cut-off diaphragm.*

Disassembly

Note: *Work on one carburetor at a time to avoid mixing up the parts, and to give you a*

"reference carburetor" to refer to if you can't remember how things go back together. As you disassemble each carburetor, store the parts for each sub-assembly in a clearly labeled plastic bag so you don't lose anything.

1   Remove the carburetors (see Section 12), then place them on a clean working surface.
2   Carefully study how the air and fuel hoses are routed **(see illustrations)**, mark them with adhesive labels or colored electrical tape, then detach them from the carburetors. Use the accompanying photos to help you route the hoses correctly during reassembly.
3   Remove the starting enrichment valves **(see illustrations)**.
4   It's not necessary to separate the carburetors in order to disassemble them. If you're simply rebuilding the carburetors, skip the following Steps and proceed to Step 7. If you are replacing a carburetor, proceed to the next Step.

13.3c Each starting enrichment valve assembly consists of the valve itself (1), the spring (2), the collar (3) and the choke cable end (4)

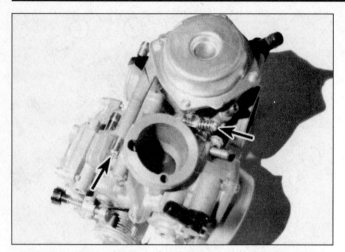

13.5 Back off the synchronization adjusting screw (right arrow) and remove the two carburetor attaching screws (arrow) (the other attaching screw, not visible in this photo, is in exactly the same location on the side of the other carburetor)

13.6 Pull the two carburetors apart, remove the thrust spring (arrow) and put it in a plastic bag so you don't lose it

13.7 Remove the float chamber cover screws and remove the float chamber cover

13.8 Remove the float pivot pin and remove the float, the float valve and the float valve retainer (the small metal retainer that attaches the float valve to the float)

5   Back off the synchronization adjusting screw and remove the two carburetor attaching screws (**see illustration**).
6   Pull the two carburetors apart (**see illustration**), remove the thrust spring and put it in a plastic bag so you don't lose it.
7   Remove the float chamber cover screws (**see illustration**) and remove the float chamber cover.
8   Remove the float pivot pin (**see illustration**) and remove the float, the float valve and the float valve retainer.
9   Unscrew and remove the float valve seat, the main jet and the slow jet (**see illustration**). Don't lose the washer for the float valve seat.
10   Center punch the plug for the pilot screw, then drill out the plug with a 4 mm (5/32-inch) drill bit (**see illustration**). To protect the pilot screw from damage, use a drill stop set to prevent the drill bit from going deeper than 3 mm (1/8-inch). Make sure you

13.9 Unscrew and remove the float valve seat (1), the main jet (2) and the slow jet (3); don't lose the washer for the float valve seat

13.10 Center punch the plug for the pilot screw, then drill out the plug with a 4 mm (5/32-inch) drill bit; to protect the pilot screw from damage, use a drill stop set to prevent the drill bit from going deeper than 3 mm (1/8-inch)

13.11 Screw a self-tapping 4 mm screw into the drilled-out plug, grasp the head of the screw and pull out the plug

13.12a Carefully counting the number of turns it takes to seat the screw, screw in the pilot screw until it seats lightly and jot down the number for assembly

13.12b Remove the pilot screw, washer and O-ring; the bypass hole (arrow) is an alignment mark for throttle adjustment

13.13 Remove the vacuum chamber screws and remove the vacuum chamber cover, the spring and the piston/diaphragm assembly

don't damage the pilot screw.

11   Screw a self-tapping 4 mm screw into the drilled-out plug, grasp the head of the self-tapping screw and pull out the plug **(see illustration)**.

12   Carefully counting the number of turns, screw in the pilot screw until it seats lightly.

Caution: Do NOT keep turning the pilot screw in after you feel it stop; this will damage the screw.

Jot down the number of turns it took to seat the screw; you'll need this number when reassembling the carburetor. Remove the pilot screw, the washer and the O-ring **(see illustrations)**.

13   Remove the vacuum chamber screws and remove the vacuum chamber cover **(see illustration)**. Remove the spring and the piston/diaphragm assembly.

14   Using a Phillips screwdriver, push down on the jet needle holder **(see illustration)**, turn it counterclockwise 90 degrees to unlock it, and remove the jet needle holder, the spring and the jet needle.

15   Remove the air cut-off valve cover screws and remove the air cut-off valve cover, the spring and the diaphragm **(see illustration)**. Remove and discard the old O-ring.

13.14 Using a Phillips screwdriver, push down on the jet needle holder, turn it counterclockwise 90 degrees to unlock it, then remove the jet needle holder, the spring and the jet needle

13.15 Remove the air cut-off valve cover screws and remove the air cut-off valve cover, the spring and the diaphragm; remove and discard the old O-ring

13.17a Float assembly, jets and pilot screw assembly

1	Drain screw	9	Float valve seat filter
2	Float chamber cover	10	Main jet
3	Float valve pin	11	Needle jet holder
4	Float	12	Slow jet
5	Retainer	13	Pilot screw
6	Float valve	14	Spring
7	Float valve seat	15	Washer
8	Float valve seat washer	16	O-ring

13.17b Vacuum chamber and air cut-off diaphragm assemblies

1	Vacuum chamber cover screws	9	Air cut-off diaphragm cover screw/bracket
2	Vacuum chamber cover	10	Air cut-off diaphragm cover
3	Spring	11	Spring
4	Piston/diaphragm	12	Diaphragm
5	Jet needle holder	13	O-ring
6	Spring	14	Elbow fitting for sub-air cleaner hose
7	Jet needle		
8	Air cut-off diaphragm cover screw		

Inspection

16   Clean or wipe off all the parts well enough to inspect them.

17   Lay out all the parts for inspection (see illustrations).

18   Operate the throttle shaft to make sure the throttle butterfly valve opens and closes smoothly. If it doesn't, replace the carburetor.

19   Inspect the carburetor body, the float chamber cover and the vacuum chamber cover for cracks, distorted sealing surfaces and other damage. If either cover is damaged, replace it. If the carburetor body is damaged, you'll have to replace the entire carburetor.

20   Inspect the float for damage. Make sure it's not cracked or leaking (this is usually apparent by the presence of fuel inside the float).

21   Inspect the float valve and the float valve seat for scratches and scoring; if a pronounced groove has formed on the tapered portion of the valve, replace the valve. Make sure there are no deposits on the sealing surface of the valve or the valve seat which might prevent the valve from fully closing against the seat. Make sure that no deposits on the bore of the seat are blocking fuel flow through the seat. If any of these parts are damaged, replace them. There's a small filter in the seat; make sure it's not clogged or damaged.

22   Inspect the jets. Make sure that the passages through the jets are clean and free of deposits.

23   Inspect the tapered part of the pilot screw for wear and damage. Make sure the spring is in good shape. Replace any worn or damaged parts.

24   Inspect the spring for the vacuum piston; make sure it's not kinked or distorted. Inspect the vacuum chamber diaphragm for cracks, holes, tears and general deterioration (holding it up to a light will help to reveal problems of this nature). Inspect the surface of the vacuum chamber piston for scratches, scoring and excessive wear. Insert the piston in the piston bore in the carburetor body and note whether it moves up and down smoothly in the piston bore. If it doesn't move smoothly in the bore, replace the carburetor. Inspect the tip of the jet needle for excessive wear. Make sure it's not bent. A good way to check the jet needle for straightness is to roll it on a flat surface, such as a piece of glass. If the jet needle is damaged, replace it.

25   Inspect the spring for the air cut-off diaphragm; make sure it's in good shape. Inspect the air cut-off diaphragm for cracks, holes and tears. If it's damaged, replace it.

Cleaning

Caution: Use only a petroleum based solvent for carburetor cleaning. Don't use caustic cleaners.

26   Submerge the metal components in the solvent for about thirty minutes (or longer, if the directions recommend it).

27   After the carburetor has soaked long enough for the cleaner to loosen and dissolve most of the varnish and other deposits, use a brush to remove the stubborn deposits. Rinse it again, then dry it with compressed air. Blow out all of the fuel and air passages in the main body.

Caution: Never clean the jets or passages with a piece of wire or a drill bit, as they will be enlarged, causing the fuel and air metering rates to be upset.

28   Thoroughly wash the vacuum chamber diaphragm and the air cut-off valve diaphragm with soap and water, then rinse them off with clean water.

Reassembly

Note: *When reassembling the carburetors, be sure to use the new O-rings, gaskets and other parts supplied in the rebuild kit.*

29   Install a new O-ring with its flat side toward the carburetor. Install the air cut-off diaphragm, spring and cover. Tighten the cover screws securely.

30   Install the jet needle, spring, and jet needle holder in the vacuum piston. Push down on the jet needle holder and turn it clockwise 90 degrees to lock it into place.

31   Install the vacuum diaphragm/piston assembly in the piston bore. Make sure that the lip on the underside of the diaphragm is seated in the groove in the carburetor casting and the positioning tab on the edge of the diaphragm is aligned with the cavity in the groove (see illustration).

32   Install the spring and the vacuum chamber cover. As you compress the spring, make sure you keep it straight. And don't pinch the diaphragm. Install the cover screws and tighten them securely.

13.31 Align the positioning tab on the edge of the diaphragm with the notches in the cover and carburetor body

33   Install the needle jet holder, main jet and slow jet.

Caution: Don't overtighten the jets. Because they're made of soft brass, it's easy to strip the threads.

34   Install the float valve seat/filter. Again, don't overtighten it.
35   Assemble the float valve, retainer and float **(see illustrations)**.
36   Place the float assembly in position and secure it with the float pin. Make sure that the float valve is correctly seated on the float valve seat and the float valve retainer is correctly engaged with the float **(see illustration)**.
37   Using a carburetor float level gauge (Honda special tool 07401-0010000), check the float level. Place the carburetor(s) on a bench with the float chamber on its side, so that the float is hanging from its pivot pin. Place the gauge so that it's perpendicular to the machined face of the float chamber and position it so that it's aligned with the main jet. Check the float level and compare your measurement to the float level listed in this Chapter's Specifications. If the float level is

incorrect, replace the float assembly.
38   Install the float chamber cover with a new O-ring, install the cover screws and tighten them securely.
39   Install the pilot screw, return it to its original position in accordance with your notes

13.35a Reassemble the float valve and the retainer . . .

and install a new sealing plug. If you're installing a new pilot screw, establish a baseline by setting it at the same position as the old pilot screw, then - after the carburetors are installed and synchronized - adjust it (see Section 14). Don't install a sealing plug at this time if you're using a new pilot screw.
40   Repeat Steps 7 through 39 for the other carburetor.
41   If you separated the carburetors, reattach them as follows. If not, go to Step 50.
42   Back off the synchronizer adjusting screw **(see illustration 13.5)** to remove spring tension.
43   Install the thrust spring **(see illustration 13.6)** between the throttle links.
44   Reattach the carburetors with the two carburetor attaching screws **(see illustration 13.5)** and tighten the screws securely.
45   Make sure the synchronizer spring is correctly positioned **(see illustration)**, then tighten the synchronizer adjusting screw.
46   Open the throttle slightly by rotating the throttle valve, then release the throttle. It should close quickly and smoothly, without dragging.

13.35b . . . then attach them to the float

13.36 Place the float assembly in position and secure it with the float pin; make sure that the float valve is correctly seated on the float valve seat and the float valve retainer is correctly engaged with the float

13.45 Make sure that each synchronizer spring is correctly positioned, then tighten the synchronizer adjusting screw

13.47 Use the idle stop screw (arrow) to adjust the throttle valve of the carburetor for the rear cylinder so that it's aligned with the by-pass hole

47   Turn the throttle stop screw (see illustration) to align the throttle valve in the rear carburetor with the edge of the by-pass hole (see illustration 13.12b).

48   Turn the synchronizer adjusting screw (see illustration 13.5) to align the throttle valve in the front carburetor with the edge of the by-pass hole.

49   Operate the throttle and verify that it operates smoothly and that both throttle valves are aligned with their respective by-pass holes.

50   Reattach the starting enrichment valves. Make sure the valve, spring and collar are correctly assembled on the end of each choke cable (see illustration 13.3c) and tighten them securely.

51   Referring to the accompanying photos (see illustrations 13.2a through 13.2f), reattach all air and fuel hoses.

52   Install the carburetors (see Section 12).

53   Synchronize the carburetors (see Chapter 1).

14 Idle fuel/air mixture - adjustment

Dual carburetors

1   Because of emissions regulations of the Environmental Protection Agency (EPA), and the regulatory bodies of some state governments as well, the idle fuel/air mixture is a critical adjustment. In order to comply with these regulations, each carburetor has a sealing plug in the pilot screw hole to prevent tampering. These plugs should only be removed during a complete carburetor overhaul, after which the screws must be returned to their original settings.

2   If you replaced the pilot screws during a carburetor overhaul, adjust the idle fuel/air mixture as follows. Make sure that the carburetors are synchronized (see Chapter 1) before proceeding.

3   Remove each pilot screw plug, if necessary (see Steps 10 and 11 in Section 13).

4   Turn each pilot screw clockwise until it seats lightly, then back it out to the initial opening listed in this Chapter's Specifications.

Caution: Do NOT overtighten the pilot screw; overtightening it will damage it.

5   Start the engine and warm it up to its normal operating temperature.

6   Turn off the engine and hook up a tachometer in accordance with the manufacturer's instructions.

7   Start the engine and adjust the engine idle speed to the idle speed listed in the Chapter 1 Specifications with the throttle stop screw.

8   Back out each pilot screw 1/2-turn from its initial setting.

9   If the engine speed increases by 50 rpm or more, back out each pilot screw another 1/2 turn and continue doing so until the engine speed no longer increases.

10   Adjust the idle speed to the idle speed listed in the Chapter 1 Specifications with the throttle stop screw.

11   Turn in the pilot screw for the rear cylinder carburetor until the engine speed drops 50 rpm.

12   Back out the pilot screw for the rear cylinder carburetor to the final opening listed in this Chapter's Specifications.

13   Adjust the idle speed with the throttle stop screw.

14   Repeat Steps 11, 12 and 13 and adjust the pilot screw for the front cylinder carburetor.

15   Install new sealing plugs into the pilot screw holes with a 7 mm guide driver (Honda special tool 07942-8230000, or equivalent). When each plug is fully seated, its surface is recessed 1 mm (1/32-inch).

16   If the engine runs extremely rough or blows black smoke at idle or continually stalls, and a carburetor overhaul, followed by the preceding adjustment, does not cure the problem, take the motorcycle to a Honda dealer service department, or a motorcycle repair shop, equipped with an exhaust gas analyzer. They will be able to correctly adjust the idle fuel/air mixture to achieve a smooth idle and restore low speed performance.

Single carburetor models

17   You'll need a tune-up tachometer and vacuum pump for this procedure. Since the pilot screw is difficult to reach, you'll also need a pilot screw wrench or equivalent (for US models, Honda tools 07MMA-MT3010B and 07PMA-MZ2011A; for non-US VT600 models, 07PMA-MZ2011A; for non-US VT750 models, 07KMA-MS60102 and 07PMA-MZ2011A).

18   Warm the engine to normal operating temperature (10 minutes of stop-and-go riding).

19   Remove the fuel tank (see Section 2).

20   Disconnect the vacuum hose from the PAIR control valve and plug the disconnected end (see Section 16). Connect a vacuum pump to hose fitting on the PAIR valve, then pump it to more than the standard test setting listed in this Chapter's Specifications. This will temporarily deactivate the PAIR system so it won't affect the adjustment.

21   Connect a temporary fuel source to the carburetor inlet or reinstall the fuel tank temporarily.

22   Turn the pilot screw in until it seats lightly.

Caution: Do not bottom the pilot screw forcefully or its tip will be damaged. Turn the screw back out the number of turns listed in this Chapter's Specifications (initial adjustment setting).

23   Start the engine and let it idle. Idle speed should be 1200 +/- 100 rpm. Adjust it if necessary, referring to Chapter 1.

24   Adjust the pilot screw, turning it slowly in or out to obtain the highest idle speed. Once this is done, rev the engine two or three times.

25   Turn the pilot screw clockwise until idle speed drops to 50 rpm lower than the speed obtained in Step 23.

26   Turn the pilot screw out to the final adjustment setting.

27   Disconnect the vacuum pump from the PAIR valve, then unplug the vacuum hose and connect it to the PAIR valve fitting.

28   Recheck idle speed on the tachometer and readjust it to 1200 +/- 100 rpm if necessary.

29   Disconnect the tachometer. Disconnect the temporary fuel source and reinstall the fuel tank (see Section 2).

15 Exhaust system - removal and installation

 Warning: Make sure the engine is cool before performing this procedure.

1   Unless you're replacing the exhaust pipe covers or the exhaust pipes themselves, it's unnecessary to remove the covers. However, at least on VT600 models, this might be

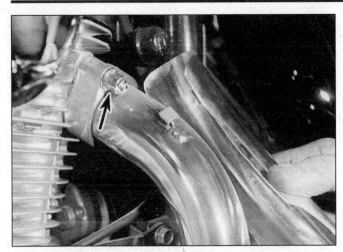

15.2a Unbolt the cover for access to the front exhaust pipe nuts on a VT600 (lower nut hidden)

15.2b Remove the clamp (arrow) and rear bolt (not shown) to detach the VT600 rear exhaust pipe cover . . .

15.2c . . . and lift the cover off

15.4 Remove the two nuts that secure the rear exhaust pipe to the rear cylinder head

a good time to inspect each pipe for corrosion and other damage, including the part of the pipe behind the cover (especially if you live in a damp climate). On VT750 models, however, you do NOT want to remove the exhaust pipe covers unless you're replacing them. If you remove them, they must be replaced; once removed, VT750 covers cannot be re-used.

2   If you're replacing the exhaust pipes or the exhaust pipe covers on a VT600 model, remove the bolts that attach the exhaust pipe covers to the exhaust pipes and remove the covers (see illustrations).

3   If you're replacing the exhaust pipe cover on a VT750 model, knock the cover loose by hitting the end of the cover with a plastic or rubber-tipped mallet. Strike the cover hard enough to break the lock tab, then disengage the cover from the exhaust pipe and discard the cover (once the lock tab is broken, the cover must be replaced).

4   Remove the two nuts that secure the front exhaust pipe to the front cylinder head

(see illustration 15.2a) and the rear pipe to the rear cylinder head (see illustration).

5   On VT600 models, remove the muffler

15.5a The VT600 upper muffler is attached to its bracket by this nut . . .

mounting nut and bolt (see illustrations).

6   On VT750 models, remove the muffler mounting nuts (they're below the muffler).

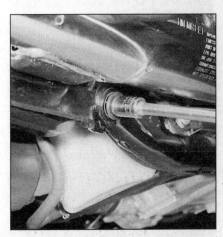

15.5b . . . and the lower muffler is attached to its bracket by this bolt

15.7 Slide back the joint, pull the exhaust pipe out of the head and remove the split collar (arrows) (front pipe shown, rear pipe similar)

15.8 After the exhaust pipes have been removed, carefully pry out the old gaskets (arrow) (rear exhaust pipe gasket shown, front gasket similar)

7 Slide back the exhaust pipe joints, pull the pipes out of the cylinder heads, remove the collars **(see illustration)**, disengage the mufflers from their mounting brackets and remove the exhaust pipes and mufflers.

8 Dig out the old gaskets **(see illustration)** from the cylinder heads and discard them.

9 Installation is the reverse of removal. Be sure to use new gaskets and tighten all fasteners securely. If you removed either exhaust pipe cover on a VT750 model, install a new cover: align the slots on the backside of the cover with the tabs on the exhaust pipe and slide the cover into place until the lock tab on the cover locks into place.

16 PAIR system - inspection and component replacement

1 The PAIR system uses exhaust gas pulses to suck fresh air into the exhaust ports, where it mixes with hot combustion gases. The additional oxygen provided by the fresh air allows combustion to continue for a longer time, reducing unburned hydrocarbons in the exhaust. Reed valves (one for each cylinder) allow the flow of air into the ports and prevent exhaust gas from flowing into the system. An air filter filters the air that the system draws in.

2 Inspection of the hoses is described in Chapter 1.

3 The reed valves are mounted in the valve covers. To remove the front one, remove the air cleaner housing for access. This isn't necessary to remove the rear reed valve. Unbolt the reed valve from the valve cover and lift it out. If the reed is cracked or otherwise damaged, replace the reed valve as a unit. The valve should also be replaced as a unit if the

gasket is damaged or deteriorated.

4 To test the control valve, warm up the engine (10 minutes of stop-and-go riding is sufficient). Disconnect the air inlet hose from the air filter. Disconnect the vacuum hose from the PAIR control valve and plug the disconnected end. Connect a vacuum pump to the hose fitting on the PAIR valve. Start the engine and let it idle. Raise engine speed slightly and check to make sure air is sucked into the system. If it isn't, check to make sure the air supply hose isn't kinked or plugged.

5 Slowly apply vacuum to the control valve with the vacuum pump. Air should stop flowing into the supply hose when vacuum reaches the amount listed in this Chapter's Specifications. Stop pumping at this point. The vacuum reading should remain steady without dropping. If air keeps flowing, or if vacuum bleeds down, replace the control valve. To do this, disconnect its hoses and unbolt it. Bolt in a new valve and reconnect the hoses.

6 Blow low-pressure air into the air filter (an arrow molded into the filter indicates the direction of air flow). If air doesn't flow, replace the filter.

7 Once repairs are made, reconnect the hoses. Hose routing is printed on a vacuum diagram, mounted on the frame under the fuel tank.

17 Throttle position sensor - check and replacement

Check

1 Remove the fuel tank (see Section 2).

2 Locate the 3-pin TPS connector (it can be identified by its wire colors).

3 Unplug the connector and connect an

ohmmeter between the blue and black wire terminals in the TPS side of the connector (not the wiring harness side). The reading should be between 2 and 4 ohms.

4 Connect the ohmmeter between the yellow and black wire terminals in the TPS side of the connector. When the throttle is moved form closed to open, the resistance should increase. When the throttle is moved from open to closed, the resistance should decrease.

5 If the TPS doesn't perform as described, replace it as described below.

6 If the TPS does give the correct reading, check its wiring harness. To do this, unplug the 22-pin connector from the ignition control module. Connect the ohmmeter to the harness side of the ICM connector, between the blue/green and yellow/red wire terminals (all except 2008 VT750) or blue and black/red wire terminals (2008 VT750). The reading should be between 2 and 4 ohms. If not, check the wires between the connector and the throttle position sensor for breaks or bad connections.

7 Check the TPS input voltage. Unplug the 3-pin TPS connector. Connect a voltmeter to the harness side of the connector, between the blue/green and yellow/red wire terminals (all except 2008 VT750) or blue and black/red wire terminals (2008 VT750). Turn the ignition key to On and the kill switch to Run. The reading should be 5 volts. If not, check the wires between the connector and the throttle position sensor for breaks or bad connections.

8 If the wiring and throttle position sensor are good, but the TPS still doesn't perform properly, the ignition control module may be at fault. Since this is an expensive component that can't be returned once purchased, have it tested by a dealer service department or other qualified shop.

Chapter 5
Ignition system

Contents

Degrees of difficulty

Easy, suitable for novice with little experience		Fairly easy, suitable for beginner with some experience		Fairly difficult, suitable for competent DIY mechanic		Difficult, suitable for experienced DIY mechanic		Very difficult, suitable for expert DIY or professional	

Specifications

Ignition coil (1988 and 1989, 1991 through 1996 VT600 only*)
Primary resistance .... 1.89 to 2.32 ohms
Secondary resistance
    With plug wires attached .... 23.55 to 30.45 k-ohms
    Without plug wires attached .... 19.8 to 24.2 k-ohms

Ignition pulse generator(s) (1988 and 1989, 1991 through 1996 VT600 only*)
Coil resistance .... 450 to 550 ohms

Ignition timing
VT600
    1988, 1989, 1991 through 1996 .... 6.2 degrees BTDC at idle
    1997 on .... 6.5 degrees BTDC at idle
VT750 .... 8 degrees BTDC at idle

* 1997 and later VT600 and all VT750 models must be tested by a Honda dealer.

Torque specifications
Ignition pulse generator bolts .... 12 Nm (108 in-lbs)

1 General information

These motorcycles are equipped with a battery-operated, fully transistorized, break-erless ignition system. The system consists of the following components:

    Ignition control module
    Ignition pulse generator(s) and
        timing rotor
    Battery and fuse
    Ignition coils
    Spark plugs
    Ignition (main) and engine kill (stop)
        switches
    Primary and secondary circuit wiring

The ignition pulse generators are the timing devices that enable the ignition control module to control the primary voltage to the ignition coils. VT600 models are equipped with two ignition pulse generators, one for each cylinder. VT750 models use one pulse generator for both cylinders. Every time a tip of the timing rotor sweeps by the ignition pulse generator, the pulse generator produces a low-voltage output signal to the ignition control module. The module switches primary voltage to the coils on and off in accordance with these signals from the pulse generator(s). With the exception of spark plug replacement, ignition system service is eliminated.

Ignition system components can be checked but they can't be repaired. If ignition system problems occur, the faulty component(s) must be replaced. Most electrical parts cannot be returned, so don't buy anything until you're sure that you have identified the problem.

2 Ignition system - check

2.16 A simple spark gap testing fixture can be made from a block of wood, a large alligator clip, two nails, a screw and a piece of wire

⚠ **Warning: Because of the very high voltage generated by the ignition system, extreme care should be taken when these checks are performed.**

1   If the ignition system is the suspected cause of poor engine performance or failure to start, a number of checks can be made to isolate the problem.
2   Make sure the engine kill switch is in the Run position.

Engine will not start

3   Disconnect one of the spark plug wires (there are two for each cylinder), connect the wire to a spare spark plug and lay the plug on the engine with the threads of the plug in contact with the engine. If necessary, hold the spark plug with an insulated tool. Crank the engine over and make sure a well-defined, blue spark occurs between the spark plug electrodes.

⚠ **Warning: Don't remove one of the spark plugs from the engine to perform this check - atomized fuel being pumped out of the open spark plug hole could ignite, causing severe injury!**

4   If no spark occurs, repeat the same test on the *other* spark plug lead of the same coil.
5   If the plug sparks when the second lead is attached, then the first plug wire or cap is defective. Install a new wire and cap and retest.
6   If neither plug wire produces a spark on a 1988, 1989 or 1991 through 1996 VT600 model, check and, if necessary, replace the coil (see Section 3).
7   If neither plug wire produces a spark on a 1997 or later VT600 model, or on any VT750 model, try swapping the coils (see Section 3). If the plug wires of the second coil produce a good spark, replace the first coil. No further testing of the ignition coil on these later models is possible without a special diagnostic tester. The coils must be checked by a Honda service department with the necessary diagnostic equipment.
8   Repeat Steps 3 through 5 for the other ignition coil.
9   If both coils are operating satisfactorily, inspect the rest of the ignition system. Make sure that all electrical connectors are clean and tight. Check all wires for shorts, opens and make sure that they're correctly installed.
10   Check the battery voltage with a voltmeter and - on models equipped with batteries having removable filler caps - check the specific gravity with a hydrometer (see Chapter 1). If the voltage is less than 12-volts or if the specific gravity is low, recharge the battery.
11   Check the ignition fuse and the fuse connections (see Chapter 9). If the fuse is blown, replace it; if the connections are loose or corroded, clean or repair them.
12   Check the ignition switch, engine kill switch, neutral switch and sidestand switch.
13   On 1988, 1989 or 1991 through 1996 VT600 models, check the ignition pulse generator resistance (see Section 4).
14   On 1997 and later VT600 models, and on VT750 models, no testing of the ignition pulse generator(s) is possible without a special diagnostic tester. Have the pulse generator(s) checked by a Honda service department with the necessary diagnostic equipment.

Engine starts but misfires
15   If the engine starts but misfires, make the following checks before deciding that the ignition system is at fault.
16   The ignition system must be able to produce a spark across a six millimeter (1/4-inch) gap (minimum). A simple test fixture **(see illustration)** can be constructed to make sure the minimum spark gap can be jumped. Make sure the fixture electrodes are positioned six millimeters apart.
17   Connect one of the spark plug wires to the protruding test fixture electrode, then attach the fixture's alligator clip to a good engine ground/earth.
18   Crank the engine over (it will probably start and run on the remaining cylinders) and see if well-defined, blue sparks occur between the test fixture electrodes. If the minimum spark gap test is positive, the ignition coil for that cylinder is functioning properly. Repeat the check on one of the spark plug wires connected to the other coil. If the spark will not jump the gap during either test, or if it is weak (orange colored), refer to Steps 3 through 8.

3 Ignition coils - check and replacement

Check

1   Inspect the coils for cracks and other damage. If either coil is obviously damaged, replace it. If the coils are undamaged, proceed to the next Step.
2   The following tests apply only to the ignition coils used on 1988 and 1989 and 1991 through 1996 VT600 models. To determine whether an ignition coil on a 1997 or

3.4 Test 1: Check coil primary resistance between the primary terminals. Test 2: Check secondary resistance between the two spark plug wire caps, then unscrew the plug leads from the coil and check secondary resistance between the two high tension terminals

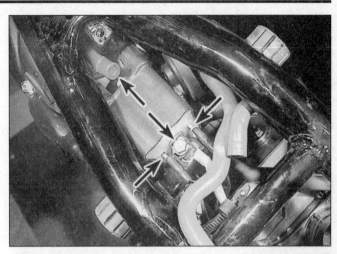

3.6 To remove the coil for the front cylinder, unplug the primary leads (arrows) and remove the coil mounting bolts (arrows); don't forget to reattach the ground wire attached to the rear bolt when installing the coil (VT600 shown, VT750 similar)

later VT600 model, or a VT750 model, is defective, have it tested by a Honda dealer service department equipped with the necessary diagnostic equipment.

3   To access the coil for the front cylinder, remove the fuel tank (see Chapter 4) and remove the crankcase breather separator (see Chapter 4). (The separator is the white plastic tank above the coil; it's part of the crankcase emission control system.) To check or replace the coil for the rear cylinder, remove the right side cover (see Chapter 8).

4   To check the primary resistance of a coil, unplug the electrical connectors from the primary terminals and, using an ohmmeter, measure the resistance between these two terminals (see illustration). Compare

[image description]

3.7 To remove the coil for the rear cylinder, unplug the primary leads from the rear end of the coil (not visible in this photo) and remove the coil mounting bolts (arrows) (VT600 shown, VT750 similar, except that coil is installed vertically)

your measurement to the primary resistance listed in this Chapter's Specifications. If the indicated primary resistance is outside the specified range, replace the coil. If the primary resistance is within range, check the coil secondary resistance.

5   To check the coil secondary resistance, measure the resistance between the two spark plug leads and compare your measurement to the secondary resistance listed in this Chapter's Specifications. If the indicated secondary resistance is outside the specified range, unscrew the spark plug leads from the coil, measure the resistance between the two coil high tension terminals and compare your measurement to the secondary resistance listed in this Chapter's Specifications. If the indicated secondary resistance is now within the specified range, replace the spark plug high tension leads. If the indicated resistance is still not within the specified range, replace the coil.

Replacement

6   To replace the coil for the front cylinder, remove the fuel tank (see Chapter 4) and remove the crankcase breather separator (see Chapter 4). (The separator is the white plastic tank above the coil; it's part of the crankcase emission control system.) Before detaching the coil, clearly label the primary electrical connectors (see illustration), then unplug them from the primary terminals. Detach the spark plug caps from the front cylinder plugs, remove the two coil mounting bolts, pull back the ground wire eyelet (attached to the rear mounting bolt) and remove the coil. (The accompanying photo depicts the front coil on a VT600 model. The front coil on VT750 models is also located in the same general location; it's bolted to the left side of the upper frame tube.)

7   To replace the coil for the rear cylinder,

remove the right side cover (see Chapter 8). The rear coil (see illustration) is removed basically the same way as the front coil. (The accompanying photo depicts the rear coil on a VT600 model. The rear coil on VT750 models is also located behind the right side cover, except that it's mounted vertically.)

8   Installation is the reverse of removal.

4   Ignition pulse generator(s) - check and replacement

Check

1   The following test applies only to the pulse generators used on 1988 and 1989 and 1991 through 1996 VT600 models. In order to determine whether one of the ignition pulse generators on a 1997 or later VT600 model, or the single pulse generator on a VT750 model, is defective, have it tested by a Honda dealer service department equipped with the necessary diagnostic equipment.

2   Remove the fuel tank (see Chapter 4) and the left steering head cover (see Chapter 8).

3   Unplug the white four-pin connector for the ignition pulse generators (see illustration).

4   Using an ohmmeter, measure the resistance between the white/yellow wire and the yellow wire (front ignition pulse generator), and between the white/blue wire and the blue wire (rear ignition pulse generator). Compare your measurements to the ignition pulse generator coil resistance listed in this Chapter's Specifications. If the resistance of either coil is outside the specified range, replace that ignition pulse generator.

4.3 To check the ignition pulse generators, measure resistance at the white four-pin connector (on the left side, directly behind the steering head)

4.8 To detach either ignition pulse generator, remove the four retaining bolts (arrows)

Replacement

5   Remove the fuel tank (see Chapter 4) and the left steering head cover (see Chapter 8).

6   Unplug the white four-pin connector for the ignition pulse generators (**see illustration 4.3**). Carefully pull the harness down the right frame tube. If the connector snags on anything, stop and disengage it before pulling the harness down.

7   Remove the right crankcase cover (see "Clutch - removal and installation" in Chapter 2).

8   Remove the ignition pulse generator mounting bolts (**see illustration**) and remove the ignition pulse generator(s).

9   Installation is the reverse of removal. Tighten the pulse generator mounting bolts to the torque listed in this Chapter's Specifications. The wires for the ignition pulse

generators exit the engine through a hole in the crankcase, directly in front of the pulse generators. Make sure that the two grommets are correctly installed (**see illustration**) before installing the right crankcase cover. And before routing the harness up the right frame tube and plugging in the electrical connector up top, be sure to route the harness through the harness guide welded onto the frame (**see illustration**).

5   Timing rotor - removal and installation

The timing rotor is attached to the primary drive gear by the primary drive gear retaining bolt. It's removed and installed with the primary drive gear (see Chapter 2).

6   Ignition control module - check and replacement

Check

1   The ignition control module is basically diagnosed by a process of elimination. It should never even be *checked* until *after absolutely all other possible causes have been checked and eliminated.* Because a new module is expensive and cannot be returned, it's a good idea to have a Honda dealer test the old module before you buy a new unit.

Replacement
VT600 models

2   Remove the left side cover (see Chapter 8). Locate the six-pin and four-pin electri-

4.9a When installing the ignition pulse generator(s), make sure that the grommets are correctly installed (left grommet); do not install the right crankcase cover with the grommets unseated (right grommet), or water will get into the crankcase (and oil will get out!)

4.9b Before plugging in the electrical connector for the ignition pulse generators, make sure that the harness is routed correctly through this guide, then up the right frame tube

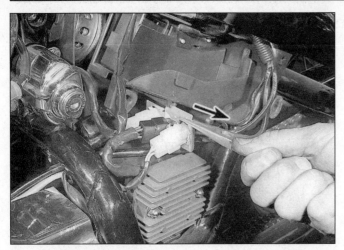

6.3 To detach the electrical connector plates from the underside of the tool tray, pull them straight out (VT600 models)

7.1 Align the timing mark (left arrow) with the index mark (right arrow)

cal connectors for the ignition control module. The module can be identified by its wire colors, referring to wiring diagrams at the end of the book.

3   Disengage the electrical connector plates from the underside of the tool tray **(see illustration)**.

4   Remove the tool tray.

5   Unplug the six-pin and four-pin electrical connectors from the ignition control module.

6   Disengage the module from its mounting stay.

7   Installation is the reverse of removal.

VT750 models

8   Remove the seat (see Chapter 8).

9   Remove the ignition control module from the battery case cover.

10   Unplug the 16-pin or 22-pin connector and remove the module.

11   Installation is the reverse of removal.

7 Ignition timing - check

1   Remove the timing hole cap from the left side of the engine **(see illustration)**.

2   Hook up an inductive timing light in accordance with the manufacturer's instructions to one of the rear (No. 1 cylinder) spark plug wires.

3   Warm up the engine to its normal operating temperature.

4   With the engine at its normal idle speed (see Chapter 1), check the timing mark with the timing light. The ignition timing is correct if the firing (F) mark on the flywheel is aligned with the stationary index mark on the edge of the timing hole in the left crankcase cover **(see illustration 7.1)**.

5   Increase the engine speed and verify that the advance marks on the flywheel are aligned with the stationary index mark on the edge off the timing hole.

6   Stop the engine, remove the inductive pickup from the rear cylinder spark plug wire and hook it up to one of the front (cylinder No. 2) spark plug wires.

7   Start the engine and allow it to return to its normal idle.

8   Check the timing for the front cylinder the same way (see Steps 4 and 5).

9   The ignition timing is not adjustable. If it's incorrect, either the ignition control module or an ignition pulse generator is defective. Have the system checked out by a Honda dealer with the necessary system diagnostic equipment.

Notes

Chapter 6
Steering and suspension

Contents

Degrees of difficulty

Easy, suitable for novice with little experience	**Fairly easy,** suitable for beginner with some experience	**Fairly difficult,** suitable for competent DIY mechanic	**Difficult,** suitable for experienced DIY mechanic	**Very difficult,** suitable for expert DIY or professional

Specifications

Front fork

Spring free length
  VT600
    1988 and 1989, 1991 through 1992 .... 305 mm (12 inches)
    1993 on.. 333.9 mm (13-5/32 inches)
  VT750
    2003 and earlier.. 303.4 mm (11-61/64 inches)
    2004 and later
      VT750C Aero
        Standard.. 367.8 mm (14.48 inches)
        Limit... 360.4 mm (14.19 inches)
      VT750C2 Spirit
        Standard.. 371.8 mm (14.64 inches)
        Limit... 364.4 mm (14.35 inches)

Fork oil
  Type... Honda SS-8 (10W), or equivalent
  Capacity
    VT600 .... 449 cc (16.9 ounces)
    VT750
      2003 and earlier.. 512 cc (17.3 ounces)
      2004 .... 469 +/- 2.5 cc (15.9 +/- 0.08 ounces)
      2005 and later
        VT750C Aero .... 474 +/- 2.5 cc (16.0 +/- 0.08 ounces)
        VT750C2 Shadow Spirit .... 478 +/- 2.5 cc (16.2 +/- 0.08 ounces)
  Distance from top of fork tube
    VT600 .... 4.4 inches
    VT750
      2003 and earlier.. 4.3 inches
      2004 .... 4.1 inches
      2005 and later .... 3.9 inches

Rear shock absorber and spring

Spring free length

1988, 1989, 1991 through 1996 VT600	135 mm (5-5/16 inches)
All other models	Do not disassemble shock

Torque specifications

Front forks

Axle pinch bolts	22 Nm (16 ft-lbs)
Fork caps	
VT600	23 Nm (17 ft-lbs)
VT750	22 Nm (16 ft-lbs)
Damper rod bolts	29 Nm (21 ft-lbs)*

Handlebar brackets

Upper bracket bolts	
VT600	30 Nm (22 ft-lbs)
VT750	23 Nm (17 ft-lbs)
Lower bracket-to-upper triple clamp nuts	
Handlebars with removable upper caps	23 Nm (17 ft-lbs)
Handlebars with integral risers	54 Nm (40 ft-lbs)

Rear shock absorber

Upper and lower mounting bolts/nuts	
VT600	45 Nm (33 ft-lbs)
VT750	
2003 and earlier	26 Nm (19 ft-lbs)
2004 and later	
Upper	26 Nm (19 ft-lbs)
Lower right	34 Nm (25 ft-lbs)
Lower left	23 Nm (17 ft-lbs)
Damper rod locknut (pre-1997 VT600)	70 Nm (52 ft-lbs)
Steering stem head nut	103 Nm (76 ft-lbs)

Triple clamp/fork tube pinch bolts

VT600	
Upper	11 Nm (96 in-lbs)
Lower	50 Nm (37 ft-lbs)
VT750	
2003 and earlier	
Upper	26 Nm (19 ft-lbs)
Lower	50 Nm (37 ft-lbs)
2004 and later	
VT750C Aero	
Upper	26 Nm (19 ft-lbs)
Lower	49 Nm (36 ft-lbs)
VT750C2 Spirit	
Upper	22 Nm (16 ft-lbs)
Lower	49 Nm (36 ft-lbs)

Swingarm pivot bolt/nut

VT600	88 Nm (65 ft-lbs)
VT750	
2003 and earlier	
Pivot adjusting bolt	25 Nm (18 ft-lbs)
Pivot locknut	64 Nm (47 ft-lbs)
2004 and later	
Left pivot bolt	103 Nm (76 ft-lbs)
Right pivot bolt	
Initial setting	28 Nm (21 ft-lbs)
Second setting	Loosen 1/4-turn
Final setting	22 Nm (16 ft-lbs)
Right pivot bolt locknut	
Indicated when using special tool	103 Nm (76 ft-lbs)
Actual	93 Nm (69 ft-lbs)

* Use non-permanent thread locking agent on the threads.

2.1 To get to the handlebar bracket bolts on models with removable handlebar risers, pry out these four caps (arrows) with a small screwdriver

2.2 To remove the clutch lever bracket, remove these bolts (arrows)

1 General information

The front forks are a conventional coil-spring, hydraulically-damped telescopic type, designed to run at atmospheric pressure (they're not pressurized).

The rear suspension on VT600 models consists of a single nitrogen-charged shock absorber/coil spring assembly and a swingarm. The rear suspension on VT750 models consists of two shock absorbers and a swingarm.

The single shock on VT600 models and the twin shocks on VT750 models have spring preload adjusters which allow seven spring preload settings. Setting one is for light loads and/or good roads; setting seven is for heavy loads and/or bad roads. Setting two is the standard setting.

2 Handlebar - removal and installation

1   If the handlebar is being removed only to service other components, such as the steering head or fork tubes, it's only necessary to detach it from the bike and set it aside. It isn't necessary to disconnect the brake hose, the clutch or throttle cables, or the wire harnesses for the handlebar switches, but it is a good idea to support the handlebar assembly with a piece of wire or rope, to avoid excessive strain on the brake hose, the cables and the harnesses. If the handlebar is secured to the risers by removable upper brackets, pry out the trim caps **(see illustration)**, remove the bolts under them and lift the caps and handlebar off. If the handlebar has integral risers, remove the nuts from the bottoms of the risers (accessible from the underside of the

upper triple clamp) and lift the handlebar out.
2   If the handlebar itself is being replaced, disconnect the clutch cable (see Chapter 2), remove the clutch lever bracket **(see illustration)**, remove the switch housings (see Chapter 9), disconnect the throttle cables (see Chapter 4), remove the brake master cylinder (see Chapter 7), and unbolt the handlebar (see Step 1).
3   To remove the lower halves of the handlebar brackets from the upper triple clamp, remove the bracket nuts from the underside of the upper triple clamp **(see illustration)** and pull the brackets out of the triple clamp. Remove the rubber bushings.
4   Inspect the rubber bushings for cracks and distortion. If they're damaged or worn, replace them.
5   Inspect the handlebar for cracks and distortion and replace it if any damage is found.
6   Installation is the reverse of removal. Be sure to tighten the handlebar bracket bolts to the torque listed in this Chapter's Specifications.

3 Fork oil change

Note: *The following procedure applies to a fork oil change unassociated with rebuilding the front forks. If you are going to rebuild the forks, it's much easier to simply pour out the old fork oil after the forks have been removed from the bike.*

1   Support the bike securely so it can't be knocked over during this procedure. The front wheel must be raised off the ground using a hydraulic lift, a shop stand, a jack and wood support under the crankcase, axle stands, etc.
2   Remove the front wheel (see Chapter 7).
3   Place a drain pan under the fork legs

2.3 To detach the lower halves of the handlebar brackets from the upper triple clamp, remove these nuts (arrows)

3.3a Back out the damper rod bolt from the lower end of the fork leg . . .

3.3b . . . remove the bolt, discard the sealing washer and drain the fork oil

3.4 Remove the fork cap

and remove the damper rod bolts **(see illustrations)**. Discard the old sealing washers. Damper rod bolts can be difficult to remove, because the damper rod turns with the bolt. If this happens, use an air wrench to back out the bolt. If you don't have air tools, have an assistant compress the fork while you loosen the damper rod bolt (compressing the fork makes it harder for the damper rod to turn with the bolt). If you still can't loosen the bolt, remove the fork (see Section 4), put it in a bench vise (be sure to protect the fork with brass or plastic jaw protectors) and, again, have an assistant compress the fork while you loosen the damper rod bolt (it's easier to compress the fork when it's in a bench vise than when it's on the bike).

4   Remove the fork caps **(see illustration)**.

5   After most of the oil has drained, alternate between *slowly* compressing and releasing the forks to pump out the remaining oil. Don't try to compress the forks too quickly or you will squirt oil everywhere!

6   Clean the threads of the damper rod bolts with solvent, then dry them with compressed air, if available. You'll also need to clean and dry the damper rod threads inside the fork, because the thread locking agent won't work if the threads are oily. Apply non-permanent thread locking agent to the bolt threads, then install them with new sealing washers and tighten them to the torque listed in this Chapter's Specifications.

7   Remove the fork springs from the forks.

8   Pour the type and amount of fork oil listed in this Chapter's Specifications into the fork tube through the opening at the top **(see illustration)**.

9   Measure the level of the oil in the fork with the fork fully compressed and without the spring in position **(see illustration)**. Compare it to the value listed in this Chapter's Specifications. Add or remove oil as necessary.

10   Install the springs with their more closely-wound coils at the top.

11   Install the fork caps and tighten them to the torque listed in this Chapter's Specifications.

12   The remainder of installation is the reverse of the removal steps.

4   Forks - removal and installation

Removal

1   The front end of the bike must be off the ground for this procedure. Raise the bike on a hydraulic lift or shop stand, or put it on a milk crate or some other suitable support. Make sure that whatever you use is strong enough to support the bike securely.

2   Remove the front wheel (see Chapter 7).

3   Remove the front fender (see Chapter 8).

4   If you're planning to remove the left fork, disconnect the brake hose clamp and unbolt the brake caliper (see Chapter 7). Hang the caliper with a piece of wire or rope to protect the brake hose. This is a good time to inspect

3.8 Add the specified type and amount of fork oil (fork removed from bike for clarity; it's not necessary to remove the forks to add new fork oil)

3.9 Measure the distance from the top of the fork tube to the fork oil with the spring removed and the fork fully compressed

4.6a To detach a fork tube from the triple clamps, remove each plug (arrow) (lower triple clamp shown) . . .

4.6b . . . and remove each fork tube pinch bolt (arrow) (upper triple clamp shown)

the caliper and brake pads for wear (see Chapter 7).

5   The tops of the fork tubes are flush with the top surface of the upper triple clamp. The tube(s) must be reinstalled in exactly the same position.

6   Loosen the fork upper and lower triple clamp bolt caps and bolts **(see illustrations)**.

VT600 models

7   Remove the fork(s) from the triple clamps with a twisting motion.

VT750CD models

8   Remove the upper triple clamp (see Section 5).

9   Pull the fork tube(s) down slightly and remove the O-ring(s) between the upper fork cover(s) and the fork tube(s).

10   Remove the upper fork cover bolts and remove the upper fork cover(s).

11   Remove the fork(s) from the triple clamps with a twisting motion.

12   Remove the lower fork cover(s).

Installation

13   Installation is the reverse of removal. On VT750CD models, don't forget to install the lower and upper fork cover(s); be sure to use new O-rings with the upper cover(s). Do NOT torque any of the triple clamp bolts until the front wheel is installed.

14   After removing the bike from the lift, milk crate, etc., pump the front brake lever several times to bring the pads into contact with the disc.

5   Forks - disassembly, inspection and reassembly

Disassembly

Note: *Work on one fork leg at a time to avoid mixing up the parts.*

1   *Loosen* (do NOT remove), the damper rod bolts **(see illustration 3.3a)** and the fork tube caps **(see illustration 3.4)**.

2   Remove the forks (see Section 4).

3   Place a fork leg in a bench vise (clamp the vise jaws onto the slider; do not clamp onto the friction surface of the fork tube itself) and remove the fork cap and O-ring, the spacer, the spring seat and the fork spring. Discard the old fork cap O-ring.

4   Remove the fork from the bench vise and pour out the fork oil.

5   Place the fork leg back in the bench vise again. To finish disassembling the fork, you must remove the damper rod bolt (it's a large Allen bolt) from the bottom of the slider **(see illustration 3.3b)**. This bolt attaches the damper rod to the fork slider. When removing the Allen bolt, retrieve the old copper sealing washer and discard it. This washer must be replaced when the fork is reassembled. Sometimes, the damper rod bolt is so tight that the damper rod turns when you try to loosen the bolt. If this happens, try removing the bolt with an air tool, if you have it. If not, have an assistant push the inner fork tube firmly into the slider; compressing the fork spring is usually sufficient to lock the damper rod cylinder into place while the damper rod bolt is loosened. If that doesn't work, try compressing the fork spring *and* loosening the bolt with an air tool. And if that doesn't work? There are aftermarket tools designed to hold the damper rod; see your dealer parts department or an aftermarket motorcycle accessory shop. If you can't find a suitable special tool, have a dealer service department loosen the bolt.

6   Pry the dust seal out of the fork slider with a small screwdriver and slide it up the fork tube, so it's out of the way **(see illustration)**.

Caution: If you plan to reuse the dust seal, make sure you don't slide it over rust spots or spots where the chrome is flaking off, or you'll ruin it.

7   Slide the dust seal up the fork tube and pry out the stopper ring **(see illustration)**.

8   To separate the fork tube from the slider, hold the slider and yank the tube upward repeatedly (like a slide hammer) until the seal,

5.6 Pry the dust seal from the fork slider

5.7 Carefully pry the stopper ring out of its groove in the fork slider without distorting it

back-up ring and slider bushing pop loose from the slider **(see illustration)**. Remove the dust seal, stopper ring, seal and back-up ring from the fork tube. Discard the dust seal and fork seal. If the stopper ring is fatigued, replace it too.

9   Remove the oil lock piece from the damper rod **(see illustrations)**. If it's not there, it's probably still in the bottom of the fork slider.

10   Invert the tube and remove the damper rod and rebound spring.

5.8 Pull the slider and fork tube in opposite directions with a few sharp jerks (like a slide hammer); the slider bushing (A), back-up ring (B) and oil seal (C) will pop out of the slider with the tube

5.9a Remove the oil lock piece . . .

5.9b . . . and remove the damper rod and rebound spring from the other (upper) end of the fork tube

5.11a Fork tube bushing (A) and slider bushing (B)

5.11b Pry the fork tube bushing apart at the slit and slide it off; don't pry the bushing apart any more than necessary, to avoid distorting it

5.11c The slider bushing can be removed by simply sliding it off

11   The smaller-diameter fork tube bushing and the larger-diameter slider bushing are on the lower end of the fork tube (see illustration). The fork tube bushing fits tightly around the end of the fork tube and is seated against a shoulder on the end of the tube, while the slider bushing slides freely up and down the fork tube and is seated against a shoulder inside the fork slider. You need not remove either bushing unless it appears worn or scratched. If it's necessary to replace the fork tube bushing (the lower bushing on the tube, the one that doesn't slide up and down), pry it apart at the slit and slide it off (see illustration). To remove the slider bushing, simply slide it off the fork tube (see illustration).

Inspection

12   Clean all parts in solvent and blow them dry with compressed air, if available. Lay out the parts for inspection (see illustration).
13   Inspect the fork tube and slider, the bushings and the damper rod for score marks and scratches. Inspect the chrome surface of the fork tube for flaking and excessive wear. Look for dents in the tube. If the fork tube is

damaged or worn, replace it.
14   Have the fork tube checked for runout at a dealer service department or other repair shop.

⚠️ **Warning: If the fork tube is bent, replace it; don't try to have it straightened.**

15   Measure the overall length of the fork spring and check it for cracks and other damage. Compare the length to the minimum length listed in this Chapter's Specifications. If it's defective or sagged, replace both fork springs. Never replace only one spring.

Reassembly

16   Lightly lubricate all parts with clean fork oil as they're reassembled.
17   Install the new fork tube bushing, if the old bushing was removed. Do not pry open the bushing any more than necessary to install it. Be extremely careful not to damage the bushing friction surface. Make sure the bushing is seated at the bottom of the fork tube, against the shoulder.

18   Install the slider bushing on the fork tube.
19   Install the rebound spring on the damper rod. Install the damper rod into the fork tube, then let it slide slowly down until it protrudes from the bottom of the fork tube (see illustration).
20   Install the oil lock piece over the end of the damper rod that protrudes from the fork tube (see illustration).
21   Holding the fork slider upside down (so the lock piece doesn't fall off the lower end of the damper rod), insert the fork tube and damper rod into the slider.
22   Apply a non-permanent thread-locking agent to the damper rod bolt, then install the bolt and a new sealing washer (see illustration) and tighten it as much as you can. (Don't try to tighten to the torque listed in this Chapter's Specifications at this time unless you have a suitable tool for holding the damper rod.) If the bolt won't tighten up, the damper rod is not correctly aligned with the bolt. Using a flashlight and a Phillips screwdriver with a taped tip, align the threaded bore in the lower end of the damper rod with

5.12 The front fork assembly:

1	Fork cap and O-ring	10	Damper rod and rebound spring
2	Spacer		
3	Spring seat	11	Lock piece
4	Fork spring	12	Fork tube and fork tube bushing
5	Dust seal		
6	Stopper ring	13	Fork slider
7	Fork seal	14	Damper rod bolt and sealing washer
8	Back-up ring		
9	Slider bushing		

5.19 Insert the damper rod (with its rebound spring) into the upper end of the fork tube and let it drop through the smaller opening in the lower end

5.20 Install the lock piece on the lower end of the damper rod

5.22 This is the relationship of the damper rod bolt to the lock piece and damper rod when the damper rod bolt is installed through the bottom end of the slider, into the lower end of the damper rod; if the damper rod isn't aligned correctly with the hole in the slider, the bolt won't thread into it

the bore in the bottom of the slider.
23 Slide the back-up ring down the fork tube **(see illustration)**.

5.23 Install the back-up ring on the fork tube

24 Using a suitable bushing driver **(see illustrations)**, drive the slider bushing into place until it's fully seated. If you don't have one of these tools, drive the bushing into place with a section of pipe and an old guide bushing **(see illustration)**. Wrap tape around the ends of the pipe to prevent it from scratching the fork tube. If you're unable to fabricate a suitable bushing driver, take the fork assembly to a Honda dealer service department or a motorcycle machine shop or repair shop to have the bushing installed.
25 Lubricate the lip and the outer circumference of the new oil seal with the fork oil listed in this Chapter's Specifications and slide the seal down the fork tube with the part number side of the seal facing up **(see illustrations)**. Drive the seal into place with a seal driver (or use the same tool used to drive in the slider bushing) **(see illustrations)** or make something that will do the job **(see illustration)**. Again, if you don't have a suitable tool for this job, take the fork assembly to a Honda dealer service department or other motorcycle repair shop to have the seal installed. If you're extremely careful, the seal

can even be installed with a hammer and a drift punch. Work around the circumference of the seal, tapping gently on the outer edge of the seal until it's seated. Be careful! If you distort or damage the seal, you'll have to dig it out, which might mean disassembling the fork again (and taking it to a dealer!).
26 Install the stopper ring **(see illustration)**. Make sure the ring is correctly seated in its groove in the fork slider.
27 Install the dust seal and drive it into place with the same tool used to install the oil seal **(see illustration)**, or use the tool used to install the slider bushing driver. Make sure the dust seal is fully seated.
28 Add the recommended type and amount of fork oil (see Section 3).
29 Install the fork spring, with the closer-wound coils at the top.
30 Install the spring seat, the spacer and the fork cap. Use a new O-ring on the fork cap.
31 Install the fork assembly (see Section 4). If you won't be installing the fork right away, store it in an upright position.
32 Repeat this procedure for the other fork.

5.24a Using a split-type seal driver (this is a Kent-Moore, but any suitable equivalent will work) . . .

5.24b . . . tap down gently and repeatedly to seat the slider bushing; make sure the bushing is fully seated against the shoulder inside the slider

5.24c If you don't have a bushing driver, use a section of pipe instead; be sure to tape the ends of the pipe so it doesn't scratch the fork tube

5.25a Coat the inner lip and the outer circumference of the new seal with grease or fork oil . . .

5.25b . . . and install the seal on the fork tube; be careful not to damage the seal lip on the upper edge of the fork tube

5.25c Tap the seal gently and repeatedly with a seal driver until it's fully seated into the fork slider (but don't keep hitting it after it bottoms)

5.25d You can also use a bushing driver to tap the seal into place (one half of the bushing driver has been removed for clarity)

5.25e You can even drive the seal into place with two PVC plumbing fittings of the correct diameter; place one fitting on the seal and strike it with the other fitting (like a slide hammer)

5.26 Compress the stopper ring and fit it securely into its groove in the fork slider (if the stopper doesn't "snap" into place, it might be too fatigued to re-use)

5.27 Use any of the tools previously shown to drive the dust seal into place

6.4a Remove the steering stem nut . . .

6.4b . . . and remove the washer

6.5 Straighten the tabs on the lockwasher with a
small screwdriver

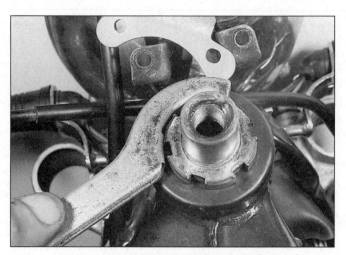

6.6a Loosen the locknut with ring nut wrench
(also known as a C-spanner)

6.6b Remove the locknut and the lockwasher (arrow)

6.7 Remove the bearing adjustment nut and the upper bearing
dust seal (arrow)

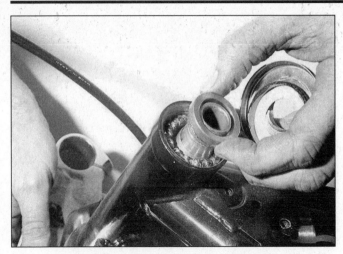

6.8 Remove the upper bearing inner race

6.9 Carefully pull the steering stem/lower triple clamp assembly from the steering head

6 Steering stem and bearings - removal, inspection and installation

Removal

1 If the steering head bearing check/adjustment (see Chapter 1) does not remedy excessive play or roughness in the steering head bearings, the entire front end must be disassembled and the bearings and races replaced.

2 Remove the fuel tank (see Chapter 4) and the steering head covers (see Chapter 8).

3 Remove the front forks (see Section 4).

4 Remove the steering stem nut and washer **(see illustrations)**, then lift off the upper triple clamp (sometimes called the fork bridge or crown). Unless you plan to replace the upper triple clamp, it isn't necessary to remove the handlebars - just set the upper triple clamp aside with everything attached.

Caution: If any of the electrical harnesses for the handlebar switches are pulled tight, unplug them (see Chapter 9). It isn't necessary to disconnect the brake hydraulic hose, but make sure that the handlebar/triple clamp assembly is neither hanging by the hose or putting any strain on the hose.

5 The locknut is secured by four lockwasher tabs. Straighten these tabs with a screwdriver **(see illustration)**.

6 Using a ring nuts wrench (also known as a C-spanner wrench), remove the locknut and the lockwasher **(see illustrations)**. There should be a suitable spanner in the bike's tool kit; if not, you can obtain the right wrench from a dealer or motorcycle accessory shop.

7 Remove the bearing locknut and the dust seal **(see illustration)**.

8 Remove the upper bearing inner race **(see illustration)** and remove the upper

bearing assembly.

9 Pull down on the lower triple clamp and remove the steering stem/lower bearing/lower triple clamp assembly **(see illustration)**. If it's stuck, gently tap on the top of the steering stem with a plastic mallet or a hammer and a wood block.

Inspection

10 Clean all the parts with solvent and dry them thoroughly, using compressed air, if available. Wipe the old grease out of the steering head and bearing races.

11 Examine the outer races in the steering head for cracks, dents, and pits. If even the slightest amount of wear or damage is evident, the races should be replaced.

12 To remove the outer races from the steering head, drive them out with a hammer and drift punch **(see illustrations)**. A slide hammer with the right internal-jaw puller will also work.

6.12a Insert a long punch or rod from below to tap out the upper steering head outer race . . .

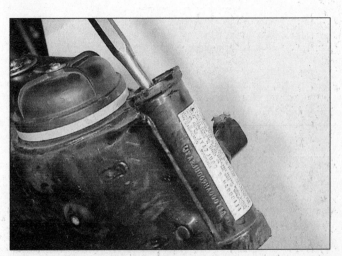

6.12b . . . and from above to tap out the lower bearing outer race

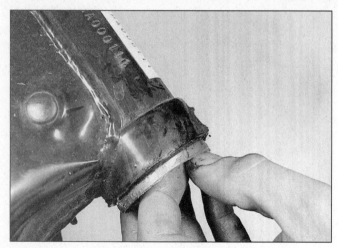

6.13a **Position the lower bearing outer race in the steering head . . .**

6.13b **. . . and tap it into position with a socket slightly smaller in diameter than the race**

13 Since the outer races are an "inter-ference-fit" in the frame, installation will be easier if the new races are left overnight in a refrigerator freezer. The frozen races will contract slightly, and slip into place in the frame with very little effort. When installing the races, tap them gently into place with a hammer and punch or a large socket **(see illustrations)**. Do not strike the bearing surface or the race will be damaged.

14 Inspect the bearings **(see illustration)** for wear. Look for cracks, dents, and pits in the races and flat spots on the bearings. If either bearing assembly is damaged or worn, replace both the upper or lower steering head bearings as a set.

15 Inspect the lower bearing inner race (the one that's pressed onto the steering stem) for cracks, dents, and pits. If even the slightest amount of wear or damage is evident, replace the lower inner race. Examine the dust seal under the lower bearing; if it's damaged, replace it.

16 To remove the lower bearing inner race, use a bearing puller (available at tool rental

yards, if you don't have one). A hammer and drift punch will also work **(see illustration)**. Don't remove this race unless it, or the dust seal, must be replaced. Removing the race will damage the dust seal, so replace the seal if the bearing is removed.

17 Inspect the steering stem/lower triple clamp assembly for cracks and other damage. Do not attempt to repair this component. If any damage is evident, replace the steering stem/lower triple clamp assembly.

18 Install a new dust seal and the lower bearing inner onto the steering stem **(see illustrations)**. Drive the lower bearing onto the steering stem using a bearing driver. If you don't have access to these tools, a section of pipe with the same diameter as the inner race can be used. Drive the bearing on until it's fully seated.

Installation

19 Pack the bearings with high-quality grease (preferably a moly-based grease). Coat the outer races in the steering head with grease also.

20 Install the lower steering head bearing assembly on the steering stem, then insert the steering stem/lower triple clamp into the lower end of the steering head. Install the upper bearing, inner race, dust seal and bearing adjustment nut. Using the spanner wrench (C-spanner), tighten the adjuster nut while moving the lower triple clamp back and forth. Continue to tighten the nut, 1/8-turn at a time, until all play has been removed from the steering head bearings. However, don't overtighten the adjustment nut, or the steering will be too firm and the new bearings and/or races will wear out prematurely.

21 Once the adjustment nut is tight and all bearing play has been removed, install the lockwasher and the locknut. Bend up the tabs on the lockwasher to secure the lock-nut, then install the upper triple clamp on the steering stem. Install the washer and steering stem nut but don't tighten the nut yet.

22 Install the forks and tighten the lower triple clamp bolts to the torque listed in this Chapter's Specifications.

23 Tighten the steering stem nut to the

6.13c **Tap the upper bearing outer race into position with the same tools**

6.13d **. . . the upper bearing outer race should look like this when installed**

6.14 The steering stem/lower triple clamp assembly

6.16 Tap the seal and lower bearing bottom race off the steering stem

1 Bearing adjustment nut
2 Dust seal
3 Upper steering head
   bearing inner race
4 Upper steering head
   bearing assembly

5 Lower steering head
   bearing assembly
6 Lower steering head
   bearing inner race

torque listed in this Chapter's Specifications.
24 Check the alignment of the fork tubes with the top surface of the upper triple clamp. The tops of the fork tubes must be even with the surface of the triple clamp. If necessary, loosen the lower triple clamp bolts and adjust the position of the fork tubes. Tighten the upper (and lower, if loosened) triple clamp bolts to the torque listed in this Chapter's Specifications.
25 Install the handlebar assembly, if removed (see Section 2).
26 Install the steering head covers (see Chapter 8) and fuel tank (see Chapter 4).

7 Rear shock absorber (VT600 models) - removal, inspection and installation

Removal

⚠ **Warning: Do not attempt to disassemble this shock absorber. It is nitrogen-charged under high pressure. Improper disassembly could result in serious injury. Instead, take the shock to a dealer service department with the proper equipment to do the job.**

1 The bike must be supported with the rear wheel off the ground for this procedure. Raise the bike on a hydraulic lift or shop stand, or put it on a milk crate or some other suitable support. Make sure that whatever you use is strong enough to support the bike securely.
2 Remove the seat and both side covers (see Chapter 8).
3 Remove the fuel pump and the fuel pump relay (see Chapter 4).
4 Remove the rear ignition coil mounting bolts (see Chapter 5).
5 Remove the turn signal relay from the fuel pump bracket (see Chapter 9).
6 Remove the front bolt from the rear igni-

6.18a Install a new seal with its concave side down . . .

6.18b . . . then install the lower bearing inner race with its bearing surface facing up, and press the race onto the stem with a section of pipe (taped to protect the bearing surface)

tion coil bracket **(see illustration)**.

7　Locate the fuel pump bracket mounting nut on the left side of the bike, right above the rear end of the ignition control module and remove it **(see illustration)**.

8　Remove the fuel pump bracket **(see illustration)**.

9　Remove the upper and lower shock absorber nuts and bolts **(see illustrations)**.

10　Remove the shock absorber from the top **(see illustration)**.

Inspection

11　Inspect the shock absorber for obvious physical damage, such as a worn damper rod seal or a bent damper rod. Inspect the coil spring for looseness or signs of fatigue. Inspect the shock for evidence that it's leaking shock oil or nitrogen gas.

12　If the shock absorber or the coil spring is damaged or obviously worn, replace the shock and coil spring as a single assembly.

On 1988 and 1989 and 1991 through 1996 VT600 models, either component could be replaced separately at one time. Check with your dealer for availability. Unless the parts department has the older separate parts in stock, you will probably discover that older models are being fitted with the newer unit, which is only available as a single assembly. Even if you do find the parts separately, however, special tools are needed to disassemble the shock/coil spring assembly. Have

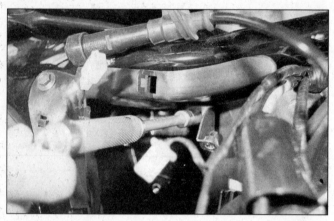

7.6 Remove the front bolt from the rear ignition coil bracket

7.7 Remove the fuel pump bracket mounting nut (on the left side of the bike, right above the rear end of the ignition control module)

7.8 Remove the fuel pump bracket

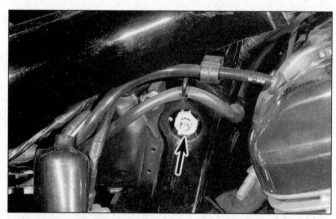

7.9a Remove the upper shock absorber nut and bolt

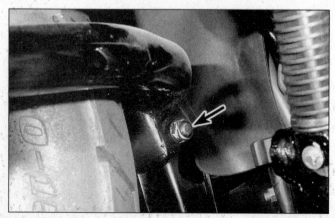

7.9b Remove the lower shock absorber nut and bolt

7.10 Remove the shock absorber from the top

the unit disassembled and the coil spring or shock absorber replaced by a dealer service department with the right tools.

Installation

13   Installation is the reverse of removal. Be sure to tighten the shock absorber nuts and bolts to the torque listed in this Chapter's Specifications.

8   Rear shock absorbers (VT750 models) - removal, inspection and installation

⚠ **Warning: Do not attempt to disassemble this shock absorber. It is nitrogen-charged under high pressure. Improper disassembly could result in serious injury. Instead, take the shock to a dealer service department with the proper equipment to do the job.**

Removal

1   The bike must be supported with the rear wheel off the ground for this procedure. Raise the bike on a hydraulic lift or shop stand, or put it on a milk crate or some other suitable support. Make sure that whatever you use is strong enough to support the bike securely.
2   Remove the upper and lower mounting bolts and the washers from *one* shock absorber **(see illustration)**. Do NOT remove both shocks at the same time!

Inspection

3   Inspect the shock for oil leaks and obvious external damage. Inspect the upper and lower mounting bolt bushings for cracks and excessive wear. If any damage is evident, replace the shock. It cannot be overhauled.

Installation

4   Install the shock absorber, install the washers and mounting bolts and tighten the bolts to the torque listed in this Chapter's Specifications.

5   Repeat Steps 2 through 4 for the other shock.
6   Remove the bike from its support.

9   Swingarm bearings - check

1   Remove the rear wheel (see Chapter 7).
2   Remove the rear shock absorber(s) (VT600 models, see Section 7; VT750 models, see Section 8).
3   Grasp the rear of the swingarm with one hand and place your other hand at the junction of the swingarm and the frame. Try to move the rear of the swingarm from side-to-side. Any wear (play) in the bearings should be felt as movement between the swingarm and the frame at the front. The swingarm will actually be felt to move forward and backward at the front (not from side-to-side).
4   Move the swingarm up and down through its full travel. It should move freely, without any binding or rough spots. If it doesn't move up and down freely, either the swingarm pivot is too tight or the swingarm bearings and/or bushings are damaged.
5   If the swingarm has too much play or is stiff, remove the swingarm (VT600 models, see Section 10; VT750 models, see Sec-

tion 11) and replace the swingarm bearings and/or bushings (see Section 12).

10   Swingarm (VT600 models) - removal, inspection and installation

Removal

1   The bike must be supported with the rear wheel off the ground for this procedure. Raise the bike on a hydraulic lift or shop stand, or put it on a milk crate or some other suitable support. Make sure that whatever you use is strong enough to support the bike securely.
2   Remove the gearshift arm from the gearshift spindle (see Chapter 2).
3   Remove the rear wheel (see Chapter 7).
4   Remove the chain guard and the drive sprocket (see Chapters 8 and 7).
5   On California models, remove the evaporative emission control system canister (see Chapter 4).
6   Remove the coolant reservoir (see Chapter 3).
7   Remove the shock absorber lower mounting nut and bolt and disengage the lower end of the shock absorber from the swingarm (see Section 7).
8   Remove the swingarm pivot bolt and nut **(see illustrations)**.

8.2 **VT750 shock absorber mounting bolts and washers (arrows)**

10.8a **To detach the VT600 swingarm from the frame, remove the pivot bolt caps from both ends, remove the nut . . .**

10.8b **. . . and remove the pivot bolt (arrow)**

10.10a Remove the left side pivot bushing and the dust seals (arrow) from the swingarm (outer dust seal not visible in this photo)

10.10b Remove the right side pivot collars and the dust seals (arrow) from the swingarm (outer dust seal not visible in this photo)

9   Remove the swingarm. If you're replacing the swingarm, unbolt the stopper arm (the arm between the swingarm and the rear brake) and detach the drive chain protector (it's attached by two bolts: one on top, one on bottom).

Inspection

10   Remove the bushing from the left swingarm pivot **(see illustration)** and remove the two collars from the right pivot **(see illustration)**.
11   Inspect the swingarm pivot bolt, the left pivot bushing and the right pivot collars **(see illustration)** for scoring and excessive wear. If any of these parts are damaged or worn, replace them.
12   Inspect the swingarm bearings **(see illustration)** for dryness, damage and excessive wear. If they're dry, lubricate them; if they're damaged or worn, replace them (see Section 12).

Installation

13   Installation is the reverse of removal. Tighten the pivot bolt and the shock absorber lower mounting nut and bolt to the torque listed in this Chapter's Specifications.
14   Adjust the drive chain when you're done (see Chapter 1).

---

11 Swingarm (VT750 models) - removal, inspection and installation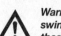

⚠️ *Warning: Tightening the swingarm pivot bolt safely on these models requires special tools for which there are no adequate substitutes. If you don't have the correct tools, take the bike to a Honda dealer or other properly equipped shop to have the bolt removed and installed.*

Removal

1   The bike must be supported with the rear wheel off the ground for this procedure. Raise the bike on a hydraulic lift or shop stand, or put it on a milk crate or some other suitable support. Make sure that whatever you use is strong enough to support the bike securely.
2   Remove the exhaust pipe (see Chapter 4).
3   Remove the rear wheel (see Chapter 7).
4   Remove the rear shock absorbers (see Section 8).
5   If you're working on a chain drive model, unbolt the chain guard. If you're working on a shaft drive model, remove the final drive unit (see Chapter 7).
6   Remove the swingarm pivot bolt caps.

Chain drive models

7   Remove the swingarm pivot bolt nut.
8   Hold the pivot bolt and remove the

10.11 Inspect the swingarm pivot nut (1), bolt (2), the left side pivot bushing (3) and right side pivot collars (4)

10.12 Inspect the swingarm bearings; if they're dry, lubricate them with multi-purpose grease and if they're worn, replace them

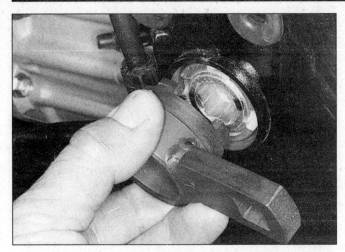

11.8a Use this tool to loosen and tighten the swingarm locknut

11.8b Unscrew the locknut from the pivot bolt

swingarm pivot bolt locknut (see illustrations).

9   Loosen the swingarm adjusting bolt by turning the pivot bolt (see illustration).

10   Pull out the pivot bolt and remove the swingarm. If you're replacing the swingarm, unbolt the stopper arm (the arm between the swingarm and the rear brake) and detach the drive chain protector (it's attached by two bolts: one on top, one on bottom).

Shaft drive models

11   Undo the locknut on the left pivot bolt, using Honda tool 07908-4690003 (see illustrations 11.8a and 11.8b). While you're undoing the locknut, hold the pivot bolt from turning with a 17mm Allen bolt bit. These are available from tool stores.

12   Unscrew the swingarm pivot bolts with the 17mm Allen bolt bit and remove both bolts (see illustrations).

13   Pull the swingarm back and remove it from the frame. The U-joint may bind a little on the output shaft splines, but it will come loose if you pull it firmly.

14   Remove the old U-joint dust boot from the swingarm, then pull the U-joint out of the swingarm (see illustration).

15   Check the pivot bearings in the swingarm for dryness or wear (see Section 12). Lubricate or replace them as necessary.

11.9 Unscrew the pivot bolt with an Allen bolt bit

11.12a Use a 17mm Allen bolt bit in a socket to hold the right pivot bolt while you turn the locknut, and to unscrew both pivot bolts

11.12b Remove the pivot bolts

11.14 After pulling off the old U-joint dust boot, remove the U-joint from the swingarm

Inspection

Chain drive models

16   Remove the two collars from the left and right pivots **(see illustration 10.10b)**.

17   Inspect the swingarm pivot bolt and the left and right pivot collars for scoring and excessive wear. If any of these parts are damaged or worn, replace them.

18   Inspect the swingarm bearings **(see illustration 10.12)** for dryness, damage and excessive wear. If they're dry, lubricate them with multi-purpose grease. If they're damaged or worn, replace them (see Section 12).

Shaft drive models

19   Check the pivot bolts and locknut for wear or damage and replace as needed.

20   Check the tapered roller bearing in each side of the swingarm for dryness, damage or excessive wear. If they're dry, lubricate them with multi-purpose grease. If they're damaged or worn, replace them (see Section 12).

Installation

Chain drive models

21   Place the swingarm in position and install the swingarm adjusting bolt. Make sure that the tip of the bolt doesn't protrude in too far (if the end of the bolt *does* protrude in too far, you won't able to install the swingarm).

22   Apply a coat of grease to the swingarm pivot bolt and install the pivot bolt.

23   Screw in the adjusting bolt by hand.

24   Push the hex shank of the pivot bolt into the socket head of the adjusting bolt.

25   Tighten the pivot bolt and adjusting bolt to the torque listed in this Chapter's Specifications.

26   Install the swingarm pivot adjusting bolt locknut and tighten it by hand, then tighten the locknut to the torque listed in this Chapter's Specifications. A special tool (07GMA-KT70200, or a suitable equivalent) is needed

to hold the pivot bolt while torquing the locknut. If you're unable to obtain this special tool or a suitable equivalent (consult your dealer parts department), take the bike to a dealer and have the locknut tightened to the correct torque by the service department.

 Warning: Don't ride the bike until the locknut has been properly tightened to the specified torque.

27   Installation is otherwise the reverse of removal. Be sure to tighten the shock absorber mounting bolts to the torque listed in this Chapter's Specifications.

28   Adjust the drive chain when you're done (see Chapter 1).

Shaft drive models

29   Lubricate the universal joint splines with multi-purpose grease. Make sure the universal joint dust boot is in place, then install the universal joint in the swingarm and push it onto the forward end of the driveshaft.

30   Place the swingarm in the installed position in the frame, but don't install the universal joint on the output shaft yet. Grease the tips of the pivot bolts and thread them into their holes, making sure the tips fit into the swingarm bearings. Don't tighten the pivot bolts yet.

31   Slide the universal joint forward onto the output shaft **(see illustration)**. If it hangs upon the output shaft splines, turn the rear end of the driveshaft back and forth while pushing forward until you feel the universal joint slide onto the output shaft splines.

32   Tighten the left pivot bolt to the torque listed in this Chapter's Specifications. **Note:** *The swingarm pivot bolts and locknut must be tightened in the specified sequence and to the correct torque settings.*

33   Tighten the right pivot bolt after tightening the left pivot bolt. The right pivot bolt is tightened in three stages, listed in this Chap-

11.31 The universal joint splines must slide onto the splines on the output shaft (arrow)

ter's Specifications. Tighten to the initial setting, then loosen the bolt 1/4 turn. Raise and lower the swingarm a few times to seat the bearings, then retighten the right pivot bolt to the final torque listed in this Chapter's Specifications.

34   Thread the locknut onto the right pivot bolt as far as you can with your fingers. Attach the special wrench to a torque wrench. Hold the pivot bolt with the 17mm Allen bolt bit so it won't turn, then tighten the locknut to the torque listed in this Chapter's Specifications. **Note:** *The extra length of the special wrench will amplify the effect of the torque wrench, so it will tighten the locknut to a higher torque than that indicated on the torque wrench. Tighten the locknut to the indicated torque listed in this Chapter's Specifications, not to the actual torque.*

35   The remainder of installation is the reverse of the removal steps.

12.4a Pry out the old grease seals for the swingarm with a seal removal tool or screwdriver

12.4b Remove the seal and bearing from each end of the swingarm pivot bore

12.6 Replace the outer races and bearings as a set if either race is worn; don't forget to install the grease retainer (arrow) in each end

12 Swingarm bearings - replacement

Chain drive models

1   Remove the swingarm (VT600 models, see Section 10; VT750 models, see Section 11).

2   Special tools are needed to press out the old bearings and press in new ones. Take the swingarm to a dealer service department or to a motorcycle machine shop with the right tools and have the old bearings replaced.

3   Install the swingarm.

Shaft drive models

4   Pry out the seals and remove the bearings from the swingarm (see illustrations).

5   Clean the parts with solvent and dry them thoroughly, using compressed air, if available. If you do use compressed air, don't let the bearings spin as they're dried - this could ruin them. Wipe the old grease out of the swingarm and bearing races.

6   Examine the bearings and races (see illustration) for cracks, dents or pits. If any wear is evident, the races should be replaced. If one race (or one bearing) needs to be replaced, replace both of the bearings, as well as their races and seals, as a set.

7   To remove the bearing races, drive them out of the swingarm with a hammer and long rod. To do this, drill a hole in the internal grease retainer on one side of the swingarm, then insert the rod through the hole to drive out the grease retainer and bearing race on the opposite side. Pull out the rod, insert it through the opposite side of the swingarm and drive out the remaining grease retainer and outer race.

8   Since the races are an interference fit with the swingarm, installation will be easier if the new races are left overnight in a freezer. This will cause them to contract and slip into place in the frame with very little effort. When installing the races, tap them gently into place with a hammer and bearing driver or large socket. Do not strike the bearing surface or the race will be damaged.

Notes

Chapter 7
Brakes, wheels, tires and final drive

Contents

Degrees of difficulty

Easy, suitable for novice with little experience		**Fairly easy,** suitable for beginner with some experience		**Fairly difficult,** suitable for competent DIY mechanic		**Difficult,** suitable for experienced DIY mechanic	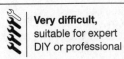	**Very difficult,** suitable for expert DIY or professional	

Specifications

Brakes
Brake fluid type .... See Chapter 1
Front brake disc thickness
  VT600
    Standard.. 5.0 mm (0.20 inch)
    Minimum*... 4.0 mm (0.16 inch)
  VT750
    Standard.. 5.8 to 6.2 mm (0.23 to 0.24 inch)
    Minimum*... 5.0 mm (0.2 inch)
Disc runout limit .... 0.30 mm (0.012 inch)
Front brake pad minimum thickness.. To bottom of wear groove
Rear brake drum inside diameter
  VT600
    Standard.. 160 mm (6.30 inches)
    Maximum... 161 mm (6.34 inches)*
  VT750
    Standard.. 180 to 180.3 mm (7.09 to 7.10 inches)
    Maximum... 181 mm (7.13 inches)*
Rear brake shoe lining thickness
  Standard .... 5 mm (0.20 inch)
  Minimum .... 2 mm (0.08 inch)

*Refer to marks on the disc or drum (they supersede information printed here)

Wheels and tires

Wheel runout
  Radial (up-and-down) .... 2.0 mm (0.08 inch)
  Axial (side-to-side) .... 2.0 mm (0.08 inch)
Tire pressures.. See Chapter 1
Tire sizes
  Front
    VT600 .... 100/90-19 57S
    VT750
      2003 and earlier.. 120/90-17 64S
      2004 and later
        VT750C Aero .... 120/90-17 M/C 64S
        VT750C2 Spirit .... 90/90-21 M/C 54S
  Rear
    All VT600, 2003 and earlier VT750 .... 170/80-15 M/C 77S
    2004 and later VT750 .... 160/80-15 M/C 74S

Torque specifications

Brake disc mounting bolts
  VT600
    1988 through 1998 .... 39 Nm (29 ft-lbs)
    1999 on.. 42 Nm (31 ft-lbs)
  VT750 .... 42 Nm (31 ft-lbs)
Brake caliper bracket mounting bolts
  1988, 1989, 1991 through 1993 VT600 .... 27 Nm (20 ft-lbs)
  1994 on VT600, VT750... 30 Nm (22 ft-lbs)
Brake hose banjo bolt .... 34 Nm (25 ft-lbs)
Brake lever pivot bolt nut .... 6 Nm (53 in-lbs)
Brake pad pin... 18 Nm (159 in-lbs)
Drive sprocket bolts .... 10 Nm (7 ft-lbs)
VT600 driven sprocket nuts .... 65 Nm (47 ft-lbs)
VT750 driven sprocket nuts (chain drive)..................................... 88 Nm (65 ft-lbs)
Final drive unit mounting nuts (shaft drive) .... 64 Nm (47 ft-lbs)
Coupling flange Allen bolts (shaft drive)....................................... 20 Nm (15 ft-lbs)
Front axle
  VT600 .... 74 Nm (55 ft-lbs)
  VT750
    2003 and earlier.. 59 Nm (44 ft-lbs)
    2004 through 2007 VT750C Aero .... 74 Nm (54 ft-lbs)
    2008 VT750C Aero, 2007 and later VT750C2 Spirit (axle bolt)..... 59 Nm (44 ft-lbs)
Front axle pinch bolts.. 22 Nm (16 ft-lbs)
Master cylinder mounting bolts.. 12 Nm (108 in-lbs)
Rear axle nut
  VT600
    1988 and 1989, 1991 through 1996 .... 90 Nm (66 ft-lbs)
    1997 on.. 88 Nm (65 ft-lbs)
  VT750
    2003 and earlier.. 93 Nm (69 ft-lbs)
    2004 and later... 88 Nm (65 ft-lbs)
Rear brake stopper arm bolts/nuts
  VT600 .... 22 Nm (16 ft-lbs)
  VT750
    2003 and earlier.. 20 Nm (15 ft-lbs)
    2004 and later... 22 Nm (16 ft-lbs)

2.3 Unscrew and remove the pad pin plug

2.4 Unscrew the pad pin

1 General information

The models covered in this Chapter are equipped with a hydraulic disc brake at the front and a mechanical drum brake at the rear. All models are equipped with wire spoke wheels and tube-type tires. And all models are chain-driven.

Caution: Disc brake components rarely require disassembly. Do not disassemble components unless absolutely necessary. If any hydraulic brake line connection in the system is loosened, the entire system should be disassembled, drained, cleaned and then properly filled and bled upon reassembly. Do not use solvents on internal brake components. Solvents will cause seals to swell and distort. Use only clean brake fluid, brake cleaner or alcohol for cleaning. Use care when working

with brake fluid as it can injure your eyes and it will damage painted surfaces and plastic parts.

2 Brake pads - replacement

⚠️ *Warning: The dust created by the brake system is harmful to your health. Never blow it out with compressed air and don't inhale any of it. An approved filtering mask should be worn when working on the brakes.*

1   Turn the handlebar so that the brake master cylinder is level, then remove the master cylinder reservoir cover, set plate and diaphragm (see Section 5).
2   Depress the caliper pistons by pushing the caliper in (toward the disc) with your

thumbs. Watch the level of the brake fluid in the master cylinder reservoir; it will rise as you depress the caliper pistons. If it gets too close to the top, siphon off a little fluid from the reservoir. If you can't depress the pistons with thumb pressure, try using a C-clamp. If the pistons stick, remove the caliper and overhaul it (see Section 3).
3   Remove the pad pin plug **(see illustration)**.
4   Remove the pad pin **(see illustration)**.
5   Remove the brake pads **(see illustration)**.
6   If the pads have removable shims, remove the shims from the old pads.
7   Note whether the friction material on the pads has been worn down to the bottom of the wear grooves (if the wear grooves have disappeared, or are about to disappear) **(see illustration)**. If so, replace the pads, as a pair. If the pads are fouled with oil or are damaged, replace them.
8   Inspect the condition of the brake disc (see Section 4). If it needs to be machined or

2.5 Pull out the pad pin plug and remove the brake pads; the holes for the pad pin at the lower end of the caliper

2.7 There are grooves in new pads (left); if they're worn away (right), replace the pads immediately

2.9 Replace the pad retainer (left arrow) and pad spring (right arrow) if they're damaged or worn

2.12 This is how the pads and the pad pin should look right before the pad pin is screwed into the caliper

replaced, follow the procedure in that Section to remove it. If the disc is okay, deglaze it with sandpaper or emery cloth, using a swirling motion.

9   Inspect the condition of the pad retainer and the pad spring (see illustration). If either of them is distorted or damaged, replace it. If you remove the retainer or the spring, make sure that the new part fits into the caliper exactly as shown. If either of these parts is incorrectly installed, the pads will not fit into the caliper correctly.

10   Install the shims on the new brake pads.

11   Install the pads in the caliper so that their upper ends rest against the pad retainer.

12   Push the pads against the pad spring, align the holes in the lower ends of the pads with the hole in the caliper, insert the pad pin (see illustration) and tighten it to the torque listed in this Chapter's Specifications.

13   Install the pad pin plug and tighten it securely.

14   Refill the master cylinder reservoir (see Chapter 1) and install the diaphragm and cover.

15   Operate the brake lever several times to bring the pads into contact with the disc. Check the operation of the brakes carefully before riding the motorcycle.

3   Brake caliper - removal, overhaul and installation

⚠️ *Warning: The dust created by the brake system is harmful to your health. Never blow it out with compressed air and don't inhale any of it. An approved filtering mask should be worn when working on the brakes. Do not, under any circumstances, use petroleum-based solvents to clean brake parts. Use brake cleaner or denatured alcohol only!*

Note: *The brake caliper on 2008 models is mounted on the right fork leg instead of the left fork leg, but service procedures are the same.*

Removal

1   Remove the cover, set plate and diaphragm from the master cylinder and siphon out all of the old brake fluid.

2   Detach the brake hose from the fork slider (see illustration). Disconnect the brake hose from the caliper (see illustration). Remove the brake hose banjo bolt and discard the sealing washers. Place the end of the hose in a container and operate the brake lever to pump out the rest of the brake fluid. After all the fluid has been expelled, wrap a clean shop rag tightly around the hose fitting to soak up any drips and prevent contamination.

3   Remove the caliper bracket mounting bolts (see illustration) and separate the caliper from the fork slider.

Overhaul

4   Clean the exterior of the caliper with denatured alcohol or brake system cleaner.

5   Remove the brake pad pin and the brake pads (see Section 2).

3.2a Brake hose clamp (upper arrow); the neck of the hose must be in this notch (lower arrow)

3.2b To disconnect the brake hose from the caliper, remove the banjo bolt; discard the old sealing washers

3.3 To detach the brake caliper from the fork slider, remove these two bolts (arrows)

3.6 Pull the caliper and bracket apart; inspect the caliper pin dust boot (A) and the bracket pin boot (B)

6   Separate the caliper bracket from the caliper (see illustration).

7   Remove the caliper pin dust boot and the pad retainer from the caliper bracket. Inspect the dust boot for cracks, tears and deterioration; replace it if it's damaged or worn. Make sure the retainer is neither bent nor damaged; if it is, replace it.

8   Remove the caliper bracket pin dust boot and the pad spring from the caliper. Inspect the boot for cracks, tears and deterioration; replace it if it's damaged or worn. Make sure the pad spring is neither bent nor damaged; if it is, replace it.

9   Place a few rags between the piston and the caliper frame to act as a cushion, lay the caliper on the work bench so that the pistons are facing down, toward the work bench surface, then use compressed air, directed into the fluid inlet, to remove the pistons. Use only small quick blasts of air to ease the pistons out of the bore. If a piston is blown out with too much force, it might be damaged.

⚠ Warning: Never place your fingers in front of the pistons in an attempt to catch or protect them when applying compressed air. Doing so could result in serious injury.

10   If compressed air isn't available, reconnect the caliper to the brake hose and pump the brake lever until the piston is free. (You'll have to put brake fluid in the master cylinder reservoir and get most of the air out of the hose to use this method.)

11   Once the pistons are protruding from the caliper, remove them (see illustration).

12   Using a wood or plastic tool, remove the dust seals and the piston seals (see illustration).

13   Clean the pistons and the piston bores with denatured alcohol, fresh brake fluid or brake system cleaner and dry them off with filtered, unlubricated compressed air. Inspect the surfaces of the pistons (see illustration) and the piston bores for nicks and burrs and loss of plating. If you find defects on the surface of either piston or piston bore,

replace the caliper assembly (the pistons are matched to the caliper). If the caliper is in bad shape, inspect the master cylinder too.

14   Lubricate the new piston seals and dust

3.11 After popping the pistons loose with compressed air, insert a pair of pliers inside each piston and pull them out of their bores

3.12 Remove the dust (outer) seals and the piston (inner) seals from both bores; be careful not to scratch the surface of the bores

3.13 Front brake caliper assembly

1	Pistons	3	Piston seal	5	Caliper
2	Dust seal	4	Pad springs		

4.3 Set up a dial indicator with the probe touching the surface of the disc, turn the wheel slowly and measure runout

4.4a Use a micrometer to measure the thickness of the disc at several points

seals with clean brake fluid and install them in their grooves in the caliper bore. Make sure they're not twisted and are fully and correctly seated.

15 Lubricate the pistons with clean brake fluid and install them into their bores in the caliper. Using your thumbs, push each piston all the way in; make sure it doesn't become cocked in the bore.

16 The caliper body should be able to slide in relation to its mounting bracket. If it was seized or operated stiffly prior to disassembly, inspect the slider pins on the caliper and the bracket for excessive wear. Minor blemishes can be cleaned up with crocus or emery cloth. If either pin shows signs of serious damage, replace it. The pins can be unscrewed from the bracket and caliper. If you remove either pin, be sure to tighten the new pin to the torque listed in this Chapter's Specifications. Coat the pins with high-temperature disc brake grease.

17 Reassemble the caliper and the caliper bracket. Make sure that the two parts slide smoothly in and out on the pins.

18 If the pad retainer or pad spring was removed, install it now **(see illustration 2.9)**.

19 Install the brake pads (see Section 2).

Installation

20 Install the caliper on the fork slider, install the caliper bracket mounting bolts and tighten them to the torque listed in this Chapter's Specifications.

21 Connect the brake hose to the caliper, using new sealing washers on each side of the banjo bolt.

22 Fill the master cylinder with the recommended brake fluid (see Chapter 1) and bleed the system (see Section 7). Check for leaks.

23 Check the operation of the brakes carefully before riding the motorcycle.

4 Brake disc - inspection, removal and installation

Inspection

1 Support the bike securely so it can't be knocked over during this procedure.

2 Visually inspect the surface of the disc for score marks and other damage. Light scratches are normal after use and won't affect brake operation, but deep grooves and heavy score marks will reduce braking efficiency and accelerate pad wear. If the disc is badly grooved it must be machined or replaced.

3 To check disc runout, mount a dial indicator to the fork leg with the plunger on the indicator touching the surface of the disc about 1/2-inch from the outer edge **(see illustration)**. Slowly turn the wheel and

4.4b The minimum thickness is also stamped into the disc (if it differs from the value listed in this Chapter's Specifications, the information here supersedes the specs)

4.6 To detach the disc from the wheel, remove these five Allen bolts in a criss-cross fashion

5.4 Reservoir cover screws (left arrows) and brake hose banjo bolt (right arrow)

5.7 Detach the master cylinder mounting bolts (arrows); the UP mark must be upright when the master cylinder is installed

watch the indicator needle, comparing your reading with the limit listed in this Chapter's Specifications or stamped on the disc itself. If the runout is greater than allowed, replace the disc.

4   The disc must not be machined or allowed to wear down to a thickness less than the minimum allowable thickness, listed in this Chapter's Specifications. The thickness of the disc can be checked with a micrometer **(see illustration)**. If the thickness of the disc is less than the minimum allowable, it must be replaced. The minimum thickness is also stamped into the disc **(see illustration)**.

Removal

5   Remove the wheel (see Section 11).
6   Mark the relationship of the disc to the wheel, so it can be installed in the same position. Remove the bolts that retain the disc to the wheel hub **(see illustration)**. Loosen the bolts a little at a time, in a criss-cross pattern, to avoid distorting the disc. Once all the bolts are loose, take the disc off.
7   Take note of any paper shims that may be present where the disc mates to the hub. If there are any, mark their position and be sure to include them when installing the disc.

Installation

8   Position the disc on the wheel, aligning the previously applied match marks (if you're reinstalling the original disc). Make sure the arrow (stamped on the disc) marking the direction of rotation is pointing in the correct direction (the direction that the wheel rotates when the bike is moving forward).
9   Apply a non-hardening thread locking compound to the threads of the bolts. Install the bolts with new lockwashers, tightening them a little at a time, in a criss-cross pattern, until the torque listed in this Chapter's Specifications is reached. Clean off all grease from the brake disc using acetone or brake

system cleaner.
10   Install the wheel (see Section 11).
11   Operate the brake lever several times to bring the pads into contact with the disc. Check the operation of the brakes carefully before riding the motorcycle.

> ### 5 Front brake master cylinder - removal, overhaul and installation

1   If the master cylinder is leaking fluid, or if the lever does not produce a firm feel when the brake is applied, and bleeding the brakes does not help, master cylinder overhaul is recommended.
2   Before disassembling the master cylinder, read through the entire procedure and make sure that you have the correct rebuild kit. Also, you will need some new, clean brake fluid of the recommended type, some clean rags and internal snap-ring pliers. **Note:** *To prevent damage to the paint from spilled brake fluid, always cover the top cover or upper fuel tank when working on the master cylinder.*

Caution: Disassembly, overhaul and reassembly of the brake master cylinder must be done in a spotlessly clean work area to avoid contamination and possible failure of the brake hydraulic system components.

Removal

3   Remove the rear view mirror.
4   Remove the reservoir cover retaining screws **(see illustration)**. Remove the reservoir, the set plate and the rubber diaphragm. Siphon as much brake fluid from the reservoir as you can to avoid spilling it on the bike.
5   Unplug the electrical connectors from the brake light switch (see Chapter 9).
6   Pull back the rubber dust boot, loosen

the brake hose banjo bolt **(see illustration 5.4)** and separate the brake hose from the master cylinder. Wrap the end of the hose in a clean rag and suspend the hose in an upright position or bend it down carefully and place the open end in a clean container. The objective is to prevent excessive loss of brake fluid, fluid spills and system contamination.
7   Remove the master cylinder mounting bolts **(see illustration)** and separate the master cylinder from the handlebar.

Caution: Do not tip the master cylinder upside down or any brake fluid still in the reservoir will run out.

Overhaul

8   Remove the brake lever pivot bolt nut, remove the pivot bolt and remove the lever.
9   Carefully remove the rubber dust boot from the end of the piston **(see illustration)**. Using snap-ring pliers, remove the snap-ring

5.9a Remove the rubber dust boot (arrow) . . .

5.9b . . . and remove the snap-ring from the bore

5.9c Pry the baffle plate from the bottom of the reservoir

(see illustration) and slide out the piston assembly and the spring. Remove the baffle from the bottom of the reservoir (see illustration).

10   Lay the parts out in the order in which they're removed to prevent confusion during reassembly (see illustration).

11   Clean all of the parts with brake system cleaner (available at motorcycle dealerships and auto parts stores), isopropyl alcohol or clean brake fluid.

Caution: Do not, under any circumstances, use a petroleum-based solvent to clean brake parts. If compressed air is available, use it to dry the parts thoroughly (make

sure it's filtered and unlubricated). Check the master cylinder bore for corrosion, scratches, nicks and score marks. If damage is evident, the master cylinder must be replaced with a new one. If the master cylinder is in poor condition, then the calipers should be checked as well.

12   The dust seal, piston assembly and spring are included in the rebuild kit. Use all of the new parts, regardless of the apparent condition of the old ones.

13   Before reassembling the master cylinder, soak the piston and the rubber cup seals in clean brake fluid for ten or fifteen minutes. Lubricate the master cylinder bore with clean

brake fluid, then carefully insert the piston and related parts in the reverse order of disassembly. Make sure the lips on the cup seals do not turn inside out when they are slipped into the bore.

14   Depress the piston, then install the snap-ring (make sure the snap-ring is properly seated in the groove). Install the rubber dust boot (make sure the lip is seated properly in the piston groove).

15   Lubricate the brake lever pivot bolt and the friction surface on the lever that pushes against the piston assembly (see illustration).

5.10 Master cylinder assembly

1	Reservoir cover	
2	Set plate	
3	Rubber diaphragm	
4	Master cylinder body	
5	Brake hose banjo bolt	
6	Sealing washers	
7	Master cylinder mounting bracket	
8	Brake lever pivot bolt nut	

9	Brake lever pivot bolt	
10	Brake lever	
11	Rubber dust boot	
12	Snap-ring	
13	Washer	
14	Piston/spring assembly	
15	Brake light switch mounting screw	
16	Brake light switch	

5.15 Lubricate the brake lever pivot bolt and the part of the lever (arrow) that pushes against the piston assembly

7.5a Remove the rubber dust boot from the bleed valve, place a box wrench over the bleed valve . . .

7.5b . . . then connect a length of clear plastic tubing to the valve and submerge the other end of the tubing in a jar of clean brake fluid

Installation

16   Attach the master cylinder to the handlebar and tighten the bolts to the torque listed in this Chapter's Specifications.
17   Connect the brake hose to the master cylinder, using new sealing washers. Tighten the banjo bolt to the torque listed in this Chapter's Specifications.
18   Fill the master cylinder with the recommended brake fluid (see Chapter 1), then bleed the air from the system (see Section 7).

6   Brake hose - inspection and replacement

Inspection

1   Once a week or, if the motorcycle is used less frequently, before every ride, check the condition of the brake hose.
2   Twist and flex the rubber hoses while looking for cracks, bulges and seeping fluid. Check extra carefully around the areas where the hoses connect with the banjo bolts, as these are common areas for hose failure.
3   Inspect the metal banjo fittings connected to the brake hoses. If the fittings are rusted, scratched or cracked, replace them.

Replacement

4   The brake hose has a banjo fitting on each end of the hose. Cover the surrounding area with plenty of rags and unscrew the union bolt on either end of the hose. Detach the hose from any clips that may be present and remove the hose.
5   Position the new hose, making sure it isn't twisted or otherwise strained, between the two components. Install the union bolts, using new sealing washers on both sides of the fittings, and tighten them to the torque listed in this Chapter's Specifications.
6   Flush the old brake fluid from the system, refill the system with the recommended

fluid (see Chapter 1) and bleed the air from the system (see Section 7). Check the operation of the front brake carefully before riding the motorcycle.

7   Brake system bleeding

1   Bleeding the brake system removes all the air bubbles from the brake fluid reservoirs, the lines and the brake calipers. Bleeding is necessary whenever a brake system hydraulic connection is loosened, when a component or hose is replaced, or when the master cylinder or caliper is overhauled. Leaks in the system may also allow air to enter, but leaking brake fluid will reveal their presence and warn you of the need for repair.
2   To bleed the brakes, you will need some new, clean brake fluid of the recommended type (see Chapter 1), a length of clear vinyl or plastic tubing, a small container partially filled with clean brake fluid, some rags and a wrench to fit the brake caliper bleeder valves.
3   Cover the fuel tank and any other painted surfaces near the reservoir to prevent damage in the event that brake fluid is spilled.
4   Remove the reservoir cover screws and remove the cover, set plate and diaphragm. Slowly pump the brake lever a few times, until no air bubbles can be seen floating up from the holes at the bottom of the reservoir. Doing this bleeds the air from the master cylinder end of the line. Top up the reservoir with new fluid, then install the reservoir diaphragm, set plate and cover, but don't tighten the screws; you may have to remove the cover, plate and diaphragm several times during the procedure.
5   Remove the rubber dust cover from the bleeder valve (see illustration) and slip a box wrench over the caliper bleed valve. Attach one end of the clear vinyl or plastic tubing to

the bleed valve (see illustration) and submerge the other end in the brake fluid in the container.
6   Carefully pump the brake lever three or four times and hold it while opening the caliper bleeder valve. When the valve is opened, brake fluid will flow out of the caliper into the clear tubing and the lever will move toward the handlebar. Retighten the bleed valve, then release the brake lever gradually.
7   Repeat this procedure until no air bubbles are visible in the brake fluid leaving the caliper and the lever is firm when applied. Note: *Remember to add fluid to the reservoir as the level drops. Use only new, clean brake fluid of the recommended type. Never re-use the fluid lost during bleeding.*
8   Keep an eye on the fluid level in the reservoir, especially if there's a lot of air in the system. Every time you crack the bleed valve open, the fluid level in the reservoir drops a little. Do not allow the fluid level to drop below the lower mark during the bleeding process. If the level looks low, remove the reservoir cover, set plate and diaphragm and add some fluid.
9   When you're done, inspect the fluid level in the reservoir one more time, add some fluid if necessary, then install the diaphragm, set plate and reservoir cover and tighten the screws securely. Wipe up any spilled brake fluid and check the entire system for leaks. Note: *If bleeding is difficult, it may be necessary to let the brake fluid in the system stabilize for a few hours (it may be aerated). Repeat the bleeding procedure when the tiny bubbles in the system have settled out.*

8   Drum brake - removal, inspection and installation

Removal and disassembly

1   Before you start, inspect the rear brake wear indicator (see Chapter 1). If the shoes are excessively worn, replace them.

8.2 Push the brake arm forward, unscrew the adjuster nut from the brake rod and disengage the rod from the clevis pin

8.3a To detach the stopper arm from the brake panel, remove the cotter pin . . .

8.3b . . . remove the nut and the metal and rubber washers from the bolt, slide off the stopper arm and remove the bolt

8.5 Remove the brake panel from the wheel

2   Disconnect the brake rod from the brake arm **(see illustration)**. Store the adjuster nut, the clevis pin and the brake rod spring in a plastic bag.
3   Disconnect the rear brake stopper arm **(see illustrations)**. Store the nut, bolt and metal and rubber washers in a plastic bag.
4   Remove the rear wheel (see Section 12).

5   Remove the brake panel from the wheel **(see illustration)**.
6   Remove the brake arm pinch bolt **(see illustration 12.3b)** and remove the brake arm from the splined spindle end of the brake cam. Note the punch mark on the end of the brake cam spindle **(see illustration 12.3b)**; this mark indicates the location of the wider

spline on the spindle. This wider spline must be aligned with the corresponding wider spline on the brake arm when the arm is installed. Remove the indicator plate and the felt seal **(see illustrations)**. Pull the brake cam out of the brake panel.
7   Remove the cotter pins from the anchor pins **(see illustration)** and remove the set plate (the oblong-shaped spacer that fits over the ends of both anchor pins). To remove the shoes from the brake panel, spread them apart slightly to clear the ridges on the brake cam, then slide them up and off the anchor pins **(see illustration)**. Disengage the shoes and springs **(see illustration)**.

Inspection

8   Inspect the linings for wear, damage and signs of contamination from road dirt and water. If the linings are visibly defective, replace them.
9   Measure the thickness of the lining material (just the lining material, not the metal backing) and compare your measurements to the minimum thickness listed in this Chapter's Specifications. If the lining material is worn to less than the minimum, replace the shoes.
10   Inspect the ends of the shoes, where

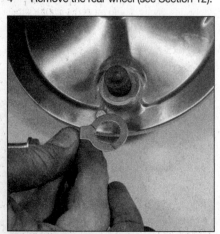

8.6a Remove the indicator plate from the brake cam spindle

8.6b Remove the felt seal from the brake cam spindle

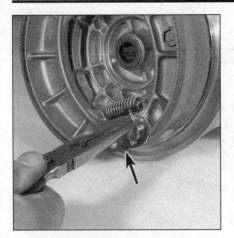

8.7a Remove the cotter pins from the anchor pins and remove the set plate (arrow)

8.7b Pull the upper ends of the shoes apart and pull the shoes off the anchor pins

8.7c Disengage the brake shoes and springs

they contact the brake cam and where they slip over the anchor pins. If there's visible wear, replace the shoes.

11   Check the fit of the brake cam in the brake panel hole. If it feels loose, replace the brake cam or the panel, depending on which part is worn. Inspect the anchor pins for wear and damage. If the anchor pins are worn, replace the brake panel.

12   Inspect the brake drum (inside the wheel) for wear or damage. Measure the diameter at several points with a brake drum micrometer (or have this done by a Honda dealer). If the measurements are uneven (the brake drum is "out-of-round") or if there are scratches deep enough to snag a fingernail, have the drum turned by a dealer service department or a motorcycle machine shop to correct the surface. If the drum has to be turned beyond the wear limit to remove the defects, replace it. You'll find the maximum diameter of the drum cast into the wheel **(see illustration)**. If the specified maximum diameter on the wheel is different from the maximum diameter listed in this Chapter's Specifications, the spec on the wheel super-sedes the value in the Specifications.

8.12 The maximum diameter of the brake drum is cast into the drum; if it differs from that listed in this Chapter's Specifications, use the specification on the drum

Installation

13   Apply high-temperature brake grease to the ends of the springs, the brake cam and the anchor pins. Install the brake cam, the felt seal and the indicator plate. Install the brake arm. Make sure the punch marks on the brake arm and the brake cam spindle are aligned. Install the brake arm pinch bolt and tighten it securely.

14   Hook the springs to the shoes. Position the shoes over the brake panel, slide the lower ends of the shoes onto the ends of the anchor pins, spread the upper ends of the shoes apart far enough to clear the ridges on the brake cam, push the shoes down onto the anchor pins and release the upper ends of the shoes. Make sure the upper ends of the shoes fit correctly against the brake cam and the lower ends are fully seated on the anchor pins **(see illustrations)**. Install the set plate and install new cotter pins on the anchor pins **(see illustration)**.

8.14a When installing the brake shoes, make sure the upper ends of the shoes are correctly seated against the brake cam . . .

8.14b . . . and the lower ends are correctly seated against the shoulders at the lower ends of the anchor pins

8.14c Once the shoes are correctly positioned on the brake panel, install the set plate and secure the plate with a pair of new cotter pins in the anchor pins

8.17 To attach the brake rod to the brake arm clevis pin, push the brake arm forward and install the adjuster nut

9.2 The middle brake rod connects the brake shaft arm (left arrow) and brake pedal arm (right arrow)

15 Install the brake panel and brake shoe assembly in the wheel.
16 Install the wheel (see Section 12).
17 To reattach the brake rod to the brake arm clevis pin, install the spring on the rod, insert the rod in the hole in the clevis, push the brake arm forward and install the adjuster nut **(see illustration)**.
18 Align the wheels (see Section 15).
19 Adjust the rear brake pedal freeplay (see Chapter 1).
20 Adjust the rear brake light switch (see Chapter 1).

---

9 Rear brake pedal and linkage - removal and installation

1 If you're planning to service either the middle brake rod or the brake pedal assembly, remove the exhaust system (see Chapter 4).

Middle brake rod

2 Remove the cotter pins, nuts and bolts from both ends of the middle brake rod and disconnect the rod from the rear brake pedal and from the brake shaft arm (VT600 models) **(see illustration)** or the middle rod joint (VT750 models). On VT750 models, note the return spring for the rod (at the middle rod joint) and the return spring for the rear brake light switch (at the pedal). Disengage both springs from the rod.
3 Installation is the reverse of removal. Tighten the nuts securely and install new cotter pins. Check and, if necessary, adjust the brake pedal height and the rear brake light switch (see Chapter 1).

Brake pedal

4 Disconnect the middle brake rod from the rear brake pedal **(see illustration)**.
5 Unbolt the right footpeg bracket from the frame **(see illustration 9.4)**.
6 On VT600 models, remove the brake pedal, the pivot collar (bushing) and the dust

seals from the footpeg bracket. On VT750C/CD models, remove the pedal pivot bolt, pedal and washer. On VT750DC models, remove the snap-ring and bushing washer. Clean the parts thoroughly and dry them off for inspection. Clean out the pivot bore of the pedal (that fits over the collar or pivot bolt) with a cylindrical wire brush.
7 Inspect the collar or pivot bolt for scoring and other damage. If it's worn or damaged, replace it.
8 On VT600 models, inspect the dust seals **(see illustration)**. If they're torn, cracked or deteriorated, replace them.
9 Grease the collar **(see illustration)** or pivot bolt. Make sure the surface of the bore in the pedal that fits over the collar or pivot bolt is clean and free of debris and old grease.
10 On VT600 models, reassemble the collar, dust seals and brake pedal **(see illustration)**. On VT750 models, install the washer, pedal and pivot bolt; tighten the pivot bolt securely.

9.4 Disconnect the middle brake rod from the brake pedal arm (lower arrow) and remove the footpeg bracket bolts (arrows) (VT600 shown; VT750 similar)

9.8 The open side of each seal faces inward

9.9 Grease the collar and the inside of the pivot bore in the pedal before reassembling them

9.10 The assembled footpeg bracket and rear brake pedal should look like this (VT600 shown)

11   Installation is the reverse of removal. Tighten the footpeg bracket bolts securely.

12   Reconnect the middle brake rod to the brake pedal and install a new cotter pin.

13   Check and, if necessary, adjust the rear brake pedal height and the rear brake light switch (see Chapter 1).

Brake rod

VT600

14   Disconnect the middle brake rod from the brake shaft arm **(see illustration)**.

15   Disconnect the brake rod from the brake arm (see Section 8).

16   Remove the rear wheel (see Section 12).

17   Remove the swingarm (see Chapter 6).

18   Remove the pinch bolt from the middle brake arm **(see illustration)** and slide the middle brake arm off the brake shaft arm spindle. Note the punch marks on the brake shaft arm spindle and on the middle brake arm. These marks must be aligned when the middle brake arm is reinstalled on the brake

shaft arm spindle.

19   Disengage the middle brake arm return spring and the brake light switch return spring and remove the middle brake arm.

20   Pull the brake shaft arm out of the frame.

VT750 models

21   Disconnect the brake rod from the brake arm (see Section 8).

22   Remove the cotter pin, pull out the clevis pin and disconnect the brake rod from the middle rod joint.

All models

23   Clean and inspect the parts for wear and damage. Replace worn or damaged parts. Be sure to clean out the bore in the frame for the brake shaft arm spindle.

24   Installation is the reverse of removal. Grease the brake shaft arm spindle before inserting it through the frame. Make sure that the punch marks on the brake shaft arm spindle and on the middle brake arm are aligned. Don't forget to install the middle brake arm

return spring and the brake light switch arm.

25   Check and, if necessary, adjust the rear brake pedal height and freeplay and the rear brake light switch (see Chapter 1).

10 Wheels - inspection and repair

1   Clean the wheels thoroughly to remove mud and dirt that may interfere with the inspection procedure or mask defects. Make a general check of the wheels and tires as described in Chapter 1.

2   Support the bike securely so it can't be knocked over during this procedure. Place a jack beneath the engine to raise the front wheel off the ground, or beneath the frame to raise the rear wheel off the ground. Attach a dial indicator to the fork slider or the swingarm and position the stem against the side of the rim. Spin the wheel slowly and check the side-to-side (axial) runout of

9.14 Disconnect the middle brake rod from the brake shaft arm (arrow)

9.18 Middle brake arm pinch bolt (lower arrow), middle brake arm return spring (middle arrow) and brake light switch return spring (upper arrow)

10.2 Measure wheel runout with a dial indicator, if available, or with a flat piece of metal and feeler gauge

1 *Radial (up-and-down) runout*
2 *Axial (side-to-side) runout*

10.5 If a spoke is loose, tighten the spoke nipple with a spoke wrench (available at any motorcycle dealership or accessory store)

the rim, then compare your readings with the value listed in this Chapter's Specifications **(see illustration)**. In order to accurately check radial runout with the dial indicator, the wheel would have to be removed from the machine and the tire removed from the wheel. With the axle clamped in a vise, the wheel can be rotated to check the runout.

3   An easier, though slightly less accurate, method is to attach a stiff wire pointer to the fork or the swingarm and position the end a fraction of an inch from the wheel (where the wheel and tire join). If the wheel is true, the distance from the pointer to the rim will be constant as the wheel is rotated. Repeat the procedure to check the runout of the rear

wheel. **Note:** *If wheel runout is excessive, refer to the appropriate Section in this Chapter and check the wheel bearings very carefully before replacing the wheel or paying to have it trued.*

4   The wheels should also be visually inspected for cracks, flat spots on the rim, bent spokes and other damage.

5   Tap the spokes with a metal screwdriver blade or similar tool and listen to the sound. If the spoke makes a "clunk" or low-pitched sound, it's loose. Tighten the spoke **(see illustration)**.

6   If damage is evident, or if runout in either direction is excessive, the wheel will have to be trued or, if damage is severe, replaced with a new one.

11 Front wheel - removal and installation

Removal

1   Support the bike securely so it can't be knocked over during this procedure. Raise

the front wheel off the ground by placing a floor jack, with a wood block on the jack head, under the engine.

2   Disconnect the speedometer cable from the speedometer gearbox (see Chapter 9).

3   If you're working on a 2008 VT750, unscrew the axle bolt from the right-hand end of the axle. On all models, loosen the axle pinch bolts and unscrew the axle **(see illustrations)**.

4   Support the wheel, then pull out the axle and carefully lower the wheel from the forks.

5   Remove the speedometer gearbox unit from the left side of the wheel and remove the collar from the right side **(see illustrations)**. Set the wheel aside.

Caution: When you lay down the wheel and allow it to rest on the brake disc - the disc could become warped. Set the wheel on wood blocks so the disc doesn't support the weight of the wheel.

Note: *Don't operate the front brake lever with the wheel removed.*

Inspection

6   Roll the axle on a flat surface such as a piece of plate glass. If it's bent, replace it.

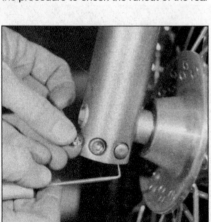

11.3a Pry out the pinch bolt plugs . . .

11.3b . . . loosen the axle pinch bolts . . .

11.3c . . . and unscrew the axle

11.5a Remove the speedometer drive unit from the left side of the wheel . . .

11.5b . . . and remove the collar from the right side

If the axle is corroded, remove the corrosion with fine emery cloth.

7   Inspect the wheel bearings (see Section 13).

Installation

8   Installation is the reverse of removal. Apply a thin coat of grease to the seal lip, then slide the axle into the hub. Slide the wheel into place. Make sure the lugs in the speedometer drive clutch line up with the notches in the speedometer drive unit **(see illustration)**. Make sure the protrusion on the inner side of the left fork fits into the notch in the speedometer drive unit.

9   Slip the axle into place, then tighten the axle to the torque listed in this Chapter's Specifications. Tighten the axle pinch bolts to the torque listed in this Chapter's Specifications.

10   Apply the front brake, pump the forks up and down several times and check for binding and proper brake operation.

12 Rear wheel - removal and installation

Removal

1   Support the bike securely so it can't be knocked over during this procedure. Raise the rear wheel off the ground.

2   Detach the brake rod from the brake arm and the stopper arm from the brake panel (see Section 8).

Chain drive models

3   Remove the axle nut **(see illustrations)** and unscrew the drive chain adjusters from the adjuster collars (see "Drive chain and sprockets - check, adjustment and lubrication" in Chapter 1).

4   Support the wheel, pull out the axle and remove the adjuster collars and the spac-

11.8 When installing the speedometer drive unit, make sure the tangs align with the slots

12.3a Hold the rear axle bolt . . .

12.3b . . . and remove the axle nut (right arrow); the punch mark on the end of the brake cam spindle (left arrow) is used for brake arm and spindle alignment

12.4a Remove the left side collar . . .

12.4b . . . remove the left spacer . . .

12.4c . . . remove the right side collar . . .

12.4d . . . remove the right spacer . . .

12.4e . . . disengage the driven sprocket from the drive chain
and remove the wheel

ers **(see illustrations)**. Pull the wheel to the right and disengage the drive chain from the sprocket **(see illustration)**.

Shaft drive models

5   Where necessary for access to the axle bolt, remove the exhaust system (see Chapter 4).

6   Loosen the pinch bolt that clamps the right side of the swingarm to the axle bolt. Hold the axle bolt head with an Allen bolt bit in a socket and unscrew the axle nut **(see illustration)**.

7   Support the wheel, pull the axle out and remove the spacer collar that fits between the brake panel and the right side of the swingarm.

8   Lower the wheel away from the bike and roll it out.

9   Remove the spacer collar from inside the final drive unit.

All models

10   Before installing the wheel, check the axle for straightness by rolling it on a flat surface such as a piece of plate glass (if the axle is corroded, first remove the corrosion with fine emery cloth). If the axle is bent, replace it.

11   Inspect the sprocket (chain drive models) (see Section 17) and inspect the driven flange and the rubber dampers (see Section 18).

12   Inspect the seals and the wheel bearings (see Section 13).

Installation

13   Installation is the reverse of removal. Apply a light coat of multi-purpose lithium-based grease to the lips of the oil seals. Tighten the axle nut to the torque listed in the Chapter 1 Specifications.

14   Adjust the drive chain (chain drive models) (see "Drive chain and sprockets - check, adjustment and lubrication" in Chapter 1).

15   Adjust the rear brake pedal (see Chapter 1).

16   Carefully check the operation of the brake before riding the motorcycle.

13 Wheel bearings - inspection and maintenance

1   Support the bike securely so it can't be knocked over during this procedure and remove the wheel. Remove the front wheel

(see Section 11) or remove the rear wheel (see Section 12).

2   Set the wheel on blocks so as not to allow the weight of the wheel to rest on the brake disc or hub.

Front wheel bearings

3   From the left side of the wheel, remove the speedometer gearbox unit **(see illustration 11.5a)**, then pry out the grease seal **(see illustration)** and remove the speedometer clutch **(see illustration)**.

4   From the right side of the wheel, remove the collar **(see illustration 11.5b)**.

5   The usual method of removing wheel bearings is to insert a brass punch through one side of the hub, place it against the inner race of the opposite bearing, then tap on the punch to drive the bearing out. There may not be enough clearance for this method; if not, you'll need Honda special tools or equivalents **(see illustration)**. The remover head goes inside the bearing to be removed. The wedge part of the remover rod is then tapped into the slot of the remover head from the opposite side of the hub. This expands the remover head and locks it to the bearing. Tapping some more on the rod will drive

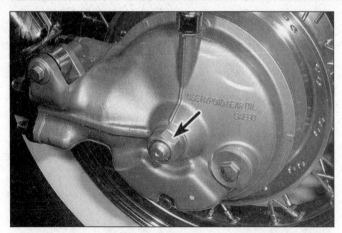

12.6 Hold the rear axle from the other side of the wheel with a hex bit and remove the axle nut (arrow)

13.3a Pry out the left side seal from the front wheel hub with a seal removal tool

13.3b Remove the speedometer clutch

13.5a Bearing remover head (right) and wedged shaft (left)

13.5b Tap the head into place (the slotted end goes into the bearing)

the remover head and bearing out of the hub **(see illustrations)**.

6   Turn the wheel over and pry out the right side grease seal.

7   Remove the right side bearing the same way you removed the left one.

8   Clean the bearings with a high flash-point solvent (one which won't leave any residue) and blow them dry with compressed air (don't let the bearings spin as you dry them). Apply a few drops of oil to the bearing. Hold the outer race of the bearing and rotate the inner race - if the bearing doesn't turn smoothly, has rough spots or is noisy, replace it with a new one.

9   If the bearing checks out okay and will be re-used, wash it in solvent once again and dry it, then pack the bearing with high-quality bearing grease.

10   Thoroughly clean the hub area of the wheel. Install the left side bearing into the recess in the hub, with the marked or sealed side facing out. Using a bearing driver or a socket large enough to contact the outer race of the bearing, drive in the bearing until it's completely seated **(see illustration)**.

13.5c From the other side of the wheel, tap the wedge end of the shaft into the head's slot and drive out the bearing

11   Install the speedometer gearbox retainer on top of the new bearing. Make sure the tangs on the retainer are aligned with the slots in the hub. Install a new left side grease

13.10 Install the new bearings with a seal driver or socket

seal with its closed side out. It should be possible to push the seal in with even finger pressure but, if necessary, use a seal driver, a large socket or a flat piece of wood to drive

13.17a Install the 17 mm bearing remover head . . .

13.17b . . . from the other side of the wheel, install the bearing remover shaft and drive out the left side bearing

13.17c Install the new bearings with a seal driver or socket

the seal into place.

12   Turn the wheel over and install the right side bearing as described in Step 10. Install a new right side seal as described in Step 11.

13   Install the speedometer gearbox unit, making sure the tangs on the speedometer gearbox are aligned with the slots in the retainer **(see illustration 11.8)**.

14   Clean off all grease from the brake disc using acetone or brake system cleaner.

15   Make sure the right side collar is in place **(see illustration 11.5b)** and install the wheel (see Section 11).

Rear wheel bearings

16   Remove the sprocket, driven flange and rubber dampers (see Section 18).

17   The rear wheel bearings are removed the same way as the front wheel bearings, in Steps 5 through 10 above **(see illustrations)**.

18   While the rear wheel is removed, inspect the drive chain (see Section 16), the driven sprocket (see Section 17) and the driven flange (see Section 18). The driven flange has an outer dust seal, a bearing, an O-ring and a collar that should be inspected for wear and, if necessary, replaced.

14 Tires - general information

1   Tires with tubes are used as standard equipment on this motorcycle. They are generally easier to change than tubeless tires.

2   Before changing a tire yourself, check with your local dealership or repair shop to find out the labor charge for changing a tire. Although the procedure is not complicated, it is time-consuming, and for safety, it must be done correctly. For these reasons, it may be more practical to have the job done. Watching a professional technician do the job before attempting it yourself can provide valuable information.

3   The accompanying illustrations can be used to replace a tube-type tire in an emergency.

15 Wheels - alignment check

1   Misalignment of the wheels, which may be due to a cocked rear wheel or a bent frame or triple clamps, can cause strange and possibly serious handling problems. If the frame or triple clamps are at fault, repair by a frame specialist or replacement with new parts are the only alternatives.

2   To check the alignment you will need

an assistant, a length of string or a perfectly straight piece of wood and a ruler graduated in 1/64 inch increments. A plumb bob or other suitable weight will also be required.

3   Support the motorcycle in a level position, then measure the width of both tires at their widest points. Subtract the smaller measurement from the larger measurement, then divide the difference by two. The result is the amount of offset that should exist between the front and rear tires on both sides.

4   If a string is used, have your assistant hold one end of it about half way between the floor and the rear axle, touching the rear sidewall of the tire.

5   Run the other end of the string forward and pull it tight so that it is roughly parallel to the floor. Slowly bring the string into contact with the front sidewall of the rear tire, then turn the front wheel until it is parallel with the string. Measure the distance from the front tire sidewall to the string.

6   Repeat the procedure on the other side of the motorcycle. The distance from the front tire sidewall to the string should be equal on both sides.

7   As was previously pointed out, a perfectly straight length of wood may be substituted for the string. The procedure is the same.

8   If the distance between the string and tire is greater on one side, or if the rear wheel appears to be cocked, make sure the swingarm pivot bolt and nut are tight ("Swingarm bearings - check" in Chapter 6).

9   If the front-to-back alignment is correct, the wheels still may be out of alignment vertically.

10   Using the plumb bob, or other suitable weight, and a length of string, check the rear wheel to make sure it is vertical. To do this, hold the string against the tire upper sidewall and allow the weight to settle just off the floor. When the string touches both the upper and lower tire sidewalls and is perfectly straight, the wheel is vertical.

TIRE CHANGING SEQUENCE - TUBED TIRES

 1 Deflate the tire and loosen the rim lock nut. After pushing the tire beads away from the rim flanges push the tire bead into the well of the rim at the point opposite the valve. Insert the tire lever adjacent to the valve and work the bead over the edge of the rim.

2 Use two levers to work the bead over the edge of the rim. Note the use of rim protectors

3 Remove the inner tube from the tire

4 When the first bead is clear, remove the tire as shown. If the bead isn't too tight, rim protectors won't be necessary

5 To install, partially inflate the inner tube and insert it in the tire. Make sure there's a nut on the valve stem

6 Work the first bead over the rim and feed the valve through the hole in the rim. Partially screw on the retaining nut to hold the valve in place. (The nut should be removed after the tire has been inflated)

7 Check that the inner tube is positioned correctly and work the second bead over the rim using the tire levers. Start at a point between the valve stem and the rim lock

8 Work final area of the bead over the rim while pushing the valve inwards to ensure that the inner tube is not trapped. Also push the rim lock inwards and, if necessary, pry the tire bead over the rim lock. After inflating the tire, tighten the rim lock nut securely

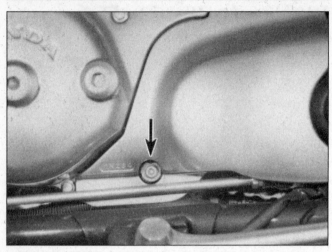

16.2a To remove the left rear cover, remove this Allen bolt . . .

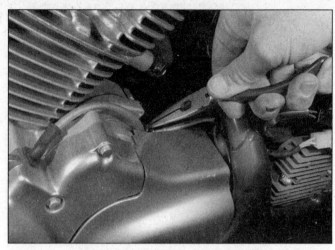

16.2b . . . pull off this retaining clip (only on VT600 models) . . .

11   Once the rear wheel is vertical, check the front wheel in the same manner. If both wheels are not perfectly vertical, the frame and/or major suspension components are bent.

16 Drive chain - removal, cleaning and installation

Removal

1   Loosen the rear axle nut and back off the axle adjuster bolts to loosen the drive chain (see "Drive chain and sprockets - check, adjustment and lubrication" in Chapter 1). Push the rear wheel forward as far as possible to create as much chain slack as possible.
2   Remove the Allen bolt from the left rear cover, remove the retaining clip (VT600 models only) and pull off the left rear cover (see illustrations). After removing the cover on VT750 models, remove the collar for the bolt.
3   Remove the gearshift lever from the gearshift spindle (see "Gearshift linkage - removal, inspection and installation" in Chapter 1).
4   Remove the rear wheel and lift the chain off the driven sprocket (see Section 12).
5   Detach the swingarm from the frame (see Chapter 6). Pull the swingarm back far enough to allow the chain to slip between the frame and the front of the swingarm. Lift chain off the drive sprocket and remove it.

Cleaning

6   Soak the chain in kerosene or diesel fuel for approximately five or six minutes.

Caution: Don't use gasoline or other cleaning fluids. Remove the chain, wipe it off then dry it with compressed air immediately. The entire process shouldn't take longer than ten minutes - if it does, the O-rings in the chain rollers could be damaged.

Installation

7   Installation is the reverse of removal. Be sure to tighten the suspension fasteners to the torque listed in the Chapter 6 Specifications. Tighten the rear axle nut to the torque listed in this Chapter's Specifications.
8   On VT750 models, don't forget to install the collar before installing the left rear cover. To install the left rear cover, place it in position, push the cover positioning pin into the grommet and align the bolt hole in the cover with the threaded hole in the bracket on the engine (see illustration). Install the left rear cover Allen bolt and tighten it securely. On VT600 models, install the retaining clip.
9   Lubricate and adjust the chain (see Chapter 1).

16.2c . . . and remove the cover (VT600 model shown; on VT750 models, don't forget to retrieve the collar for the bolt); the post (arrow) . . .

16.2d . . . engages this grommet

17.4 Remove the sprocket bolts and retaining plate

17.8 To remove the driven sprocket, remove these nuts (arrows) . . .

17 Sprockets - check and replacement

Check

1   Whenever the drive chain is inspected, the sprockets should be inspected also. If you are replacing the chain, replace the sprockets as well. Likewise, if the sprockets are in need of replacement, install a new chain also.
2   Remove the left rear cover from the engine **(see illustrations 16.2a through 16.2c)**.
3   Inspect the wear pattern on the sprockets. If the sprocket teeth are worn excessively, replace the chain and sprockets.

Replacement

Drive sprocket

4   With the chain installed and the rear tire on the ground, have an assistant apply the rear brake while you loosen the sprocket retaining bolts **(see illustration)**. Remove the bolts and remove the sprocket setting plate.
5   Disengage the drive sprocket from the chain and remove the sprocket.
6   Installation is the reverse of removal. Be sure to tighten the sprocket retaining bolts to the torque listed in this Chapter's Specifications.

Driven sprocket

7   If you're going to remove the drive sprocket, do it before removing the chain. Remove the rear wheel (see Section 12).
8   Remove the sprocket retaining nuts **(see illustration)** and detach the driven sprocket from the driven flange.
9   While the rear wheel is removed, inspect the wheel bearings (see Section 13) and inspect the driven flange seal, collar, bearing and rubber dampers (see Section 18).
10   Installation is the reverse of removal. Be sure to apply a non-hardening thread locking compound to the threads of the studs and tighten the sprocket retaining nuts to the torque listed in this Chapter's Specifications.

18 Driven flange and rubber dampers (chain drive) - removal, inspection and installation

1   Remove the rear wheel (see Section 12).
2   Lift the sprocket/driven flange off the wheel **(see illustration)** from the wheel and check it for cracks, hardening and general deterioration. Replace it with a new one if necessary.
3   Remove the collar from the driven flange **(see illustration)**.
4   Inspecting and replacing the driven flange bearing and seal is just like checking and replacing a wheel bearing and seal (see Section 13).

18.2 . . . and lift the sprocket/driven flange assembly from the wheel

18.3 Remove the collar from the driven flange

19.2 Loosen these four final drive-to-swingarm nuts (arrows) now, before removing the wheel and the shocks (fourth nut not visible in this photo)

19.5 Pull the final drive unit to the rear; the driveshaft will come with it

5   Inspect the rubber dampers inside the wheel hub. If they're cracked, torn, dried out or deteriorated, replace them.

6   Installation is the reverse of removal.

Caution: Don't forget to install the collar, or the coupling bearing will be damaged when the axle nut is tightened.

19 Final drive unit and driveshaft - removal, inspection and installation

Removal

1   Drain the final drive oil (see Chapter 1).

2   Loosen, but don't remove, the four final drive nuts **(see illustration)**.

3   Remove the rear wheel (see Chapter 7).

4   Support the swingarm and remove the shock absorbers (see Chapter 6).

5   Remove the final drive mounting nuts **(see illustration 19.2)** and separate the final drive from the swingarm **(see illustration)**.

6   To remove the driveshaft from the final drive unit, slip the axle and spacer back into the final drive unit. Grasp the forward end of the driveshaft and wiggle it in a circle while pulling it away from the final drive unit. The stopper ring will provide some resistance, then the driveshaft should pull free of the final drive unit. Remove the spring, oil seal and stopper from the driveshaft.

Inspection

7   Look into the axle holes and check for obvious signs of wear and damage such as broken gear teeth **(see illustration)**. Also check the seals for signs of leakage. Slip the

driveshaft into its splines (if it was removed) and turn the pinion by hand.

8   Final drive overhaul is a complicated procedure that requires several special tools, for which there are no readily available substitutes. If there's visible wear or damage, or if the gear rotation is rough or noisy, have it inspected further by a dealer service department or other qualified shop.

9   Check the coupling flange in the rear wheel for wear or damage **(see illustration)**. If necessary, pull the flange out of the coupling. To remove the rubber dampers, unbolt the mounting plate, lift it off and take the rubber dampers out of the wheel.

10   Inspect the splines of the driveshaft for damage and wear. If they're damaged or worn, replace the driveshaft.

11   To remove the U-joint, remove the swingarm (see Chapter 6).

19.7 Inspect the final drive unit oil seal for leaks; make sure this spacer is in position before installing the wheel

19.9 Inspect the splines on the wheel hub coupling for damage

12 Inspect the U-joint splines for wear or damage. Verify that the U-joint operates smoothly, without binding or noise. If the U-joint is damaged or worn, replace it.

Installation

13 Installation is the reverse of the removal steps, with the following additions:

a) *Install a new driveshaft oil seal if you removed the driveshaft from the final drive unit.*

b) *Install a new stopper ring.*

c) *If you removed the rubber dampers from the coupling, install them with the Out Side marks facing out. Install the plate over the dampers with its Out Side mark facing out and its arrow mark between the two projections on the hub.*

d) *Lubricate splines of the U-joint and final drive unit with Honda Moly 60 grease or equivalent.*

e) *Install the final drive unit loosely. Do not tighten the final drive to the torque listed in this Chapter's Specifications until after the rear axle is installed.*

f) *Check the final drive unit oil level (see Chapter 1).*

Notes

Chapter 8
Frame and bodywork

Contents

Degrees of difficulty

| Easy, suitable for novice with little experience | Fairly easy, suitable for beginner with some experience | Fairly difficult, suitable for competent DIY mechanic | Difficult, suitable for experienced DIY mechanic | Very difficult, suitable for expert DIY or professional |

1 General information

The models covered in this manual use a steel frame of round-section tubing. The front fender is steel; the rear fender and side covers are plastic.

2 Frame - inspection and repair

1 The frame should not require attention unless accident damage has occurred. In most cases, frame replacement is the only satisfactory remedy for such damage.

A few frame specialists have the jigs and other equipment necessary for straightening the frame to the required standard of accuracy, but even then there is no simple way of assessing to what extent the frame may have been overstressed.
2 After the machine has accumulated a lot of miles, the frame should be examined closely for signs of cracking or splitting at the welded joints. Corrosion can

3.3 To replace a footpeg, remove the cotter pin and washer and pull out the pivot pin; the spring is used only on VT750 models

3.4 VT750 right footpeg and brake pedal assembly

A   Mounting bolts   B   Brake light switch

also cause weakness at these joints. Loose engine mount bolts can cause elongation of the bolt holes or fracturing of the mounting tabs. Minor damage can often be repaired by welding, depending on the extent and nature of the damage.

3   Remember that a frame which is out of alignment will cause handling problems. If misalignment is suspected as the result of an accident, it will be necessary to strip the machine completely so the frame can be thoroughly checked.

3 Footpegs - removal and installation

1   The front footpegs are mounted on brackets that also serve as the mounting brackets for the gearshift linkage on the left side (see Chapter 2) and the rear brake pedal linkage on the right side (see Chapter 7). The rear footpegs are mounted on brackets bolted to the frame.

2   To replace a footpeg pad on a VT600 model, work the rubber pad off the end of the footpeg. The pad is a tight fit, so this may be difficult. Cutting off the old pad, then heating the new pad in hot water and lubricating it with soap, will make the job easier. (The footpegs and pads on VT750 models are a single assembly.)

3   To replace a footpeg, remove the cotter pin and the washer (see illustration), pull out the clevis pin and separate the footpeg from the bracket. On VT750 models, note how the spring is installed, with one end hooked over the rear clevis pin boss on the footpeg and the other end hooked into the bracket. Installation is the reverse of removal. Grease the footpeg clevis pin before installing it.

4   To replace a front footpeg assembly (footpeg and bracket), remove the bolts that secure the bracket to the frame (see illus-

tration). If you're removing the left footpeg assembly on a VT600 model, detach the gearshift pedal from the back of the bracket (see "Gearshift linkage - removal, inspection and installation" in Chapter 2). If you're removing the right footpeg assembly on a VT600 model, detach the brake pedal from the back of the bracket (see "Rear brake pedal and linkage - removal and installation" in Chapter 7). (On VT750 models, the footpeg brackets can be removed separately; they're not connected to the gearshift pedal or brake pedal.) Installation is the reverse of removal. Tighten the bracket bolts securely.

4 Sidestand - maintenance

1   The sidestand is attached to a bracket on the frame. A return spring anchored to a bracket on the frame ensures that the stand remains in the extended or retracted position (see illustration).

2   Make sure the pivot bolt is tight and the return spring is not fatigued. An accident could occur if the stand extends while the machine is in motion, and damage to the machine could occur if the stand retracts while the machine is resting on the stand.

5 Sidestand - removal and installation

1   Support the bike securely so it can't be knocked over during this procedure.

2   Unhook the sidestand spring (see illustration 4.1).

3   Remove the sidestand switch (see Chapter 9).

4   Remove the dust cap (see illustration 4.1).

5   Remove the sidestand switch pivot bolt and nut.

6   Installation is the reverse of removal. Be sure to grease the pivot bolt and tighten the nut securely.

4.1 Make sure the sidestand spring is in good condition and correctly installed; the sidestand pivot bolt is under this cap (arrow)

6.1 To detach the seat on VT600 models, remove the Allen bolt from each side (arrow)

6.2 Grasp the seat firmly and slide it to the rear to disengage the retaining lugs

6 Seat - removal and installation

VT600 models

1   Remove the two Allen bolts (one on each side) from under the seat (see illustration).
2   Grasp the seat firmly and slide it to the rear (see illustration).
3   To install the seat, place it in position, then slide it forward. Make sure that the lug under the forward end of the seat slides under the small crossmember on the frame (see illustration) and the two smaller lugs under the rear end of the seat slide under the two retainers on the fender (see illustration).
4   Install the two retaining bolts and tighten them securely.

VT750C/CD/C2 models

5   Remove the passenger seat retaining bolt (see illustration).
6   To remove the rear seat, slide it forward and lift it up.
7   Remove the front seat mounting bolt.
8   To remove the front seat, slide it back and lift it up.
9   To install the front seat, place it in position, then slide it forward. Make sure that the lug on the forward end of the seat slides under the small crossmember on the frame (see illustration 6.3a).
10   Align the hole in the front seat retaining bolt flange with the hole in the fender, install the bolt and tighten it securely.
11   To install the rear seat, insert the lug on the forward end of the seat over the front seat mounting bolt, then slide the seat to the rear.
12   Align the hole in the rear seat retaining bolt flange with the hole in the fender, install the bolt and tighten it securely.

VT750DC models

13   Remove the bolt and washer on each end of the passenger grab strap. Remove the strap.
14   Slide the seat readward to disengage its front hook from the bracket. Lift the seat off the bike.
15   Installation is the reverse of the removal steps.

7 Steering head covers (VT600 and VT750C/CD models) - removal and installation

1   The steering head covers conceal and protect wiring harnesses and connectors in the area between the steering head and the fuel tank.
2   Remove the fuel tank (see Chapter 4).

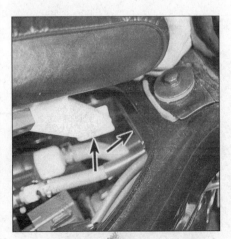

6.3a To install the VT600 seat, insert the forward retaining lug under this crossmember in the frame (arrow) . . .

6.3b . . . and insert the two rear lugs under their retainers, then slide the seat forward and install the two mounting bolts

A   Seat retainers
B   Rear fender upper mounting bolt

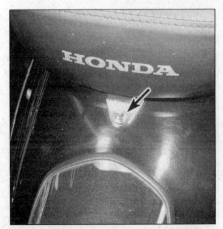

6.5 To remove the rear seat on VT750C/CD models, remove this bolt (arrow), slide the seat forward and lift it up (there's another bolt just like this at the rear of the front seat)

7.3a To remove the joint cover (arrow) from the steering covers on VT600 models . . .

7.3b . . . carefully pry it off (joint cover and steering covers removed for clarity)

7.4 On VT600 models, remove the steering cover retaining screw (arrow)

7.5a To detach the steering covers from the bike, grasp each cover half at the rear and pull it off . . .

7.5b . . . to disengage each mounting lug and grommet (arrows)

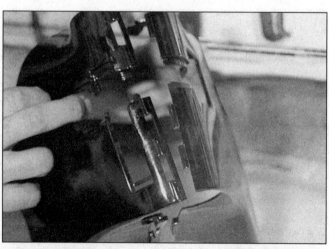

7.5c On VT600 models, the steering cover halves are hinged at the front; lift the left cover up slightly and pull the tangs out of the slots (steering covers removed for clarity)

VT600 models

3   To remove the joint cover **(see illustrations)**, carefully pry it out.

4   Remove the retaining screw **(see illustration)**.

5   Pull the two steering cover halves apart from the rear to disengage their mounting lugs from the grommets on the frame **(see illustrations)**, disengage the tangs and slots of the two cover halves at the steering head **(see illustration)** and remove the covers.

6   Installation is the reverse of removal. Make sure that neither cover half interferes with any wiring harnesses or connectors.

VT750C/CD models

7   Remove the two trim clips, one per side, from each steering cover half.

8   Pull the two steering cover halves apart to disengage their mounting lugs from the grommets on the frame **(see illustrations 7.5a and 7.5b)**.

9   Remove the joint clip and remove the covers.

10   Installation is the reverse of removal. Make sure that neither cover half interferes with any wiring harnesses or connectors.

VT750C2 Spirit models

11   Remove the speedometer (see Chapter 9).

12   Slide the retaining clip to the rear to separate the top edges of the cover halves.

13   Remove the bolts from the underside of the covers.

14   Slip the left cover's tab out of the right cover's slot, separate the cover and halves and take them off the motorcycle.

15   Installation is the reverse of the removal steps.

8   Side covers - removal and installation

VT600 models

1   To remove a side cover, put your fingers under the lower edge of the side cover **(see illustration)** and pull out, disengaging the two mounting bosses on the side cover **(see illustration)** from their respective grommets on the frame **(see illustration)**.

2   To install a side cover, insert the three positioning tabs across the top of the side cover under the lower edge of the rear fender bodywork **(see illustration)**, then push in the lower edge of the side cover and pop the two bosses into their grommets.

8.1a   To remove a VT600 side cover, put your fingers under the lower edge of the side cover and pull out . . .

8.1b   . . . disengaging the two mounting bosses (side cover removed for clarity) . . .

8.1c   . . . from the two grommets (arrows) on the frame

8.2   To install a VT600 side cover, insert these three tabs under the lower edge of the rear fender bodywork, then push in the lower edge of the cover and pop the two mounting bosses into their grommets

9.1 Remove the front chain guard mounting bolt
(VT600 model shown)

9.2 Remove the rear chain guard mounting bolt and, on VT600
models, disengage the guard from the grommet on the
swingarm (arrows)

VT750 models

3   To remove a side cover, grasp the side cover with both hands and pull it off, disengaging the three mounting bosses (one on top, one near the front end, one near the lower rear corner) from their respective grommets on the frame.
4   Installation is the reverse of removal. Simply position the side cover with the three mounting bosses aligned with their corresponding grommets and push in the cover.

9 Chain guard - removal and installation

1   Remove the front chain guard mounting bolt (see illustration).
2   Remove the rear chain guard mounting

bolt and, on VT600 models, disengage the guard from the grommet on the swingarm (see illustration).
3   Installation is the reverse of removal. Tighten the bolts securely.

10 Front fender - removal and installation

1   Remove the front wheel (see Chapter 7).
2   Unbolt the fender from the forks (see illustration).
3   Installation is the reverse of the removal steps. Tighten the bolts securely. Don't forget to route the speedometer cable through the loop on the left side of the fender.

11 Rear fender - removal and installation

1   On VT600 models, remove the seat; on VT750 models, remove the front and rear seat (see Section 6).
2   On VT600 models, remove the left and right side covers; on VT750 models, remove the right side cover (see Section 8).

VT600

3   Remove the fuel tank (see Chapter 4).
4   Remove the rear fender mounting bolts (see illustration).
5   Disengage the taillight wiring harness from its clips (see illustration) and unplug the electrical connectors for the harness (see illustration).

10.2 To detach the fender from the forks, remove these two bolts
from the left side and the two bolts from the other side

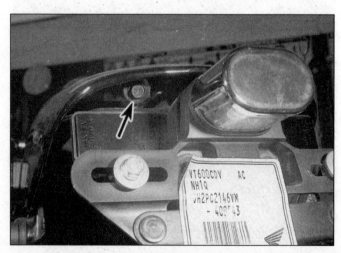

11.4 Remove the two VT600 rear fender bolts (arrow)
(left bolt shown)

11.5a Disengage the taillight harness from these clips . . .

11.5b . . . and unplug the electrical connectors (arrows) for the taillights (2003 and earlier shown)

6   Remove the taillight assembly from the rear fender (see Chapter 9).

7   Remove the rear fender mounting bolt **(see illustration 6.3b)** and nut (see "Taillight assembly - removal and installation" in Chapter 9).

8   Installation is the reverse of removal.

VT750 models

9   Unplug the electrical connectors for the taillight.

10   Remove the fender mounting bolts **(see illustration)**.

11   Remove the fender. If you're replacing the fender, the taillight assembly or the license plate/turn signal assembly, remove the taillight assembly and the license plate light/turn signal assembly (see Chapter 9).

12   Installation is the reverse of removal.

12 Rear sub-frame (VT600 models) - removal and installation

1   Remove the rear fender (see Section 11).

2   Unplug the electrical connectors for the left and right turn signal lights **(see illustration 11.5b)**. The wires for the left turn signal are green and orange; the wires for the right turn signal are green and light blue.

3   Remove the two rear sub-frame mounting bolts **(see illustration)**.

4   Remove the rear sub-frame from the frame.

5   Installation is the reverse of removal. Be sure to tighten the rear sub-frame mounting bolts securely.

13 Rear grab rails (VT750 models) - removal and installation

1   Remove the rear fender (see Section 11).

2   To remove the left fender grab rail, loosen the mounting nut located at the upper end of the left shock absorber, then remove the grab rail mounting bolt and washer. Remove the left grab rail.

3   To remove the right fender grab rail, remove the right shock absorber (see Chapter 6), then remove the grab rail mounting bolts. Remove the right grab rail.

4   Installation is the reverse of removal.

11.10 To detach a VT750 rear fender from the grab rails, remove the fender mounting bolts (arrows) (2003 and earlier right side shown)

12.3 To detach the VT600 rear sub-frame from the frame, remove the two sub-frame mounting bolts (arrow) (left bolt shown)

Notes

Chapter 9
Electrical system

Contents

Degrees of difficulty

Easy, suitable for novice with little experience	**Fairly easy,** suitable for beginner with some experience	**Fairly difficult,** suitable for competent DIY mechanic	**Difficult,** suitable for experienced DIY mechanic 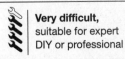	**Very difficult,** suitable for expert DIY or professional

Specifications

Battery type
VT600	12 V, 8 Ah
VT750	
VT750C/CD (2003 and earlier)	12V, 14 Ah
VT750DC (2003 and earlier)	12V, 12 Ah
VT750C Aero, VT750C2 Spirit (2004 and later)	12V, 10 or 11 Ah

Fuse specifications
Main fuse	30 amps
All others	
1988 and 1989 VT600 models	Six 10-amp and one 15-amp
1990-on VT600 models	Three 10-amp and one 15-amp
VT750 models	
2003 and earlier	Four 10-amp and one 15-amp
2004 and later	
VT750C Aero (2004 through 2007)	Five 10-amp, one 5-amp
VT750C Aero (2008)	Five 10-amp, one 20-amp
VT750C2 Spirit	Five 10-amp and one 20-amp

Bulb specifications

Headlight bulb	60/55W
Brake light/taillight bulbs	
1988, 1989, 1991 through 1996 VT600	32/3 cp or 27/8W
1997 on VT600..	32/3 cp
VT750C (2003 and earlier)	
VT750C/CD..	32/3 cp
VT750DC..	21/5W
VT750 (2004 and later)...	21/5W
Front turn signal bulbs	
1988, 1989, 1991 through 1996 VT600	32/3 cp or 23/8W
1997 and 1998 VT600..	32/3 cp
1999-on VT600, VT750	21/5W
Rear turn signal bulbs	
1988, 1989, 1991 through 1996 VT600	32 cp or 23W
1997 and 1998 VT600..	32 cp
1999-on VT600, VT750	21W
License plate bulb	
VT600	4 cp
VT750	5W
Speedometer light bulb	
VT600, 2003 and earlier VT750..................................	3.4W
2004 and later VT750	LED
Indicator bulbs	
VT600	1.7W
VT750 C/CD (2003 and earlier)	3.4W
VT750DC..	LED
VT750C Aero	
2004 through 2007	LED
2008...	3.4W
VT750C2 Spirit...	LED

Charging system

Stator coil resistance	
VT600, VT750DC	0.1 to 1.0 ohms
VT750C/CD	0.1 to 0.3 ohms
Charging system output	
VT600, VT750C/CD..	345 watts at 5,000 rpm
VT750DC..	333 watts at 5,000 rpm
Regulated voltage output	
1988, 1989, 1991 through 1996 VT600	14.3 to 15.1 volts at 5,000 rpm
1997 on VT600..	13.5 to 14 volts at 5,000 rpm
VT750C/CD..	14 to 15 volts at 4,000 rpm
VT750DC..	Less than 15.5 volts
Maximum current leakage	
VT600	1.3 mA
VT750	1.0 mA

Starter

Starter brush length	
Standard	12.5 mm (0.49 inch)
Minimum	6.5 mm (0.26 inch)
Starter driven gear hub	
VT600	
Inside diameter..	37.10 mm (1.461 inches)
Outside diameter	57.60 mm (2.268 inches)
VT750	
Inside diameter..	40.10 mm (1.579 inches)
Outside diameter	57.73 mm (2.273 inches)

Torque specifications

Neutral switch..	12 Nm (108 in-lbs)
Oil pressure switch	10 Nm (84 in-lbs)
Sidestand switch retaining bolt	
VT600	9 Nm (78 in-lbs)
VT750	10 Nm (84 in-lbs)
Rotor (rotor) bolt	128 Nm (94 ft-lbs)
Stator assembly retaining bolts	12 Nm (108 in-lbs)
Left crankcase cover bolts	12 Nm (108 in-lbs)
Rotor-to-clutch housing bolts	29 Nm (22 ft-lbs)

1 General information

The machines covered by this manual are equipped with a 12-volt electrical system.

The charging system uses an alternator consisting of a rotor (rotor) with permanent magnets that rotates around a stator coil of copper wire. The alternator produces alternating current, which is converted to direct current by the regulator/rectifier. The regulator/rectifier also controls the charging system output.

An electric starter mounted behind the rear cylinder is standard equipment. The starter has four brushes. The starting system includes the motor, the battery, the starter relay switch and the wiring harnesses and switches. When the engine kill switch and the ignition switch are both in the On position, the starter relay switch allows the starter motor to operate only if the transmission is in Neutral (Neutral switch on) or the clutch lever is pulled in (clutch switch on) and the sidestand is up (sidestand switch on). **Note:** *Keep in mind that electrical parts, once purchased, can't be returned. To avoid unnecessary expense, make very sure the faulty component has been positively identified before buying a replacement part.*

2 Electrical troubleshooting

A typical electrical circuit consists of an electrical component, the switches, relays, etc. related to that component and the wiring and connectors that hook the component to both the battery and the frame. To aid in locating a problem in any electrical circuit, complete wiring diagrams of each model are included at the end of this Chapter.

Before tackling any troublesome electrical circuit, first study the appropriate diagrams thoroughly to get a complete picture of what makes up that individual circuit. Trouble spots, for instance, can often be narrowed down by noting if other components related to that circuit are operating properly or not. If several components or circuits fail at one time, chances are the fault lies in the fuse or ground connection, as several circuits often are routed through the same fuse and ground connections.

Electrical problems often stem from simple causes, such as loose or corroded connections or a blown fuse. Prior to any electrical troubleshooting, always visually check the condition of the fuse, wires and connections in the problem circuit. Intermittent failures can be especially frustrating, since you can't always duplicate the failure when it's convenient to test. In such situations, a good practice is to clean all connections in the affected circuit, whether or not they appear to be good. All of the connections and wires should also be wiggled to check for looseness which can cause intermittent failure.

If testing instruments are going to be utilized, use the diagrams to plan where you will make the necessary connections in order to accurately pinpoint the trouble spot.

The basic tools needed for electrical troubleshooting include a test light or voltmeter, a continuity tester (which includes a bulb, battery and set of test leads) and a jumper wire, preferably with a circuit breaker incorporated, which can be used to bypass electrical components. Specific checks described later in this Chapter may also require an ohmmeter.

Voltage checks should be performed if a circuit is not functioning properly. Connect one lead of a test light or voltmeter to either the negative battery terminal or a known good ground. Connect the other lead to a connector in the circuit being tested, preferably nearest to the battery or fuse. If the bulb lights, voltage is reaching that point, which means the part of the circuit between that connector and the battery is problem-free. Continue checking the remainder of the circuit in the same manner. When you reach a point where no voltage is present, the problem lies between there and the last good test point. Most of the time the problem is due to a loose connection. Keep in mind that some circuits only receive voltage when the ignition key is in the On position.

One method of finding short circuits is to remove the fuse and connect a test light or voltmeter in its place to the fuse terminals. There should be no load in the circuit (it should be switched off). Move the wiring harness from side-to-side while watching the test light. If the bulb lights, there is a short to ground somewhere in that area, probably where insulation has rubbed off a wire. The same test can be performed on other components in the circuit, including the switch.

A ground check should be done to see if a component is grounded properly. Disconnect the battery and connect one lead of a self-powered test light (continuity tester) to a known good ground. Connect the other lead to the wire or ground connection being tested. If the bulb lights, the ground is good. If the bulb does not light, the ground is not good.

A continuity check is performed to see if a circuit, section of circuit or individual component is capable of passing electricity through it. Disconnect the battery and connect one lead of a self-powered test light (continuity tester) to one end of the circuit being tested and the other lead to the other end of the circuit. If the bulb lights, there is continuity, which means the circuit is passing electricity through it properly. Switches can be checked in the same way.

Remember that all electrical circuits are designed to conduct electricity from the battery, through the wires, switches, relays, etc. to the electrical component (light bulb, motor, etc.). From there it is directed to the frame (ground) where it is passed back to the battery. Electrical problems are basically an interruption in the flow of electricity from the battery or back to it.

3 Battery - removal, inspection, maintenance and installation

1   Most battery damage is caused by heat, vibration, and/or low electrolyte levels, so make sure the battery is securely mounted, check the electrolyte level frequently (if the battery is a conventional unit) and make sure the charging system is functioning properly.

Removal and installation
VT600 models

2   Remove the left and right side covers (see Chapter 8).
3   On the right side, peel back the protective rubber cover from the fuse box (see Section 5), pull off the fuse box and remove the battery case cover screws **(see illustration)**.
4   Lift up the cover and disconnect the

3.3 To remove the battery case cover on VT600 models, remove these two screws (arrows)

3.4a On VT600 models, disconnect the negative cable (left terminal) first . . .

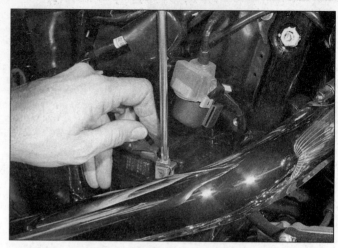

3.4b . . . then disconnect the positive cable (right terminal)

battery cables from the battery terminals, negative cable (left terminal) first, then positive **(see illustrations)**.

5   Remove the battery from the battery case and inspect it (see below).

6   Installation is the reverse of removal. Be sure to attach the positive cable (right terminal) first, then negative. Tighten the cables securely. Don't forget to put the protective cap back on the positive terminal.

VT750 models

7   Remove the seat (see Chapter 8).

8   Remove the ignition control module from the battery case cover (see Chapter 5).

9   Remove the three battery case cover screws.

10   Disconnect the battery cables from the battery terminals, negative cable (right terminal) first, then positive.

11   Lift the battery out of the battery case and inspect it (see below).

12   Installation is the reverse of removal. Be sure to attach the positive cable (left terminal) first, then negative. Tighten the cables securely. Don't forget to put the protective cap back on the positive terminal.

Inspection and maintenance

13   All machines covered in this manual are originally equipped with maintenance-free batteries. However, if you or a previous owner have installed a conventional battery, check the electrolyte level and specific gravity (see Chapter 1).

14   Check around the base inside of the battery for sediment, which is the result of sulfation caused by low electrolyte levels. These deposits will cause internal short circuits, which can quickly discharge the battery. Look for cracks in the case and replace the battery if either of these conditions is found.

15   Check the battery terminals and cable ends for tightness and corrosion. If corrosion is evident, remove the cables from the battery and clean the terminals and cable ends with a wire brush or knife and emery paper. Reconnect the cables and apply a thin coat of petroleum jelly to the connections to slow further corrosion.

16   The battery case should be kept clean to prevent current leakage, which can discharge the battery over a period of time (especially when it sits unused). Wash the outside of the case with a solution of baking soda and water. Do not get any baking soda solution in the battery cells. Rinse the battery thoroughly, then dry it.

17   If acid has been spilled on the frame or battery box, neutralize it with the baking soda and water solution, dry it thoroughly, then touch up any damaged paint. If the battery is equipped with a vent tube, make sure it's correctly routed and is not kinked or pinched.

18   If the motorcycle sits unused for long periods of time, disconnect the cables from the battery terminals. Charge the battery about once a month (see Section 4).

4   Battery - charging

1   If the machine sits idle for extended periods or if the charging system malfunctions, the battery can be charged from an external source.

Maintenance-free batteries

2   Charging the maintenance-free battery used on these models requires a digital voltmeter and a variable-voltage charger with a built-in ammeter.

3   When charging the battery, always remove it from the machine and be sure to check the electrolyte level by looking through the translucent battery case before hooking up the charger. If the electrolyte level is low, the battery must be discarded; never remove the sealing plug to add water.

4   Disconnect the battery cables (negative cable first), then connect a digital voltmeter between the battery terminals and measure the voltage.

5   If terminal voltage is 12.6 volts or higher, the battery is fully charged. If it's lower, recharge the battery. Refer to the accompanying illustration for charging rate and time **(see illustration)**.

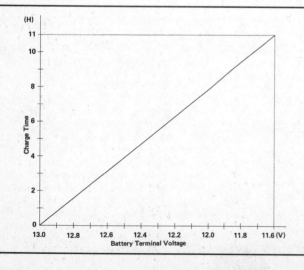

4.5 Battery charge-time table (maintenance-free batteries)

6   A quick charge can be used in an emergency, provided the maximum charge rates and times are not exceeded (exceeding the maximum rate or time may ruin the battery). A quick charge should always be followed as soon as possible by a charge at the standard rate and time.

7   Hook up the battery charger leads (positive lead to battery positive terminal, negative lead to battery negative terminal), then, and only then, plug in the battery charger.

 Warning: The hydrogen gas escaping from a charging battery is explosive, so keep open flames and sparks well away from the area. Also, the electrolyte is extremely corrosive and will damage anything it comes in contact with.

8   Start charging at a high voltage setting (no more than 25 volts) and watch the ammeter for about 5 minutes. If the charging current doesn't increase, replace the battery.

9   When the charging current increases beyond the specified maximum, reduce the charging voltage to reduce the charging current to the rate listed in this Chapter's Specifications. Do this periodically as the battery charges.

10   Allow the battery to charge for the specified time listed in this Chapter's Specifications. If the battery overheats or gases excessively, the charging rate is too high. Either disconnect the charger or lower the charging rate to prevent damage to the battery.

11   After the specified time, unplug the charger first, then disconnect the leads from the battery.

12   Wait 30 minutes, then measure voltage between the battery terminals. If it's 12.6 volts or higher, the battery is fully charged. If it's between 12.0 and 12.6 volts, charge the battery again (refer to this Chapter's Specifications and **illustration 4.5** for charge rate and time). If it's less than 12.0 volts, it's time for a new battery.

13   When the battery is fully charged, unplug the charger first, then disconnect the leads from the battery. Wipe off the outside of the battery case and install the battery in the bike.

Conventional batteries

14   To properly charge the battery, you will need a charger of the correct rating, a hydrometer, a clean rag and a syringe for adding distilled water to the battery cells.

15   The maximum charging rate for any battery is 1/10 of the rated amp/hour capacity. As an example, the maximum charging rate for a 12 amp/hour battery would be 1.2 amps and the maximum charging rate for a 14 amp/hour battery would be 1.4 amps. If the battery is charged at a higher rate, it could be damaged.

16   Do not allow the battery to be subjected to a so-called quick charge (high rate

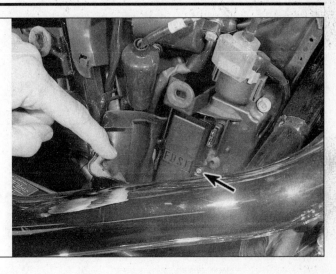

5.2 The VT600 fuse box is located behind the right side cover; to open the fuse box, remove this screw (arrow); the main (30A) fuse is located directly above the fuse box

of charge over a short period of time) unless you are prepared to buy a new battery.

17   When charging the battery, always remove it from the machine and be sure to check the electrolyte level before hooking up the charger. Add distilled water to any cells that are low.

18   Loosen the cell caps, hook up the battery charger leads (red to positive, black to negative), cover the top of the battery with a clean rag, then, and only then, plug in the battery charger.

 Warning: Remember, the gas escaping from a charging battery is explosive, so keep open flames and sparks well away from the area. Also, the electrolyte is extremely corrosive and will damage anything it comes in contact with.

19   Allow the battery to charge until the specific gravity is as specified (refer to Chapter 1 for specific gravity checking procedures). The charger must be unplugged and disconnected from the battery when making specific gravity checks. If the battery overheats or gases excessively, the charging rate is too high. Either disconnect the charger or lower the charging rate to prevent damage to the battery.

20   It's time for a new battery if:

a) One or more of the cells is significantly lower in specific gravity than the others after a long slow charge.

b) The battery as a whole doesn't seem to want to take a charge.

c) Battery voltage won't increase.

d) The electrolyte doesn't bubble.

e) The plates are white (indicating sulfation) or debris has accumulated in the bottom of a cell.

f) The plates or insulators are warped or buckled.

21   When the battery is fully charged, unplug the charger first, then disconnect the leads from the battery. Install the cell caps and wipe any electrolyte off the outside of the battery case.

5   Fuses - check and replacement

1   Some fuses are located in the fuse block, which is located on the right side of the bike, behind the right side cover. Remove the right side cover (see Chapter 8).

2   On VT600 models, peel back the protective rubber cover **(see illustration)** and remove the fuse cover screw. The fuse box houses six 10-amp fuses and one 15-amp fuse (1988 and 1989 models) or three 10-amp fuses and one 15-amp fuse (1990 and later VT600 models). The main (30-amp) fuse is located right above the fuse box.

3   On VT750 models, remove the cover from the fuse box. The main (30-amp) fuse is on the left side. To check or replace it, remove the left side cover (see Chapter 8).

4   Other fuses (turn signal/dimmer/horn switch, fan motor switch, oil pressure switch, neutral switch, sidestand switch, brake light switches, fuel pump, etc.) are installed inline, often near the electrical connector for each circuit device. Most of these fuses are easy to find when troubleshooting a circuit. For further help in locating inline fuses, refer to the wiring diagrams at the end of this Chapter.

5   If you have a test light, all of the fuses can be checked without removing them. Turn the ignition key to the On position, connect one end of the test light to a good ground, then probe each terminal on top of the fuse. If the fuse is good, there will be voltage available at both terminals. If the fuse is blown, there will only be voltage present at one of the terminals.

6   The fuses can also be tested with an ohmmeter or self-powered test light. Remove the fuse and connect the tester to the ends of the fuse. If the ohmmeter shows continuity or the test lamp lights, the fuse is good. If the ohmmeter shows infinite resistance or the test lamp stays out, the fuse is blown.

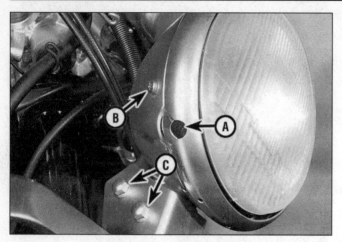

7.1 VT600 headlight assembly

A   *Headlight adjusting screw (1 of 2)*
B   *Headlight retaining screw (1 of 2)*
C   *Headlight assembly nuts and bolts*

7.2 Tilt the headlight out and disconnect the wiring connector (arrow)

7.3 The TOP mark on the dust cover (arrow) goes upward

7.4 Remove the headlight bulb retainer

7.5 Lift out the bulb; don't touch the glass on the new bulb

8.3 The headlight adjusting screws are located on either side of the headlight assembly (headlight removed for clarity; the screws can be adjusted without removing the headlight)

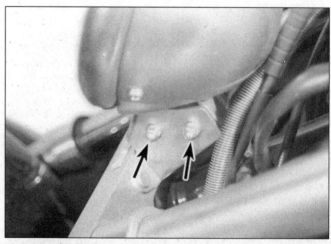

9.3 To detach the headlight housing from the bracket, remove these two nuts (arrows) and pull out the bolts (VT600 models)

7   The fuses can be removed and checked visually. If you can't pull the fuse out with your fingertips, use a pair of needle-nose pliers. A blown fuse is easily identified by a break in the element.

8   If a fuse blows, be sure to check the wiring harnesses very carefully for evidence of a short circuit. Look for bare wires and chafed, melted or burned insulation. If a fuse is replaced before the cause is located, the new fuse will blow immediately. Occasionally a fuse will blow or cause an open circuit for no obvious reason. Corrosion of the fuse ends and fuse block terminals may occur and cause poor fuse contact. If this happens, remove the corrosion with a wire brush or emery paper, then spray the fuse end and terminals with electrical contact cleaner.

9   Fuse ratings are listed in this Chapter's Specifications. Fuse ratings are also marked on the fuses themselves. Never, under any circumstances, use a higher rated fuse or bridge the fuse block terminals, as damage to the electrical system could result.

6   Lighting system - check

1   The battery provides power for operation of the headlight, taillight, brake light, license plate light, instrument and warning lights. If none of the lights operate, always check battery voltage before proceeding. Low battery voltage indicates either a faulty battery, low battery electrolyte level or a defective charging system. If the bike has a conventional battery, check the battery electrolyte level and the specific gravity (see Chapter 1). Inspect the battery; make sure it's fully charged (see Sections 3 and 4). Check the condition of the fuses and replace any blown fuses (see Section 5). Check the charging system (see Sections 29 and 30).

Headlight

2   If the headlight is out when the engine is running, check the fuse first with the key or switch On (see Section 5), then unplug the electrical connector for the headlight and use jumper wires to connect the bulb directly to the battery terminals (see Section 7). If the light comes on, the problem lies in the wiring (see the wiring diagrams at the end of this Chapter).

Turn signal lights/brake light/ taillight/license plate light

3   If a light fails to work, check the bulb and the bulb terminal first, then check for battery voltage at the electrical connector. If voltage is present, check the ground circuit for an open or poor connection.

4   If no voltage is indicated, check the wiring between the taillight and the ignition switch, then check the switch.

Brake light switches

5   See Section 12 for the brake light switch checking procedure.

Speedometer light and indicator lights

6   If the speedometer light fails to operate when the key switch is On, check the fuse (see Section 5) and the bulb (see Section 16). If the bulb and fuses are in good condition, check for battery voltage at the connector. If the turn signal indicator light fails to operate when the turn signal switch is in the LEFT or RIGHT position, or if the high-beam indicator light fails to operate when the dimmer switch is in the HI position, see Section 18. If the neutral indicator light fails to operate when the transmission in Neutral, see Section 20.

7   Headlight bulb - replacement

   Warning: If the bulb has just burned out, allow it to cool. It will be hot enough to burn your fingers.

1   Remove the headlight retaining screws (see illustration).

2   Tilt the headlight forward out of the headlight housing and unplug the electrical connector (see illustration).

3   Remove the dust cover (see illustration).

4   Remove the bulb retainer (see illustration).

5   Remove the bulb (see illustration).

6   Installation is the reverse of removal. Be sure not to touch the bulb glass with your fingers - oil from your skin will cause the bulb to overheat and fail prematurely. If you do touch the bulb, wipe it off with a clean rag dampened with rubbing alcohol.

8   Headlight aim - check and adjustment

1   An improperly adjusted headlight may cause problems for oncoming traffic or provide poor, unsafe illumination of the road ahead. Before adjusting the headlight, be sure to consult with local traffic laws and regulations.

2   The headlight beam can be adjusted both vertically and horizontally. Before performing the adjustment, make sure the fuel tank is at least half full and have an assistant sit on the seat.

3   The adjusting screws are located in the lower edge of the headlight (see illustration).

9   Headlight assembly - removal and installation

1   Remove the headlight (see Section 7).

2   Clearly label, then disconnect, all electrical connectors inside the headlight housing, then remove the wiring from the housing. Be careful not to cut any wires when pulling them through the holes in the housing.

VT600 models

3   If you just want to remove the headlight housing itself, remove the bracket-to-housing nuts (see illustration) and bolts (see illustration 7.1) and remove the housing.

4   If you want to remove the headlight housing bracket from the lower triple clamp, remove the nuts (see illustration) from the bracket studs on the underside of the lower triple clamp.

9.4 To detach the headlight housing bracket from the lower triple clamp, remove these two nuts (VT600 models)

9.5 Headlight housing assembly (VT600 models)

1 Nuts
2 Bolts
3 Headlight housing (with one bushing and set of collars assembled)
4 Collars
5 Bushing
6 Headlight housing bracket

10.1 Remove the turn signal lens retaining screws (arrows) and remove the lens

5 Remove the collars and bushings from the bracket **(see illustration)**, clean and inspect them, remove any corrosion, lubricate them lightly and reassemble.
6 Installation is the reverse of removal.

VT750 models
7 Remove the handlebar and the upper triple clamp (see Chapter 6).
8 Remove the headlight and turn signal assembly. Lift the assembly's mounting posts out of the grommets in the lower triple clamp.
9 If you're replacing a turn signal assembly, or if you're replacing the headlight assembly itself, remove the turn signal(s).
10 Installation is the reverse of removal.

---

10 Turn signal, tail/brake light and license plate bulbs - replacement

Turn signal bulbs
1 To replace a turn signal bulb, remove the lens retaining screws **(see illustration)**.
2 Push the bulb in and turn it counterclockwise to remove it.
3 Check the socket terminals for corrosion and clean them if necessary. Line up the pins on the new bulb with the slots in the socket, push in and turn the bulb clockwise until it locks in place.
4 Position the lens on the housing and

install the screws. Be careful not to overtighten them or the lens will crack.

Tail/brake light bulbs
5 Remove the lens screws **(see illustration)** and take the lens off.
6 To remove a brake or taillight bulb, push the bulb in and turn it counterclockwise **(see illustration)**.
7 Install the bulb (see Steps 3 and 4).

License plate bulb
VT600 models
8 Remove the license plate bracket **(see illustrations)**.
9 Remove the two license plate lens/ housing retaining bolts from the back of the

10.5 Remove the brake/taillight lens screws (arrows) (VT600 shown) and take off the lens

10.6 To remove a brake or taillight bulb, press the bulb into its socket and turn it counterclockwise

10.8a To remove the license plate bracket from the rear sub-frame on VT600 models, remove these two bolts (arrows) . . .

10.8b . . . and remove this nut from the back

license plate bracket **(see illustration)**.
10   Remove the lens and the housing **(see illustration)**.
11   Push the bulb in, turn it counterclockwise and remove it **(see illustration)**.
12   Installation is the reverse of removal.

VT750C/CD models (2003 and earlier)

13   Remove the license light cover screws and remove the license light cover.
14   License plate bulb replacement on these models is otherwise identical to the procedure for replacing the bulb on a VT600 model (except that the lens and housing are retained by two nuts instead of two bolts). Refer to Steps 9, 10 and 11 above.
15   Installation is the reverse of removal.

VT750 models (2004 and later)

16   Remove the screws that secure the cover to the license plate light and take it off.
17   Pull the bulb straight out of the socket

and press a new one in.
18   Installation is the reverse of the removal steps. Inspect the cover gasket and replace it if it's damaged or deteriorated.

11 Turn signal circuit and relay - check

Circuit

1   Battery voltage powers the turn signal lights, so if they don't operate, check battery voltage first and, on bikes with a conventional battery, the electrolyte level and specific gravity (see Chapter 1). Low battery voltage indicates either a defective battery (see Sections 3 and 4) or a malfunction in the charging system (see Sections 29 and 30). Also, check the fuses (see Section 5).
2   Most turn signal problems are the result of a burned out bulb or corroded socket.

This is even more likely when the turn signal lights flash correctly on one side but not on the other. Check the bulbs and the sockets (see Section 10).

10.9 License plate lens and housing bolts (VT600; VT750 uses two nuts)

10.10 Remove the license plate lens and housing from the license plate bracket

10.11 To remove the license plate bulb, push it in and turn it counterclockwise; to install it, push it in and turn it clockwise

11.4 The turn signal relay is located under the seat on VT600 and VT750C2 Spirit models (VT600 shown)

12.5 Disconnect the two electrical leads from the front brake light switch (VT600 shown, VT750 similar)

3   If the bulbs and sockets check out okay, check the turn signal relay.

Turn signal relay

4   On VT600 and VT750C2 Spirit models, remove the seat (see Chapter 8) and detach the turn signal relay **(see illustration)**.
5   On VT750 models, remove the headlight (see Section 7) and remove the turn signal relay from the headlight housing.
6   Locate the terminals of the turn signal relay connector for the black/brown wire (fuse side of circuit) and the gray wire (switch side of circuit) (on 1988 and 1989 VT600 models, there's a white/green wire, instead of a black/brown wire). Connect the two terminals together with a jumper wire.
7   Turn the ignition switch to ON and operate the turn signal switch.
8   If the turn signal lights *don't* come on, check the turn signal switch for an open circuit (see Section 18). If the turn signal switch is okay, look for an open circuit in the black/

brown (green/white) wire or in the gray wire.
9   If the turn signal lights *do* come on, check for continuity between the terminal for the green wire and the ground terminal at the connector. If there is no continuity, there is an open circuit in the green wire. If there is continuity, either there's a loose (intermittent) or poor contact in the turn signal relay connector, or the turn signal relay is defective.

12 Brake light switches - check and replacement

Circuit check

1   Before checking any electrical circuit, check the fuses (see Section 5).
2   Using a test light connected to a good ground, check for voltage at the brake light switch. If there's no voltage present, check the wire between the switch and the fuse box

(see the wiring diagrams at the end of this Chapter).
3   If voltage is available, touch the probe of the test light to the other terminal of the switch, then pull the brake lever or depress the brake pedal - if the test light doesn't light up, replace the switch.
4   If the test light does light, check the wiring between the switch and the brake lights (see the wiring diagrams at the end of this Chapter).

Switch replacement
Front brake lever switch

5   Disconnect the two electrical leads from the switch **(see illustration)**.
6   Remove the switch retaining screw **(see illustration)**.
7   Installation is the reverse of removal. Make sure that the positioning pin on the switch is aligned with the hole in the master cylinder **(see illustration)**.

12.6 To detach the front brake light switch from the master cylinder, remove this retaining screw (arrow) (VT600 shown, VT750 similar)

12.7 Make sure that the positioning pin on the brake switch is aligned with the hole (arrow) in the master cylinder (VT600 shown, VT750 similar)

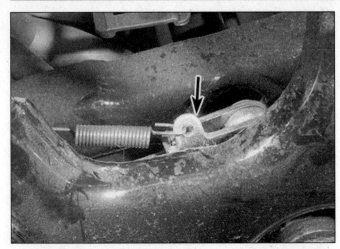

12.10 On VT600 models, disengage the rear brake light switch return spring from the middle brake arm (arrow)

12.11 To remove the rear brake light switch, turn the adjusting nut (arrow), not the switch, and take the switch out of the bracket

Rear brake pedal switch

VT600 models

8   Remove the right side cover (see Chapter 8).

9   Unplug the switch electrical connector (it can be identified by its wire colors, referring to wiring diagrams at the end of the book).

10   Unhook the switch spring **(see illustration)**.

11   Back off the switch locknut and slide the switch out of its mounting bracket **(see illustration)**.

12   Installation is the reverse of removal.

13   Adjust the switch (see Chapter 1).

VT750 models

14   The switch used on VT750 models is identical in design to the switch used on VT600 models, except that it's located up front, next to the rear brake pedal **(see illustration 3.4 in Chapter 8)**.

15   To replace the switch on a VT750

model, follow the procedure outlined above for VT600 models. The electrical connector for the switch is a black two-pin connector. On VT750C/CD models, it's behind the seat. On VT750DC models, remove the right side radiator mounting bolt and pull the grille forward for access to the connector.

13 Turn signal assembly - removal and installation

Front turn signals

All except 2004 and later VT750C Aero

1   On VT600 models, the front turn signal wires and connectors are located right behind the steering head. Remove the fuel tank (see Chapter 4) and the steering head covers (see Chapter 8).

2   On VT750 models, the front turn signal wires and connectors are located inside the headlight housing. Remove the headlight from the housing (see Section 7).

3   Locate the electrical leads for the front turn signals. On all models, the three left turn signal wires are green, orange and orange/white; the three right turn signal wires are green, light blue and light blue/white. Unplug the leads for the turn signal you are removing.

4   On VT600 models, remove the turn signal assembly pinch bolt, remove the chrome cover and pull the turn signal assembly from the fork tube **(see illustrations)**.

5   On VT750 models, remove the turn signal assembly together with the headlight assembly (see Section 9).

6   Installation is the reverse of removal.

2004 and later VT750C Aero

7   Remove the headlight assembly (see Section 9).

13.4a To detach a VT600 front turn signal assembly from the fork tube, remove this pinch bolt (arrow) . . .

13.4b . . . remove the chrome cover (note the bolt collar). . .

13.4c . . . and pull off the turn signal assembly

13.15a To detach a VT600 rear turn signal assembly, detach the wiring harness from all clips and clamps . . .

13.15b . . . and remove the turn signal assembly mounting nut (note how the harness is routed through the hole in the bracket)

8   Locate the turn signal connectors inside the headlight housing and unplug them.
9   Unbolt the cover for the front of the turn signal crossbar. Remove the bolts, collars and crossbar.
10   Unbolt the turn signals and stays and remove them from the motorcycle.
11   Installation is the reverse of the removal steps. Align the tab on the right turn signal light with the slot in its stay.

Rear turn signals

12   On VT600 models, the rear turn signal wires and connectors are located on under the seat. Remove the seat (see Chapter 8).
13   On VT750 models, the rear turn signal wires and connectors are located behind the right side cover. Remove the right side cover (see Chapter 8).
14   Locate the electrical leads for the rear turn signals. On all models, the two left turn signal wires are green and orange; the two right turn signal wires are green and light

blue. Unplug the leads for the turn signal you are removing.
15   On VT600 models, trace the routing of the harness back to the turn signal, detach the harness from all clips and clamps on the frame, then remove the turn signal assembly mounting nut (see illustrations).
16   On VT750 models, remove two screws from the underside of the license light cover and lift the cover off. Disconnect the wires running to each turn signal stalk and remove the stalk mounting nut.
17   Installation is the reverse of removal.

14 Brake light/taillight assembly - removal and installation

VT600 models

1   Remove the seat (see Chapter 8).
2   The wires for the brake light and taillight

are brown, green and green/yellow. Trace the wires to the electrical connector(s) in the dust boot to the right of the fuel pump. Unplug the connector.
3   Trace the harness back to the brake light/taillight assembly and detach all clips and clamps.
4   From underneath the fender, remove the brake light/taillight assembly mounting nuts (see illustration) and remove the brake light/taillight assembly (see illustration) and pull out the harness.
5   Installation is the reverse of removal.

VT750 models

2003 and earlier

6   Remove the right side cover (see Chapter 8).
7   The wires for the brake light and taillight are brown, green and green/yellow. Trace the wires to the electrical connector(s) in the dust boot behind the right side cover. Unplug the connector.

14.4a To detach the VT600 brake light/taillight assembly from the rear fender, remove these two nuts (arrows) . . .

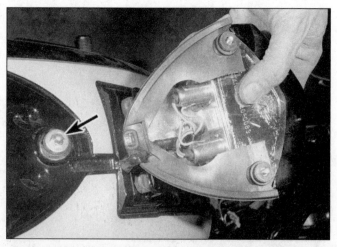

14.4b . . . lift the assembly out of the fender and carefully pull the wire harness out - pull on the harness, not the taillight (there's a fender mounting nut [arrow] under the taillight)

15.2 Speedometer (VT600 shown; VT750 similar)

A Speedometer housing screws
B Speedometer cable nut

15.3 To disconnect the lower end of the speedometer cable from the speedometer gearbox, remove this screw and pull out the cable

8   Trace the harness back to the brake light/taillight assembly and detach all clips and clamps.

9   From underneath the fender, remove the brake light/taillight assembly mounting nuts, remove the brake light/taillight assembly and pull out the harness.

10   Installation is the reverse of removal.

2004 and later

11   Remove the rear fender (see Chapter 8). If you're working on a VT750C2 Spirit, remove the upper portion of the fender from the lower part.

12   Working inside the fender, remove the nuts and collars that secure the taillight to the fender. Lift the taillight off the fender.

13   Installation is the reverse of the removal steps.

---

15 Speedometer and cable or speed sensor - removal and installation

1   Depending on the model, the speedometer is either mounted on the upper triple clamp and driven by a cable, or on top of the fuel tank and connected by a wiring harness to a speed sensor at the front wheel.

Speedometer cable

2   Unscrew the upper speedometer cable end from the speedometer (see illustration) and detach the cable from the speedometer.

3   Note how it's routed, then unscrew the speedometer cable from the speedometer gearbox at the front fork (see illustration).

4   Installation is the reverse of the removal steps. Be sure the speedometer cable is routed so that it doesn't cause the steering to bind or interfere with other components. The squared-off ends of the cable must fit into their spindles in the speedometer and gearbox.

Speed sensor

5   To test the speed sensor, follow the wiring harness to the connector and disconnect it (it's inside the headlight housing on VT750DC models). Connect a voltmeter to the terminals in the speed sensor side of the connector. Place a screwdriver in the sensor slot and spin it. The voltmeter should indicate pulsing voltage between zero and 5 volts. If not, and if the wires are good, replace the sensor.

6   On 2003 and earlier models, remove the mounting screw at the bottom of the speed sensor and take it off the fork leg. On 2004 and later models, the speed sensor is mounted on the left side of the crankcase, directly below the ignition lock. Disconnect its wiring connector, free the wiring harness from its retainers, remove the sensor mounting bolts and take it off the engine.

7   Installation is the reverse of the removal steps.

Speedometer

Mounted on triple clamp

8   Disconnect the cable from the speedometer (see illustration 15.2).

9   On VT600 models, remove the fuel tank (see Chapter 4) and the steering head covers (see Chapter 8). Follow the speedometer wires to the black six-pin connector behind the steering head and unplug the connector. Also, unplug the connector for the yellow/black wire.

10   On VT750 models, remove the headlight (see Section 7). Follow the speedometer wires to the black six-pin connector behind the steering head and unplug the connector.

11   Remove the bolt and nut (see illustration) and detach the speedometer from the mounting bracket.

Mounted on fuel tank

12   If you're working on a VT750C/CD model, unbolt the fuel tank, lift it up and

15.11 To detach the speedometer assembly from its mounting bracket, remove this nut (arrow) and pull out the bolt

disconnect the speedometer connector. Remove two bolts from the front of the speedometer cover and two bolts from the top rear. Remove the fuel tank cap and lift the speedometer off.

13   If you're working on a VT750DC, VT750C Aero or VT750C2 Spirit (2004 and later), remove the two bolts at the top rear of the speedometer cover. Slide the speedometer forward to disengage its front retainer from the tank, then lift the speedometer and disconnect its electrical connector.

14   Installation is the reverse of the removal steps. If you're working on a VT750DC model, be sure the rubber mounting pad is in position on the tank bracket.

16.4a To replace the light bulb that illuminates the speedometer face, pull the bulb socket out of the speedometer assembly . . .

16.4b . . . then pull the bulb out of the socket

16 Speedometer light and indicator lights - replacement

Speedometer light bulb

1   The speedometer illumination bulb on models with conventional bulbs can be replaced. On models with a light-emitting diode (LED), the light can't be replaced separately from the speedometer. See this Chapter's Specifications for bulb types.

2   Remove the speedometer (see Section 15).

3   Remove the speedometer cover screws **(see illustration 15.2)** and remove the cover.

4   Remove the bulb socket **(see illustration)**, then pull the bulb out of the socket **(see illustration)**. If the socket contacts are dirty or corroded, they should be scraped clean and sprayed with electrical contact cleaner before new bulbs are installed.

5   Carefully push the new bulb into position,

then push the socket into the speedometer.

6   Installation is otherwise the reverse of removal.

Indicator lights

7   The indicator lights (turn signal, neutral and high beam) on VT600 and VT750C/CD models are located in the upper triple clamp. The bulbs can be replaced. On VT750DC models, the indicator lights are light emitting diodes that can't be replaced.

8   To replace an indicator light bulb on a VT600 or 2008 VT750C Aero, pull down the socket for the bulb you wish to replace **(see illustration)**, pull out the bad bulb from the socket, install a new bulb in the socket and install the new bulb and socket into its receptacle in the triple clamp. Make sure it's firmly seated.

9   To replace an indicator light bulb on a VT750C/CD, remove the indicator light lens and pull the socket out of the triple clamp and replace the bulb as described in the previous step.

16.8 The bulbs for the indicator lights (arrows) are accessible from the underside of the triple clamp

17 Ignition main (key) switch - check and replacement

Check

1   Remove the left side cover (see Chapter 8).

2   Trace the wiring harness from the ignition switch to the four-pin white connector and disconnect it. The wires between the ignition switch are red, red/black and blue/orange (these are, respectively, the battery, ignition and fan motor wires). On 1988 and 1989 VT600 models, there's also a brown/white wire to this connector, and two more wires, brown and yellow/blue, lead to a black two-pin connector which must be disconnected (the extra wires on these models are for the Park position, which was eliminated after 1989).

3   Using an ohmmeter, check the continuity of the terminal pairs indicated in the following steps. Connect the ohmmeter to the *switch* side of the connector, not the wiring harness side.

4   In the OFF position, there should be no continuity between any of the wires.

5   In the ON position, there should be continuity between the red, red/blue and blue/orange wires (and, on 1988 and 1989 VT600 models, between the brown/white and brown wires).

6   In the PARK position, on 1988 and 1989 VT600 models, there should be continuity between the red and yellow/blue wires.

7   If the switch fails any of the tests, replace it.

Replacement

8   Disconnect the electrical connector, if you haven't already done so. Free the wiring harness from any clips or retainers.

9   Remove the ignition switch cover screw **(see illustration)** and remove the cover.

17.9 To remove the ignition switch cover, remove its retaining screw (arrow)

17.10 To detach the ignition switch from its mounting bracket, drill out these two "break-off bolts"

10   Drill out the two "break-off bolts" **(see illustration)** and remove the ignition switch.
11   Installation is the reverse of removal. Be sure to use new break-off bolts (available at the dealer parts department). Tighten them until their heads snap off.

 18 Handlebar switches - check

1   Most handlebar switch problems are caused by dirty or corroded contacts, or by worn or broken internal parts. If some part of a switch breaks, the switch assembly must be replaced. Individual parts are not available.
2   If a handlebar switch malfunctions, check it for continuity with an ohmmeter or a continuity test light. Be sure to disconnect the battery negative cable to prevent a short circuit, before making the checks.
3   On VT600 models, remove the fuel tank (see Chapter 4) and the steering head covers (see Chapter 8).
4   On VT750 models, remove the headlight (see Section 7).
5   Trace the wiring harness from the suspect switch and unplug the electrical connector(s).
6   Using an ohmmeter, check the continuity of the terminal pairs indicated in the following steps. Connect the ohmmeter to the *switch* side of the connector, not the wiring harness side.

Left handlebar switches

7   The wire colors for the **left** handlebar switches are as follows:
  a) The **dimmer switch** wires are blue/white, blue and white on all models.
  b) The **turn signal switch** wires on 1988, 1989 and 1991 VT600 models are green, light blue, orange, brown/blue, orange/white and light blue/white.
  c) The **turn signal switch** wires on all other models are green, light blue, orange, brown/blue, light blue/white and orange/white (yes, they're the same colors, but the last two wire colors are switched, which is important to remember when making the following continuity tests).
  d) The **horn switch** wires on 1988, 1989 and 1991 VT600 models, as well as 2004 and later VT750 models, are white/green and light green.
  e) The **horn switch** wires on all other models are black/brown and light green.

Dimmer switch
8   LO position - continuity between blue/white and white.
9   HI position - continuity between blue/white and blue.

Turn signal switch
1988, 1989 and 1991 VT600 models
10   LEFT - continuity between green and orange, and between brown/black and orange/white.
11   RIGHT - continuity between green and light blue, and between brown/black and light blue/white.

All other models
12   LEFT - continuity between green and orange, and between brown/black and light blue/white.
13   RIGHT - continuity between green and light blue, and between brown/black and orange/white.

Horn switch
1988, 1989 and 1991 VT600 models
14   RELEASED - no continuity.
15   DEPRESSED - continuity between white/green and light green.

All other models
16   RELEASED - no continuity.
17   DEPRESSED - continuity between black/brown and light green.

Right handlebar switches
18   The wire colors for the **right** handlebar switches are as follows:
  a) The **starter switch** wires on 1988, 1989 and 1991 through 1993 VT600 models are black, yellow/red, black/red and blue/white.
  b) The **starter switch** wires on 1994 through 1996 VT600 models are black/white, yellow/red, black/red and blue/white.
  c) The **starter switch** wires on all other models are black/white and yellow/red.
  d) The **kill switch** wires on 1988, 1989 and 1991 through 1993 VT600 models are black and black/white.
  e) The **kill switch** wires on all other models are black/green and black/white.

Starter switch
1988, 1989 and 1991 through 1993 VT600 models
19   RELEASED - continuity between black/red and blue/white.
20   DEPRESSED - continuity between black and yellow/red.

1994 through 1996 VT600 models
21   RELEASED - continuity between black/red and blue/white.
22   DEPRESSED - continuity between black/white and yellow/red.

All other models
23   RELEASED - no continuity.
24   DEPRESSED - continuity between black/white and yellow/red.

Kill switch
1988, 1989 and 1991 through 1993 VT600 models
25   OFF - no continuity.
26   RUN - continuity between black and black/white.

19.1a The handlebar switches are held together by screws (arrows); this is the throttle side . . .

19.1b . . . the clutch side switches are also held together by screws (arrows)

All other models

27   OFF - no continuity.
28   RUN - continuity between black/green and black/white.
29   If any continuity check indicates a problem, remove the switch (see Section 19), spray the switch contacts with electrical contact cleaner, then retest. The contacts can also be scraped clean with a knife or polished with crocus cloth, if they're accessible. If the switch still fails to check out as described above, or if it's obviously damaged or broken, replace the switch.

19 Handlebar switches - removal and installation

1   The handlebar switches are composed of two halves that clamp around the bars. They are easily removed for cleaning or inspection by taking out the clamp screws and pulling the switch halves away from the

handlebars (see illustrations).
2   To completely remove the switches, the electrical connectors in the wiring harness should be unplugged.
3   When installing the switches, make sure the wiring harnesses are properly routed to avoid pinching or stretching the wires.

20 Neutral switch - check and replacement

Check

1   Make sure the transmission is in neutral.
2   On VT600 models, remove the left side cover (see Chapter 8). On 2003 and earlier VT750 models, remove the right side cover. On all models, remove the decorative cover from the left rear corner of the engine. To do this, pull the clip out of the bolt, unscrew the bolt and take the cover off.
3   On all VT600 and 2003 and earlier

VT750 models, follow the wiring harness from the neutral switch to the connector and unplug it. On 2004 and later VT750 models, unplug the wire from the switch.
4   Ground the terminal on the harness side of the connector to bare metal on the motorcycle frame with a short length of wire. The neutral indicator light on the upper triple clamp should come on.
5   If the light doesn't come on, check the bulb (if equipped) (see Section 16) and the wiring between the ignition switch and the neutral switch (see wiring diagrams at the end of this Chapter). Remove the left rear cover (see "Drive chain - removal, cleaning and installation" in Chapter 7) and locate the switch, right in front of the drive sprocket (see illustration). Make sure that the electrical lead is connected to the switch.
6   If the neutral indicator light comes on, the neutral switch might be bad. Connect an ohmmeter between the terminal on the switch side of the connector and ground. Shift through the gears. The ohmmeter should indicate continuity in neutral and no

19.1c Separate the switch halves for access to the individual switches

20.5 Neutral switch (left arrow) and oil pressure switch (right arrow)

continuity in all other gears.

7   If the neutral switch doesn't operate as described, replace it.

Replacement

8   Remove the left rear cover (see "Drive chain - removal, cleaning and installation" in Chapter 7).

9   Locate the neutral switch, directly in front of the drive sprocket **(see illustration 20.5)** and disconnect the electrical lead.

10   Some oil is going to come out when you unscrew the switch and remove it from the crankcase, so be prepared to catch it with a drain pan.

11   Apply thread sealant to the threads of the new switch and tighten it to the torque listed in this Chapter's Specifications.

12   Installation is otherwise the reverse of removal. Be sure to route the wire harness for the oil pressure switch and the neutral switch correctly so that it's not damaged by the drive chain.

21 Oil pressure switch - check and replacement

Check

1   When the ignition switch is turned to ON, the oil pressure warning light on the speedometer should come on. This verifies that the oil pressure switch and circuit are functioning normally.

2   If the oil pressure warning light doesn't come on when the ignition switch is turned to ON, remove the left rear cover (see "Drive chain - removal, cleaning and installation" in Chapter 7).

3   Locate the oil pressure switch **(see illustration 20.5)**, directly behind the water pump. Remove the dust boot, remove the electrical lead retaining screw **(see illustra-**

tion) and detach the lead from the switch.

4   Short the switch lead to ground with a jumper wire. Turn the ignition switch to ON. The oil pressure warning indicator light should now come on.

5   If the oil pressure warning light still doesn't come on, check the 10A inline mini-fuse and check the switch circuit for an open circuit somewhere.

6   Start the engine and verify that the oil pressure warning light goes out.

7   If the oil pressure warning light doesn't go out, have the oil pressure checked by a Honda dealer service department.

8   If the oil pressure is normal, replace the oil pressure switch.

Replacement

9   On VT600 models, remove the left side cover; on VT750 models, remove the right side cover (see Chapter 8).

10   Unplug the electrical connector for the oil pressure switch. It's the same electrical connector the neutral switch uses (see Section 20).

11   Remove the left rear cover (see "Drive chain - removal, cleaning and installation" in Chapter 7).

12   Locate the oil pressure switch **(see illustration 20.5)**, directly behind the water pump. Remove the dust boot, remove the electrical lead retaining screw and disconnect the lead from the switch.

13   Some oil is going to come out when you unscrew the switch, so be prepared to catch it with a drain pan.

14   Apply thread sealant to the threads of the new switch, install the switch and tighten it to the torque listed in this Chapter's Specifications.

15   Installation is otherwise the reverse of removal. Be sure to route the wire harness for the oil pressure switch and the neutral switch correctly so that it's not damaged by the drive chain.

22 Sidestand switch - check and replacement

Check

1   On VT600 models, remove the left side cover; on VT750 models, remove the right side cover (see Chapter 8).

2   The wires in the sidestand switch circuit are green/white, yellow/black and green. Follow the wiring harness from the switch (at the upper end of the sidestand) to the green three-pin electrical connector, then unplug the connector.

3   Connect the leads of an ohmmeter to the terminals for the indicated wire colors.

4   With the sidestand in the down position, there should be continuity between the terminals for the yellow/blue and green wires.

5   With the sidestand in the up position, there should be continuity between the terminals for the green/white and green wires.

6   If the sidestand switch fails either of these tests, replace it.

Replacement

7   On VT600 models, remove the left side cover; on VT750 models, remove the right side cover (see Chapter 8).

8   Unplug the electrical connector for the sidestand switch (see Step 2).

VT600 models

9   Remove the sidestand switch bolt, switch holder, washer and switch **(see illustration)**.

10   When installing the new sidestand switch, align the positioning pin on the switch with the hole in the sidestand and align the groove in the switch with the pin on the sidestand.

11   Install the sidestand switch holder, install the retaining bolt and tighten it to the torque listed in this Chapter's Specifications.

21.3 Remove the screw to disconnect the oil pressure switch wire

22.9 VT600 sidestand switch

22.13 To remove the VT750 sidestand switch, remove this bolt (arrow) and pull off the switch

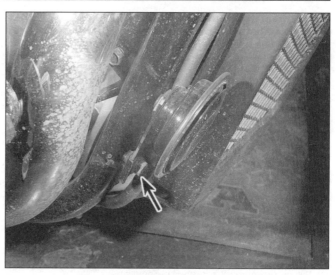

24.1 Unplug the electrical connectors from the horn and remove its mounting bolt (arrow)

12   Installation is otherwise the reverse of the removal procedure. Be sure to route the electrical lead correctly.

VT750 models

13   Remove the sidestand switch bolt **(see illustration)** and remove the switch.
14   When installing the new sidestand switch, align the positioning pin on the switch with the hole in the sidestand and align the groove in the switch with the pin on the sidestand.
15   Install the sidestand switch retaining bolt and tighten it to the torque listed in this Chapter's Specifications.
16   Installation is otherwise the reverse of the removal procedure. Be sure to route the electrical lead correctly.

23 Clutch switch - check and replacement

Check

1   Disconnect the electrical connectors from the clutch switch **(see illustration 19.1b)**.
2   Connect an ohmmeter to the terminals of the clutch switch. With the clutch lever pulled in, the ohmmeter should show continuity. With the lever out, the ohmmeter should show no continuity.
3   If the switch doesn't check out as described, replace it.

Replacement

4   Disconnect the electrical connectors from the clutch switch **(see illustration 19.1b)**.
5   Remove the clutch switch from the handlebar bracket.
6   Installation is the reverse of removal.

24 Horn - check and replacement

Check

1   Disconnect the electrical connectors from the horn **(see illustration)**. Using two jumper wires, apply battery voltage directly to the terminals on the horn. If the horn sounds, check the switch (see Section 18) and the wiring between the switch and the horn (see the wiring diagrams at the end of this Chapter). The horn wiring harness is connected to the main harness at a black two-pin connector (same connector as the fan motor) behind the steering head. To get to it, remove the steering head covers (see Chapter 8).
2   If the horn doesn't sound, replace it.

Replacement

3   Disconnect the electrical connectors and unbolt the horn **(see illustration 24.1)**.
4   Installation is the reverse of removal.

25 Starter relay switch - check and replacement

Check

1   Make sure the battery is fully charged.
2   Remove the right side cover (see Chapter 8).

⚠️ **Warning: Make sure the transmission is in neutral for this step.**

3   Turn the ignition switch to ON and the engine kill switch to RUN. When you push the starter button, the starter relay switch should click.
4   If the starter relay switch doesn't click, unplug the starter relay switch 4-pin electri-

25.4 The starter relay (arrow) is mounted in a rubber holder

27.2a Starter cable nut and mounting bolts (early models); the left bolt secures a ground wire

27.2b On later models, the starter cable nut is beneath a boot (upper arrow); the right mounting bolt secures a ground wire (lower arrows indicate the mounting bolts)

cal connector **(see illustration)** and check for continuity between the terminal for the green/red wire (on the harness side of the connector) and ground.

5   If there is continuity when the transmission is in Neutral or when the clutch is disengaged and the sidestand is up (sidestand switch closed), the ground circuit is okay (you will note a slight resistance in the circuit because of the clutch diode).

6   Reconnect the starter relay switch electrical connector, shift the transmission into Neutral and, using a voltmeter, measure the voltage between the terminal for the yellow/red wire (backprobe the connector) and ground. Battery voltage should be indicated when the starter button is pushed with the ignition switch ON.

7   Unplug the starter relay switch connector again, remove the cable attaching bolts or nuts and disconnect the cables from the relay. Using jumper wires, hook up the positive terminal of a 12-volt battery to the starter relay switch terminal for the yellow/red wire and hook up the negative terminal of the battery to the starter relay terminal for the green/red wire. Using an ohmmeter hooked up to the starter relay cable terminals, verify that there is continuity when the battery is connected to the relay. Disconnect the battery from the relay and verify that there is no continuity across the relay terminals.

8   If the starter relay switch fails any of these tests, replace it.

Replacement

9   Disconnect the battery negative cable.

10   Remove the right side cover (see Chapter 8).

11   Unplug the starter relay switch electrical connector **(see illustration 25.4).**

12   Remove the cable attaching bolts or nuts and disconnect the cables from the starter relay switch.

13   Remove the starter relay switch.

14   Installation is the reverse of removal. Reconnect the negative battery cable after all the other electrical connections are made.

26 Clutch diode - check and replacement

1   The clutch diode on VT600 models is located in the wiring harness and covered with tape. On VT750 models, it's mounted in the fuse box.

2   The clutch diode has three terminals, one for the green/red wire, one for the light green/red wire and one for the light green wire. The clutch diode allows current to flow through the first two terminals and out the third terminal, but it does not allow current the flow the other way. Think of the first two terminals (green/red wire and light green/red wire) as the "in" terminals; think of the third terminal (light green wire) as the "out" terminal.

3   Using an ohmmeter, verify that there is continuity between each of the "in" terminals and the "out" terminal in one direction, but NOT in the other direction.

4   If the clutch diode fails either of these tests, replace it.

5   Installation is the reverse of removal.

27 Starter motor - removal and installation

Removal

1   Disconnect the cable from the negative terminal of the battery.

2   Pull back the rubber cover, remove the nut retaining the starter cable to the starter and disconnect the cable **(see illustrations).**

3   Remove the starter mounting bolts.

4   Lift the end of the starter slightly and disengage the starter from the crankcase by pulling it out to the right **(see illustration).**

5   Inspect the O-ring on the end of the starter and replace it if necessary. Also inspect the teeth on the starter pinion gear and on the reduction gear; make sure the gear teeth are neither chipped nor excessively worn. (With a flashlight, you can inspect the reduction gear teeth through the hole in the case for the starter.)

Installation

6   Apply a little engine oil to the O-ring. Installation is otherwise the reverse of removal. Tighten the starter mounting bolts to the torque listed in this Chapter's Specifications.

27.4 Lift the right end of the starter slightly and slide it out to the right; inspect the O-ring (lower arrow)

28 Starter motor - disassembly, inspection and reassembly

1 Remove the starter motor (see Section 27).

Disassembly

2 Mark the position of the housing to each end cover. Remove the two through-bolts and their lockwashers and detach both end covers **(see illustration)**.

3 Remove the nut and push the terminal bolt through the starter housing, then reinstall the washers and nut on the bolt so you don't forget how they go. Pull the armature out of the housing and remove the brush plate.

4 Remove the two brushes with the plastic holder from the housing.

Inspection

5 The parts of the starter motor most likely to require attention are the brushes. Measure the length of the brushes and compare the results to the brush length listed in this Chapter's Specifications **(see illustration)**. If any of the brushes are worn beyond the specified limits, replace the brush holder assembly. If the brushes are not worn excessively, cracked, chipped, or otherwise damaged, they may be re-used.

6 Inspect the commutator **(see illustration)** for scoring, scratches and discoloration. The commutator can be cleaned and polished with crocus cloth, but do not use sandpaper or emery paper. After cleaning, wipe away any residue with a cloth soaked in an electrical system cleaner or denatured alcohol. Measure the commutator diameter and compare it to the diameter listed in this Chapter's Specifications. If it is less than the service limit, the motor must be replaced.

7 Using an ohmmeter or a continuity test light, check for continuity between the com-

28.2 Starter - exploded view

1   Through-bolt
2   Lockwasher
3   Brush end cover
4   Brush plate
5   Plastic brush housing
6   Cable
7   O-rings
8   Starter housing
9   O-ring
10 Armature
11 Bolt
12 Washer

mutator bars **(see illustration)**. Continuity should exist between each bar and all of the others. Also, check for continuity between the commutator bars and the armature shaft **(see illustration)**. There should be no continuity between the commutator and the shaft. If the checks indicate otherwise, the armature is defective.

8 Check for continuity between the brush plate and the brushes **(see illustration)**. The meter should read close to 0 ohms. If it doesn't, the brush plate has an open and must be replaced.

9 Using the highest range on the ohmmeter, measure the resistance between the

brush holders and the brush plate **(see illustration)**. The reading should be infinite. If there is any reading at all, replace the brush plate.

10 Check the starter pinion gear for worn, cracked, chipped and broken teeth. If the gear is damaged or worn, replace the starter motor.

Reassembly

11 Install the brush holder into the housing. Make sure the terminal bolt and washers are assembled in their original order. Tighten the terminal nut securely.

12 Detach the brush springs from the

28.5 Measure the length of the brushes and compare the length of the shortest brush with the length listed in this Chapter's Specifications

28.6 Check the commutator for cracks and discoloring, then measure the diameter and compare it with the minimum diameter listed in this Chapter's Specifications

28.7a Continuity should exist between the commutator bars

28.7b There should be no continuity between the commutator bars and the armature shaft

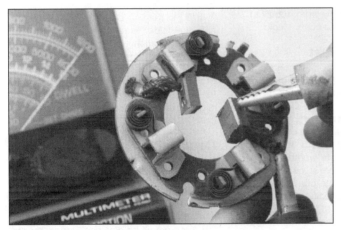

28.8 There should be almost no resistance (0 ohms) between the brushes and the brush plate

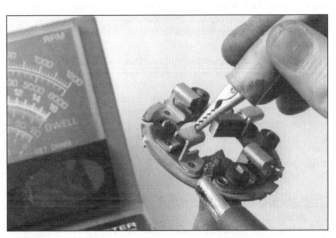

28.9 There should be no continuity between the brush plate and the brush holders (the resistance reading should be infinite)

brush plate (this will make armature installation much easier). Install the brush plate into the housing, routing the brush leads into the notches in the plate. Make sure the tongue on the brush plate fits into the notch in the housing.

13   Install the brushes into their holders and slide the armature into place. Install the brush springs.

14   Install any washers that were present on the end of the armature shaft **(see illustration)**.

15   Install the end covers, aligning the previously applied match marks (be sure to install the large O-rings between the starter housing and end covers). Install the O-rings and washers (if equipped) on the two through-bolts, then install the through-bolts and tighten them securely.

29 Charging system testing - general information and precautions

1   If the performance of the charging system is suspect, the system as a whole should be checked first, followed by testing of the individual components (the alternator and the voltage regulator/rectifier). **Note:** *Before beginning the checks, make sure the battery is fully charged and that all system connections are clean and tight.*

2   Checking the output of the charging system and the performance of the various components within the charging system requires the use of special electrical test equipment. A voltmeter or a multimeter are the absolute minimum tools required. In addition, an ohmmeter is generally required for checking the remainder of the system.

28.14 Be sure the shims and washers are in place on both ends of the armature shaft

3   When making the checks, follow the procedures carefully to prevent incorrect connections or short circuits, as irreparable damage to electrical system components may result if short circuits occur. Because of the special tools and expertise required, it is recommended that the job of checking the charging system be left to a dealer service department or a reputable motorcycle repair shop.

30 Charging system - check

Caution: Never disconnect the battery cables from the battery while the engine is running. If the battery is disconnected, the alternator and regulator/rectifier will be damaged.

1   To check the charging system output, you will need a voltmeter or a multimeter with a voltmeter function.
2   On VT600 models, remove both side covers; on VT750 models, remove the front seat (see Chapter 8).
3   The battery must be fully charged (charge it from an external source if necessary) and the engine must be at normal operating temperature to obtain an accurate reading.

Regulated voltage output test

4   Attach the positive (red) voltmeter lead to the positive (+) battery terminal and the negative (black) lead to the battery negative (-) terminal. The voltmeter selector switch (if equipped) must be in a DC volt range greater than 15 volts.
5   Start the engine and allow it to warm up to its normal operating temperature. With the headlight on LOW beam and the engine running at the rpm indicated in this Chapter's

Specifications, note the regulated voltage output of the charging system and compare your measurement to the regulated output listed in this Chapter's Specifications. Turn off the engine.
6   If the charging system fails to produce the specified regulated voltage output, there could be an open or a short circuit, or a loose, corroded or shorted connector, somewhere in the charging system wire harness; there could be an open or short in the alternator (see Section 31); or the voltage regulator/rectifier could be defective (see Section 32).
7   If the charging system produces a higher-than-specified voltage output, the regulator/rectifier is either poorly grounded or it's defective (see Section 32), or the battery is defective (see Section 3).
8   If the indicated regulated voltage output is within the specified range, but the battery is frequently discharged, this is an indication that the battery is probably worn out. But it's also possible that there's a current leak.

Current leakage test

9   To test for a current leak, disconnect the negative battery cable (see Section 3) and hook up a digital ammeter capable of readings in the milliampere range. Connect the positive probe of the ammeter to the battery negative cable and the negative probe to the battery negative terminal. With the ignition switch turned to OFF, note whether there is any current leakage. If there is, compare your reading to the permissible current leakage listed in this Chapter's Specifications.
10   If the indicated current leakage exceeds the specified allowable maximum, there's a short circuit somewhere. To locate the circuit where the short is occurring, unplug the harness electrical connectors one by one until the leak stops.
11   If the indicated current leakage is less than the specified allowable maximum, but the battery is frequently discharged, replace the battery (see Section 3).

31 Alternator - check and replacement

Check

1   Remove the left side cover (see Chapter 8) and the engine sprocket cover (see Chapter 7).
2   Trace the three-wire harness (all three wires are yellow on all models) from the alternator, on the left side of the engine, to the three-pin white electrical connector and disconnect the connector **(see illustrations)**.
3   Using an ohmmeter, measure the resistance between each terminal and each of the other two terminals of the connector (on the alternator side of the connector, not the wiring harness side). Compare your measurements to the stator coil resistance listed in this Chapter's Specifications.
4   If the reading between any two terminals is outside the range listed in this Chapter's Specifications, replace the stator.
5   If the reading is within the Specifications, refer to the wiring diagrams at the end of the book and check the charging circuit for breaks or poor connections. If the wiring is good, check the voltage regulator/rectifier (see Section 32).

Replacement
Stator

6   Remove the left side cover (see Chapter 8).
7   Trace the three-wire harness (all three wires are yellow on all models) from the alternator, on the left side of the engine, to the three-pin white electrical connector and disconnect the connector **(see illustrations 31.2a and 31.2b)**.
8   Loosen the left crankcase cover mounting bolts **(see illustration)** evenly in a criss-cross pattern and remove the cover. Remove the dowel pins **(see illustration)**.
9   Remove the two stator wire holder retaining bolts **(see illustration 31.8b)** and remove

31.2a Alternator wire harness routing

31.2b The alternators on all models use a white, three-pin connector located on the left side of the bike, in the area covered by the left side cover

31.8a To remove the left crankcase cover, remove these 11 bolts (arrows) evenly, in a criss-cross fashion

31.8b The stator is mounted inside the left crankcase cover

A	Cover dowels	B	Stator Allen bolts

the stator wire holder. Note how the wire harness is routed in the cover, then disengage it from the cover. Remove the stator retaining bolts and remove the stator assembly.

10 Thoroughly clean the left engine cover with solvent and blow it dry with compressed air.

11 Insert the wire harness and grommets in the cover, install the stator wire holder and the holder bolts, and tighten the holder bolts securely. Install the stator retaining bolts and tighten them to the torque listed in this Chapter's Specifications.

12 Clean all traces of old gasket sealer from the cover and its mating surface on the engine.

13 Make sure there are no metal particles stuck to the rotor magnets.

14 Install the dowel pins. Position a new gasket over the dowels.

15 Install the cover and tighten the cover bolts evenly, in a criss-cross pattern, to the torque listed in this Chapter's Specifications. Route the wiring harness across the top of the crankcase and through the guide attached to the left rear cover bracket **(see illustration)**. Connect the electrical connector.

Rotor (flywheel)

16 Remove the left crankcase cover (see Steps 6, 7 and 8).

17 Install a rotor holder tool (Honda 07725-0040000, or equivalent) to lock the rotor in place. If you don't have a suitable rotor holder tool, shift the transmission into gear

and have an assistant apply the rear brake. Remove the rotor bolt and washer **(see illustration)**. Note: *The rotor bolt is reverse thread; turn it clockwise to loosen it.*

18 Thread a rotor puller (Honda 07733-0020001, or 07933-3290001, or equivalent) into the rotor **(see illustration)**. Remove the

31.15 Note the harness routing under the cover; place the alternator harness in its clip (arrow)

31.17 To detach the rotor (flywheel) from the crankshaft, remove this (reverse-thread) bolt (arrow) . . .

31.18a . . . use a tool like this one to separate the rotor from the crankshaft . . .

31.18b . . . then take the rotor off . . .

31.18c . . . and lift the Woodruff key (upper arrow) out of its slot; as long as the rotor is removed, this is a good time to inspect the starter clutch needle bearing (lower arrow)

rotor from the end of the crankshaft and take the Woodruff key out of its slot **(see illustrations)**.

19 Remove and inspect the starter clutch assembly, if necessary (see Section 33).

20 Installation is the reverse of the removal steps. Be sure to reinstall the Woodruff key.

Caution: Make sure no metal objects have stuck to the magnets inside the rotor. Tighten the rotor bolt to the torque listed in this Chapter's Specifications.

32 Voltage regulator/rectifier - check and replacement

Check

1 On VT600 models, remove the left side cover; on VT750 models, remove the right side cover (see Chapter 8).

2 Trace the wiring harness from the regulator/rectifier to the connector **(see illustration)**. VT600 models use a four-pin connector. VT750C/CD models use a six-pin connector. VT750DC models use two connectors, one with two pins and one with three.

3 Using a voltmeter, verify that there is voltage between the terminals for the red/white and green wires. There shouldn't be any voltage between them (if there is voltage between them, there is a short in the connector).

4 If there is no voltage between the terminals for the red/white and green wires, verify that there *is* voltage between the terminal for the red/white wire and ground. If there is, then you know that there is power to the regulator/rectifier. Finally, using an ohmmeter, verify that there is continuity between the terminal for the green wire and ground. If there is, then you know that the regulator/rectifier output line is good. Replace the voltage regulator/rectifier.

Replacement

5 On VT600 models, remove the left side cover; on VT750 models, remove the right side cover (see Chapter 8).

6 Trace the wiring harness from the regulator/rectifier to the connector(s) (see Step 2).

7 Remove the regulator/rectifier mounting nuts **(see illustration 32.2 and the accompanying illustration)**.

8 Installation is the reverse of removal.

33 Starter clutch assembly - removal, inspection and installation

1 Remove the left engine cover (see Section 31).

2 Remove the reduction gear and shaft, and the idle gear and shaft **(see illustrations)**. Inspect the reduction gear and idle

32.2 On VT600 models, remove the regulator/rectifier mounting nuts (arrows) . . .

32.7 . . . and remove the unit

33.2a Remove the starter reduction gear (arrow) . . .

33.2b . . . remove the reduction gear shaft . . .

gear for wear and chipped teeth. Inspect the gear shafts for scoring and excessive wear. Replace any worn or damaged parts.

3   Remove the rotor (see Section 31). Remove the needle bearing from the crankshaft **(see illustration 31.18c)**.

4   Holding the rotor in one hand, with the rotor facing down and the starter clutch facing toward you, verify that the starter clutch turns freely in a counterclockwise direction **(see illustration)**, but not at all in a clockwise direction.

5   If the starter clutch turns in both directions, or will not turn in either direction, remove it from the rotor and inspect the starter clutch assembly.

6   Remove the starter driven gear and the big washer from the rotor **(see illustration)**. Remove the six Torx bolts from the rotor **(see illustration)** and detach the clutch housing and one-way clutch from the rotor. Remove the washer.

Caution: On VT750 models, do NOT separate the one-way clutch from the

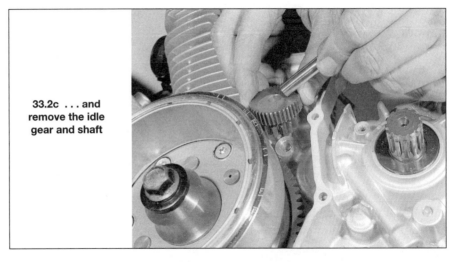

33.2c . . . and remove the idle gear and shaft

clutch housing unless you are definitely planning to replace it.

7   Clean all parts thoroughly in clean solvent and blow them dry with compressed air.

8   Inspect the needle bearing, the one-way clutch sprag **(see illustration 33.6a)** and the clutch housing for scoring or other signs of excessive wear. Replace all worn or damaged parts.

33.4 The starter driven gear should turn in one direction only

33.6a Remove the starter driven gear from the rotor, remove the big washer (A) and inspect the sprag (B)

33.6b To detach the clutch housing from the rotor, remove these six Torx bolts

9   Measure the inside diameter (I.D.) and outside diameter (O.D.) of the starter driven gear and compare your measurements to the I.D. and O.D. listed in this Chapter's Specifications. If the starter gear hub I.D. is greater than the specified I.D., or if the hub O.D. is less than the specified O.D., replace the starter gear.

10   Apply clean engine oil to the one-way clutch sprags and install the one-way clutch unit into the clutch housing. Install the housing with its flange toward the rotor, install the six Torx bolts and tighten them to the torque listed in this Chapter's Specifications.

11   Lubricate the big washer and install it on the backside of the rotor.

12   Lubricate the outer surface of the starter driven gear hub and install the gear into the clutch housing.

13   The remainder of installation is the reverse of removal.

34 Wiring diagrams

Prior to troubleshooting a circuit, check the fuses to make sure they're in good condition. Make sure the battery is fully charged and check the cable connections.

When checking a circuit, make sure all connectors are clean, with no broken or loose terminals or wires. When unplugging a connector, don't pull on the wires - pull only on the connector housings themselves.

Refer to the table in Chapter 9 for the wire color codes.

Wiring diagrams on the following pages

Wiring diagram - 1988 and 1989 VT600 models (1 of 2)

Wiring diagram - 1988 and 1989 VT600 models (2 of 2)

(1) Not used on 2001 and later models

Wiring diagram - 1991 through 2003 VT600 models (1 of 2)

Wiring diagram - 1991 through 2003 VT600 models (2 of 2)

Wiring diagram - 2004 and later VT600 models (1 of 2)

Wiring diagram - 2003 and earlier VT750 models (1 of 2)

Wiring diagram - 2003 and earlier VT750 models (2 of 2)

Wiring diagram - 2004 and later VT750 models (1 of 2)

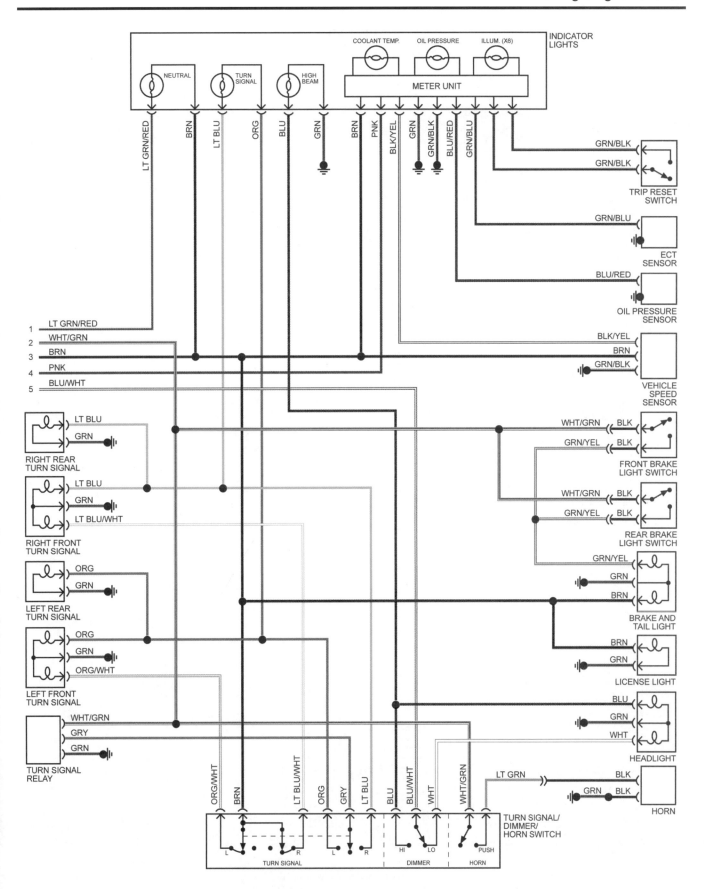

Wiring diagram - 2004 and later VT750 models (2 of 2)

Notes

Dimensions and weights

600 models

Frame and suspension

Wheelbase

1988 through 1998	1605 mm (63.2 inches)
1999 and later	1600 mm (63.0 inches)

Overall length .... 2310 mm (90.9 inches)

Overall width

1988 and 1989, 1991 through 1994	760 mm (29.9 inches)
1995 through 1998	890 mm (35.0 inches)
1999 and later	880 mm (34.6 inches)

Overall height

1988 through 1998	1125 mm (44.3 inches)
1999 and later	1120 mm (44.1 inches)

Seat height

1988 through 1998	690 mm (27.2 inches)
1999 and later	650 mm (25.6 inches)

Dry weight (2003 and earlier)

1988 and 1999, 1991 through 1993	196 kg (432 pounds)
1994	199 kg (439 pounds)

1995 and 1996

VT600C	199 kg (439 pounds)
VT600CD	202 kg (445 pounds)

1997 and 1998

VT600C	199 kg (439 pounds)

VT600CD

Except California	202 kg (445 pounds)
California	203 kg (448 pounds)

1999 through 2003

VT600C

Except California	205 kg (442 pounds)
California	206 kg (454 pounds)

VT600CD

Except California	208 kg (459 pounds)
California	209 kg (461 pounds)

Curb weight (2004 and later)

VT600C

Except California	214 kg (472 lbs)
California	216 kg (476 lbs)

VT600CD

Except California

2004 and 2005	217 kg (478 lbs)
2006 and later	216 kg (476 lbs)
California	218 kg (481 lbs)

Front suspension .... Telescopic fork

Rear suspension	Single shock absorber/coil spring
Front brake	Single hydraulic disc with 2-piston caliper
Rear brake	Mechanically-actuated drum brake
Fuel capacity	
1988 and 1989, 1991 through 1993	9 liters (2.4 US gallons)
1994 on	11 liters (2.9 US gallons)

Engine

Type	Liquid-cooled, 4-stroke, SOHC 52-degree V-twin
Displacement	583 cc
Compression ratio	9.2 to 1
Ignition system	Transistorized
Carburetor type	
1988 through 1998	Two 34 mm Keihin CV carburetors
1999 on	Single 34 mm Keihin CV carburetor
Transmission	4-speed, constant mesh

750 models

Frame and suspension - VT750C/CD Shadow/Shadow Deluxe American Classic Edition 750 (2003 and earlier)

Wheelbase	1615 mm (63.6 inches)
Overall length	2450 mm (96.5 inches)
Overall width	980 mm (38.6 inches)
Overall height	
VT750C	1135 mm (44.7 inches)
VT750CD and CD2	
1998 through 2000	1135 mm (44.7 inches)
2001 and later	1110 mm (43.7 inches)
VT750C3 and CD3	1110 mm (43.7 inches)
Seat height	700 mm (27.6 inches)
Dry weight	229 kg (505 pounds)
Front suspension	Telescopic fork
Rear suspension	Dual shock absorbers/coil springs
Front brake	Single hydraulic disc with 2-piston caliper
Rear brake	Mechanically-actuated drum brake
Fuel capacity	14 liters (3.7 US gallons)

VT750C (2004 and later)

Wheelbase	1640 mm (64.6 inches)
Overall length	2510 mm (98.8 inches)
Overall height	1125 mm (44.3 inches)
Seat height	660 mm (26.0 inches)
Curb weight	
Except California	
2007 through 2007	252 kg (556 lbs)
2008	251 kg (553 lbs)
California	
2007 through 2007	253 kg (558 lbs)
2008	254 kg (560 lbs)
Front suspension	Telescopic fork
Rear suspension	Dual shock absorbers/coil springs
Front brake	Single hydraulic disc with 2-piston caliper
Rear brake	Mechanically actuated drum brake
Fuel capacity	13 liters (3.43 US gallons)

VT750C2 Spirit (2007 and later)

Wheelbase	1655 mm (65.2 inches)
Overall length	2430 mm (95.7 inches)
Overall height	1130 mm (44.5 inches)
Seat height	655 mm (25.8 inches)
Curb weight	
Except California	243 kg (536 lbs)
California	246 kg (542 lbs)
Front suspension	Telescopic fork
Rear suspension	Dual shock absorbers/coil springs
Front brake	Single hydraulic disc with 2-piston caliper
Rear brake	Mechanically actuated drum brake
Fuel capacity	13 liters (3.43 US gallons)

Frame and suspension - VT750DC Shadow Spirit 750

Wheelbase	1645 mm (64.8 inches)
Overall length	2335 mm (91.9 inches)
Overall width	800 mm (31.5 inches)
Overall height	1071 mm (42.1 inches)
Seat height	675 mm (26.6 inches)
Dry weight	
Except California	224.5 kg (494.9 pounds)
California	225.7 kg (497.6 pounds)
Front suspension	Telescopic fork

Rear suspension.. Dual shock absorbers/coil springs
Front brake .... Single hydraulic disc with 2-piston caliper
Rear brake .... Mechanically-actuated drum brake
Fuel capacity .... 13 liters (3.43 US gallons)

Engine - all 750 models

Type .... Liquid-cooled, 4-stroke, SOHC
52-degree V-twin
Displacement... 745 cc
Compression ratio .... 9.0 to 1
Ignition system .... Transistorized
Carburetor type
    2003 and earlier .... Two 34mm Keihin CV carburetors
    2004 and later .... One 40mm Keihin CV carburetor with accelerator pump

Transmission... 5-speed, constant mesh

Buying tools

A good set of tools is a fundamental requirement for servicing and repairing a motorcycle. Although there will be an initial expense in building up enough tools for servicing, this will soon be offset by the savings made by doing the job yourself. As experience and confidence grow, additional tools can be added to enable the repair and overhaul of the motorcycle. Many of the special tools are expensive and not often used so it may be preferable to rent them, or for a group of friends or motorcycle club to join in the purchase.

As a rule, it is better to buy more expensive, good quality tools. Cheaper tools are likely to wear out faster and need to be replaced more often, nullifying the original savings.

> ⚠️ **Warning: To avoid the risk of a poor quality tool breaking in use, causing injury or damage to the component being worked on, always aim to purchase tools which meet the relevant national safety standards.**

The following lists of tools do not represent the manufacturer's service tools, but serve as a guide to help the owner decide which tools are needed for this level of work. In addition, items such as an electric drill, hacksaw, files, soldering iron and a workbench equipped with a vise, may be needed. Although not classed as tools, a selection of bolts, screws, nuts, washers and pieces of tubing always come in useful.

For more information about tools, refer to the Haynes *Motorcycle Workshop Practice Techbook* (Bk. No. 3470).

Manufacturer's service tools

Inevitably certain tasks require the use of a service tool. Where possible an alternative tool or method of approach is recommended, but sometimes there is no option if personal injury or damage to the component is to be avoided. Where required, service tools are referred to in the relevant procedure.

Service tools can usually only be purchased from a motorcycle dealer and are identified by a part number. Some of the commonly-used tools, such as rotor pullers, are available in aftermarket form from mail-order motorcycle tool and accessory suppliers.

Maintenance and minor repair tools

1 *Set of flat-bladed screwdrivers*
2 *Set of Phillips head screwdrivers*
3 *Combination open-end and box wrenches*
4 *Socket set (3/8 inch or 1/2 inch drive)*
5 *Set of Allen keys or bits*

6 *Set of Torx keys or bits*
7 *Pliers, cutters and self-locking grips (vise grips)*
8 *Adjustable wrenches*
9 *C-spanners*
10 *Tread depth gauge and tire pressure gauge*

11 *Cable oiler clamp*
12 *Feeler gauges*
13 *Spark plug gap measuring tool*
14 *Spark plug wrench or deep plug sockets*
15 *Wire brush and emery paper*

16 *Calibrated syringe, measuring cup and funnel*
17 *Oil filter adapters*
18 *Oil drainer can or tray*
19 *Pump type oil can*
20 *Grease gun*

21 *Straight-edge and steel rule*
22 *Continuity tester*
23 *Battery charger*
24 *Hydrometer (for battery specific gravity check)*
25 *Antifreeze tester (for liquid-cooled engines)*

Repair and overhaul tools

1 *Torque wrench (small and mid-ranges)*
2 *Conventional, plastic or soft-faced hammers*
3 *Impact driver set*
4 *Vernier caliper*
5 *Snap-ring pliers (internal and external, or combination)*
6 *Set of cold chisels and punches*
7 *Selection of pullers*
8 *Breaker bars*
9 *Chain breaking/ riveting tool set*
10 *Wire stripper and crimper tool*
11 *Multimeter (measures amps, volts and ohms)*
12 *Stroboscope (for dynamic timing checks)*
13 *Hose clamp (wingnut type shown)*
14 *Clutch holding tool*
15 *One-man brake/clutch bleeder kit*

Special tools

1 *Micrometers (external type)*
2 *Telescoping gauges*
3 *Dial gauge*
4 *Cylinder compression gauge*
5 *Vacuum gauges (left) or manometer (right)*
6 *Oil pressure gauge*
7 *Plastigage kit*
8 *Valve spring compressor (4-stroke engines)*
9 *Piston pin drawbolt tool*
10 *Piston ring removal and installation tool*
11 *Piston ring clamp*
12 *Cylinder bore hone (stone type shown)*
13 *Stud extractor*
14 *Screw extractor set*
15 *Bearing driver set*

1 Workshop equipment and facilities

The workbench

● Work is made much easier by raising the bike up on a ramp - components are much more accessible if raised to waist level. The hydraulic or pneumatic types seen in the dealer's workshop are a sound investment if you undertake a lot of repairs or overhauls **(see illustration 1.1)**.

1.1 Hydraulic motorcycle ramp

● If raised off ground level, the bike must be supported on the ramp to avoid it falling. Most ramps incorporate a front wheel locating clamp which can be adjusted to suit different diameter wheels. When tightening the clamp, take care not to mark the wheel rim or damage the tire - use wood blocks on each side to prevent this.
● Secure the bike to the ramp using tie-downs **(see illustration 1.2)**. If the bike has only a sidestand, and hence leans at a dangerous angle when raised, support the bike on an auxiliary stand.

1.2 Tie-downs are used around the passenger footrests to secure the bike

● Auxiliary (paddock) stands are widely available from mail order companies or motorcycle dealers and attach either to the wheel axle or swingarm pivot **(see illustration 1.3)**. If the motorcycle has a centerstand, you can support it under the crankcase to prevent it toppling while either wheel is removed **(see illustration 1.4)**.

1.3 This auxiliary stand attaches to the swingarm pivot

1.4 Always use a block of wood between the engine and jack head when supporting the engine in this way

Fumes and fire

● Refer to the Safety first! page at the beginning of the manual for full details. Make sure your workshop is equipped with a fire extinguisher suitable for fuel-related fires (Class B fire - flammable liquids) - it is not sufficient to have a water-filled extinguisher.
● Always ensure adequate ventilation is available. Unless an exhaust gas extraction system is available for use, ensure that the engine is run outside of the workshop.
● If working on the fuel system, make sure the workshop is ventilated to avoid a build-up of fumes. This applies equally to fume build-up when charging a battery. Do not smoke or allow anyone else to smoke in the workshop.

Fluids

● If you need to drain fuel from the tank, store it in an approved container marked as suitable for the storage of gasoline **(see illustration 1.5)**. Do not store fuel in glass jars

1.5 Use an approved can only for storing gasoline

or bottles.
● Use proprietary engine degreasers or solvents which have a high flash-point, such as kerosene, for cleaning off oil, grease and dirt - never use gasoline for cleaning. Wear rubber gloves when handling solvent and engine degreaser. The fumes from certain solvents can be dangerous - always work in a well-ventilated area.

Dust, eye and hand protection

● Protect your lungs from inhalation of dust particles by wearing a filtering mask over the nose and mouth. Many frictional materials still contain asbestos which is dangerous to your health. Protect your eyes from spouts of liquid and sprung components by wearing a pair of protective

1.6 A fire extinguisher, goggles, mask and protective gloves should be at hand in the workshop

goggles **(see illustration 1.6)**.
● Protect your hands from contact with solvents, fuel and oils by wearing rubber gloves. Alternatively apply a barrier cream to your hands before starting work. If handling hot components or fluids, wear suitable gloves to protect your hands from scalding and burns.

What to do with old fluids

● Old cleaning solvent, fuel, coolant and oils should not be poured down domestic drains or onto the ground. Package the fluid up in old oil containers, label it accordingly, and take it to a garage or disposal facility. Contact your local disposal company for location of such sites.

Note: It is illegal to dump oil down the drain. Check with your local auto parts store, disposal facility or environmental agency to see if they accept the oil for recycling.

2 Fasteners - screws, bolts and nuts

Fastener types and applications

Bolts and screws

● Fastener head types are either of hexagonal, Torx or splined design, with internal and external versions of each type **(see illustrations 2.1 and 2.2)**; splined head fasteners are not in common use on motorcycles. The conventional slotted or Phillips head design is used for certain screws. Bolt or screw length is always measured from the underside of the head to the end of the item **(see illustration 2.11)**.

2.1 Internal hexagon/Allen (A), Torx (B) and splined (C) fasteners, with corresponding bits

2.2 External Torx (A), splined (B) and hexagon (C) fasteners, with corresponding sockets

● Certain fasteners on the motorcycle have a tensile marking on their heads, the higher the marking the stronger the fastener. High tensile fasteners generally carry a 10 or higher marking. Never replace a high tensile fastener with one of a lower tensile strength.

Washers (see illustration 2.3)

● Plain washers are used between a fastener head and a component to prevent damage to the component or to spread the load when torque is applied. Plain washers can also be used as spacers or shims in certain assemblies. Copper or aluminum plain washers are often used as sealing washers on drain plugs.

2.3 Plain washer (A), penny washer (B), spring washer (C) and serrated washer (D)

● The split-ring spring washer works by applying axial tension between the fastener head and component. If flattened, it is fatigued and must be replaced. If a plain (flat) washer is used on the fastener, position the spring washer between the fastener and the plain washer.

● Serrated star type washers dig into the fastener and component faces, preventing loosening. They are often used on electrical ground connections to the frame.

● Cone type washers (sometimes called Belleville) are conical and when tightened apply axial tension between the fastener head and component. They must be installed with the dished side against the component and often carry an OUTSIDE marking on their outer face. If flattened, they are fatigued and must be replaced.

● Tab washers are used to lock plain nuts or bolts on a shaft. A portion of the tab washer is bent up hard against one flat of the nut or bolt to prevent it loosening. Due to the tab washer being deformed in use, a new tab washer should be used every time it is removed.

● Wave washers are used to take up endfloat on a shaft. They provide light springing and prevent excessive side-to-side play of a component. Can be found on rocker arm shafts.

Nuts and cotter pins

● Conventional plain nuts are usually six-sided **(see illustration 2.4)**. They are sized by thread diameter and pitch. High tensile nuts carry a number on one end to denote their tensile strength.

2.4 Plain nut (A), shouldered locknut (B), nylon insert nut (C) and castellated nut (D)

● Self-locking nuts either have a nylon insert, or two spring metal tabs, or a shoulder which is staked into a groove in the shaft - their advantage over conventional plain nuts is a resistance to loosening due to vibration. The nylon insert type can be used a number of times, but must be replaced when the friction of the nylon insert is reduced, i.e. when the nut spins freely on the shaft. The spring tab type can be reused unless the tabs are damaged. The shouldered type must be replaced every time it is removed.

● Cotter pins are used to lock a castellated nut to a shaft or to prevent loosening of a plain nut. Common applications are wheel axles and brake torque arms. Because the cotter pin arms are deformed to lock around the nut a new cotter pin must always be used on installation - always use the correct size cotter pin which will fit snugly in the shaft hole. Make sure the cotter pin arms are correctly located around the nut **(see illustrations 2.5 and 2.6)**.

2.5 Bend cotter pin arms as shown (arrows) to secure a castellated nut

2.6 Bend cotter pin arms as shown to secure a plain nut

Caution: If the castellated nut slots do not align with the shaft hole after tightening to the torque setting, tighten the nut until the next slot aligns with the hole - never loosen the nut to align its slot.

● R-pins (shaped like the letter R), or slip pins as they are sometimes called, are sprung and can be reused if they are otherwise in good condition. Always install R-pins with their closed end facing forwards **(see illustration 2.7)**.

2.7 Correct fitting of R-pin. Arrow indicates forward direction

Snap-rings (see illustration 2.8)

● Snap-rings (sometimes called circlips) are used to retain components on a shaft or in a housing and have corresponding external or internal ears to permit removal. Parallel-sided (machined) snap-rings can be installed either way round in their groove, whereas stamped snap-rings (which have a chamfered edge on one face) must be installed with the chamfer facing away from the direction of thrust load **(see illustration 2.9)**.

2.8 External stamped snap-ring (A), internal stamped snap-ring (B), machined snap-ring (C) and wire snap-ring (D)

● Always use snap-ring pliers to remove and install snap-rings; expand or compress them just enough to remove them. After installation, rotate the snap-ring in its groove to ensure it is securely seated. If installing a snap-ring on a splined shaft, always align its opening with a shaft channel to ensure the snap-ring ends are well supported and unlikely to catch **(see illustration 2.10)**.

2.9 Correct fitting of a stamped snap-ring

2.10 Align snap-ring opening with shaft channel

● Snap-rings can wear due to the thrust of components and become loose in their grooves, with the subsequent danger of becoming dislodged in operation. For this reason, replacement is advised every time a snap-ring is disturbed.

● Wire snap-rings are commonly used as piston pin retaining clips. If a removal tang is provided, long-nosed pliers can be used to dislodge them, otherwise careful use of a small flat-bladed screwdriver is necessary. Wire snap-rings should be replaced every time they are disturbed.

Thread diameter and pitch

● Diameter of a male thread (screw, bolt or stud) is the outside diameter of the threaded portion **(see illustration 2.11)**. Most motorcycle manufacturers use the ISO (International Standards Organization) metric system expressed in millimeters. For example, M6 refers to a 6 mm diameter thread. Sizing is the same for nuts, except that the thread diameter is measured across the valleys of the nut.

● Pitch is the distance between the peaks of the thread **(see illustration 2.11)**. It is expressed in millimeters, thus a common bolt size may be expressed as 6.0 x 1.0 mm (6 mm thread diameter and 1 mm pitch). Generally pitch increases in proportion to thread diameter, although there are always exceptions.

● Thread diameter and pitch are related for conventional fastener applications and the accompanying table can be used as a guide. Additionally, the AF (Across Flats), wrench or socket size dimension of the bolt or nut **(see illustration 2.11)** is linked to thread and pitch specification. Thread pitch can be measured with a thread gauge **(see illustration 2.12)**.

2.11 Fastener length (L), thread diameter (D), thread pitch (P) and head size (AF)

2.12 Using a thread gauge to measure pitch

AF size	Thread diameter x pitch (mm)
8 mm	M5 x 0.8
8 mm	M6 x 1.0
10 mm	M6 x 1.0
12 mm	M8 x 1.25
14 mm	M10 x 1.25
17 mm	M12 x 1.25

● The threads of most fasteners are of the right-hand type, ie they are turned clockwise to tighten and counterclockwise to loosen. The reverse situation applies to left-hand thread fasteners, which are turned counterclockwise to tighten and clockwise to loosen. Left-hand threads are used where rotation of a component might loosen a conventional right-hand thread fastener.

Seized fasteners

● Corrosion of external fasteners due to water or reaction between two dissimilar metals can occur over a period of time. It will build up sooner in wet conditions or in countries where salt is used on the roads during the winter. If a fastener is severely corroded it is likely that normal methods of removal will fail and result in its head being ruined. When you attempt removal, the fastener thread should be heard to crack free and unscrew easily - if it doesn't, stop there before damaging something.

● A smart tap on the head of the fastener will often succeed in breaking free corrosion which has occurred in the threads **(see illustration 2.13)**.

● An aerosol penetrating fluid (such as WD-40) applied the night beforehand may work its way down into the thread and ease removal. Depending on the location, you may be able to make up a modeling-clay well around the fastener head and fill it with penetrating fluid.

2.13 A sharp tap on the head of a fastener will often break free a corroded thread

● If you are working on an engine internal component, corrosion will most likely not be a problem due to the well lubricated environment. However, components can be very tight and an impact driver is a useful tool in freeing them **(see illustration 2.14)**.

2.14 Using an impact driver to free a fastener

● Where corrosion has occurred between dissimilar metals (e.g. steel and aluminum alloy), the application of heat to the fastener head will create a disproportionate expansion rate between the two metals and break the seizure caused by the corrosion. Whether heat can be applied depends on the location of the fastener - any surrounding components likely to be damaged must first be removed **(see illustration 2.15)**. Heat can be applied using a paint stripper heat gun or clothes iron, or by immersing the component in boiling water - wear protective gloves to prevent scalding or burns to the hands.

2.15 Using heat to free a seized fastener

● As a last resort, it is possible to use a hammer and cold chisel to work the fastener head unscrewed **(see illustration 2.16)**. This will damage the fastener, but more importantly extreme care must be taken not to damage the surrounding component.

Caution: Remember that the component being secured is generally of more value than the bolt, nut or screw - when the fastener is freed, do not unscrew it with force, instead work the fastener back and forth when resistance is felt to prevent thread damage.

2.16 Using a hammer and chisel to free a seized fastener

Broken fasteners and damaged heads

● If the shank of a broken bolt or screw is accessible you can grip it with self-locking grips. The knurled wheel type stud extractor tool or self-gripping stud puller tool is particularly useful for removing the long studs which screw into the cylinder mouth surface of the crankcase or bolts and screws from which the head has broken off **(see illustration 2.17)**. Studs can also be removed by locking two nuts together on the threaded end of the stud and using a wrench on the lower nut **(see illustration 2.18)**.

2.17 Using a stud extractor tool to remove a broken crankcase stud

2.18 Two nuts can be locked together to unscrew a stud from a component

● A bolt or screw which has broken off below or level with the casing must be extracted using a screw extractor set. Centerpunch the fastener to centralize the drill bit, then drill a hole in the fastener **(see illustration 2.19)**. Select a drill bit which is approximately half

2.19 When using a screw extractor, first drill a hole in the fastener . . .

to three-quarters the diameter of the fastener and drill to a depth which will accommodate the extractor. Use the largest size extractor possible, but avoid leaving too small a wall thickness otherwise the extractor will merely force the fastener walls outwards wedging it in the casing thread.

● If a spiral type extractor is used, thread it counterclockwise into the fastener. As it is screwed in, it will grip the fastener and unscrew it from the casing **(see illustration 2.20)**.

2.20 . . . then thread the extractor counterclockwise into the fastener

● If a taper type extractor is used, tap it into the fastener so that it is firmly wedged in place. Unscrew the extractor (counter-clockwise) to draw the fastener out.

> *Warning: Stud extractors are very hard and may break off in the fastener if care is not taken - ask a machine shop about spark erosion if this happens.*

● Alternatively, the broken bolt/screw can be drilled out and the hole retapped for an oversize bolt/screw or a diamond-section thread insert. It is essential that the drilling is carried out squarely and to the correct depth, otherwise the casing may be ruined - if in doubt, entrust the work to a machine shop.

● Bolts and nuts with rounded corners cause the correct size wrench or socket to slip when force is applied. Of the types of wrench/socket available always use a six-point type rather than an eight or twelve-point type - better grip

2.21 Comparison of surface drive box wrench (left) with 12-point type (right)

is obtained. Surface drive wrenches grip the middle of the hex flats, rather than the corners, and are thus good in cases of damaged heads **(see illustration 2.21)**.

● Slotted-head or Phillips-head screws are often damaged by the use of the wrong size screwdriver. Allen-head and Torx-head screws are much less likely to sustain damage. If enough of the screw head is exposed you can use a hacksaw to cut a slot in its head and then use a conventional flat-bladed screwdriver to remove it. Alternatively use a hammer and cold chisel to tap the head of the fastener around to loosen it. Always replace damaged fasteners with new ones, preferably Torx or Allen-head type.

A dab of valve grinding compound between the screw head and screwdriver tip will often give a good grip.

Thread repair

● Threads (particularly those in aluminum alloy components) can be damaged by overtightening, being assembled with dirt in the threads, or from a component working loose and vibrating. Eventually the thread will fail completely, and it will be impossible to tighten the fastener.

● If a thread is damaged or clogged with old locking compound it can be renovated with a thread repair tool (thread chaser) **(see illustrations 2.22 and 2.23)**; special thread

2.22 A thread repair tool being used to correct an internal thread

2.23 A thread repair tool being used to correct an external thread

chasers are available for spark plug hole threads. The tool will not cut a new thread, but clean and true the original thread. Make sure that you use the correct diameter and pitch tool. Similarly, external threads can be cleaned up with a die or a thread restorer file **(see illustration 2.24)**.

2.24 Using a thread restorer file

● It is possible to drill out the old thread and retap the component to the next thread size. This will work where there is enough surrounding material and a new bolt or screw can be obtained. Sometimes, however, this is not possible - such as where the bolt/screw passes through another component which must also be suitably modified, also in cases where a spark plug or oil drain plug cannot be obtained in a larger diameter thread size.

● The diamond-section thread insert (often known by its popular trade name of Heli-Coil) is a simple and effective method of replacing the thread and retaining the original size. A kit can be purchased which contains the tap, insert and installing tool **(see illustration 2.25)**. Drill out the damaged thread with the size drill specified **(see illustration 2.26)**. Carefully retap the thread **(see illustration 2.27)**. Install the

2.25 Obtain a thread insert kit to suit the thread diameter and pitch required

2.26 To install a thread insert, first drill out the original thread . . .

2.27 . . . tap a new thread . . .

2.28 . . . fit insert on the installing tool . . .

2.29 . . . and thread into the component . . .

2.30 . . . break off the tang when complete

insert on the installing tool and thread it slowly into place using a light downward pressure **(see illustrations 2.28 and 2.29)**. When positioned between a 1/4 and 1/2 turn below the surface withdraw the installing tool and use the break-off tool to press down on the tang, breaking it off **(see illustration 2.30)**.

● There are epoxy thread repair kits on the market which can rebuild stripped internal threads, although this repair should not be used on high load-bearing components.

Thread locking and sealing compounds

● Locking compounds are used in locations where the fastener is prone to loosening due to vibration or on important safety-related items which might cause loss of control of the motorcycle if they fail. It is also used where important fasteners cannot be secured by other means such as lockwashers or cotter pins.

● Before applying locking compound, make sure that the threads (internal and external) are clean and dry with all old compound removed. Select a compound to suit the component being secured - a non-permanent general locking and sealing type is suitable for most applications, but a high strength type is needed for permanent fixing of studs in castings. Apply a drop or two of the compound to the first few threads of the fastener, then thread it into place and tighten to the specified torque. Do not apply excessive thread locking compound otherwise the thread may be damaged on subsequent removal.

● Certain fasteners are impregnated with a dry film type coating of locking compound on their threads. Always replace this type of fastener if disturbed.

● Anti-seize compounds, such as copper-based greases, can be applied to protect threads from seizure due to extreme heat and corrosion. A common instance is spark plug threads and exhaust system fasteners.

3 Measuring tools and gauges

Feeler gauges

● Feeler gauges (or blades) are used for measuring small gaps and clearances (see illustration 3.1). They can also be used to measure endfloat (sideplay) of a component on a shaft where access is not possible with a dial gauge.

● Feeler gauge sets should be treated with care and not bent or damaged. They are etched with their size on one face. Keep them clean and very lightly oiled to prevent corrosion build-up.

3.1 Feeler gauges are used for measuring small gaps and clearances - thickness is marked on one face of gauge

● When measuring a clearance, select a gauge which is a light sliding fit between the two components. You may need to use two gauges together to measure the clearance accurately.

Micrometers

● A micrometer is a precision tool capable of measuring to 0.01 or 0.001 of a millimeter. It should always be stored in its case and not in the general toolbox. It must be kept clean and never dropped, otherwise its frame or measuring anvils could be distorted resulting in inaccurate readings.

● External micrometers are used for measuring outside diameters of components and have many more applications than internal micrometers. Micrometers are available in different size ranges, typically 0 to 25 mm, 25 to 50 mm, and upwards in 25 mm steps; some large micrometers have interchangeable anvils to allow a range of measurements to be taken. Generally the largest precision measurement you are likely to take on a motorcycle is the piston diameter.

● Internal micrometers (or bore micrometers) are used for measuring inside diameters, such as valve guides and cylinder bores. Telescoping gauges and small hole gauges are used in conjunction with an external micrometer, whereas the more expensive internal micrometers have their own measuring device.

External micrometer

Note: *The conventional analogue type instrument is described. Although much easier to read, digital micrometers are considerably more expensive.*

● Always check the calibration of the micrometer before use. With the anvils closed (0 to 25 mm type) or set over a test gauge

3.2 Check micrometer calibration before use

(for the larger types) the scale should read zero **(see illustration 3.2)**; make sure that the anvils (and test piece) are clean first. Any discrepancy can be adjusted by referring to the instructions supplied with the tool. Remember that the micrometer is a precision measuring tool - don't force the anvils closed, use the ratchet (4) on the end of the micrometer to close it. In this way, a measured force is always applied.

● To use, first make sure that the item being measured is clean. Place the anvil of the micrometer (1) against the item and use the thimble (2) to bring the spindle (3) lightly into contact with the other side of the item **(see illustration 3.3)**. Don't tighten the thimble down because this will damage the micrometer - instead use the ratchet (4) on the end of the micrometer. The ratchet mechanism applies a measured force preventing damage to the instrument.

● The micrometer is read by referring to the linear scale on the sleeve and the annular scale on the thimble. Read off the sleeve first to obtain the base measurement, then add the fine measurement from the thimble to obtain the overall reading. The linear scale on the sleeve represents the measuring range of the micrometer (eg 0 to 25 mm). The annular scale

3.3 Micrometer component parts

1 Anvil	3 Spindle	5 Frame
2 Thimble	4 Ratchet	6 Locking lever

on the thimble will be in graduations of 0.01 mm (or as marked on the frame) - one full revolution of the thimble will move 0.5 mm on the linear scale. Take the reading where the datum line on the sleeve intersects the thimble's scale. Always position the eye directly above the scale otherwise an inaccurate reading will result.

In the example shown the item measures 2.95 mm **(see illustration 3.4)**:

Linear scale	2.00 mm
Linear scale	0.50 mm
Annular scale	0.45 mm
Total figure	**2.95 mm**

3.5 **Micrometer reading of 46.99 mm on linear and annular scales . . .**

3.7 **Expand the telescoping gauge in the bore, lock its position . . .**

3.6 **. . . and 0.004 mm on vernier scale**

3.4 **Micrometer reading of 2.95 mm**

3.8 **. . . then measure the gauge with a micrometer**

Most micrometers have a locking lever (6) on the frame to hold the setting in place, allowing the item to be removed from the micrometer.

● Some micrometers have a vernier scale on their sleeve, providing an even finer measurement to be taken, in 0.001 increments of a millimeter. Take the sleeve and thimble measurement as described above, then check which graduation on the vernier scale aligns with that of the annular scale on the thimble **Note:** *The eye must be perpendicular to the scale when taking the vernier reading - if necessary rotate the body of the micrometer to ensure this.* Multiply the vernier scale figure by 0.001 and add it to the base and fine measurement figures.

In the example shown the item measures 46.994 mm **(see illustrations 3.5 and 3.6)**:

Linear scale (base)	46.000 mm
Linear scale (base)	00.500 mm
Annular scale (fine)	00.490 mm
Vernier scale	00.004 mm
Total figure	**46.994 mm**

Internal micrometer

● Internal micrometers are available for measuring bore diameters, but are expensive and unlikely to be available for home use. It is suggested that a set of telescoping gauges and small hole gauges, both of which must be used with an external micrometer, will suffice for taking internal measurements on a motorcycle.

● Telescoping gauges can be used to

measure internal diameters of components. Select a gauge with the correct size range, make sure its ends are clean and insert it into the bore. Expand the gauge, then lock its position and withdraw it from the bore **(see illustration 3.7)**. Measure across the gauge ends with a micrometer **(see illustration 3.8)**.

● Very small diameter bores (such as valve guides) are measured with a small hole gauge. Once adjusted to a slip-fit inside the component, its position is locked and the gauge withdrawn for measurement with a micrometer **(see illustrations 3.9 and 3.10)**.

Vernier caliper

Note: *The conventional linear and dial gauge type instruments are described. Digital types are easier to read, but are far more expensive.*

● The vernier caliper does not provide the precision of a micrometer, but is versatile in being able to measure internal and external diameters. Some types also incorporate a depth gauge. It is ideal for measuring clutch plate friction material and spring free lengths.

● To use the conventional linear scale vernier, loosen off the vernier clamp screws (1) and set its jaws over (2), or inside (3), the item to be measured **(see illustration 3.11)**. Slide the jaw into contact, using the thumb-wheel (4) for fine movement of the sliding scale (5) then tighten the clamp screws (1). Read off the main scale (6) where the zero on the sliding scale (5) intersects it, taking the whole number to the left of the zero; this provides the base measurement. View along the sliding scale and select the division which lines up exactly

3.9 **Expand the small hole gauge in the bore, lock its position . . .**

3.10 **. . . then measure the gauge with a micrometer**

with any of the divisions on the main scale, noting that the divisions usually represents 0.02 of a millimeter. Add this fine measurement to the base measurement to obtain the total reading.

3.11 Vernier component parts (linear gauge)

1 Clamp screws	3 Internal jaws	5 Sliding scale	7 Depth gauge
2 External jaws	4 Thumbwheel	6 Main scale	

In the example shown the item measures 55.92 mm **(see illustration 3.12)**:

Base measurement	55.00 mm
Fine measurement	00.92 mm
Total figure	**55.92 mm**

3.12 Vernier gauge reading of 55.92 mm

● Some vernier calipers are equipped with a dial gauge for fine measurement. Before use, check that the jaws are clean, then close them fully and check that the dial gauge reads zero. If necessary adjust the gauge ring accordingly. Slacken the vernier clamp screw (1) and set its jaws over (2), or inside (3), the item to be measured **(see illustration 3.13)**. Slide the jaws into contact, using the thumbwheel (4) for fine movement. Read off the main scale (5) where the edge of the sliding scale (6) intersects it, taking the whole number to the left of the zero; this provides the base measurement. Read off the needle position on the dial gauge (7) scale to provide the fine measurement; each division represents 0.05 of a millimeter. Add this fine measurement to the base measurement to obtain the total reading.

In the example shown the item measures 55.95 mm **(see illustration 3.14)**:

Base measurement	55.00 mm
Fine measurement	00.95 mm
Total figure	**55.95 mm**

3.13 Vernier component parts (dial gauge)

1 Clamp screw	5 Main scale
2 External jaws	6 Sliding scale
3 Internal jaws	7 Dial gauge
4 Thumbwheel	

3.14 Vernier gauge reading of 55.95 mm

Plastigage

● Plastigage is a plastic material which can be compressed between two surfaces to measure the oil clearance between them. The width of the compressed Plastigage is measured against a calibrated scale to determine the clearance.

● Common uses of Plastigage are for measuring the clearance between crankshaft journal and main bearing inserts, between crankshaft journal and big-end bearing inserts, and between camshaft and bearing surfaces. The following example describes big-end oil clearance measurement.

● Handle the Plastigage material carefully to prevent distortion. Using a sharp knife, cut a length which corresponds with the width of the bearing being measured and place it carefully across the journal so that it is parallel with the shaft **(see illustration 3.15)**. Carefully install both bearing shells and the connecting rod. Without rotating the rod on the journal tighten its bolts or nuts (as applicable) to the specified torque. The connecting rod and bearings are then disassembled and the crushed Plastigage examined.

3.15 Plastigage placed across shaft journal

● Using the scale provided in the Plastigage kit, measure the width of the material to determine the oil clearance **(see illustration 3.16)**. Always remove all traces of Plastigage after use using your fingernails.

Caution: Arriving at the correct clearance demands that the assembly is torqued correctly, according to the settings and sequence (where applicable) provided by the motorcycle manufacturer.

3.16 Measuring the width of the crushed Plastigage

Dial gauge or DTI (Dial Test Indicator)

● A dial gauge can be used to accurately measure small amounts of movement. Typical uses are measuring shaft runout or shaft endfloat (sideplay) and setting piston position for ignition timing on two-strokes. A dial gauge set usually comes with a range of different probes and adapters and mounting equipment.

● The gauge needle must point to zero when at rest. Rotate the ring around its periphery to zero the gauge.

● Check that the gauge is capable of reading the extent of movement in the work. Most gauges have a small dial set in the face which records whole millimeters of movement as well as the fine scale around the face periphery which is calibrated in 0.01 mm divisions. Read off the small dial first to obtain the base measurement, then add the measurement from the fine scale to obtain the total reading.

Base measurement	1.00 mm
Fine measurement	0.48 mm
Total figure	**1.48 mm**

3.17 Dial gauge reading of 1.48 mm

In the example shown the gauge reads 1.48 mm **(see illustration 3.17)**:
● If measuring shaft runout, the shaft must be supported in vee-blocks and the gauge mounted on a stand perpendicular to the shaft. Rest the tip of the gauge against the center of the shaft and rotate the shaft slowly while watching the gauge reading **(see illustration 3.18)**. Take several measurements along the length of the shaft and record the

3.18 Using a dial gauge to measure shaft runout

maximum gauge reading as the amount of runout in the shaft. **Note:** *The reading obtained will be total runout at that point - some manufacturers specify that the runout figure is halved to compare with their specified runout limit.*

● Endfloat (sideplay) measurement requires that the gauge is mounted securely to the surrounding component with its probe touching the end of the shaft. Using hand pressure, push and pull on the shaft noting the maximum endfloat recorded on the gauge **(see illustration 3.19)**.

3.19 Using a dial gauge to measure shaft endfloat

● A dial gauge with suitable adapters can be used to determine piston position BTDC on two-stroke engines for the purposes of ignition timing. The gauge, adapter and suitable length probe are installed in the place of the spark plug and the gauge zeroed at TDC. If the piston position is specified as 1.14 mm BTDC, rotate the engine back to 2.00 mm BTDC, then slowly forwards to 1.14 mm BTDC.

Cylinder compression gauges

● A compression gauge is used for measuring cylinder compression. Either the rubber-cone type or the threaded adapter type can be used. The latter is preferred to ensure a perfect seal against the cylinder head. A 0 to 300 psi (0 to 20 Bar) type gauge (for gasoline engines) will be suitable for motorcycles.

● The spark plug is removed and the gauge either held hard against the cylinder head (cone type) or the gauge adapter screwed into the cylinder head (threaded type) **(see illustration 3.20)**. Cylinder compression is measured with the engine turning over, but not running - carry out the compression test as described in

3.20 Using a rubber-cone type cylinder compression gauge

Troubleshooting Equipment. The gauge will hold the reading until manually released.

Oil pressure gauge

● An oil pressure gauge is used for measuring engine oil pressure. Most gauges come with a set of adapters to fit the thread of the take-off point **(see illustration 3.21)**. If the take-off point specified by the motorcycle manufacturer is an external oil pipe union, make sure that the specified replacement union is used to prevent oil starvation.

3.21 Oil pressure gauge and take-off point adapter (arrow)

● Oil pressure is measured with the engine running (at a specific rpm) and often the manufacturer will specify pressure limits for a cold and hot engine.

Straight-edge and surface plate

● If checking the gasket face of a component for warpage, place a steel rule or precision straight-edge across the gasket face and measure any gap between the straight-edge and component with feeler gauges **(see illustration 3.22)**. Check diagonally across the component and between mounting holes **(see illustration 3.23)**.

3.22 Use a straight-edge and feeler gauges to check for warpage

3.23 Check for warpage in these directions

- Checking individual components for warpage, such as clutch plain (metal) plates, requires a perfectly flat plate or piece of plate glass and feeler gauges.

4 Torque and leverage

What is torque?

- Torque describes the twisting force around a shaft. The amount of torque applied is determined by the distance from the center of the shaft to the end of the lever and the amount of force being applied to the end of the lever; distance multiplied by force equals torque.
- The manufacturer applies a measured torque to a bolt or nut to ensure that it will not loosen in use and to hold two components securely together without movement in the joint. The actual torque setting depends on the thread size, bolt or nut material and the composition of the components being held.
- Too little torque may cause the fastener to loosen due to vibration, whereas too much torque will distort the joint faces of the component or cause the fastener to shear off. Always stick to the specified torque setting.

Using a torque wrench

- Check the calibration of the torque wrench and make sure it has a suitable range for the job. Torque wrenches are available in Nm (Newton-meters), kgf m (kilograms-force meter), lbf ft (pounds-feet), lbf in (inch-pounds). Do not confuse lbf ft with lbf in.
- Adjust the tool to the desired torque on the scale **(see illustration 4.1)**. If your torque wrench is not calibrated in the units specified, carefully convert the figure (see *Conversion Factors*). A manufacturer sometimes gives a torque setting as a range (8 to 10 Nm) rather than a single figure - in this case set the tool midway between the two settings. The same torque may be expressed as 9 Nm ± 1 Nm. Some torque wrenches have a method of locking the setting so that it isn't inadvertently altered during use.

4.1 Set the torque wrench index mark to the setting required, in this case 12 Nm

- Install the bolts/nuts in their correct location and secure them lightly. Their threads must be clean and free of any old locking compound. Unless specified the threads and flange should be dry - oiled threads are necessary in certain circumstances and the manufacturer will take this into account in the specified torque figure. Similarly, the manufacturer may also specify the application of thread-locking compound.
- Tighten the fasteners in the specified sequence until the torque wrench clicks, indicating that the torque setting has been reached. Apply the torque again to double-check the setting. Where different thread diameter fasteners secure the component, as a rule tighten the larger diameter ones first.
- When the torque wrench has been finished with, release the lock (where applicable) and fully back off its setting to zero - do not leave the torque wrench tensioned. Also, do not use a torque wrench for loosening a fastener.

Angle-tightening

- Manufacturers often specify a figure in degrees for final tightening of a fastener. This usually follows tightening to a specific torque setting.
- A degree disc can be set and attached to the socket **(see illustration 4.2)** or a protractor can be used to mark the angle of movement on the bolt/nut head and the surrounding casting **(see illustration 4.3)**.

4.2 Angle tightening can be accomplished with a torque-angle gauge ...

4.3 ... or by marking the angle on the surrounding component

Loosening sequences

- Where more than one bolt/nut secures a component, loosen each fastener evenly a little at a time. In this way, not all the stress of the joint is held by one fastener and the components are not likely to distort.
- If a tightening sequence is provided, work in the REVERSE of this, but if not, work from the outside in, in a criss-cross sequence **(see illustration 4.4)**.

4.4 When loosening, work from the outside inwards

Tightening sequences

- If a component is held by more than one fastener it is important that the retaining bolts/nuts are tightened evenly to prevent uneven stress build-up and distortion of sealing faces. This is especially important on high-compression joints such as the cylinder head.
- A sequence is usually provided by the manufacturer, either in a diagram or actually marked in the casting. If not, always start in the center and work outwards in a criss-cross pattern **(see illustration 4.5)**. Start off by securing all bolts/nuts finger-tight, then set the torque wrench and tighten each fastener by a small amount in sequence until the final torque is reached. By following this practice,

4.5 When tightening, work from the inside outwards

the joint will be held evenly and will not be distorted. Important joints, such as the cylinder head and big-end fasteners often have two- or three-stage torque settings.

Applying leverage

● Use tools at the correct angle. Position a socket or wrench on the bolt/nut so that you pull it towards you when loosening. If this can't be done, push the wrench without curling your fingers around it **(see illustration 4.6)** - the wrench may slip or the fastener loosen suddenly, resulting in your fingers being crushed against a component.

4.6 If you can't pull on the wrench to loosen a fastener, push with your hand open

● Additional leverage is gained by extending the length of the lever. The best way to do this is to use a breaker bar instead of the regular length tool, or to slip a length of tubing over the end of the wrench or socket.
● If additional leverage will not work, the fastener head is either damaged or firmly corroded in place (see *Fasteners*).

5 Bearings

Bearing removal and installation

Drivers and sockets

● Before removing a bearing, always inspect the casing to see which way it must be driven out - some casings will have retaining plates or a cast step. Also check for any identifying markings on the bearing and, if installed to a certain depth, measure this at this stage. Some roller bearings are sealed on one side - take note of the original installed position.
● Bearings can be driven out of a casing using a bearing driver tool (with the correct size head) or a socket of the correct diameter. Select the driver head or socket so that it contacts the outer race of the bearing, not the balls/rollers or inner race. Always support the casing around the bearing housing with wood blocks, otherwise there is a risk of fracture. The bearing is driven out with a few blows on the driver or socket from a heavy mallet. Unless access is severely restricted (as with wheel bearings), a pin-punch is not recommended unless it is moved around the bearing to keep it square in its housing.

● The same equipment can be used to install bearings. Make sure the bearing housing is supported on wood blocks and line up the bearing in its housing. Install the bearing as noted on removal - generally they are installed with their marked side facing outwards. Tap the bearing squarely into its housing using a driver or socket which bears only on the bearing's outer race - contact with the bearing balls/rollers or inner race will destroy it **(see illustrations 5.1 and 5.2)**.
● Check that the bearing inner race and balls/rollers rotate freely.

5.1 Using a bearing driver against the bearing's outer race

5.2 Using a large socket against the bearing's outer race

Pullers and slide-hammers

● Where a bearing is pressed on a shaft a puller will be required to extract it **(see illustration 5.3)**. Make sure that the puller clamp or legs fit securely behind the bearing and are unlikely to slip out. If pulling a bearing

5.3 This bearing puller clamps behind the bearing and pressure is applied to the shaft end to draw the bearing off

off a gear shaft for example, you may have to locate the puller behind a gear pinion if there is no access to the race and draw the gear pinion off the shaft as well **(see illustration 5.4)**.

> **Caution: Ensure that the puller's center bolt locates securely against the end of the shaft and will not slip when pressure is applied. Also ensure that puller does not damage the shaft end.**

5.4 Where no access is available to the rear of the bearing, it is sometimes possible to draw off the adjacent component

● Operate the puller so that its center bolt exerts pressure on the shaft end and draws the bearing off the shaft.
● When installing the bearing on the shaft, tap only on the bearing's inner race - contact with the balls/rollers or outer race will destroy the bearing. Use a socket or length of tubing as a drift which fits over the shaft end **(see illustration 5.5)**.

5.5 When installing a bearing on a shaft use a piece of tubing which bears only on the bearing's inner race

● Where a bearing locates in a blind hole in a casing, it cannot be driven or pulled out as described above. A slide-hammer with knife-edged bearing puller attachment will be required. The puller attachment passes through the bearing and when tightened expands to fit firmly behind the bearing **(see illustration 5.6)**. By operating the slide-hammer part of the tool the bearing is jarred out of its housing **(see illustration 5.7)**.
● It is possible, if the bearing is of reasonable weight, for it to drop out of its housing if the casing is heated as described opposite. If

5.6 Expand the bearing puller so that it locks behind the bearing . . .

5.7 . . . attach the slide hammer to the bearing puller

this method is attempted, first prepare a work surface which will enable the casing to be tapped face down to help dislodge the bearing - a wood surface is ideal since it will not damage the casing's gasket surface. Wearing protective gloves, tap the heated casing several times against the work surface to dislodge the bearing under its own weight **(see illustration 5.8)**.

5.8 Tapping a casing face down on wood blocks can often dislodge a bearing

● Bearings can be installed in blind holes using the driver or socket method described above.

Drawbolts

● Where a bearing or bushing is set in the eye of a component, such as a suspension linkage arm or connecting rod small-end, removal by drift may damage the component. Furthermore, a rubber bushing in a shock absorber eye cannot successfully be driven out of position. If access is available to a hydraulic press, the task is straightforward. If not, a drawbolt can be fabricated to extract the bearing or bushing.

5.9 Drawbolt component parts assembled on a suspension arm

1 Bolt or length of threaded bar
2 Nuts
3 Washer (external diameter greater than tubing internal diameter)
4 Tubing (internal diameter sufficient to accommodate bearing)
5 Suspension arm with bearing
6 Tubing (external diameter slightly smaller than bearing)
7 Washer (external diameter slightly smaller than bearing)

5.10 Drawing the bearing out of the suspension arm

● To extract the bearing/bushing you will need a long bolt with nut (or piece of threaded bar with two nuts), a piece of tubing which has an internal diameter larger than the bearing/bushing, another piece of tubing which has an external diameter slightly smaller than the bearing/bushing, and a selection of washers **(see illustrations 5.9 and 5.10)**. Note that the pieces of tubing must be of the same length, or longer, than the bearing/bushing.
● The same kit (without the pieces of tubing) can be used to draw the new bearing/bushing back into place **(see illustration 5.11)**.

5.11 Installing a new bearing (1) in the suspension arm

Temperature change

● If the bearing's outer race is a tight fit in the casing, the aluminum casing can be heated to release its grip on the bearing. Aluminum will expand at a greater rate than the steel bearing outer race. There are several ways to do this, but avoid any localized extreme heat (such as a blow torch) - aluminum alloy has a low melting point.
● Approved methods of heating a casing are using a domestic oven (heated to 100°C/200°F) or immersing the casing in boiling water **(see illustration 5.12)**. Low temperature range localized heat sources such as a paint stripper heat gun or clothes iron can also be used **(see illustration 5.13)**. Alternatively, soak a rag in boiling water, wring it out and wrap it around the bearing housing.

> ⚠️ **Warning: All of these methods require care in use to prevent scalding and burns to the hands. Wear protective gloves when handling hot components.**

5.12 A casing can be immersed in a sink of boiling water to aid bearing removal

5.13 Using a localized heat source to aid bearing removal

● If heating the whole casing note that plastic components, such as the neutral switch, may suffer - remove them beforehand.
● After heating, remove the bearing as described above. You may find that the expansion is sufficient for the bearing to fall out of the casing under its own weight or with a light tap on the driver or socket.
● If necessary, the casing can be heated to aid bearing installation, and this is sometimes the recommended procedure if the motorcycle manufacturer has designed the housing and bearing fit with this intention.

● Installation of bearings can be eased by placing them in a freezer the night before installation. The steel bearing will contract slightly, allowing easy insertion in its housing. This is often useful when installing steering head outer races in the frame.

Bearing types and markings

● Plain shell bearings, ball bearings, needle roller bearings and tapered roller bearings will all be found on motorcycles (see illustrations 5.14 and 5.15). The ball and roller types are usually caged between an inner and outer race, but uncaged variations may be found.

5.14 Shell bearings are either plain or grooved. They are usually identified by color code (arrow)

5.15 Tapered roller bearing (A), needle roller bearing (B) and ball journal bearing (C)

● Shell bearings (often called inserts) are usually found at the crankshaft main and connecting rod big-end where they are good at coping with high loads. They are made of a phosphor-bronze material and are impregnated with self-lubricating properties.
● Ball bearings and needle roller bearings consist of a steel inner and outer race with the balls or rollers between the races. They require constant lubrication by oil or grease and are good at coping with axial loads. Taper roller bearings consist of rollers set in a tapered cage set on the inner race; the outer race is separate. They are good at coping with axial loads and prevent movement along the shaft - a typical application is in the steering head.
● Bearing manufacturers produce bearings to ISO size standards and stamp one face of the bearing to indicate its internal and external diameter, load capacity and type (see illustration 5.16).
● Metal bushings are usually of phosphor-bronze material. Rubber bushings are used in suspension mounting eyes. Fiber bushings have also been used in suspension pivots.

5.16 Typical bearing marking

Bearing troubleshooting

● If a bearing outer race has spun in its housing, the housing material will be damaged. You can use a bearing locking compound to bond the outer race in place if damage is not too severe.
● Shell bearings will fail due to damage of their working surface, as a result of lack of lubrication, corrosion or abrasive particles in the oil (see illustration 5.17). Small particles of dirt in the oil may embed in the bearing material whereas larger particles will score the bearing and shaft journal. If a number of short journeys are made, insufficient heat will be generated to drive off condensation which has built up on the bearings.

5.17 Typical bearing failures

● Ball and roller bearings will fail due to lack of lubrication or damage to the balls or rollers. Tapered-roller bearings can be damaged by overloading them. Unless the bearing is sealed on both sides, wash it in kerosene to remove all old grease then allow it to dry. Make a visual inspection looking to dented balls or rollers, damaged cages and worn or pitted races (see illustration 5.18).
● A ball bearing can be checked for wear by listening to it when spun. Apply a film of light oil to the bearing and hold it close to the ear - hold the outer race with one hand and spin the

5.18 Example of ball journal bearing with damaged balls and cages

5.19 Hold outer race and listen to inner race when spun

inner race with the other hand (see illustration 5.19). The bearing should be almost silent when spun; if it grates or rattles it is worn.

6 Oil seals

Oil seal removal and installation

● Oil seals should be replaced every time a component is dismantled. This is because the seal lips will become set to the sealing surface and will not necessarily reseal.
● Oil seals can be pried out of position using a large flat-bladed screwdriver (see illustration 6.1). In the case of crankcase seals, check first that the seal is not lipped on the inside, preventing its removal with the crankcases joined.

6.1 Pry out oil seals with a large flat-bladed screwdriver

● New seals are usually installed with their marked face (containing the seal reference code) outwards and the spring side towards the fluid being retained. In certain cases, such as a two-stroke engine crankshaft seal, a double lipped seal may be used due to there being fluid or gas on each side of the joint.

● Use a bearing driver or socket which bears only on the outer hard edge of the seal to install it in the casing - tapping on the inner edge will damage the sealing lip.

Oil seal types and markings

● Oil seals are usually of the single-lipped type. Double-lipped seals are found where a liquid or gas is on both sides of the joint.

● Oil seals can harden and lose their sealing ability if the motorcycle has been in storage for a long period - replacement is the only solution.

● Oil seal manufacturers also conform to the ISO markings for seal size - these are molded into the outer face of the seal (see illustration 6.2).

6.2 These oil seal markings indicate inside diameter, outside diameter and seal thickness

7 Gaskets and sealants

Types of gasket and sealant

● Gaskets are used to seal the mating surfaces between components and keep lubricants, fluids, vacuum or pressure contained within the assembly. Aluminum gaskets are sometimes found at the cylinder joints, but most gaskets are paper-based. If the mating surfaces of the components being joined are undamaged the gasket can be installed dry, although a dab of sealant or grease will be useful to hold it in place during assembly.

● RTV (Room Temperature Vulcanizing) silicone rubber sealants cure when exposed to moisture in the atmosphere. These sealants are good at filling pits or irregular gasket faces, but will tend to be forced out of the joint under very high torque. They can be used to replace a paper gasket, but first make sure that the width of the paper gasket is not essential to the shimming of internal components. RTV sealants should not be used on components containing gasoline.

● Non-hardening, semi-hardening and hard setting liquid gasket compounds can be used with a gasket or between a metal-to-metal joint. Select the sealant to suit the application: universal non-hardening sealant can be used on virtually all joints; semi-hardening on joint faces which are rough or damaged; hard setting sealant on joints which require a permanent bond and are subjected to high temperature and pressure. **Note:** *Check first if the paper gasket has a bead of sealant*

impregnated in its surface before applying additional sealant.

● When choosing a sealant, make sure it is suitable for the application, particularly if being applied in a high-temperature area or in the vicinity of fuel. Certain manufacturers produce sealants in either clear, silver or black colors to match the finish of the engine. This has a particular application on motorcycles where much of the engine is exposed.

● Do not over-apply sealant. That which is squeezed out on the outside of the joint can be wiped off, whereas an excess of sealant on the inside can break off and clog oilways.

Breaking a sealed joint

● Age, heat, pressure and the use of hard setting sealant can cause two components to stick together so tightly that they are difficult to separate using finger pressure alone. Do not resort to using levers unless there is a pry point provided for this purpose (see illustration 7.1) or else the gasket surfaces will be damaged.

● Use a soft-faced hammer (see illustration 7.2) or a wood block and conventional hammer to strike the component near the mating surface. Avoid hammering against cast extremities since they may break off. If this method fails, try using a wood wedge between the two components.

> **Caution: If the joint will not separate, double-check that you have removed all the fasteners.**

7.1 If a pry point is provided, apply gentle pressure with a flat-bladed screwdriver

7.2 Tap around the joint with a soft-faced mallet if necessary - don't strike cooling fins

Removal of old gasket and sealant

● Paper gaskets will most likely come away complete, leaving only a few traces stuck

Most components have one or two hollow locating dowels between the two gasket faces. If a dowel cannot be removed, do not resort to gripping it with pliers - it will almost certainly be distorted. Install a close-fitting socket or Phillips screwdriver into the dowel and then grip the outer edge of the dowel to free it.

on the sealing faces of the components. It is imperative that all traces are removed to ensure correct sealing of the new gasket.

● Very carefully scrape all traces of gasket away making sure that the sealing surfaces are not gouged or scored by the scraper (see illustrations 7.3, 7.4 and 7.5). Stubborn deposits can be removed by spraying with an aerosol gasket remover. Final preparation of

7.3 Paper gaskets can be scraped off with a gasket scraper tool . . .

7.4 . . . a knife blade . . .

7.5 . . . or a household scraper

7.6 Fine abrasive paper is wrapped around a flat file to clean up the gasket face

7.7 A kitchen scourer can be used on stubborn deposits

the gasket surface can be made with very fine abrasive paper or a plastic kitchen scourer **(see illustrations 7.6 and 7.7)**.

● Old sealant can be scraped or peeled off components, depending on the type originally used. Note that gasket removal compounds are available to avoid scraping the components clean; make sure the gasket remover suits the type of sealant used.

8 Chains

Breaking and joining final drive chains

● Drive chains for all but small bikes are continuous and do not have a clip-type connecting link. The chain must be broken using a chain breaker tool and the new chain securely riveted together using a new soft rivet-type link. Never use a clip-type connecting link instead of a rivet-type link, except in an emergency. Various chain breaking and riveting tools are available, either as separate tools or combined as illustrated in the accompanying photographs - read the instructions supplied with the tool carefully.

> ⚠ *Warning: The need to rivet the new link pins correctly cannot be overstressed - loss of control of the motorcycle is very likely to result if the chain breaks in use.*

● Rotate the chain and look for the soft link. The soft link pins look like they have been

8.1 Tighten the chain breaker to push the pin out of the link . . .

8.2 . . . withdraw the pin, remove the tool . . .

8.3 . . . and separate the chain link

deeply center-punched instead of peened over like all the other pins **(see illustration 8.9)** and its sideplate may be a different color. Position the soft link midway between the sprockets and assemble the chain breaker tool over one of the soft link pins **(see illustration 8.1)**. Operate the tool to push the pin out through the chain **(see illustration 8.2)**. On an O-ring chain, remove the O-rings **(see illustration 8.3)**. Carry out the same procedure on the other soft link pin.

> *Caution: Certain soft link pins (particularly on the larger chains) may require their ends to be filed or ground off before they can be pressed out using the tool.*

● Check that you have the correct size and strength (standard or heavy duty) new soft link - do not reuse the old link. Look for the size marking on the chain sideplates **(see illustration 8.10)**.

● Position the chain ends so that they are

8.4 Insert the new soft link, with O-rings, through the chain ends . . .

8.5 . . . install the O-rings over the pin ends . . .

8.6 . . . followed by the sideplate

engaged over the rear sprocket. On an O-ring chain, install a new O-ring over each pin of the link and insert the link through the two chain ends **(see illustration 8.4)**. Install a new O-ring over the end of each pin, followed by the sideplate (with the chain manufacturer's marking facing outwards) **(see illustrations 8.5 and 8.6)**. On an unsealed chain, insert the link through the two chain ends, then install the sideplate with the chain manufacturer's marking facing outwards.

● Note that it may not be possible to install the sideplate using finger pressure alone. If using a joining tool, assemble it so that the plates of the tool clamp the link and press the sideplate over the pins **(see illustration 8.7)**. Otherwise, use two small sockets placed over

8.7 Push the sideplate into position using a clamp

8.8 Assemble the chain riveting tool over one pin at a time and tighten it fully

8.9 Pin end correctly riveted (A), pin end unriveted (B)

the rivet ends and two pieces of the wood between a C-clamp. Operate the clamp to press the sideplate over the pins.

● Assemble the joining tool over one pin (following the manufacturer's instructions) and tighten the tool down to spread the pin end securely **(see illustrations 8.8 and 8.9)**. Do the same on the other pin.

> ⚠ **Warning: Check that the pin ends are secure and that there is no danger of the sideplate coming loose. If the pin ends are cracked the soft link must be replaced.**

Final drive chain sizing

● Chains are sized using a three digit number, followed by a suffix to denote the chain type **(see illustration 8.10)**. Chain type is either standard or heavy duty (thicker sideplates), and also unsealed or O-ring/X-ring type.

● The first digit of the number relates to the pitch of the chain, ie the distance from the center of one pin to the center of the next pin **(see illustration 8.11)**. Pitch is expressed in eighths of an inch, as follows:

8.10 Typical chain size and type marking

8.11 Chain dimensions

Sizes commencing with a 4 (for example 428) have a pitch of 1/2 inch (12.7 mm)
Sizes commencing with a 5 (for example 520) have a pitch of 5/8 inch (15.9 mm)
Sizes commencing with a 6 (for example 630) have a pitch of 3/4 inch (19.1 mm)

● The second and third digits of the chain size relate to the width of the rollers, for example the 525 shown has 5/16 inch (7.94 mm) rollers **(see illustration 8.11)**.

9 Hoses

Clamping to prevent flow

● Small-bore flexible hoses can be clamped to prevent fluid flow while a component is worked on. Whichever method is used, ensure that the hose material is not permanently distorted or damaged by the clamp.

 a) A brake hose clamp available from auto parts stores **(see illustration 9.1)**.
 b) A wingnut type hose clamp **(see illustration 9.2)**.

9.1 Hoses can be clamped with an automotive brake hose clamp . . .

9.2 . . . a wingnut type hose clamp . . .

 c) Two sockets placed on each side of the hose and held with straight-jawed self-locking pliers **(see illustration 9.3)**.
 d) Thick card stock on each side of the hose held between straight-jawed self-locking pliers **(see illustration 9.4)**.

9.3 . . . two sockets and a pair of self-locking grips . . .

9.4 . . . or thick card and self-locking grips

Freeing and fitting hoses

● Always make sure the hose clamp is moved well clear of the hose end. Grip the hose with your hand and rotate it while pulling it off the union. If the hose has hardened due to age and will not move, slit it with a sharp knife and peel its ends off the union **(see illustration 9.5)**.

● Resist the temptation to use grease or soap on the unions to aid installation; although it helps the hose slip over the union it will equally aid the escape of fluid from the joint. It is preferable to soften the hose ends in hot water and wet the inside surface of the hose with water or a fluid which will evaporate.

9.5 Cutting a coolant hose free with a sharp knife

Length (distance)
Inches (in)	X	25.4	= Millimeters (mm)	X 0.0394	= Inches (in)
Feet (ft)	X	0.305	= Meters (m)	X 3.281	= Feet (ft)
Miles	X	1.609	= Kilometers (km)	X 0.621	= Miles

Volume (capacity)
Cubic inches (cu in; in^3)	X	16.387	= Cubic centimeters (cc; cm^3)	X 0.061	= Cubic inches (cu in; in^3)
Imperial pints (Imp pt)	X	0.568	= Liters (l)	X 1.76	= Imperial pints (Imp pt)
Imperial quarts (Imp qt)	X	1.137	= Liters (l)	X 0.88	= Imperial quarts (Imp qt)
Imperial quarts (Imp qt)	X	1.201	= US quarts (US qt)	X 0.833	= Imperial quarts (Imp qt)
US quarts (US qt)	X	0.946	= Liters (l)	X 1.057	= US quarts (US qt)
Imperial gallons (Imp gal)	X	4.546	= Liters (l)	X 0.22	= Imperial gallons (Imp gal)
Imperial gallons (Imp gal)	X	1.201	= US gallons (US gal)	X 0.833	= Imperial gallons (Imp gal)
US gallons (US gal)	X	3.785	= Liters (l)	X 0.264	= US gallons (US gal)

Mass (weight)
Ounces (oz)	X	28.35	= Grams (g)	X 0.035	= Ounces (oz)
Pounds (lb)	X	0.454	= Kilograms (kg)	X 2.205	= Pounds (lb)

Force
Ounces-force (ozf; oz)	X	0.278	= Newtons (N)	X 3.6	= Ounces-force (ozf; oz)
Pounds-force (lbf; lb)	X	4.448	= Newtons (N)	X 0.225	= Pounds-force (lbf; lb)
Newtons (N)	X	0.1	= Kilograms-force (kgf; kg)	X 9.81	= Newtons (N)

Pressure
Pounds-force per square inch (psi; lbf/in^2; lb/in^2)	X	0.070	= Kilograms-force per square centimeter (kgf/cm^2; kg/cm^2)	X 14.223	= Pounds-force per square inch (psi; lbf/in^2; lb/in^2)
Pounds-force per square inch (psi; lbf/in^2; lb/in^2)	X	0.068	= Atmospheres (atm)	X 14.696	= Pounds-force per square inch (psi; lbf/in^2; lb/in^2)
Pounds-force per square inch (psi; lbf/in^2; lb/in^2)	X	0.069	= Bars	X 14.5	= Pounds-force per square inch (psi; lbf/in^2; lb/in^2)
Pounds-force per square inch (psi; lbf/in^2; lb/in^2)	X	6.895	= Kilopascals (kPa)	X 0.145	= Pounds-force per square inch (psi; lbf/in^2; lb/in^2)
Kilopascals (kPa)	X	0.01	= Kilograms-force per square centimeter (kgf/cm^2; kg/cm^2)	X 98.1	= Kilopascals (kPa)

Torque (moment of force)
Pounds-force inches (lbf in; lb in)	X	1.152	= Kilograms-force centimeter (kgf cm; kg cm)	X 0.868	= Pounds-force inches (lbf in; lb in)
Pounds-force inches (lbf in; lb in)	X	0.113	= Newton meters (Nm)	X 8.85	= Pounds-force inches (lbf in; lb in)
Pounds-force inches (lbf in; lb in)	X	0.083	= Pounds-force feet (lbf ft; lb ft)	X 12	= Pounds-force inches (lbf in; lb in)
Pounds-force feet (lbf ft; lb ft)	X	0.138	= Kilograms-force meters (kgf m; kg m)	X 7.233	= Pounds-force feet (lbf ft; lb ft)
Pounds-force feet (lbf ft; lb ft)	X	1.356	= Newton meters (Nm)	X 0.738	= Pounds-force feet (lbf ft; lb ft)
Newton meters (Nm)	X	0.102	= Kilograms-force meters (kgf m; kg m)	X 9.804	= Newton meters (Nm)

Vacuum
Inches mercury (in. Hg)	X	3.377	= Kilopascals (kPa)	X 0.2961	= Inches mercury
Inches mercury (in. Hg)	X	25.4	= Millimeters mercury (mm Hg)	X 0.0394	= Inches mercury

Power
Horsepower (hp)	X	745.7	= Watts (W)	X 0.0013	= Horsepower (hp)

Velocity (speed)
Miles per hour (miles/hr; mph)	X	1.609	= Kilometers per hour (km/hr; kph)	X 0.621	= Miles per hour (miles/hr; mph)

Fuel consumption*
Miles per gallon, Imperial (mpg)	X	0.354	= Kilometers per liter (km/l)	X 2.825	= Miles per gallon, Imperial (mpg)
Miles per gallon, US (mpg)	X	0.425	= Kilometers per liter (km/l)	X 2.352	= Miles per gallon, US (mpg)

Temperature

Degrees Fahrenheit = (°C x 1.8) + 32   Degrees Celsius (Degrees Centigrade; °C) = (°F - 32) x 0.56

*It is common practice to convert from miles per gallon (mpg) to liters/100 kilometers (l/100km), where mpg (Imperial) x l/100 km = 282 and mpg (US) x l/100 km = 235

A number of chemicals and lubricants are available for use in motorcycle maintenance and repair. They include a wide variety of products ranging from cleaning solvents and degreasers to lubricants and protective sprays for rubber, plastic and vinyl.

• **Contact point/spark plug cleaner** is a solvent used to clean oily film and dirt from points, grim from electrical connectors and oil deposits from spark plugs. It is oil free and leaves no residue. It can also be used to remove gum and varnish from carburetor jets and other orifices.

• **Carburetor cleaner** is similar to contact point/spark plug cleaner but it usually has a stronger solvent and may leave a slight oily residue. It is not recommended for cleaning electrical components or connections.

• **Brake system cleaner** is used to remove brake dust, grease and brake fluid from the brake system, where clean surfaces are absolutely necessary. It leaves no residue and often eliminates brake squeal caused by contaminants.

• **Silicone-based lubricants** are used to protect rubber parts such as hoses and grommets, and are used as lubricants for hinges and locks.

• **Multi-purpose grease** is an all purpose lubricant used wherever grease is more practical than a liquid lubricant such as oil. Some multi-purpose grease is colored white and specially formulated to be more resistant to water than ordinary grease.

• **Gear oil** (sometimes called gear lube) is a specially designed oil used in transmissions and final drive units, as well as other areas where high friction, high temperature lubrication is required. It is available in a number of viscosities (weights) for various applications.

• **Motor oil** is the lubricant formulated for use in engines. It normally contains a wide variety of additives to prevent corrosion and reduce foaming and wear. Motor oil comes in various weights (viscosity ratings) from 0 to 50. The recommended weight of the oil depends on the season, temperature and the demands on the engine. Light oil is used in cold climates and under light load conditions. Heavy oil is used in hot climates and where high loads are encountered. Multi-viscosity oils are designed to have characteristics of both light and heavy oils and are available in a number of weights from 0W-20 to 20W-50.

• **Gasoline additives** perform several functions, depending on their chemical makeup. They usually contain solvents that help dissolve gum and varnish that build up on carburetor and inlet parts. They also serve to break down carbon deposits that form on the inside surfaces of the combustion chambers. Some additives contain upper cylinder lubricants for valves and piston rings.

• **Brake and clutch fluid** is a specially formulated hydraulic fluid that can withstand the heat and pressure encountered in break/clutch systems. Care must be taken that this fluid does not come in contact with painted surfaces or plastics. An opened container should always be resealed to prevent contamination by water or dirt.

• **Chain lubricants** are formulated especially for use on motorcycle final drive chains. A good chain lube should adhere well and have good penetrating qualities to be effective as a lubricant inside the chain and on the side plates, pins and rollers. Most chain lubes are either the foaming type or quick drying type and are usually marketed as sprays. Take care to use a lubricant marked as being suitable for O-ring chains.

• **Degreasers** are heavy duty solvents used to remove grease and grime that may accumulate on the engine and frame components. They can be sprayed or brushed on and, depending on the type, are rinsed with either water or solvent.

• **Solvents** are used alone or in combination with degreasers to clean parts and assemblies during repair and overhaul. The home mechanic should use only solvents that are non-flammable and that do not produce irritating fumes.

• **Gasket sealing compounds** may be used in conjunction with gaskets, to improve their sealing capabilities, or alone, to seal metal-to-metal joints. Many gasket sealers can withstand extreme heat, some are impervious to gasoline and lubricants, while others are capable of filling and sealing large cavities. Depending on the intended use, gasket sealers either dry hard or stay relatively soft and pliable. They are usually applied by hand, with a brush or are sprayed on the gasket sealing surfaces.

• **Thread locking compound** is an adhesive locking compound that prevents threaded fasteners from loosening because of vibration. It is available in a variety of types for different applications.

• **Moisture dispersants** are usually sprays that can be used to dry out electrical components such as the fuse block and wiring connectors. Some types an also be used as treatment for rubber and as a lubricant for hinges, cables and locks.

• **Waxes and polishes** are used to help protect painted and plated surfaces from the weather. Different types of pain may require the use of different types of wax polish. Some polishes utilize a chemical or abrasive cleaner to help remove the top layer of oxidized (dull) paint on older vehicles. In recent years, many non-wax polishes (that contain a wide variety of chemicals such as polymers and silicones) have been introduced. These non-wax polishes are usually easier to apply and last longer than conventional waxes and polishes.

Preparing for storage

Before you start

If repairs or an overhaul is needed, see that this is carried out now rather than left until you want to ride the bike again.

Give the bike a good wash and scrub all dirt from its underside. Make sure the bike dries completely before preparing for storage.

Engine

● Remove the spark plug(s) and lubricate the cylinder bores with approximately a teaspoon of motor oil using a spout-type oil can (see illustration 1). Reinstall the spark plug(s). Crank the engine over a couple of times to coat the piston rings and bores with oil. If the bike has a kickstart, use this to turn the engine over. If not, flick the kill switch to the OFF position and crank the engine over on the starter (see illustration 2). If the nature of the ignition system prevents the starter operating with the kill switch in the OFF position, remove the spark plugs and fit them back in their caps; ensure that the plugs are grounded against the cylinder head when the starter is operated (see illustration 3).

> ⚠️ **Warning: It is important that the plugs are grounded away from the spark plug holes otherwise there is a risk of atomized fuel from the cylinders igniting.**

> **HAYNES HiNT** *On a single cylinder four-stroke engine, you can seal the combustion chamber completely by positioning the piston at TDC on the compression stroke.*

● Drain the carburetor(s) otherwise there is a risk of jets becoming blocked by gum deposits from the fuel (see illustration 4).

● If the bike is going into long-term storage, consider adding a fuel stabilizer to the fuel in the tank. If the tank is drained completely, corrosion of its internal surfaces may occur if left unprotected for a long period. The tank can be treated with a rust preventative especially for this purpose. Alternatively, remove the tank and pour half a liter of motor oil into it, install the filler cap and shake the tank to coat its internals with oil before draining off the excess. The same effect can also be achieved by spraying WD40 or a similar water-dispersant around the inside of the tank via its flexible nozzle.

● Make sure the cooling system contains the correct mix of antifreeze. Antifreeze also contains important corrosion inhibitors.

● The air intakes and exhaust can be sealed off by covering or plugging the openings. Ensure that you do not seal in any condensation; run the engine until it is hot, then switch off and allow to cool. Tape a

Squirt a drop of motor oil into each cylinder

Flick the kill switch to OFF . . .

. . . and ensure that the metal bodies of the plugs (arrows) are grounded against the cylinder head

Connect a hose to the carburetor float chamber drain stub (arrow) and unscrew the drain screw

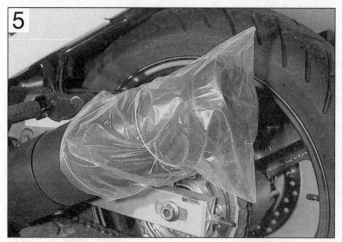

Exhausts can be sealed off with a plastic bag

Disconnect the negative lead (A) first, followed by the positive lead (B)

piece of thick plastic over the silencer end(s) **(see illustration 5)**. Note that some advocate pouring a tablespoon of motor oil into the silencer(s) before sealing them off.

Battery

● Remove it from the bike - in extreme cases of cold the battery may freeze and crack its case **(see illustration 6)**.
● Check the electrolyte level and top up if necessary (conventional refillable batteries). Clean the terminals.
● Store the battery off the motorcycle and away from any sources of fire. Position a wooden block under the battery if it is to sit on the ground.
● Give the battery a trickle charge for a few hours every month **(see illustration 7)**.

Tires

● Place the bike on its centerstand or an auxiliary stand which will support the motorcycle in an upright position. Position wood blocks under the tires to keep them off the ground and to provide insulation from damp. If the bike is being put into long-term

Use a suitable battery charger - this kit also assesses battery condition

storage, ideally both tires should be off the ground; not only will this protect the tires, but will also ensure that no load is placed on the steering head or wheel bearings.
● Deflate each tire by 5 to 10 psi, no more or the beads may unseat from the rim, making subsequent inflation difficult on tubeless tires.

Pivots and controls

● Lubricate all lever, pedal, stand and footrest pivot points. If grease nipples are fitted to the rear suspension components, apply lubricant to the pivots.
● Lubricate all control cables.

Cycle components

● Apply a wax protectant to all painted and plastic components. Wipe off any excess, but don't polish to a shine. Where fitted, clean the screen with soap and water.
● Coat metal parts with Vaseline (petroleum jelly). When applying this to the fork tubes, do not compress the forks otherwise the seals will rot from contact with the Vaseline.
● Apply a vinyl cleaner to the seat.

Storage conditions

● Aim to store the bike in a shed or garage which does not leak and is free from damp.
● Drape an old blanket or bedspread over the bike to protect it from dust and direct contact with sunlight (which will fade paint). Beware of tight-fitting plastic covers which may allow condensation to form and settle on the bike.

Getting back on the road

Engine and transmission

● Change the oil and replace the oil filter. If this was done prior to storage, check that the oil hasn't emulsified - a thick whitish substance which occurs through condensation.
● Remove the spark plugs. Using a spout-type oil can, squirt a few drops of oil into the cylinder(s). This will provide initial lubrication as the piston rings and bores comes back into contact. Service the spark plugs, or buy new ones, and install them in the engine.

● Check that the clutch isn't stuck on. The plates can stick together if left standing for some time, preventing clutch operation. Engage a gear and try rocking the bike back and forth with the clutch lever held against the handlebar. If this doesn't work on cable-operated clutches, hold the clutch lever back against the handlebar with a strong rubber band or cable tie for a couple of hours **(see illustration 8)**.
● If the air intakes or silencer end(s) were blocked off, remove the plug or cover used.
● If the fuel tank was coated with a rust

Hold the clutch lever back against the handlebar with rubber bands or a cable tie

preventative, oil or a stabilizer added to the fuel, drain and flush the tank and dispose of the fuel sensibly. If no action was taken with the fuel tank prior to storage, it is advised that the old fuel is disposed of since it will go bad over a period of time. Refill the fuel tank with fresh fuel.

Frame and running gear

● Oil all pivot points and cables.
● Check the tire pressures. They will definitely need inflating if pressures were reduced for storage.
● Lubricate the final drive chain (where applicable).
● Remove any protective coating applied to the fork tubes (stanchions) since this may well destroy the fork seals. If the fork tubes weren't protected and have picked up rust spots, remove them with very fine abrasive paper and refinish with metal polish.
● Check that both brakes operate correctly. Apply each brake hard and check that it's not possible to move the motorcycle forwards, then check that the brake frees off again once released. Brake caliper pistons can stick due to corrosion around the piston head, or on the sliding caliper types, due to corrosion of the slider pins. If the brake doesn't free after repeated operation, take the caliper off for examination. Similarly drum brakes can stick due to a seized operating cam, cable or rod linkage.
● If the motorcycle has been in long-term storage, replace the brake fluid and clutch fluid (where applicable).
● Depending on where the bike has been stored, the wiring, cables and hoses may have been nibbled by rodents. Make a visual check and investigate disturbed wiring loom tape.

Battery

● If the battery has been previously removed and given top up charges it can simply be reconnected. Remember to connect the positive cable first and the negative cable last.
● On conventional refillable batteries, if the battery has not received any attention, remove it from the motorcycle and check its electrolyte level. Top up if necessary then charge the battery. If the battery fails to hold a charge and a visual check show heavy white sulfation of the plates, the battery is probably defective and must be replaced. This is particularly likely if the battery is old. Confirm battery condition with a specific gravity check.
● On sealed (MF) batteries, if the battery has not received any attention, remove it from the motorcycle and charge it according to the information on the battery case - if the battery fails to hold a charge it must be replaced.

Starting procedure

● If a kickstart is fitted, turn the engine over a couple of times with the ignition OFF to distribute oil around the engine. If no kickstart is fitted, flick the engine kill switch OFF and the ignition ON and crank the engine over a couple of times to work oil around the upper cylinder components. If the nature of the ignition system is such that the starter won't work with the kill switch OFF, remove the spark plugs, fit them back into their caps and ground their bodies on the cylinder head. Reinstall the spark plugs afterwards.
● Switch the kill switch to RUN, operate the choke and start the engine. If the engine won't start don't continue cranking the engine - not only will this flatten the battery, but the starter motor will overheat. Switch the ignition off and try again later. If the engine refuses to start, go through the troubleshooting procedures in this manual. **Note:** *If the bike has been in storage for a long time, old fuel or a carburetor blockage may be the problem. Gum deposits in carburetors can block jets - if a carburetor cleaner doesn't prove successful the carburetors must be dismantled for cleaning.*

● Once the engine has started, check that the lights, turn signals and horn work properly.

● Treat the bike gently for the first ride and check all fluid levels on completion. Settle the bike back into the maintenance schedule.

This Section provides an easy reference-guide to the more common faults that are likely to afflict your machine. Obviously, the opportunities are almost limitless for faults to occur as a result of obscure failures, and to try and cover all eventualities would require a book. Indeed, a number have been written on the subject.

Successful troubleshooting is not a mysterious 'black art' but the application of a bit of knowledge combined with a systematic and logical approach to the problem. Approach any troubleshooting by first accurately identifying the symptom and then checking through the list of possible causes, starting with the simplest or most obvious and progressing in stages to the most complex. Take nothing for granted, but above all apply liberal quantities of common sense.

The main symptom of a fault is given in the text as a major heading below which are listed the various systems or areas which may contain the fault. Details of each possible cause for a fault and the remedial action to be taken are given. Further information should be sought in the relevant Chapter.

1 Engine doesn't start or is difficult to start

- [ ] Starter motor doesn't rotate
- [ ] Starter motor rotates but engine does not turn over
- [ ] Starter works but engine won't turn over (seized)
- [ ] No fuel flow
- [ ] Engine flooded
- [ ] No spark or weak spark
- [ ] Compression low
- [ ] Stalls after starting
- [ ] Rough idle

2 Poor running at low speed

- [ ] Spark weak
- [ ] Fuel/air mixture incorrect
- [ ] Compression low
- [ ] Poor acceleration

3 Poor running or no power at high speed

- [ ] Firing incorrect
- [ ] Fuel/air mixture incorrect
- [ ] Compression low
- [ ] Knocking or pinging
- [ ] Miscellaneous causes

4 Overheating

- [ ] Engine overheats
- [ ] Firing incorrect
- [ ] Fuel/air mixture incorrect
- [ ] Compression too high
- [ ] Engine load excessive
- [ ] Lubrication inadequate
- [ ] Miscellaneous causes

5 Clutch problems

- [ ] Clutch slipping
- [ ] Clutch not disengaging completely

6 Gearchanging problems

- [ ] Doesn't go into gear, or lever doesn't return
- [ ] Jumps out of gear
- [ ] Overselects

7 Abnormal engine noise

- [ ] Knocking or pinging
- [ ] Piston slap or rattling
- [ ] Valve noise
- [ ] Other noise

8 Abnormal driveline noise

- [ ] Clutch noise
- [ ] Transmission noise
- [ ] Final drive noise

9 Abnormal frame and suspension noise

- [ ] Front end noise
- [ ] Shock absorber noise
- [ ] Brake noise

10 Oil pressure warning light comes on

- [ ] Engine lubrication system
- [ ] Electrical system

11 Excessive exhaust smoke

- [ ] White smoke
- [ ] Black smoke

12 Poor handling or stability

- [ ] Handlebar hard to turn
- [ ] Handlebar shakes or vibrates excessively
- [ ] Handlebar pulls to one side
- [ ] Poor shock absorbing qualities

13 Braking problems

- [ ] Brakes are spongy, don't hold
- [ ] Brake lever or pedal pulsates
- [ ] Brakes drag

14 Electrical problems

- [ ] Battery dead or weak
- [ ] Battery overcharged

1 Engine doesn't start or is difficult to start

Starter motor doesn't rotate

☐ Engine kill switch OFF.

☐ Fuse blown. Check main fuse and starter circuit fuse (Chapter 9).

☐ Battery voltage low. Check and recharge battery (Chapter 9).

☐ Starter motor defective. Make sure the wiring to the starter is secure. Make sure the starter relay clicks when the start button is pushed. If the relay clicks, then the fault is in the wiring or motor.

☐ Starter relay faulty. Check it according to the procedure in Chapter 9.

☐ Starter switch not contacting. The contacts could be wet, corroded or dirty. Disassemble and clean the switch (Chapter 9).

☐ Wiring open or shorted. Check all wiring connections and harnesses to make sure that they are dry, tight and not corroded. Also check for broken or frayed wires that can cause a short to ground (see wiring diagram, Chapter 9).

☐ Ignition (main) switch defective. Check the switch according to the procedure in Chapter 9. Replace the switch with a new one if it is defective.

☐ Engine kill switch defective. Check for wet, dirty or corroded contacts. Clean or replace the switch as necessary (Chapter 9).

☐ Faulty neutral, side stand or clutch switch. Check the wiring to each switch and the switch itself according to the procedures in Chapter 9.

Starter motor rotates but engine does not turn over

☐ Starter motor clutch defective. Inspect and repair or replace (Chapter 2).

☐ Damaged idler or starter gears. Inspect and replace the damaged parts (Chapter 2).

Starter works but engine won't turn over (seized)

☐ Seized engine caused by one or more internally damaged components. Failure due to wear, abuse or lack of lubrication. Damage can include seized valves, followers/rocker arms, camshafts, pistons, crankshaft, connecting rod bearings, or transmission gears or bearings. Refer to Chapter 2 for engine disassembly.

No fuel flow

☐ No fuel in tank.

☐ Fuel tank breather hose obstructed.

☐ Fuel filter is blocked (see Chapter 1).

Engine flooded

☐ Starting technique incorrect. Under normal circumstances the machine should start with little or no throttle. When the engine is cold, the choke should be operated and the engine started without opening the throttle. When the engine is at operating temperature, only a very slight amount of throttle should be necessary.

No spark or weak spark

☐ Ignition switch OFF.

☐ Engine kill switch turned to the OFF position.

☐ Battery voltage low. Check and recharge the battery as necessary (Chapter 9).

☐ Spark plugs dirty, defective or worn out. Locate reason for fouled plugs using spark plug condition chart and follow the plug maintenance procedures (Chapter 1).

☐ Spark plug caps or secondary (HT) wiring faulty. Check condition. Replace either or both components if cracks or deterioration are evident (Chapter 5).

☐ Spark plug caps not making good contact. Make sure that the plug caps fit snugly over the plug ends.

☐ Ignition HT coils defective. Check the coils, referring to Chapter 5.

☐ IC igniter unit defective. Refer to Chapter 5 for details.

☐ Pick-up coil defective. Check the unit, referring to Chapter 5 for details.

☐ Ignition or kill switch shorted. This is usually caused by water, corrosion, damage or excessive wear. The switches can be disassembled and cleaned with electrical contact cleaner. If cleaning does not help, replace the switches (Chapter 9).

☐ Wiring shorted or broken between:

    a) Ignition (main) switch and engine kill switch (or blown fuse)
    b) IC igniter unit and engine kill switch
    c) IC igniter unit and ignition HT coils
    d) Ignition HT coils and spark plugs
    e) IC igniter unit and ignition pick-up coil.

☐ Make sure that all wiring connections are clean, dry and tight. Look for chafed and broken wires (Chapters 5 and 9).

Compression low

☐ Spark plugs loose. Remove the plugs and inspect their threads. Reinstall and tighten to the specified torque (Chapter 1).

☐ Cylinder head not sufficiently tightened down. If the cylinder head is suspected of being loose, then there's a chance that the gasket or head is damaged if the problem has persisted for any length of time. The head bolts should be tightened to the proper torque in the correct sequence (Chapter 2).

☐ Improper valve clearance. This means that the valve is not closing completely and compression pressure is leaking past the valve. Check and adjust the valve clearances (Chapter 1).

☐ Cylinder and/or piston worn. Excessive wear will cause compression pressure to leak past the rings. This is usually accompanied by worn rings as well. A top-end overhaul is necessary (Chapter 2).

☐ Piston rings worn, weak, broken, or sticking. Broken or sticking piston rings usually indicate a lubrication or fuelling problem that causes excess carbon deposits or seizures to form on the pistons and rings. Top-end overhaul is necessary (Chapter 2).

☐ Piston ring-to-groove clearance excessive. This is caused by excessive wear of the piston ring lands. Piston replacement is necessary (Chapter 2).

☐ Cylinder head gasket damaged. If a head is allowed to become loose, or if excessive carbon build-up on the piston crown and combustion chamber causes extremely high compression, the head gasket may leak. Retorquing the head is not always sufficient to restore the seal, so gasket replacement is necessary (Chapter 2).

☐ Cylinder head warped. This is caused by overheating or improperly tightened head bolts. Machine shop resurfacing or head replacement is necessary (Chapter 2).

☐ Valve spring broken or weak. Caused by component failure or wear; the springs must be replaced (Chapter 2).

☐ Valve not seating properly. This is caused by a bent valve (from over-revving or improper valve adjustment), burned valve or seat (improper fuelling) or an accumulation of carbon deposits on the seat (from fuelling or lubrication problems). The valves must be cleaned and/or replaced and the seats serviced if possible (Chapter 2).

1 Engine doesn't start or is difficult to start (continued)

Stalls after starting

- ☐ Improper choke action (carbureted models). Make sure the choke linkage shaft is getting a full stroke and staying in the out position (Chapter 4).
- ☐ Ignition malfunction. See Chapter 5.
- ☐ Carburetor or fuel injection malfunction. See Chapter 4.
- ☐ Fuel contaminated. The fuel can be contaminated with either dirt or water, or can change chemically if the machine is allowed to sit for several months or more. Drain the tank (Chapter 4).
- ☐ Intake air leak. Check for loose intake manifold retaining clips and damaged/disconnected vacuum hoses (Chapter 4).
- ☐ Engine idle speed incorrect. Turn idle adjusting screw until the engine idles at the specified rpm (Chapter 1).

Rough idle

- ☐ Ignition malfunction. See Chapter 5.
- ☐ Idle speed incorrect. See Chapter 1.
- ☐ Carburetors not synchronized (twin carburetor models). Adjust them with vacuum gauge or manometer set as described in Chapter 4.
- ☐ Carburetor or fuel injection malfunction. See Chapter 4.
- ☐ Fuel contaminated. The fuel can be contaminated with either dirt or water, or can change chemically if the machine is allowed to sit for several months or more. Drain the tank (Chapter 4).
- ☐ Intake air leak. Check for loose intake manifold retaining clips and damaged/disconnected vacuum hoses. Replace the intake ducts if they are split or deteriorated (Chapter 4).
- ☐ Air filter clogged. Replace the air filter element (Chapter 1).

2 Poor running at low speeds

Spark weak

- ☐ Battery voltage low. Check and recharge battery (Chapter 9).
- ☐ Spark plugs fouled, defective or worn out. Refer to Chapter 1 for spark plug maintenance.
- ☐ Spark plug cap or HT wiring defective. Refer to Chapters 1 and 5 for details on the ignition system.
- ☐ Spark plug caps not making contact.
- ☐ Incorrect spark plugs. Wrong type, heat range or cap configuration. Check and install correct plugs listed in Chapter 1.
- ☐ IC igniter unit or ECM faulty. See Chapter 5.
- ☐ Pick-up coil defective. See Chapter 5.
- ☐ Ignition coils defective. See Chapter 5.

Fuel/air mixture incorrect

- ☐ Pilot screws incorrectly set (Chapter 4)
- ☐ Pilot jet or air passage blocked. Remove and overhaul the carburetors (Chapter 4).
- ☐ Air filter clogged, poorly sealed or missing (Chapter 1).
- ☐ Air filter housing poorly sealed. Look for cracks, holes or loose clamps and replace or repair defective parts.
- ☐ Fuel tank breather hose obstructed.
- ☐ Intake air leak. Check for loose intake manifold retaining clips and damaged/disconnected vacuum hoses. Replace the intake ducts if they are split or deteriorated (Chapter 4).

Compression low

- ☐ Spark plugs loose. Remove the plugs and inspect their threads. Reinstall and tighten to the specified torque (Chapter 1).
- ☐ Cylinder head not sufficiently tightened down. If the cylinder head is suspected of being loose, then there's a chance that the gasket and head are damaged if the problem has persisted for any length of time. The head bolts should be tightened to the proper torque in the correct sequence (Chapter 2).
- ☐ Improper valve clearance. This means that the valve is not closing completely and compression pressure is leaking past the valve. Check and adjust the valve clearances (Chapter 1).

- ☐ Cylinder and/or piston worn. Excessive wear will cause compression pressure to leak past the rings. This is usually accompanied by worn rings as well. A top-end overhaul is necessary (Chapter 2).
- ☐ Piston rings worn, weak, broken, or sticking. Broken or sticking piston rings usually indicate a lubrication or fuelling problem that causes excess carbon deposits or seizures to form on the pistons and rings. Top-end overhaul is necessary (Chapter 2).
- ☐ Piston ring-to-groove clearance excessive. This is caused by excessive wear of the piston ring lands. Piston replacement is necessary (Chapter 2).
- ☐ Cylinder head gasket damaged. If a head is allowed to become loose, or if excessive carbon build-up on the piston crown and combustion chamber causes extremely high compression, the head gasket may leak. Retorquing the head is not always sufficient to restore the seal, so gasket replacement is necessary (Chapter 2).
- ☐ Cylinder head warped. This is caused by overheating or improperly tightened head bolts. Machine shop resurfacing or head replacement is necessary (Chapter 2).
- ☐ Valve spring broken or weak. Caused by component failure or wear; the springs must be replaced (Chapter 2).
- ☐ Valve not seating properly. This is caused by a bent valve (from over-revving or improper valve adjustment), burned valve or seat (improper fuelling) or an accumulation of carbon deposits on the seat (from fuelling, lubrication problems). The valves must be cleaned and/or replaced and the seats serviced if possible (Chapter 2).

Poor acceleration

- ☐ Fuel system fault. Remove and overhaul the carburetors or check the fuel injection system (Chapter 4).
- ☐ Engine oil viscosity too high. Using a heavier oil than that recommended in Chapter 1 can damage the oil pump or lubrication system and cause drag on the engine.
- ☐ Brakes dragging. Usually caused by debris which has entered the brake piston seals, or from a warped disc or drum or bent axle. Repair as necessary (Chapter 7).

3 Poor running or no power at high speed

Firing incorrect

- [ ] Air filter restricted. Clean or replace filter (Chapter 1).
- [ ] Spark plugs fouled, defective or worn out. See Chapter 1 for spark plug maintenance.
- [ ] Spark plug caps or HT wiring defective. See Chapters 1 and 5 for details of the ignition system.
- [ ] Spark plug caps not in good contact. See Chapter 5.
- [ ] Incorrect spark plugs. Wrong type, heat range or cap configuration. Check and install correct plugs listed in Chapter 1.
- [ ] IC igniter unit or ECM defective. See Chapter 5.
- [ ] Pick-up coil defective. See Chapter 5.
- [ ] Ignition coils defective. See Chapter 5.

Fuel/air mixture incorrect

- [ ] Fuel system fault. Remove and overhaul the carburetors or check the fuel injection system (Chapter 4).
- [ ] Air filter clogged, poorly sealed, or missing (Chapter 1).
- [ ] Air filter housing poorly sealed. Look for cracks, holes or loose clamps, and replace or repair defective parts.
- [ ] Fuel tank breather hose obstructed.
- [ ] Intake air leak. Check for loose Intake manifold retaining clips and damaged/disconnected vacuum hoses. Replace the intake ducts if they are split or deteriorated (Chapter 4).

Compression low

- [ ] Spark plugs loose. Remove the plugs and inspect their threads. Reinstall and tighten to the specified torque (Chapter 1).
- [ ] Cylinder head not sufficiently tightened down. If the cylinder head is suspected of being loose, then there's a chance that the gasket and head are damaged if the problem has persisted for any length of time. The head bolts should be tightened to the proper torque in the correct sequence (Chapter 2).
- [ ] Improper valve clearance. This means that the valve is not closing completely and compression pressure is leaking past the valve. Check and adjust the valve clearances (Chapter 1).
- [ ] Cylinder and/or piston worn. Excessive wear will cause compression pressure to leak past the rings. This is usually accompanied by worn rings as well. A top-end overhaul is necessary (Chapter 2).
- [ ] Piston rings worn, weak, broken, or sticking. Broken or sticking piston rings usually indicate a lubrication or fueling problem that causes excess carbon deposits or seizures to form on the pistons and rings. Top-end overhaul is necessary (Chapter 2).
- [ ] Piston ring-to-groove clearance excessive. This is caused by excessive wear of the piston ring lands. Piston replacement is necessary (Chapter 2).

- [ ] Cylinder head gasket damaged. If a head is allowed to become loose, or if excessive carbon build-up on the piston crown and combustion chamber causes extremely high compression, the head gasket may leak. Retorquing the head is not always sufficient to restore the seal, so gasket replacement is necessary (Chapter 2).
- [ ] Cylinder head warped. This is caused by overheating or improperly tightened head bolts. Machine shop resurfacing or head replacement is necessary (Chapter 2).
- [ ] Valve spring broken or weak. Caused by component failure or wear; the springs must be replaced (Chapter 2).
- [ ] Valve not seating properly. This is caused by a bent valve (from over-revving or improper valve adjustment), burned valve or seat (improper fuelling) or an accumulation of carbon deposits on the seat (from fuelling or lubrication problems). The valves must be cleaned and/or replaced and the seats serviced if possible (Chapter 2).

Knocking or pinging

- [ ] Carbon build-up in combustion chamber. Use of a fuel additive that will dissolve the adhesive bonding the carbon particles to the crown and chamber is the easiest way to remove the build-up. Otherwise, the cylinder head will have to be removed and decarbonized (Chapter 2).
- [ ] Incorrect or poor quality fuel. Old or improper grades of fuel can cause detonation. This causes the piston to rattle, thus the knocking or pinging sound. Drain old fuel and always use the recommended fuel grade.
- [ ] Spark plug heat range incorrect. Uncontrolled detonation indicates the plug heat range is too hot. The plug in effect becomes a glow plug, raising cylinder temperatures. Install the proper heat range plug (Chapter 1).
- [ ] Improper air/fuel mixture. This will cause the cylinders to run hot, which leads to detonation. An intake air leak can cause this imbalance. See Chapter 4.

Miscellaneous causes

- [ ] Throttle valve doesn't open fully. Adjust the throttle grip freeplay (Chapter 1).
- [ ] Clutch slipping. May be caused by loose or worn clutch components. Refer to Chapter 2 for clutch overhaul procedures.
- [ ] Engine oil viscosity too high. Using a heavier oil than the one recommended in Chapter 1 can damage the oil pump or lubrication system and cause drag on the engine.
- [ ] Brakes dragging. Usually caused by debris which has entered the brake piston seals, or from a warped disc, out-of-round drum or bent axle. Repair as necessary.

4 Overheating

Engine overheats

- [ ] Coolant level low. Check and add coolant (Chapter 1).
- [ ] Leak in cooling system. Check cooling system hoses and radiator for leaks and other damage. Repair or replace parts as necessary (Chapter 3).
- [ ] Thermostat sticking open or closed. Check and replace as described in Chapter 3.
- [ ] Faulty pressure cap. Remove the cap and have it pressure tested (Chapter 3).
- [ ] Coolant passages clogged. Have the entire system drained and flushed, then refill with fresh coolant.
- [ ] Water pump defective. Remove the pump and check the components (Chapter 3).
- [ ] Clogged radiator fins. Clean them by blowing compressed air through the fins from the backside.
- [ ] Cooling fan or fan switch fault (Chapter 3).

Firing incorrect

- [ ] Spark plugs fouled, defective or worn out. See Chapter 1 for spark plug maintenance.
- [ ] Incorrect spark plugs.
- [ ] IC igniter unit or ECM defective. See Chapter 5.
- [ ] Pick-up coil faulty. See Chapter 5.
- [ ] Faulty ignition coils. See Chapter 5.

Fuel/air mixture incorrect

- [ ] Fuel system fault. Remove and overhaul the carburetors or check the fuel injection system (Chapter 4).
- [ ] Air filter clogged, poorly sealed, or missing (Chapter 1).
- [ ] Air filter housing poorly sealed. Look for cracks, holes or loose clamps, and replace or repair defective parts.
- [ ] Fuel tank breather hose obstructed.
- [ ] Intake air leak. Check for loose intake manifold retaining clips and damaged/disconnected vacuum hoses. Replace the intake manifold(s) if they are split or deteriorated (Chapter 4).

Compression too high

- [ ] Carbon build-up in combustion chamber. Use of a fuel additive that will dissolve the adhesive bonding the carbon particles to the piston crown and chamber is the easiest way to remove the build-up. Otherwise, the cylinder head will have to be removed and decarbonized (Chapter 2).
- [ ] Improperly machined head surface or installation of incorrect gasket during engine assembly.

Engine load excessive

- [ ] Clutch slipping. Can be caused by damaged, loose or worn clutch components. Refer to Chapter 2 for overhaul procedures.
- [ ] Engine oil level too high. The addition of too much oil will cause pressurization of the crankcase and inefficient engine operation. Check Specifications and drain to proper level (Chapter 1).
- [ ] Engine oil viscosity too high. Using a heavier oil than the one recommended in Chapter 1 can damage the oil pump or lubrication system as well as cause drag on the engine.
- [ ] Brakes dragging. Usually caused by debris which has entered the brake piston seals, or from a warped disc or drum or bent axle. Repair as necessary.

Lubrication inadequate

- [ ] Engine oil level too low. Friction caused by intermittent lack of lubrication or from oil that is overworked can cause overheating. The oil provides a definite cooling function in the engine. Check the oil level (Chapter 1).
- [ ] Poor quality engine oil or incorrect viscosity or type. Oil Is rated not only according to viscosity but also according to type. Some oils are not rated high enough for use in this engine. Check the Specifications section and change to the correct oil (Chapter 1).

Miscellaneous causes

- [ ] Modification to exhaust system. Most aftermarket exhaust systems cause the engine to run leaner, which makes it run hotter.

5 Clutch problems

Clutch slipping

- [ ] Clutch cable freeplay incorrectly adjusted (cable clutch models) (Chapter 1).
- [ ] Friction plates worn or warped. Overhaul the clutch assembly (Chapter 2).
- [ ] Plain plates warped (Chapter 2).
- [ ] Clutch springs broken or weak. Old or heat-damaged (from slipping clutch) springs should be replaced with new ones (Chapter 2).
- [ ] Clutch pushrod bent. Check and, if necessary, replace (Chapter 2).
- [ ] Clutch center or housing unevenly worn. This causes improper engagement of the plates. Replace the damaged or worn parts (Chapter 2).
- [ ] Wrong type of oil used. Make sure oil with anti-friction additives (such as molybdenum disulfide) is NOT used in an engine/ transmission with a wet clutch.

Clutch not disengaging completely

- [ ] Clutch cable freeplay incorrectly adjusted (Chapter 1).
- [ ] Air in clutch hydraulic system (hydraulic clutch models). Bleed the system (Chapter 2).

- [ ] Worn master or slave cylinder (hydraulic clutch models). Inspect and repair or replace as necessary (Chapter 2).
- [ ] Clutch plates warped or damaged. This will cause clutch drag, which in turn will cause the machine to creep. Overhaul the clutch assembly (Chapter 2).
- [ ] Clutch spring tension uneven. Usually caused by a sagged or broken spring. Check and replace the springs as a set (Chapter 2).
- [ ] Engine oil deteriorated. Old, thin, worn out oil will not provide proper lubrication for the plates, causing the clutch to drag. Replace the oil and filter (Chapter 1).
- [ ] Engine oil viscosity too high. Using a heavier oil than recommended in Chapter 1 can cause the plates to stick together, putting a drag on the engine. Change to the correct weight oil (Chapter 1).
- [ ] Clutch housing bearing seized. Lack of lubrication, severe wear or damage can cause the bearing to seize on the input shaft. Overhaul of the clutch, and perhaps transmission, may be necessary to repair the damage (Chapter 2).
- [ ] Loose clutch center nut. Causes housing and center misalignment putting a drag on the engine. Engagement adjustment continually varies. Overhaul the clutch assembly (Chapter 2).

6 Gearchanging problems

Doesn't go into gear or lever doesn't return

- ☐ Clutch not disengaging. See Section 5.
- ☐ Shift fork(s) bent or seized. Often caused by dropping the machine or from lack of lubrication. Overhaul the transmission (Chapter 2).
- ☐ Gear(s) stuck on shaft. Most often caused by a lack of lubrication or excessive wear in transmission bearings and bushings. Overhaul the transmission (Chapter 2).
- ☐ Gear shift drum binding. Caused by lubrication failure or excessive wear. Replace the drum and bearing (Chapter 2).
- ☐ Gear shift lever pawl spring weak or broken (Chapter 2).
- ☐ Gear shift lever broken. Splines stripped out of lever or shaft, caused by allowing the lever to get loose or from dropping the machine. Replace necessary parts (Chapter 2).
- ☐ Gear shift mechanism stopper arm broken or worn. Full engagement and rotary movement of shift drum results. Replace the arm (Chapter 2).

- ☐ Stopper arm spring broken. Allows arm to float, causing sporadic shift operation. Replace spring (Chapter 2).

Jumps out of gear

- ☐ Shift fork(s) worn. Overhaul the transmission (Chapter 2).
- ☐ Gear groove(s) worn. Overhaul the transmission (Chapter 2).
- ☐ Gear dogs or dog slots worn or damaged. The gears should be inspected and replaced. No attempt should be made to service the worn parts.

Overselects

- ☐ Stopper arm spring weak or broken (Chapter 2).
- ☐ Return spring post broken or distorted (Chapter 2).

7 Abnormal engine noise

Knocking or pinging

- ☐ Carbon build-up in combustion chamber. Use of a fuel additive that will dissolve the adhesive bonding the carbon particles to the piston crown and chamber is the easiest way to remove the build-up. Otherwise, the cylinder head will have to be removed and decarbonized (Chapter 2).
- ☐ Incorrect or poor quality fuel. Old or improper fuel can cause detonation. This causes the pistons to rattle, thus the knocking or pinging sound. Drain the old fuel and always use the recommended grade fuel (Chapter 4).
- ☐ Spark plug heat range incorrect. Uncontrolled detonation indicates that the plug heat range is too hot. The plug in effect becomes a glow plug, raising cylinder temperatures. Install the proper heat range plug (Chapter 1).
- ☐ Improper air/fuel mixture. This will cause the cylinders to run hot and lead to detonation. Blocked carburetor jets or an air leak can cause this imbalance. See Chapter 4.

Piston slap or rattling

- ☐ Cylinder-to-piston clearance excessive. Caused by improper assembly. Inspect and overhaul top-end parts (Chapter 2).
- ☐ Connecting rod bent. Caused by over-revving, trying to start a badly flooded engine or from ingesting a foreign object into the combustion chamber. Replace the damaged parts (Chapter 2).
- ☐ Piston pin or piston pin bore worn or seized from wear or lack of lubrication. Replace damaged parts (Chapter 2).
- ☐ Piston ring(s) worn, broken or sticking. Overhaul the top-end (Chapter 2).
- ☐ Piston seizure damage. Usually from lack of lubrication or overheating. Replace the pistons and cylinders, as necessary (Chapter 2).

- ☐ Connecting rod bearing clearance excessive. Caused by excessive wear or lack of lubrication. Replace worn parts.

Valve noise

- ☐ Incorrect valve clearances. Adjust the clearances by referring to Chapter 1.
- ☐ Valve spring broken or weak. Check and replace weak valve springs (Chapter 2).
- ☐ Camshaft or cylinder head worn or damaged. Lack of lubrication at high rpm is usually the cause of damage. Insufficient oil or failure to change the oil at the recommended intervals are the chief causes. Since there are no replaceable bearings in the head, the head itself will have to be replaced if there is excessive wear or damage (Chapter 2).

Other noise

- ☐ Cylinder head gasket leaking.
- ☐ Exhaust pipe leaking at cylinder head connection. Caused by improper fit of pipe(s) or loose exhaust nuts. All exhaust fasteners should be tightened evenly and carefully. Failure to do this will lead to a leak.
- ☐ Crankshaft runout excessive. Caused by a bent crankshaft (from over-revving) or damage from an upper cylinder component failure. Can also be attributed to dropping the machine on either of the crankshaft ends.
- ☐ Engine mounting bolts loose. Tighten all engine mount bolts (Chapter 2).
- ☐ Crankshaft bearings worn (Chapter 2).
- ☐ Cam chain, tensioner or guides worn. Replace according to the procedure in Chapter 2.

8 Abnormal driveline noise

Clutch noise

☐ Clutch outer drum/friction plate clearance excessive (Chapter 2).
☐ Loose or damaged clutch pressure plate and/or bolts (Chapter 2).

Transmission noise

☐ Bearings worn. Also includes the possibility that the shafts are worn. Overhaul the transmission (Chapter 2).
☐ Gears worn or chipped (Chapter 2).
☐ Metal chips jammed in gear teeth. Probably pieces from a broken clutch, gear or shift mechanism that were picked up by the gears. This will cause early bearing failure (Chapter 2).

☐ Engine oil level too low. Causes a howl from transmission. Also affects engine power and clutch operation (Chapter 1).

Final drive noise

☐ Chain or drive belt not adjusted properly (Chapter 1).
☐ Front or rear sprocket loose. Tighten fasteners (Chapter 6).
☐ Sprockets worn. Replace sprockets (Chapter 6).
☐ Rear sprocket warped. Replace sprockets (Chapter 6).
☐ Differential worn or damaged. Have it repaired or replace it (Chapter 7).

9 Abnormal frame and suspension noise

Front end noise

☐ Low fluid level or improper viscosity oil in forks. This can sound like spurting and is usually accompanied by irregular fork action (Chapter 6).
☐ Spring weak or broken. Makes a clicking or scraping sound. Fork oil, when drained, will have a lot of metal particles in it (Chapter 6).
☐ Steering head bearings loose or damaged. Clicks when braking. Check and adjust or replace as necessary (Chapters 1 and 6).
☐ Triple clamps loose. Make sure all clamp bolts are tightened to the specified torque (Chapter 6).
☐ Fork tube bent. Good possibility if machine has been dropped. Replace tube with a new one (Chapter 6).
☐ Front axle bolt or axle pinch bolts loose. Tighten them to the specified torque (Chapter 7).
☐ Loose or worn wheel bearings. Check and replace as needed (Chapter 7).

Shock absorber noise

☐ Fluid level incorrect. Indicates a leak caused by defective seal. Shock will be covered with oil. Replace shock or seek advice on repair from a dealer (Chapter 6).
☐ Defective shock absorber with internal damage. This is in the body of the shock and can't be remedied. The shock must be replaced with a new one (Chapter 6).

☐ Bent or damaged shock body. Replace the shock with a new one (Chapter 6).
☐ Loose or worn suspension linkage components (EX250 models). Check and replace as necessary (Chapter 6).

Brake noise

☐ Squeal caused by dust on brake pads. Usually found in combination with glazed pads. Clean using brake cleaning solvent (Chapter 7).
☐ Contamination of brake pads. Oil, brake fluid or dirt causing brake to chatter or squeal. Clean or replace pads (Chapter 7).
☐ Pads glazed. Caused by excessive heat from prolonged use or from contamination. Do not use sandpaper/emery cloth or any other abrasive to roughen the pad surfaces as abrasives will stay in the pad material and damage the disc. A very fine flat file can be used, but pad replacement is suggested as a cure (Chapter 7).
☐ Disc warped. Can cause a chattering, clicking or intermittent squeal. Usually accompanied by a pulsating lever and uneven braking. Replace the disc (Chapter 7).
☐ Loose or worn wheel bearings. Check and replace as needed (Chapter 7).

10 Oil pressure warning light comes on

Engine lubrication system

☐ Engine oil pump defective, blocked oil strainer screen or failed relief valve. Carry out oil pressure check (Chapter 1).
☐ Engine oil level low. Inspect for leak or other problem causing low oil level and add recommended oil (Chapter 1).
☐ Engine oil viscosity too low. Very old, thin oil or an improper weight of oil used in the engine. Change to correct oil (Chapter 1).
☐ Camshaft or journals worn. Excessive wear causing drop in oil pressure. Replace cam and/or cylinder head. Abnormal wear could be caused by oil starvation at high rpm from low oil level or improper weight or type of oil (Chapter 1).

☐ Crankshaft and/or bearings worn. Same problems as above. Check and replace crankshaft and/or bearings (Chapter 2).

Electrical system

☐ Oil pressure switch defective. Check the switch according to the procedure in Chapter 9. Replace it if it is defective.
☐ Oil pressure indicator light circuit defective. Check for pinched, shorted, disconnected or damaged wiring (Chapter 9).

11 Excessive exhaust smoke

White smoke

☐ Piston oil ring worn. The ring may be broken or damaged, causing oil from the crankcase to be pulled past the piston into the combustion chamber. Replace the rings with new ones (Chapter 2).

☐ Cylinders worn, cracked, or scored. Caused by overheating or oil starvation. Install a new cylinder block (Chapter 2).

☐ Valve oil seal damaged or worn. Replace oil seals with new ones (Chapter 2).

☐ Valve guide worn. Perform a complete valve job (Chapter 2).

☐ Engine oil level too high, which causes the oil to be forced past the rings. Drain oil to the proper level (Chapter 1).

☐ Head gasket broken between oil return and cylinder. Causes oil to be pulled into the combustion chamber. Replace the head gasket and check the head for warpage (Chapter 2).

☐ Abnormal crankcase pressurization, which forces oil past the rings. Clogged breather is usually the cause.

Black smoke

☐ Air filter clogged. Clean or replace the element (Chapter 1).

☐ Carburetor flooding. Remove and overhaul the carburetor(s) (Chapter 4).

☐ Main jet too large. Remove and overhaul the carburetor(s) (Chapter 4).

☐ Choke cable stuck (Chapter 4).

☐ Fuel level too high. Check the fuel level (Chapter 4).

☐ Fuel injector problem (Chapter 4).

12 Poor handling or stability

Handlebar hard to turn

☐ Steering head bearing adjuster nut too tight. Check adjustment as described in Chapter 1.

☐ Bearings damaged. Roughness can be felt as the bars are turned from side-to-side. Replace bearings and races (Chapter 6).

☐ Races dented or worn. Denting results from wear in only one position (e.g., straight ahead), from a collision or hitting a pothole or from dropping the machine. Replace races and bearings (Chapter 6).

☐ Steering stem lubrication inadequate. Causes are grease getting hard from age or being washed out by high pressure car washes. Disassemble steering head and repack bearings (Chapter 6).

☐ Steering stem bent. Caused by a collision, hitting a pothole or by dropping the machine. Replace damaged part. Don't try to straighten the steering stem (Chapter 6).

☐ Front tire air pressure too low (Chapter 1).

Handlebar shakes or vibrates excessively

☐ Tires worn or out of balance (Chapter 7).

☐ Swingarm bearings worn. Replace worn bearings (Chapter 6).

☐ Wheel rim(s) warped or damaged. Inspect wheels for runout (Chapter 7).

☐ Spokes loose (see Chapter 1).

☐ Wheel bearings worn. Worn front or rear wheel bearings can cause poor tracking. Worn front bearings will cause wobble (Chapter 7).

☐ Handlebar clamp bolts loose (Chapter 6).

☐ Fork yoke bolts loose. Tighten them to the specified torque (Chapter 6).

☐ Engine mounting bolts loose. Will cause excessive vibration with increased engine rpm (Chapter 2).

Handlebar pulls to one side

☐ Frame bent. Definitely suspect this if the machine has been dropped. May or may not be accompanied by cracking near the bend. Replace the frame (Chapter 8).

☐ Wheels out of alignment. Caused by improper location of axle spacers or from bent steering stem or frame (Chapters 6 and 8).

☐ Swingarm bent or twisted. Caused by age (metal fatigue) or impact damage. Replace the arm (Chapter 6).

☐ Steering stem bent. Caused by impact damage or by dropping the motorcycle. Replace the steering stem (Chapter 6).

☐ Fork tube bent. Disassemble the forks and replace the damaged parts (Chapter 6).

☐ Fork oil level uneven. Check and add or drain as necessary (Chapter 1).

Poor shock absorbing qualities

Too hard:
   a) *Fork oil level excessive (Chapter 1).*
   b) *Fork oil viscosity too high. Use a lighter oil (see the Specifications in Chapter 1).*
   c) *Fork tube bent. Causes a harsh, sticking feeling (Chapter 6).*
   d) *Shock shaft or body bent or damaged (Chapter 6).*
   e) *Fork internal damage (Chapter 6).*
   f) *Shock internal damage.*
   g) *Tire pressure too high (Chapter 1).*

Too soft:
   a) *Fork or shock oil insufficient and/or leaking (Chapter 1).*
   b) *Fork oil level too low (Chapter 6).*
   c) *Fork oil viscosity too light (Chapter 6).*
   d) *Fork springs weak or broken (Chapter 6).*
   e) *Shock internal damage or leakage (Chapter 6).*

13 Braking problems

Brakes are spongy, don't hold

- [ ] Air in brake line. Caused by inattention to master cylinder fluid level or by leakage. Locate problem and bleed brakes (Chapter 7).
- [ ] Pad or disc worn (Chapters 1 and 7).
- [ ] Brake fluid leak. See paragraph 1.
- [ ] Contaminated pads. Caused by contamination with oil, grease, brake fluid, etc. Clean or replace pads. Clean disc thoroughly with brake cleaner (Chapter 7).
- [ ] Brake fluid deteriorated. Fluid is old or contaminated. Drain system, replenish with new fluid and bleed the system (Chapter 7).
- [ ] Master cylinder internal parts worn or damaged causing fluid to bypass (Chapter 7).
- [ ] Master cylinder bore scratched by foreign material or broken spring. Repair or replace master cylinder (Chapter 7).
- [ ] Disc warped. Replace disc (Chapter 7).

Brake lever or pedal pulsates

- [ ] Disc warped. Replace disc (Chapter 7).

- [ ] Axle bent. Replace axle (Chapter 7).
- [ ] Brake caliper bolts loose (Chapter 7).
- [ ] Wheel warped or otherwise damaged (Chapter 7).
- [ ] Wheel bearings damaged or worn (Chapter 7).
- [ ] Brake drum out of round. Replace brake drum.

Brakes drag

- [ ] Master cylinder piston seized. Caused by wear or damage to piston or cylinder bore (Chapter 7).
- [ ] Lever binding. Check pivot and lubricate (Chapter 7).
- [ ] Brake caliper piston seized in bore. Caused by wear or ingestion of dirt past deteriorated seal (Chapter 7).
- [ ] Brake caliper mounting bracket pins corroded. Clean off corrosion and lubricate (Chapter 7).
- [ ] Brake pad or shoe damaged. Material separated from backing plate. Usually caused by faulty manufacturing process or from contact with chemicals. Replace pads or shoes (Chapter 7).
- [ ] Pads improperly installed (Chapter 7).
- [ ] Drum brake springs weak. Replace springs

14 Electrical problems

Battery dead or weak

- [ ] Battery faulty. Caused by sulfated plates which are shorted through sedimentation. Also, broken battery terminal making only occasional contact (Chapter 9).
- [ ] Battery cables making poor contact (Chapter 9).
- [ ] Load excessive. Caused by addition of high wattage lights or other electrical accessories.
- [ ] Ignition (main) switch defective. Switch either grounds internally or fails to shut off system. Replace the switch (Chapter 9).
- [ ] Regulator/rectifier defective (Chapter 9).
- [ ] Alternator stator coil open or shorted (Chapter 9).
- [ ] Wiring faulty. Wiring grounded or connections loose in ignition, charging or lighting circuits (Chapter 9).

Battery overcharged

- [ ] Regulator/rectifier defective. Overcharging is noticed when battery gets excessively warm (Chapter 9).
- [ ] Battery defective. Replace battery with a new one (Chapter 9).
- [ ] Battery amperage too low, wrong type or size. Install manufacturer's specified amp-hour battery to handle charging load (Chapter 9).

Measuring open-circuit battery voltage

Float-type hydrometer for measuring battery specific gravity

Checking engine compression

● Low compression will result in exhaust smoke, heavy oil consumption, poor starting and poor performance. A compression test will provide useful information about an engine's condition and if performed regularly, can give warning of trouble before any other symptoms become apparent.

● A compression gauge will be required, along with an adapter to suit the spark plug hole thread size. Note that the screw-in type gauge/adapter set up is preferable to the rubber cone type.

● Before carrying out the test, first check the valve clearances as described in Chapter 1.

● Compression testing procedures for the motorcycles covered in this manual are described in Chapter 2C.

Checking battery open-circuit voltage

⚠ *Warning: The gases produced by the battery are explosive - never smoke or create any sparks in the vicinity of the battery. Never allow the electrolyte to contact your skin or clothing - if it does, wash it off and seek immediate medical attention.*

● Before any electrical fault is investigated the battery should be checked.

● You'll need a dc voltmeter or multimeter to check battery voltage. Check that the leads are inserted in the correct terminals on the meter, red lead to positive (+), black lead to negative (-). Incorrect connections can

damage the meter.

● A sound, fully-charged 12 volt battery should produce between 12.3 and 12.6 volts across its terminals (12.8 volts for a maintenance-free battery). On machines with a 6 volt battery, voltage should be between 6.1 and 6.3 volts.

1 Set a multimeter to the 0 to 20 volts dc range and connect its probes across the battery terminals. Connect the meter's positive (+) probe, usually red, to the battery positive (+) terminal, followed by the meter's negative (-) probe, usually black, to the battery negative terminal (-) **(see illustration 1)**.

2 If battery voltage is low (below 10 volts on a 12 volt battery or below 4 volts on a six volt battery), charge the battery and test the voltage again. If the battery repeatedly goes flat, investigate the motorcycle's charging system.

Checking battery specific gravity (SG)

⚠ *Warning: The gases produced by the battery are explosive - never smoke or create any sparks in the vicinity of the battery. Never allow the electrolyte to contact your skin or clothing - if it does, wash it off and seek immediate medical attention.*

● The specific gravity check gives an indication of a battery's state of charge.

● A hydrometer is used for measuring specific gravity. Make sure you purchase one which has a small enough hose to insert in the aperture of a motorcycle battery.

● Specific gravity is simply a measure of the electrolyte's density compared with that of water. Water has an SG of 1.000 and

fully-charged battery electrolyte is about 26% heavier, at 1.260.

● Specific gravity checks are not possible on maintenance-free batteries. Testing the open-circuit voltage is the only means of determining their state of charge.

1 To measure SG, remove the battery from the motorcycle and remove the first cell cap. Draw some electrolyte into the hydrometer and note the reading **(see illustration 2)**. Return the electrolyte to the cell and install the cap.

2 The reading should be in the region of 1.260 to 1.280. If SG is below 1.200 the battery needs charging. Note that SG will vary with temperature; it should be measured at 20°C (68°F). Add 0.007 to the reading for every 10°C above 20°C, and subtract 0.007 from the reading for every 10°C below 20°C. Add 0.004 to the reading for every 10°F above 68°F, and subtract 0.004 from the reading for every 10°F below 68°F.

3 When the check is complete, rinse the hydrometer thoroughly with clean water.

Checking for continuity

● The term continuity describes the uninterrupted flow of electricity through an electrical circuit. A continuity check will determine whether an **open-circuit** situation exists.

● Continuity can be checked with an ohmmeter, multimeter, continuity tester or battery and bulb test circuit **(see illustrations 3, 4 and 5)**.

● All of these instruments are self-powered by a battery, therefore the checks are made with the ignition OFF.

● As a safety precaution, always disconnect the battery negative (-) lead before making checks, particularly if ignition switch checks are being made.

● If using a meter, select the appropriate

Digital multimeter can be used for all electrical tests

Battery-powered continuity tester

Battery and bulb test circuit

Continuity check of front brake light switch using a meter - note cotter pins used to access connector terminals

ohms scale and check that the meter reads infinity (∞). Touch the meter probes together and check that meter reads zero; where necessary adjust the meter so that it reads zero.

● After using a meter, always switch it OFF to conserve its battery.

Switch checks

1 If a switch is at fault, trace its wiring up to the wiring connectors. Separate the wire connectors and inspect them for security and condition. A build-up of dirt or corrosion here will most likely be the cause of the problem - clean up and apply a water dispersant such as WD40.

2 If using a test meter, set the meter to the ohms x 10 scale and connect its probes across the wires from the switch (see illustration 6). Simple ON/OFF type switches, such as brake light switches, only have two wires whereas combination switches, like the ignition switch, have many internal links. Study the wiring diagram to ensure that you are connecting across the correct pair of wires. Continuity (low or no measurable resistance - 0 ohms) should be indicated with the switch ON and no continuity (high resistance) with it OFF.

3 Note that the polarity of the test probes doesn't matter for continuity checks, although care should be taken to follow specific test procedures if a diode or solid-state component is being checked.

4 A continuity tester or battery and bulb circuit can be used in the same way. Connect its probes as described above (see illustration 7). The light should come on to indicate continuity in the ON switch position, but should extinguish in the OFF position.

Wiring checks

● Many electrical faults are caused by damaged wiring, often due to incorrect routing or chaffing on frame components.

● Loose, wet or corroded wire connectors

Continuity check of rear brake light switch using a continuity tester

can also be the cause of electrical problems, especially in exposed locations.

Continuity check of front brake light switch sub-harness

A simple test light can be used for voltage checks

A buzzer is useful for voltage checks

Checking for voltage at the rear brake light power supply wire using a meter . . .

1 A continuity check can be made on a single length of wire by disconnecting it at each end and connecting a meter or continuity tester across both ends of the wire **(see illustration 8)**.

2 Continuity (low or no resistance - 0 ohms) should be indicated if the wire is good. If no continuity (high resistance) is shown, suspect a broken wire.

Checking for voltage

● A voltage check can determine whether current is reaching a component.

● Voltage can be checked with a dc voltmeter, multimeter set on the dc volts scale, test light or buzzer **(see illustrations 9 and 10)**. A meter has the advantage of being able to measure actual voltage.

● When using a meter, check that its leads are inserted in the correct terminals on the meter, red to positive (+), black to negative (-). Incorrect connections can damage the meter.

● A voltmeter (or multimeter set to the dc volts scale) should always be connected in parallel (across the load). Connecting it in series will destroy the meter.

● Voltage checks are made with the ignition ON.

1 First identify the relevant wiring circuit by referring to the wiring diagram at the end of this manual. If other electrical components share the same power supply (ie are fed from the same fuse), take note whether they are working correctly - this is useful information in deciding where to start checking the circuit.

2 If using a meter, check first that the meter leads are plugged into the correct terminals on the meter (see above). Set the meter to the dc volts function, at a range suitable for the battery voltage. Connect the meter red probe (+) to the power supply wire and the black probe to a good metal ground on the

motor-cycle's frame or directly to the battery negative (-) terminal **(see illustration 11)**. Battery voltage should be shown on the meter with the ignition switched ON.

3 If using a test light or buzzer, connect its positive (+) probe to the power supply terminal and its negative (-) probe to a good ground on the motorcycle's frame or directly to the battery negative (-) terminal **(see illustration 12)**. With the ignition ON, the test light should illuminate or the buzzer sound.

4 If no voltage is indicated, work back towards the fuse continuing to check for voltage. When you reach a point where there is voltage, you know the problem lies between that point and your last check point.

Checking the ground

● Ground connections are made either

... or a test light - note the ground connection to the frame (arrow)

A selection of jumper wires for making ground checks

directly to the engine or frame (such as sensors, neutral switch etc. which only have a positive feed) or by a separate wire into the ground circuit of the wiring harness. Alternatively a short ground wire is sometimes run directly from the component to the motor-cycle's frame.

● Corrosion is often the cause of a poor ground connection.

● If total failure is experienced, check the security of the main ground lead from the negative (-) terminal of the battery and also the main ground point on the wiring harness. If corroded, dismantle the connection and clean all surfaces back to bare metal.

1 To check the ground on a component, use an insulated jumper wire to temporarily bypass its ground connection **(see illustration 13)**. Connect one end of the jumper wire between the ground terminal or metal body

of the component and the other end to the motorcycle's frame.

2 If the circuit works with the jumper wire installed, the original ground circuit is faulty. Check the wiring for open-circuits or poor connections. Clean up direct ground connections, removing all traces of corrosion and remake the joint. Apply petroleum jelly to the joint to prevent future corrosion.

Tracing a short-circuit

● A short-circuit occurs where current shorts to ground bypassing the circuit components. This usually results in a blown fuse.

● A short-circuit is most likely to occur where the insulation has worn through due to wiring chafing on a component, allowing a direct path to ground on the frame.

1 Remove any body panels necessary to access the circuit wiring.

2 Check that all electrical switches in the circuit are OFF, then remove the circuit fuse and connect a test light, buzzer or voltmeter (set to the dc scale) across the fuse terminals. No voltage should be shown.

3 Move the wiring from side to side while observing the test light or meter. When the test light comes on, buzzer sounds or meter shows voltage, you have found the cause of the short. It will usually shown up as damaged or burned insulation.

4 Note that the same test can be performed on each component in the circuit, even the switch.

Introduction

In less time than it takes to read this introduction, a thief could steal your motorcycle. Returning only to find your bike has gone is one of the worst feelings in the world. Even if the motorcycle is insured against theft, once you've got over the initial shock, you will have the inconvenience of dealing with the police and your insurance company.

The motorcycle is an easy target for the professional thief and the joyrider alike and the official figures on motorcycle theft make for depressing reading; on average a motor-cycle is stolen every 16 minutes in the UK!

Motorcycle thefts fall into two categories, those stolen 'to order' and those taken by opportunists. The thief stealing to order will be on the look out for a specific make and model and will go to extraordinary lengths to obtain that motorcycle. The opportunist thief on the other hand will look for easy targets which can be stolen with the minimum of effort and risk.

While it is never going to be possible to make your machine 100% secure, it is estimated that around half of all stolen motorcycles are taken by opportunist thieves. Remember that the opportunist thief is always on the look out for the easy option: if there are two similar motorcycles parked side-by-side, they will target the one with the lowest level of security. By taking a few precautions, you can reduce the chances of your motorcycle being stolen.

Security equipment

There are many specialized motorcycle security devices available and the following text summarizes their applications and their good and bad points.

Once you have decided on the type of security equipment which best suits your needs, we recommended that you read one of the many equipment tests regularly carried

Ensure the lock and chain you buy is of good quality and long enough to shackle your bike to a solid object

out by the motorcycle press. These tests compare the products from all the major manufacturers and give impartial ratings on their effectiveness, value-for-money and ease of use.

No one item of security equipment can provide complete protection. It is highly recommended that two or more of the items described below are combined to increase the security of your motorcycle (a lock and chain plus an alarm system is just about ideal). The more security measures fitted to the bike, the less likely it is to be stolen.

Lock and chain

Pros: *Very flexible to use; can be used to secure the motorcycle to almost any immovable object. On some locks and chains, the lock can be used on its own as a disc lock (see below).*

Cons: *Can be very heavy and awkward to carry on the motorcycle, although some types*

will be supplied with a carry bag which can be strapped to the pillion seat.

● Heavy-duty chains and locks are an excellent security measure **(see illustration 1)**. Whenever the motorcycle is parked, use the lock and chain to secure the machine to a solid, immovable object such as a post or railings. This will prevent the machine from being ridden away or being lifted into the back of a van.

● When fitting the chain, always ensure the chain is routed around the motorcycle frame or swingarm **(see illustrations 2 and 3)**. Never merely pass the chain around one of the wheel rims; a thief may unbolt the wheel and lift the rest of the machine into a van, leaving you with just the wheel! Try to avoid having excess chain free, thus making it difficult to use cutting tools, and keep the chain and lock off the ground to prevent thieves attacking it with a cold chisel. Position the lock so that its lock barrel is facing downwards; this will make it harder for the thief to attack the lock mechanism.

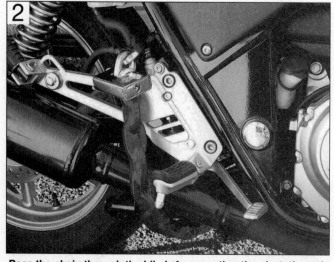

Pass the chain through the bike's frame, rather than just through a wheel . . .

. . . and loop it around a solid object

U-locks

Pros: *Highly effective deterrent which can be used to secure the bike to a post or railings. Most U-locks come with a carrier which allows the lock to be easily carried on the bike.*

Cons: *Not as flexible to use as a lock and chain.*

● These are solid locks which are similar in use to a lock and chain. U-locks are lighter than a lock and chain but not so flexible to use. The length and shape of the lock shackle limit the objects to which the bike can be secured **(see illustration 4)**.

Disc locks

Pros: *Small, light and very easy to carry; most can be stored underneath the seat.*

Cons: *Does not prevent the motorcycle being lifted into a van. Can be very embarrassing if*

A typical disc lock attached through one of the holes in the disc

U-locks can be used to secure the bike to a solid object - ensure you purchase one which is long enough

you forget to remove the lock before attempting to ride off!

● Disc locks are designed to be attached to the front brake disc. The lock passes through one of the holes in the disc and prevents the wheel rotating by jamming against the fork/brake caliper **(see illustration 5)**. Some are equipped with an alarm siren which sounds if the disc lock is moved; this not only acts as a theft deterrent but also as a handy reminder if you try to move the bike with the lock still fitted.

● Combining the disc lock with a length of cable which can be looped around a post or railings provides an additional measure of security **(see illustration 6)**.

Alarms and immobilisers

Pros: *Once installed it is completely hassle-free to use. If the system is 'Thatcham' or 'Sold Secure-approved', insurance companies may give you a discount.*

Cons: *Can be expensive to buy and complex to install. No system will prevent the motorcycle from being lifted into a van and taken away.*

● Electronic alarms and immobilizers are available to suit a variety of budgets. There are three different types of system available: pure alarms, pure immobilizers, and the more expensive systems which are combined alarm/immobilizers **(see illustration 7)**.

● An alarm system is designed to emit an audible warning if the motorcycle is being tampered with.

● An immobilizer prevents the motorcycle being started and ridden away by disabling its electrical systems.

● When purchasing an alarm/immobilizer system, check the cost of installing the system unless you are able to do it yourself. If the motorcycle is not used regularly, another consideration is the current drain of the system. All alarm/immobilizer systems are powered by the motorcycle's battery; purchasing a system with a very low current drain could prevent the battery losing its charge while the motorcycle is not being used.

A disc lock combined with a security cable provides additional protection

A typical alarm/immobilizer system

Indelible markings can be applied to most areas of the bike – always apply the manufacturer's sticker to warn off thieves

Chemically-etched code numbers can be applied to main body panels . . .

... again, always ensure that the kit manufacturer's sticker is applied in a prominent position

Security marking kits

Pros: *Very cheap and effective deterrent. Many insurance companies will give you a discount on your insurance premium if a recognized security marking kit is used on your motorcycle.*

Cons: *Does not prevent the motorcycle being stolen by joyriders.*

● There are many different types of security marking kits available. The idea is to mark as many parts of the motorcycle as possible with a unique security number **(see illustrations 8, 9 and 10)**. A form will be included with the kit to register your personal details and those of the motorcycle with the kit manufacturer. This register is made available to the police to help them trace the rightful owner of any motorcycle or components which they recover should all other forms of identification have been removed. Always apply the warning stickers provided with the kit to deter thieves.

Ground anchors, wheel clamps and security posts

Pros: *An excellent form of security which will deter all but the most determined of thieves.*

Cons: *Awkward to install and can be expensive.*

● While the motorcycle is at home, it is a good idea to attach it securely to the floor or a solid wall, even if it is kept in a securely locked garage. Various types of ground anchors, security posts and wheel clamps are available for this purpose **(see illustration 11)**. These security devices are either bolted to a solid concrete or brick structure or can be cemented into the ground.

Permanent ground anchors provide an excellent level of security when the bike is at home

Security at home

A high percentage of motorcycle thefts are from the owner's home. Here are some things to consider whenever your motorcycle is at home:

✔ Where possible, always keep the motorcycle in a securely locked garage. Never rely solely on the standard lock on the garage door, these are usual hopelessly inadequate. Fit an additional locking mechanism to the door and consider having the garage alarmed. A security light, activated by a movement sensor, is also a good investment.

✔ Always secure the motorcycle to the ground or a wall, even if it is inside a securely locked garage.
✔ Do not regularly leave the motorcycle outside your home, try to keep it out of sight wherever possible. If a garage is not available, fit a motorcycle cover over the bike to disguise its true identity.
✔ It is not uncommon for thieves to follow a motorcyclist home to find out where the bike is kept. They will then return at a later date. Be aware of this whenever you are returning

home on your motorcycle. If you suspect you are being followed, do not return home, instead ride to a garage or shop and stop as a precaution.
✔ When selling a motorcycle, do not provide your home address or the location where the bike is normally kept. Arrange to meet the buyer at a location away from your home. Thieves have been known to pose as potential buyers to find out where motorcycles are kept and then return later to steal them.

Security away from the home

As well as fitting security equipment to your motorcycle here are a few general rules to follow whenever you park your motorcycle.
✔ Park in a busy, public place.
✔ Use car parks which incorporate security features, such as CCTV.

✔ At night, park in a well-lit area, preferably directly underneath a street light.
✔ Engage the steering lock.
✔ Secure the motorcycle to a solid, immovable object such as a post or railings with an additional lock. If this is not possible,

secure the bike to a friend's motorcycle. Some public parking places provide security loops for motorcycles.
✔ Never leave your helmet or luggage attached to the motorcycle. Take them with you at all times.

A

ABS (Anti-lock braking system) A system, usually electronically controlled, that senses incipient wheel lockup during braking and relieves hydraulic pressure at wheel which is about to skid.

Aftermarket Components suitable for the motorcycle, but not produced by the motorcycle manufacturer.

Allen key A hexagonal wrench which fits into a recessed hexagonal hole.

Alternating current (ac) Current produced by an alternator. Requires converting to direct current by a rectifier for charging purposes.

Alternator Converts mechanical energy from the engine into electrical energy to charge the battery and power the electrical system.

Ampere (amp) A unit of measurement for the flow of electrical current. Current = Volts ÷ Ohms.

Ampere-hour (Ah) Measure of battery capacity.

Angle-tightening A torque expressed in degrees. Often follows a conventional tightening torque for cylinder head or main bearing fasteners **(see illustration)**.

Angle-tightening cylinder head bolts

Antifreeze A substance (usually ethylene glycol) mixed with water, and added to the cooling system, to prevent freezing of the coolant in winter. Antifreeze also contains chemicals to inhibit corrosion and the formation of rust and other deposits that would tend to clog the radiator and coolant passages and reduce cooling efficiency.

Anti-dive System attached to the fork lower leg (slider) to prevent fork dive when braking hard.

Anti-seize compound A coating that reduces the risk of seizing on fasteners that are subjected to high temperatures, such as exhaust clamp bolts and nuts.

API American Petroleum Institute. A quality standard for 4-stroke motor oils.

Asbestos A natural fibrous mineral with great heat resistance, commonly used in the composition of brake friction materials. Asbestos is a health hazard and the dust created by brake systems should never be inhaled or ingested.

ATF Automatic Transmission Fluid. Often used in front forks.

ATU Automatic Timing Unit. Mechanical device for advancing the ignition timing on early engines.

ATV All Terrain Vehicle. Often called a Quad.

Axial play Side-to-side movement.

Axle A shaft on which a wheel revolves. Also known as a spindle.

B

Backlash The amount of movement between meshed components when one component is held still. Usually applies to gear teeth.

Ball bearing A bearing consisting of a hardened inner and outer race with hardened steel balls between the two races.

Bearings Used between two working surfaces to prevent wear of the components and a build-up of heat. Four types of bearing are commonly used on motorcycles: plain shell bearings, ball bearings, tapered roller bearings and needle roller bearings.

Bevel gears Used to turn the drive through 90°. Typical applications are shaft final drive and camshaft drive **(see illustration)**.

BHP Brake Horsepower. The British measurement for engine power output. Power output is now usually expressed in kilowatts (kW).

Bevel gears are used to turn the drive through 90°

Bias-belted tire Similar construction to radial tire, but with outer belt running at an angle to the wheel rim.

Big-end bearing The bearing in the end of the connecting rod that's attached to the crankshaft.

Bleeding The process of removing air from a hydraulic system via a bleed nipple or bleed screw.

Bottom-end A description of an engine's crankcase components and all components contained therein.

BTDC Before Top Dead Center in terms of piston position. Ignition timing is often expressed in terms of degrees or millimeters BTDC.

Bush A cylindrical metal or rubber component used between two moving parts.

Burr Rough edge left on a component after machining or as a result of excessive wear.

C

Cam chain The chain which takes drive from the crankshaft to the camshaft(s).

Canister The main component in an evap-orative emission control system (California market only); contains activated charcoal granules to trap vapors from the fuel system rather than allowing them to vent to the atmosphere.

Castellated Resembling the parapets along the top of a castle wall. For example, a castellated wheel axle or spindle nut.

Catalytic converter A device in the exhaust system of some machines which

Cush drive rubber segments dampen out transmission shocks

converts certain pollutants in the exhaust gases into less harmful substances.

Charging system Description of the components which charge the battery, ie the alternator, rectifer and regulator.

Clearance The amount of space between two parts. For example, between a piston and a cylinder, between a bearing and a journal, etc.

Coil spring A spiral of elastic steel found in various sizes throughout a vehicle, for example as a springing medium in the suspension and in the valve train.

Compression Reduction in volume, and increase in pressure and temperature, of a gas, caused by squeezing it into a smaller space.

Compression damping Controls the speed the suspension compresses when hitting a bump.

Compression ratio The relationship between cylinder volume when the piston is at top dead center and cylinder volume when the piston is at bottom dead center.

Continuity The uninterrupted path in the flow of electricity. Little or no measurable resistance.

Continuity tester Self-powered bleeper or test light which indicates continuity.

Cp Candlepower. Bulb rating commonly found on US motorcycles.

Crossply tire Tire plies arranged in a criss-cross pattern. Usually four or six plies used, hence 4PR or 6PR in tire size codes.

Cush drive Rubber damper segments fitted between the rear wheel and final drive sprocket to absorb transmission shocks **(see illustration)**.

D

Degree disc Calibrated disc for measuring piston position. Expressed in degrees.

Dial gauge Clock-type gauge with adapters for measuring runout and piston position. Expressed in mm or inches.

Diaphragm The rubber membrane in a master cylinder or carburetor which seals the upper chamber.

Diaphragm spring A single sprung plate often used in clutches.

Direct current (dc) Current produced by a dc generator.

Decarbonization The process of removing carbon deposits - typically from the combustion chamber, valves and exhaust port/system.

Detonation Destructive and damaging explosion of fuel/air mixture in combustion chamber instead of controlled burning.

Diode An electrical valve which only allows current to flow in one direction. Commonly used in rectifiers and starter interlock systems.

Disc valve (or rotary valve) An induction system used on some two-stroke engines.

Double-overhead camshaft (DOHC) An engine that uses two overhead camshafts, one for the intake valves and one for the exhaust valves.

Drivebelt A toothed belt used to transmit drive to the rear wheel on some motorcycles. A drivebelt has also been used to drive the camshafts. Drivebelts are usually made of Kevlar.

Driveshaft Any shaft used to transmit motion. Commonly used when referring to the final driveshaft on shaft drive motorcycles.

E

ECU (Electronic Control Unit) A computer which controls (for instance) an ignition system, or an anti-lock braking system.

EGO Exhaust Gas Oxygen sensor. Some-times called a Lambda sensor.

Electrolyte The fluid in a lead-acid battery.

EMS (Engine Management System) A computer controlled system which manages the fuel injection and the ignition systems in an integrated fashion.

Endfloat The amount of lengthways movement between two parts. As applied to a crankshaft, the distance that the crankshaft can move side-to-side in the crankcase.

Endless chain A chain having no joining link. Common use for cam chains and final drive chains.

EP (Extreme Pressure) Oil type used in locations where high loads are applied, such as between gear teeth.

Evaporative emission control system Describes a charcoal filled canister which stores fuel vapors from the tank rather than allowing them to vent to the atmosphere. Usually only fitted to California models and referred to as an EVAP system.

Expansion chamber Section of two-stroke engine exhaust system so designed to improve engine efficiency and boost power.

F

Feeler blade or gauge A thin strip or blade of hardened steel, ground to an exact thickness, used to check or measure clearances between parts.

Final drive Description of the drive from the transmission to the rear wheel. Usually by chain or shaft, but sometimes by belt.

Firing order The order in which the engine cylinders fire, or deliver their power strokes, beginning with the number one cylinder.

Flooding Term used to describe a high fuel level in the carburetor float chambers, leading to fuel overflow. Also refers to excess fuel in the combustion chamber due to incorrect starting technique.

Free length The no-load state of a component when measured. Clutch, valve and fork spring lengths are measured at rest, without any preload.

Freeplay The amount of travel before any action takes place. The looseness in a linkage, or an assembly of parts, between the initial application of force and actual movement. For example, the distance the rear brake pedal moves before the rear brake is actuated.

Fuel injection The fuel/air mixture is metered electronically and directed into the engine intake ports (indirect injection) or into the cylinders (direct injection). Sensors supply information on engine speed and conditions.

Fuel/air mixture The charge of fuel and air going into the engine. See Stoichiometric ratio.

Fuse An electrical device which protects a circuit against accidental overload. The typical fuse contains a soft piece of metal which is calibrated to melt at a predetermined current flow (expressed as amps) and break the circuit.

G

Gap The distance the spark must travel in jumping from the center electrode to the side electrode in a spark plug. Also refers to the distance between the ignition rotor and the pickup coil in an electronic ignition system.

Gasket Any thin, soft material - usually cork, cardboard, asbestos or soft metal - installed between two metal surfaces to ensure a good seal. For instance, the cylinder head gasket seals the joint between the block and the cylinder head.

Gauge An instrument panel display used to monitor engine conditions. A gauge with a movable pointer on a dial or a fixed scale is an analog gauge. A gauge with a numerical readout is called a digital gauge.

Gear ratios The drive ratio of a pair of gears in a gearbox, calculated on their number of teeth.

Glaze-busting see **Honing**

Grinding Process for renovating the valve face and valve seat contact area in the cylinder head.

Ground return The return path of an electrical circuit, utilizing the motorcycle's frame.

Gudgeon pin The shaft which connects the connecting rod small-end with the piston. Often called a piston pin or wrist pin.

H

Helical gears Gear teeth are slightly curved and produce less gear noise that straight-cut gears. Often used for primary drives.

Helicoil A thread insert repair system. Commonly used as a repair for stripped spark plug threads **(see illustration)**.

Installing a Helicoil thread insert in a cylinder head

Honing A process used to break down the glaze on a cylinder bore (also called glaze-busting). Can also be carried out to roughen a rebored cylinder to aid ring bedding-in.

HT (High Tension) Description of the electrical circuit from the secondary winding of the ignition coil to the spark plug.

Hydraulic A liquid filled system used to transmit pressure from one component to another. Common uses on motorcycles are brakes and clutches.

Hydrometer An instrument for measuring the specific gravity of a lead-acid battery.

Hygroscopic Water absorbing. In motorcycle applications, braking efficiency will be reduced if DOT 3 or 4 hydraulic fluid absorbs water from the air - care must be taken to keep new brake fluid in tightly sealed containers.

I

lbf ft Pounds-force feet. A unit of torque. Sometimes written as ft-lbs.

lbf in Pound-force inch. A unit of torque, applied to components where a very low torque is required. Sometimes written as inch-lbs.

IC Abbreviation for Integrated Circuit.

Ignition advance Means of increasing the timing of the spark at higher engine speeds. Done by mechanical means (ATU) on early engines or electronically by the ignition control unit on later engines.

Ignition timing The moment at which the spark plug fires, expressed in the number of crankshaft degrees before the piston reaches the top of its stroke, or in the number of millimeters before the piston reaches the top of its stroke.

Infinity (∞) Description of an open-circuit electrical state, where no continuity exists.

Inverted forks (upside down forks) The sliders or lower legs are held in the yokes and the fork tubes or stanchions are connected to the wheel axle (spindle). Less unsprung weight and stiffer construction than conventional forks.

J

JASO Japan Automobile Standards Organization. JASO MA is a standard for motorcycle oil equivalent to API SJ, but designed to prevent problems with wet-type motorcycle clutches.

Joule The unit of electrical energy.

Journal The bearing surface of a shaft.

K

Kickstart Mechanical means of turning the engine over for starting purposes.

Only usually fitted to mopeds, small capacity motorcycles and off-road motorcycles.

Kill switch Handebar-mounted switch for emergency ignition cut-out. Cuts the ignition circuit on all models, and additionally prevent starter motor operation on others.

km Symbol for kilometer.

kmh Abbreviation for kilometers per hour.

L

Lambda sensor A sensor fitted in the exhaust system to measure the exhaust gas oxygen content (excess air factor). Also called oxygen sensor.

Lapping see **Grinding**.

LCD Abbreviation for Liquid Crystal Display.

LED Abbreviation for Light Emitting Diode.

Liner A steel cylinder liner inserted in an aluminum alloy cylinder block.

Locknut A nut used to lock an adjustment nut, or other threaded component, in place.

Lockstops The lugs on the lower triple clamp (yoke) which abut those on the frame, preventing handlebar-to-fuel tank contact.

Lockwasher A form of washer designed to prevent an attaching nut from working loose.

LT Low Tension Description of the electrical circuit from the power supply to the primary winding of the ignition coil.

M

Main bearings The bearings between the crankshaft and crankcase.

Maintenance-free (MF) battery A sealed battery which cannot be topped up.

Manometer Mercury-filled calibrated tubes used to measure intake tract vacuum. Used to synchronize carburetors on multi-cylinder engines.

Tappet shims are measured with a micrometer

Micrometer A precision measuring instrument that measures component outside diameters **(see illustration)**.

MON (Motor Octane Number) A measure of a fuel's resistance to knock.

Monograde oil An oil with a single viscosity, eg SAE80W.

Monoshock A single suspension unit linking the swingarm or suspension linkage to the frame.

mph Abbreviation for miles per hour.

Multigrade oil Having a wide viscosity range (eg 10W40). The W stands for Winter, thus the viscosity ranges from SAE10 when cold to SAE40 when hot.

Multimeter An electrical test instrument with the capability to measure voltage, current and resistance. Some meters also incorporate a continuity tester and buzzer.

N

Needle roller bearing Inner race of caged needle rollers and hardened outer race. Examples of uncaged needle rollers can be found on some engines. Commonly used in rear suspension applications and in two-stroke engines.

Nm Newton meters.

NOx Oxides of Nitrogen. A common toxic pollutant emitted by gasoline engines at higher temperatures.

O

Octane The measure of a fuel's resistance to knock.

OE (Original Equipment) Relates to components fitted to a motorcycle as standard or replacement parts supplied by the motorcycle manufacturer.

Ohm The unit of electrical resistance. Ohms = Volts ÷ Current.

Ohmmeter An instrument for measuring electrical resistance.

Oil cooler System for diverting engine oil outside of the engine to a radiator for cooling purposes.

Oil injection A system of two-stroke engine lubrication where oil is pump-fed to the engine in accordance with throttle position.

Open-circuit An electrical condition where there is a break in the flow of electricity - no continuity (high resistance).

O-ring A type of sealing ring made of a special rubber-like material; in use, the O-ring is compressed into a groove to provide the sealing action.

Oversize (OS) Term used for piston and ring size options fitted to a rebored cylinder.

Overhead cam (sohc) engine An engine with single camshaft located on top of the cylinder head.

Overhead valve (ohv) engine An engine with the valves located in the cylinder head, but with the camshaft located in the engine block or crankcase.

Oxygen sensor A device installed in the exhaust system which senses the oxygen content in the exhaust and converts this information into an electric current. Also called a Lambda sensor.

P

Plastigage A thin strip of plastic thread, available in different sizes, used for measuring clearances. For example, a strip of Plastigage is laid across a bearing journal. The parts are assembled and dismantled; the width of the crushed strip indicates the clearance between journal and bearing.

Polarity Either negative or positive ground, determined by which battery lead is connected to the frame (ground return). Modern motorcycles are usually negative ground.

Pre-ignition A situation where the fuel/air mixture ignites before the spark plug fires. Often due to a hot spot in the combustion chamber caused by carbon build-up. Engine has a tendency to 'run-on'.

Pre-load (suspension) The amount a spring is compressed when in the unloaded state. Preload can be applied by gas, spacer or mechanical adjuster.

Premix The method of engine lubrication on some gasoline two-stroke engines. Engine oil is mixed with the gasoline in the fuel tank in a specific ratio. The fuel/oil mix is sometimes referred to as "petrol".

Primary drive Description of the drive from the crankshaft to the clutch. Usually by gear or chain.

PS Pferdestärke - a German interpretation of BHP.

PSI Pounds-force per square inch. Imperial measurement of tire pressure and cylinder pressure measurement.

PTFE Polytetrafluroethylene. A low friction substance.

Pulse secondary air injection system A process of promoting the burning of excess fuel present in the exhaust gases by routing fresh air into the exhaust ports.

Q

Quartz halogen bulb Tungsten filament surrounded by a halogen gas. Typically used for the headlight **(see illustration)**.

Quartz halogen headlight bulb construction

R

Rack-and-pinion A pinion gear on the end of a shaft that mates with a rack (think of a geared wheel opened up and laid flat). Sometimes used in clutch operating systems.

Radial play Up and down movement about a shaft.

Radial ply tires Tire plies run across the tire (from bead to bead) and around the circumference of the tire. Less resistant to tread distortion than other tire types.

Radiator A liquid-to-air heat transfer device designed to reduce the temperature of the coolant in a liquid cooled engine.

Rake A feature of steering geometry - the angle of the steering head in relation to the vertical **(see illustration)**.

Steering geometry

Rebore Providing a new working surface to the cylinder bore by boring out the old surface. Necessitates the use of oversize piston and rings.

Rebound damping A means of controlling the oscillation of a suspension unit spring after it has been compressed. Resists the spring's natural tendency to bounce back after being compressed.

Rectifier Device for converting the ac output of an alternator into dc for battery charging.

Reed valve An induction system commonly used on two-stroke engines.

Regulator Device for maintaining the charging voltage from the generator or alternator within a specified range.

Relay A electrical device used to switch heavy current on and off by using a low current auxiliary circuit.

Resistance Measured in ohms. An electrical component's ability to pass electrical current.

RON (Research Octane Number) A measure of a fuel's resistance to knock.

rpm revolutions per minute.

Runout The amount of wobble (in-and-out movement) of a wheel or shaft as it's rotated. The amount a shaft rotates "out-of-true." The out-of-round condition of a rotating part.

S

SAE (Society of Automotive Engineers) A standard for the viscosity of a fluid.

Sealant A liquid or paste used to prevent leakage at a joint. Sometimes used in conjunction with a gasket.

Service limit Term for the point where a component is no longer useable and must be replaced.

Shaft drive A method of transmitting drive from the transmission to the rear wheel.

Shell bearings Plain bearings consisting of two shell halves. Most often used as big-end and main bearings in a four-stroke engine. Often called bearing inserts.

Shim Thin spacer, commonly used to adjust the clearance or relative positions between two parts. For example, shims inserted into or under tappets or followers to control valve clearances. Clearance is adjusted by changing the thickness of the shim.

Short-circuit An electrical condition where current shorts to ground bypassing the circuit components.

Skimming Process to correct warpage or repair a damaged surface, eg on brake discs or drums.

Slide-hammer A special puller that screws into or hooks onto a component such as a shaft or bearing; a heavy sliding handle on the shaft bottoms against the end of the shaft to knock the component free.

Small-end bearing The bearing in the upper end of the connecting rod at its joint with the gudgeon pin.

Snap-ring A ring-shaped clip used to prevent endwise movement of cylindrical parts and shafts. An internal snap-ring is installed in a groove in a housing; an external snap-ring fits into a groove on the outside of a cylindrical piece such as a shaft. Also known as a circlip.

Spalling Damage to camshaft lobes or bearing journals shown as pitting of the working surface.

Specific gravity (SG) The state of charge of the electrolyte in a lead-acid battery. A measure of the electrolyte's density compared with water.

Straight-cut gears Common type gear used on gearbox shafts and for oil pump and water pump drives.

Stanchion The inner sliding part of the front forks, held by the yokes. Often called a fork tube.

Stoichiometric ratio The optimum chemical air/fuel ratio for a gasoline engine, said to be 14.7 parts of air to 1 part of fuel.

Sulphuric acid The liquid (electrolyte) used in a lead-acid battery. Poisonous and extremely corrosive.

Surface grinding (lapping) Process to correct a warped gasket face, commonly used on cylinder heads.

T

Tapered-roller bearing Tapered inner race of caged needle rollers and separate tapered outer race. Examples of taper roller bearings can be found on steering heads.

Tappet A cylindrical component which transmits motion from the cam to the valve stem, either directly or via a pushrod and rocker arm. Also called a cam follower.

TCS Traction Control System. An electronically-controlled system which senses wheel spin and reduces engine speed accordingly.

TDC Top Dead Center denotes that the piston is at its highest point in the cylinder.

Thread-locking compound Solution applied to fastener threads to prevent loosening. Select type to suit application.

Thrust washer A washer positioned between two moving components on a shaft. For example, between gear pinions on gearshaft.

Timing chain See **Cam Chain**.

Timing light Stroboscopic lamp for carrying out ignition timing checks with the engine running.

Top-end A description of an engine's cylinder block, head and valve gear components.

Torque Turning or twisting force about a shaft.

Torque setting A prescribed tightness specified by the motorcycle manufacturer to ensure that the bolt or nut is secured correctly. Undertightening can result in the bolt or nut coming loose or a surface not being sealed. Overtightening can result in stripped threads, distortion or damage to the component being retained.

Torx key A six-point wrench.

Tracer A stripe of a second color applied to a wire insulator to distinguish that wire from another one with the same color insulator. For example, Br/W is often used to denote a brown insulator with a white tracer.

Trail A feature of steering geometry. Distance from the steering head axis to the tire's central contact point.

Triple clamps The cast components which extend from the steering head and support the fork stanchions or tubes. Often called fork yokes.

Turbocharger A centrifugal device, driven by exhaust gases, that pressurizes the intake air. Normally used to increase the power output from a given engine displacement.

TWI Abbreviation for Tire Wear Indicator. Indicates the location of the tread depth indicator bars on tires.

U

Universal joint or U-joint (UJ) A double-pivoted connection for transmitting power from a driving to a driven shaft through an angle. Typically found in shaft drive assemblies.

Unsprung weight Anything not supported by the bike's suspension (ie the wheel, tires, brakes, final drive and bottom (moving) part of the suspension).

V

Vacuum gauges Clock-type gauges for measuring intake tract vacuum. Used for carburetor synchronization on multi-cylinder engines.

Valve A device through which the flow of liquid, gas or vacuum may be stopped, started or regulated by a moveable part that opens, shuts or partially obstructs one or more ports or passageways. The intake and exhaust valves in the cylinder head are of the poppet type.

Valve clearance The clearance between the valve tip (the end of the valve stem) and the rocker arm or tappet/follower. The valve clearance is measured when the valve is closed. The correct clearance is important - if too small the valve won't close fully and will burn out, whereas if too large noisy operation will result.

Valve lift The amount a valve is lifted off its seat by the camshaft lobe.

Valve timing The exact setting for the opening and closing of the valves in relation to piston position.

Vernier caliper A precision measuring instrument that measures inside and outside dimensions. Not quite as accurate as a micrometer, but more convenient.

VIN Vehicle Identification Number. Term for the bike's engine and frame numbers.

Viscosity The thickness of a liquid or its resistance to flow.

Volt A unit for expressing electrical "pressure" in a circuit. Volts = current x ohms.

W

Water pump A mechanically-driven device for moving coolant around the engine.

Watt A unit for expressing electrical power. Watts = volts x current.

Wet liner arrangement

Wear limit see **Service limit**

Wet liner A liquid-cooled engine design where the pistons run in liners which are directly surrounded by coolant **(see illustration)**.

Wheelbase Distance from the center of the front wheel to the center of the rear wheel.

Wiring harness or loom Describes the electrical wires running the length of the motorcycle and enclosed in tape or plastic sheathing. Wiring coming off the main harness is usually referred to as a sub harness.

Woodruff key A key of semi-circular or square section used to locate a gear to a shaft. Often used to locate the alternator rotor on the crankshaft.

Wrist pin Another name for gudgeon or piston pin.

Notes

Note: *References throughout this index are in the form, "Chapter number"•"Page number"*

Notes